The Field Guide to Teaching

A Handbook for New Teachers

RICHARD J. MARCHESANI

Elmira College, Elmira, New York

Upper Saddle River, New Jersey
Columbus, Ohio

Library of Congress Cataloging-in-Publication Data
Marchesani, Richard J.
The field guide to teaching : a handbook for new teachers/Richard J. Marchesani.
p. cm.
ISBN 0-13-114990-3
1. First year teachers—Handbooks, manuals, etc. 2. Teaching—Handbooks, manuals, etc. I. Title.
LB2844.1.N4M27 2007
371.1—dc22 2006014008

Vice President and Executive Publisher: Jeffery W. Johnston
Executive Editor: Debra A. Stollenwerk
Senior Editorial Assistant: Mary Morrill
Assistant Development Editor: Elisa Rogers
Production Editor: Kris Roach
Production Coordination: Techbooks
Design Coordinator: Diane C. Lorenzo
Cover Designer: Jeff Vanik
Cover Image: Corbis
Production Manager: Susan Hannahs
Director of Marketing: David Gesell
Senior Marketing Manager: Darcy Betts Prybella
Marketing Coordinator: Brian Mounts

This book was set in Garamond by Techbooks. It was printed and bound by Banta Book Group. The cover was printed by Phoenix Color Corp.

Photo Credits:
Getty Images Inc.–Hulton Archive Photos, p. 196; George Dodson/PH College, p. 220. All other photos provided by the author.

Pearson Education Ltd.
Pearson Education Singapore Pte. Ltd.
Pearson Education Canada, Ltd.
Pearson Education—Japan
Pearson Education Australia Pty. Limited
Pearson Education North Asia Ltd.
Pearson Educación de Mexico, S.A. de C.V.
Pearson Education Malaysia Pte. Ltd.

10 9 8 7 6 5 4 3 2 1
ISBN: 0-13-114990-3

This book is dedicated to my wife, Laurie,
and to the memory of Fred Rogers,
who taught us all how to be good neighbors.

Preface

There is only one message in teaching—"If it doesn't benefit the student, then you shouldn't be doing it."

—A Retiring Teacher's Farewell Remarks

Purpose of the Text

The goal of this text is to provide very specific and practical guidance for those who are entering the teaching profession. This includes those who are engaged in student teaching, recently completed student teaching, intending to begin teaching shortly, or who are in the initial months of their first teaching job.

The text offers guidelines, hints and fundamental information geared to help the novice teacher avoid common pitfalls and to make a start on the road to becoming a professional educator. It was written from the point of view that those who read this text are unfamiliar with the profession beyond the training they have or will receive in their college teacher preparation program.

Conceptual Framework

The text lays out the processes that comprise the work of the profession, examines them where appropriate, and then makes suggestions as to what avenues of action are open for you to choose.

The essence of the text is built around two concepts: *reality* and *practicality,* comprising the fabric from which is woven a path that you might follow.

Reality

Knowledge of the true reality of the teaching profession is a foundation that any beginning teacher would like to have. This text avoids glossing the many facets of the teaching world with *desired* outcomes, and instead presents as true a picture as possible of the *actual* outcomes of teaching. Reality is presented in this sense: *as it actually occurs.*

This reality is presented through the words of many veteran teachers, administrators, and educators, as well as students and college professors. They tell it as it happened so that you can decide what meaning to attach to the narrative.

Practicality

You have already studied child and adolescent development, educational theory, curriculum design, and the methodologies of teaching. Therefore, you are most likely well prepared, with a substantial knowledge base of information on *what* to do when you begin to teach. For this reason, the text does not attempt to reteach lessons already learned; it does not reinvent the wheel.

The text is written in plain, direct language meant to describe the system within which you will work and to provide direction within that system. It does so through a portrayal of situations; descriptions of colleagues, administrators, staff, students, and parents; and a great deal of specific information that will help you make daily decisions in your work with children.

ORGANIZATION OF THE TEXT

This text is organized for a person who wants immediate and practical information on the day-to-day details of being a modern teacher. It is divided into three parts.

Part 1 Becoming a Teacher

Chapters 1 and 2 provide specific information related to the hiring process and a practical description of a typical school system. Chapter 1 is geared to be of immediate use for individuals seeking a teaching job, by providing statistical data on and procedures used in the hiring process. Chapter 2 continues with the theme of practicality by offering specific information to help support new teachers on the job.

Part 2 Learning the Teaching Process

Becoming an effective teacher involves many aspects, and most of them focus on the instructional process. Chapters 3–8 take the novice teacher through the important steps of instruction by providing information on application and implementation of the teaching process. Chapter 3 gives brief descriptions of the initial days, weeks, and months of school. Chapter 4 details the important steps of planning and organizing, which are necessary for effective instruction, and includes the standard format for organizing the year: the unit plan and daily lesson plans. Chapter 5 is an exploration of the many facets of classroom management and includes a step-by-step blueprint for organizing a typical teaching program. Chapter 6 addresses the process of instruction conceptually and practically. Chapter 7 continues with instructional prescription by providing the novice with specific activities for most subject areas. Chapter 8 concludes this part with the essentials of assessment by outlining the foundations of evaluation and presenting blueprints for grading.

Part 3 Becoming an Effective Teacher

Factors other than instructional technique will affect the new teacher's efforts to become effective. Chapters 9–13 cover these factors. Chapter 9 begins with a discussion of who today's students are and their developmental transitions. Chapter 10 covers two variables that influence the student: diversity and special needs. The all-important communication links between school and home are addressed in Chapter 11, and a discussion of the people with whom the novice teacher will interact each day follows in Chapter 12. Finally, Chapter 13 examines two important levels of development: professional and personal. It includes a discussion of the procedures the beginning teacher will likely encounter as his or her school district strives to improve teacher quality as mandated by the No Child Left Behind legislation. In conclusion, this chapter addresses the impact of the new teacher's job on his or her personal life.

FEATURES OF THE TEXT

The main feature of the text is the concise and direct flow of information, without wordy explanations that repeat information learned during curriculum and methods courses. Within each chapter, specific blocks of information serve the format of practicality.

Voices in the Classroom

Featured in each chapter are anecdotes from teachers, administrators, and students about their experiences with education. Each anecdote is a fictional composite inspired by actual events gleaned from the experiences of many educators. The value of Voices in the Classroom narratives is that they are a primary source of information about a variety of topics affecting the world of teaching. In addition, they provide real insight into the many influences on teacher effectiveness.

Legal Sidebar

In today's litigious world of education, an effective teacher is better prepared if he or she has pertinent information readily available when situations arise that might cause liability concerns. The Legal Sidebar feature highlights court cases and laws that affect teachers in the performance of their duties. Each sidebar is presented in relation to particular situations common to the typical school environment.

In Real Time

In keeping with the practicality theme, the In Real Time feature provides information related to specific situations or problem areas encountered by teachers. Frank in tone, these concise comments strike hard on the points necessary for teacher action.

Stating the Facts

The Stating the Facts feature strives to provide statistical data either from sanctioned databases or from educational, sociological, and psychological research. It functions as a source of vital information that will help make the beginning teacher more aware of the factors affecting the school environment.

Examples

In the text, practical examples are provided when feasible. Featured in boxes throughout the text, these examples translate into direct, logistical support in the areas of instructing, managing, and assessing the diverse class.

Guidepost

The Guidepost feature highlights pertinent information directly related to topics affecting the daily life of a teacher. Presented in question–answer format, each guidepost may be actionable depending on the environment and context of the teaching assignment.

Caution

Throughout the text are Caution boxes presenting the idea that sometimes things may go wrong. These warnings about pitfalls help the beginning teacher to become prepared for the likelihood of error or the presence of outside agents that may interfere with the instructional program.

Dos and Don'ts

At the conclusion of each chapter is a list of what a teacher should or should not do. The Dos and Don'ts feature is geared to act as a summary of the chapter while also alerting the teacher to points that should be noted during the teaching process.

For Your Briefcase

At the end of each chapter is a summary of the chapter given in the form of what you will need to be an effective teacher. It lists things to do that you might want to reflect on and *samples* and *templates* that are available on the CD that accompanies the text.

The Briefcase CD

Accompanying the text is a CD on which you will find samples, checklists, and tables for each chapter of the text. Some of these items are reprints of what is found in the text, but others are more detailed and provide you with direction that will aid you in your classroom activities. Also included are sample lesson plans and unit plans as well as a complete listing of Web sites that may assist you in finding more material.

Acknowledgments

Writing this book has been a journey that began in 1965, when I was inspired to become a teacher while reading Bel Kaufman's book *Up the Down Staircase.* As with teaching, writing this text for teachers could not have been done in isolation. Many people have contributed to its creation and production, including the thousands of students whom I have had the pleasure of teaching during the past 35 years. I wish I could name them all and add something about them, but neither time nor space permits.

I am greatly indebted to Debbie Stollenwerk and Elisa Rogers at Prentice Hall, who pulled me up when I was down and kept the ideas alive. I also owe a debt of thanks to the editorial staff at Prentice Hall—Mary Morrill, Dena Russell, and Kathy Termeer—and TechBooks—Linda Landis-Clark. More thanks go to Kathy Riley-King for her extensive copyediting of the manuscript.

I want to thank the reviewers for their wonderful comments and ideas. They are Karen Bosch, Virginia Wesleyan College; Carrie Dale, Baker College of Cadillac; Monique Davis, Arizona State University; Bryan L. Duke, University of Central Oklahoma; Mary Dean Dumais, Kean University; Rebecca L. Dye, Culver-Stockton College; Shirley J. Fisher, University of Arizona; Helen Harrington, University of Michigan; Dennis Holt, University of North Florida; Holly M. Hubert, College of DuPage; Ellen Jane Irons, Texas Woman's University; Michele Wilson Kamens, Rider University; Leslie Loughmiller, Texas State University; Karen E. Mayo, Stephen F. Austin State University; and Florette Reven, Tarleton State University.

Other people contributed to this book in small and large ways: graduate and undergraduate students Alicia Peters, Rebecca Parker, Emily Prestopnik, Kim Lunstead, Erin Buel, Erica Chesebro, Sara Adams-Marchesani, Erin Shane, Katie Ichiana, Hillary Stevens, and a host of others.

I am greatly in debt to my colleague Suzy Kaback for her critiques and her great spirit and to Terry Austin for her work and her cheers.

I should also mention the teachers who gave of their time and advice: David Benjamin, Rose Kramarik, Leslie Kempf, Kim Woltjen, Jill Eagen, Jill Olthof, and Julie Biviano.

Thanks to Dr. Sara Rimm-Kaufman for her kind words and assistance, Kara Schlosser from the Council of Chief State School Officers, and Caroline Arlington of MENC (National Association for Music Education).

Thanks also to the "kids" in my life—Dina, Nicole, Justin, Jay, and Rick—and their offspring: Maya, Gabriella, Ryan, Emi, James, Olivia, and the Maxster. I am indebted to the others who say little but are always there to help: Gary, David, Rachel, Colette, Joyce, Sally, and Sara—"the Teacher." My sister Barbara, a teacher who set new standards and continues to do so even today, and Gabe, "the Patriarch," also deserve many thanks.

Of course, the person who deserves the most credit for this text is the woman whose influence, brains, energy, and creativity complete my life. To my wife, Laurie, who never, ever complained of the lost hours and who always knew how to utter encouragements when I needed them most, I owe the largest debt of thanks. She is the model for many of the ideas in this book because she is the "real deal" as a teacher and, I believe, is the example all other teachers should follow.

Brief Contents

Contents

NOTE: Every effort has been made to provide accurate and current Internet information in this book. However, the Internet and information posted on it are constantly changing, so it is inevitable that some of the Internet addresses listed in this textbook will change.

Becoming a Teacher

Chapter 1

Getting Hired

Security is mostly a superstition. It does not exist in nature. Life is either a daring adventure or nothing.

—*Helen Keller, The Open Door* (1957)

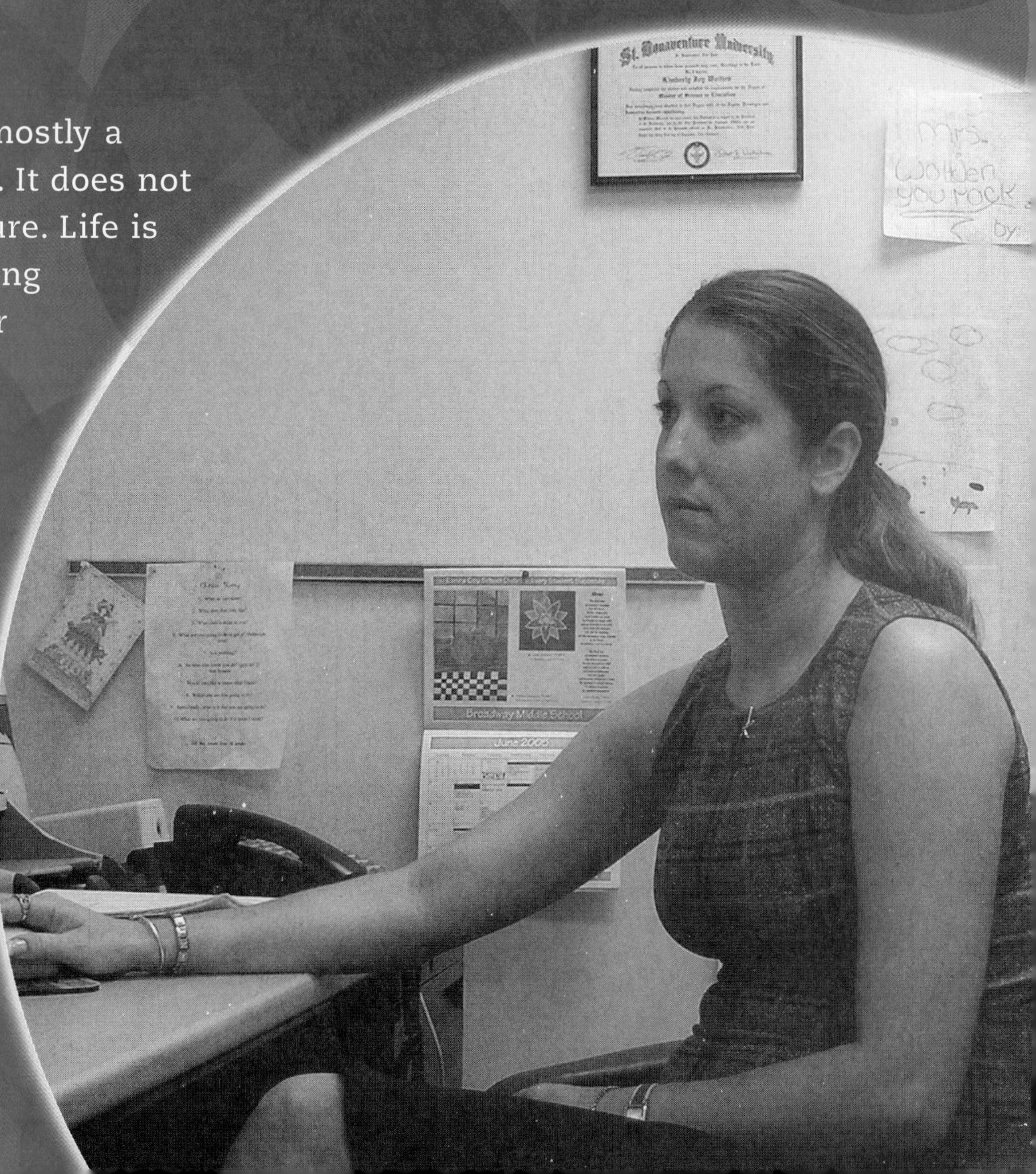

THE APPLICATION

THE PROCESS

- ☑ Become informed about the city, region, and school to which you intend to apply.
- ☑ Compile your portfolio and résumé in both binder and electronic formats.
- ☑ Request and complete the application packet.
- ☑ Prepare a list of questions for the interviewer.
- ☑ Be on time and dressed appropriately for the interview.
- ☑ Send a thank-you note to the interviewer regardless of whether you intend to take the job.

Getting a job as a teacher is an effort that follows a specific pattern and yet is often a spontaneous occurrence springing from a chance conversation or telephone call. No doubt you know someone who has been interviewing and job seeking for months without success, or someone who was hired while still student teaching. You have also probably heard how more than 100 people applied for a single position and of the individual who was signed on at a teacher recruitment fair.

Visiting the Career Placement Office

The first stop in your job search should be your college or university **career placement office**. There, you will be able to create a folder of materials that reflects your collegiate history, complete with résumé and recommendations.

Career placement offices will do the following for you:

- ☑ Maintain a confidential file of your academic profile
- ☑ Upon request, send copies of this file to prospective employers
- ☑ Provide information about graduate programs, grants, and assistantships, and contact information on prospective employers

Choosing Where You Want to Teach

Four types of school districts can be found in the United States: rural, suburban, urban, and private. Although these categories are not strictly defined, they fit the general composition of school districts in most states. Each category has a set of characteristics that you should study before deciding where to seek applications.

TYPES OF SCHOOL DISTRICTS

Type	Pros	Cons
Rural	Central organization; optimal job availability; some government incentives; stable; community oriented; moderate material and service support	Possibly longer travel time; limited hours with students; frequent budget cuts
Suburban	Generally affluent with strong budgets; more likely to have initiatives; excellent material and service support	Competitive job market; strong parental politics
Urban	High job availability; federal, state, and local teaching incentives; faster advancement; usually higher pay; high material support due to federal funding	Possibly high crime rates and more violence; lack of parental support; poor teaching conditions; many students with English as a second language (ESL) and in special education with high needs
Private	Teaching autonomy; almost a noncompetitive job market; usually organized; strong parental support; low levels of student misbehavior	Considerably lower pay; high turnover of colleagues and principals; poor-to-moderate material and service support; generally ideological

Finding Job Openings

Typically, employment opportunities fall into five categories:

1. ***Your hometown school district:*** Knowing the teachers and principals in your hometown can alert you to openings. Often, local districts look favorably on applicants whose roots are in the community. Depending on your desires, looking at your hometown district and the surrounding districts can be an excellent beginning for the job search.
2. ***Public announcements in the media and on the Internet:*** Newspapers and trade journals publicize openings for specific jobs. With the speed of the Internet, you can now access classified ads in most newspapers in the United States and abroad. Web sites such as www.aaee.org, www.careerbuilder.com, and www.teachersatwork.com provide up-to-date information on job openings throughout the nation. In addition, by going to the Web site of the education department of the state in which you would like to teach, you can find an e-mail address through which you may request applications for jobs. Alternatively, you can simply go to the Web site of the county in the state in which you want to teach and request an application (e.g., www.howard.k12.md.us/humanres/applicationinfo.html for an application for Howard County Public Schools in Maryland).
3. ***The school where you student-taught:*** This category is the most remote but occurs frequently for a select few students. After completing an outstanding student-teaching semester, and with an imminent opening in your subject or program area, the principal of the school, on strong recommendation from your cooperating teacher, may hire you. When school officials observe an obviously energetic, talented, and skillful student teacher for 2 months or more, they are more assured of future success than by the evidence provided in a résumé and an interview.
4. ***Teacher recruitment fairs:*** Attending recruitment gatherings—such as Teacher Recruitment Day in Buffalo, NY, or the Fairfax County Job Fair in Fairfax, VA—is probably the most direct method of finding a job. At such places, you will meet representatives from a variety of school districts who will be able to tell you the exact subject areas for which they are seeking teachers and the likelihood of job openings. Many prospective teachers find jobs at such fairs.
5. ***International job opportunities:*** Approximately 200 American international schools are attended by about 270,000 students and taught by 1,700 to 1,800 teachers. You can find out more information from www.tieonline.com or www.iss.edu/edustaff/edustafffaqs.html, or you can attend one of the international recruitment center fairs in Philadelphia, PA, or Boston, MA. You can also seek employment by writing to specific schools in other countries for information on their hiring policies.

Arranging Your Portfolio

For the competitive market, the best approach is to be prepared with a complete portfolio. The wise applicant will prepare a hard copy housed in a three-ring binder and an electronic copy burned onto a CD-ROM disk. The main document in your portfolio will be your résumé.

Briefcase CD CH1-1—Résumé Sample

The Résumé A standard rule to follow when you write your résumé is to keep it succinct, providing only specific facts that will be of interest to a prospective employer. Employers are busy people who will pale when confronted with a four- or five-page résumé. You should design a one- or two-page document that is easy to read but highlights your qualifications. It should contain the following information:

- ☑ Your full name, address, telephone number, and e-mail address
- ☑ The type of position or name of the position you are seeking (one short phrase)
- ☑ A list of your education from high school through college, including any summer or intersession workshops or seminars that garnered you a certificate

RÉSUMÉ SAMPLE

SIMEON BENJAMIN

One Park Place
Twainsville, NY 14901
(607) 770-0001
E-mail: sbenj@whocalled.com

Objective	A teaching position in an elementary school (Grades 1–6)
Education	B.S. in Elementary Education, concentration in Social Studies, Elmira College, NY. June 2005. GPA: 3.55/4.00. New York Childhood Education teaching certificate. Mark Twain High School, Bobsled, NY. June 2001.
Teaching Experience	***Student Teacher.*** Brookhaven Elementary School, Bradford, PA. Assisted second-grade classroom teacher, designed lesson plans, taught classes for 12 weeks. Worked with special education students and ESL children. ***Counselor.*** Camp ByeGone, Old Forge, NY. (Four summers: 1999–2002). Supervised 50 students for 8 weeks. Developed activities, taught survival and safety courses. Worked with children in a variety of situations both outdoor and indoor. ***Teaching Fieldwork.*** East Corning Middle School, Corning, NY. Assisted sixth-grade classroom teacher and taught some morning classes for 6 weeks. Most work was in literacy and social studies.
Honors	Kappa Delta Pi—National Education Honor Society Omicron Delta Pi—National Leadership Honor Society Presidential Scholar Alumni Weekend Keynote Speaker
Committees and Organizations	Orientation Leader—Responsible for 30 freshman for a semester Concert Band Orchestra Reporter for *Shout* (campus newspaper) Big Brother—Community program working with underpriveleged children Elmira Historical Society—Associate member National Council for the Teachers of Social Studies
Special Interests and Abilities	Civil War reenactor Soccer player—Played for 6 years Saxophone player
References	Dr. John H. Smith, Assistant Professor, Elmira College, One Park Place, Elmira, NY 14901. Phone: (607) 700-9000. E-mail: jhs@whocalled.com Mary Collins, Second-Grade Teacher, Brookhaven Elementary School, Bradford, PA 14333. Phone: (512) 700-0000. E-mail: mcins@whocalled.com George R. Hendricks, Sixth-Grade Teacher, East Corning Elementary School, One East Plaza, Corning, NY 14911. Phone: (607) 800-0000. E-mail: grh@whocalled.com

Briefcase CD CH1-2— Résumé Template

- ☑ A list of your work experiences, starting from high school (but not including every small job you might have had), including any service-work experience at fast-food or retail stores that demonstrates responsibility
- ☑ Your work with children in any capacity, including tutoring, student-teaching, and practicum experiences
- ☑ A list of awards and honors you received from high school forward, but not in detail
- ☑ A list of organizations and other community-related initiatives in which you participated, including your work on committees, in clubs, or in other campus programs

- ☑ Your main interests and any abilities that would enhance your qualifications for the job, in a few short words
- ☑ The names, addresses, and telephone numbers for at least three people who can speak to your strengths and overall competence, one of whom should know your potential teaching ability

Briefcase CD CH1-3—Cover Letter Sample

The Cover Letter A cover letter should accompany your résumé. As one principal said, "If they can't get my attention through the cover letter, I see no reason in reading any further" (Roden & Cardina, 1996, p. 264). Besides being the essence of brevity, your cover letter should include the following information:

- ☑ Your name and address in the heading
- ☑ Specific reference to the job for which you are applying
- ☑ Specific reference to the certificate you hold
- ☑ Reference to program initiatives ongoing in the district to which you are applying—if they were mentioned in the advertisement for the position
- ☑ A brief summary of your reasons for wanting the job and why you believe you are qualified
- ☑ A note of any special skills that might make you a more attractive candidate (e.g., soccer coach, theater experience, cardiopulmonary resuscitation certificate)
- ☑ Clear information about your availability for an interview

Briefcase CD CH1-4—Cover Letter Template

COVER LETTER SAMPLES

Cover letter A

Dear Dr. Couscous:

It is with great excitement that I seek employment with your district for the second-grade position listed in the *Reaching Star.* I am confident that my skills and experience will be a great asset to your school system.

Education is necessary so that understanding can be established at an early age. When education does not flourish, ignorance and society's ills prevail.

As a teacher, I will encourage my students to learn beyond the test and to engage in classroom activities that will stimulate intellectual growth. I will also be a role model from whom the students can learn values and strength of character. I have a great deal of experience working with young children and know that I have much to teach them.

My teaching method will be to allow the student to discover the value of the learning process and to gain knowledge through interaction and exploration. I will use a variety of strategies to help my students discover their strengths and abilities.

Please contact me at the above address or at the telephone number listed below. I am available at your convenience for an interview.

Cover letter B

Dear Dr. Couscous:

Please accept my formal application for the second-grade position posted in the *Reaching Star.* I am a New York State–certified elementary school teacher, having recently graduated from the Elmira College education program.

It has been my goal since middle school to become a teacher, and to that end I have spent many hours working with young children both in and out of the classroom. As a summer camp counselor, reading tutor, and volunteer Big Sister, I have learned the value of working with children. As stated in my résumé, I have coached intramural soccer teams and was an assistant cheerleading coach.

I am eager to join a team of professionals who are working with children every day. The Success for All program at Reaching Elementary has won praise from local legislators. As I am familiar with Success for All, I believe I would be an asset to your team and to the children whom you serve.

I am available for an interview at your convenience. I can be reached at the telephone number or e-mail address listed in the heading of this letter.

Thank you for your time. I look forward to hearing from you.

Caution: Pitfalls to Avoid in Your Cover Letter

- Self-aggrandizement
- Lengthy and metaphoric statements about your personal educational philosophy
- Extensive references to your hobbies or personal life
- Salary demands

Stating the Facts:

On New Teachers: New teachers—those who have 3 or fewer years' experience—composed 16% of all teachers in 2000. Twenty-one percent of new teachers are finding employment in schools with the highest percentages of students who are limited-English proficient and low income (Wirt et al., 2003).

Caution: Pitfalls to Avoid in Your Portfolio

- Avoid the 3- or 4-inch binder full of work from student teaching and pages of awards and honors' certificates.
- Do not ship the binder by a carrier that requires signatures, which may put the receipt of your portfolio in a negative light.
- Avoid the overly decorative and elaborately graphic-inspired binder that might indicate little substance beneath the glitter.

Although applicants in some occupations customarily state their salary parameters, in education, information on teacher salaries is widely available. You should be aware of the salary within a few hundred dollars before sending the application.

The Portfolio Binder Designing and organizing your personal teaching **portfolio binder** is considered by some individuals to be an art. Seldom does a teacher education program fail to provide workshops on or even course hours in putting together an informative portfolio. Following is a typical listing for a teaching portfolio:

- ☑ ***Table of contents:*** A convenience for people reading your portfolio. It should be concise and written in titles rather than sentences.
- ☑ ***Résumé:*** The lead document in your portfolio. It should provide a general overview of you, your education, and your work.
- ☑ ***Educational philosophy:*** A paper reflecting your ideas and concepts, supported by those of educational philosophers, theorists, and practitioners.
- ☑ ***Teaching style:*** A description reflecting your preferred mode of teaching, along with specific examples.
- ☑ ***Teacher work sample:*** A plan for a specific unit, with results of students' learning.
- ☑ ***Classroom management plan:*** A description of your overall management strategy, including homework requirements, parent conferences, grading procedures, and general discipline policy.
- ☑ ***Sample student work:*** Examples of student work acquired during your internship and student-teaching assignments.
- ☑ ***Sample thematic unit or unit plan:*** A fairly detailed plan that will demonstrate your ability to orchestrate a series of lessons that will reflect your instructional skills.

Briefcase CD CH1-5—Portfolio Binder Format

In Real Time: The Portfolio

Submitting your entire portfolio with the application when it has not been requested may place you at the bottom of the pile. However, bringing your portfolio to the interview is a must. The interviewer may or may not look at it then, but if you are being considered with others, the strength of your portfolio may make the difference in your getting the job.

Briefcase CD CH1-6—Electronic Portfolio Format

The Electronic Portfolio In this era, especially for teachers, your facility with computers is not a skill *to acquire,* it is a skill *required* before you complete your first job application. Employers expect to see an e-mail address in the heading of your résumé; in fact, e-mail communication can facilitate the entire hiring process for both the employer and the job seeker. If you do not have an e-mail address, establish one at any of the major Web servers such as Yahoo, Google, Hotmail, or AOL. However, e-mail is an elementary technological requirement; the premier reflection of your skills with technology is the electronic portfolio.

Why Is the Electronic Portfolio Effective? Fast becoming routine in the application process, the **electronic portfolio** provides a range of exposure to your background, experience, and skills that the physical binder cannot match. Darcy Plante, a successful teaching candidate, designed an electronic portfolio featuring each of her student-teaching experiences, complete with scanned copies of students' work, her supervisors' evaluations, awards certificates, and a series of photos showing her as she was teaching (National Governors Association Center for Best Practices, 2002). The portfolio also contained Word documents outlining her personal philosophy, her classroom management plan, a sample thematic unit, and recommendations from her career placement file. She burned all this material onto a CD-ROM disk, made multiple copies, and included a disk with each application. Darcy received a number of requests for interviews in which her skills with computers—as evidenced by her electronic portfolio—were mentioned and praised.

If you are more skillful, you can also include audio and video clips in which you might orally present your philosophy or give examples of your teaching strategies. After you complete the portfolio, place all the material into a single folder. If you do not have the skills to make a CD, or lack the hardware, the college media or computer center can direct you as to how to burn a CD. Be sure to provide instructions on the label of the CD for the prospective employer. A bonus accompanying the knowledge and skill you acquire

ELECTRONIC PORTFOLIO FORMAT

Content	Format
Personal philosophy of education	Word document
Student-teaching evaluation forms	Scanned and saved in JPEG format
Personal notes or teaching journal entries	Scanned and saved in JPEG format
Students' work from one of your student-teaching lessons	Scanned and saved in JPEG format
Sample lesson plan featuring introductory material	Word document
Sample lesson plan featuring project work, inquiry-based learning, or cooperative learning	Word document
Sample thematic unit or unit plan	Word or PowerPoint document
Your prescription for organizing instruction by aligning state and national standards	Word document
Your classroom management plan	Word or PowerPoint document
List of texts you have read on education, learning, teaching	Word document
Copies of awards and certificates	Scanned and saved in JPEG format
Pictures of you in the teaching context	Downloaded in JPEG format
Video clip of you tutoring a student or giving a talk on some aspect of teaching	iMovie to QuickTime format (Macintosh) Movie Maker to Windows Media format (Windows)
Audio clip of your personal philosophy or teaching strategies	QuickTime format (Macintosh) RealOne Player or Windows Media Format (Windows)

while creating such a portfolio is the ease with which you can subsequently construct a Web site featuring your teaching profile. Then, prospective employers can access your site, view your material, and become familiar with your background before or even during the interview.

THE INTERVIEW

STATING THE FACTS:

On the Interview: The results of a nationwide survey of principals and school leaders of 2,200 school districts revealed that 39% believed "the ability to present one's self professionally in an interview" was the most important factor in the decision to hire (Roden & Cardina, 1996, p. 263).

Of all the factors that affect getting hired, none equals the interview. Most applicants have the credentials (i.e., the degree, the provisional teaching certificate, and the necessary passing scores on competency tests). However, whether you get the job depends on the strength of others' recommendations, the highlights of your portfolio, and, most important, the results of your personal interview.

Format

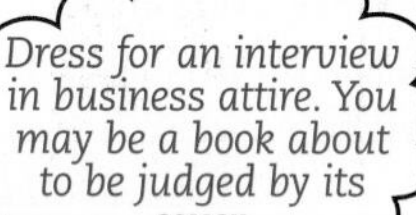

The format of the interview varies in accordance with where it is being conducted, in what manner, and with whom:

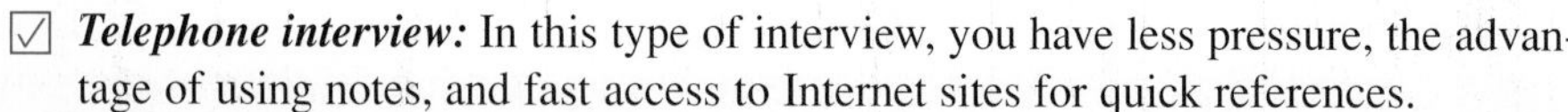

- ☑ ***Telephone interview:*** In this type of interview, you have less pressure, the advantage of using notes, and fast access to Internet sites for quick references.
- ☑ ***Face-to-face interview:*** At this type of interview, you face more pressure and your appearance is crucial, but you have a greater degree of personal interaction to highlight your strengths, and you may be able to use your notebook computer to present your electronic portfolio. The interview could be held at an off-school site.
- ☑ ***Length of interview:*** Any interview usually lasts only 15 to 30 minutes.
- ☑ ***Interviewer:*** Most often, the principal or vice-principal interviews applicants, but, alternatively, you could be interviewed by a search team of four or more people.
- ☑ ***Dress and appearance:*** Always interview in business attire and do not wear excess jewelry.

VOICES IN THE CLASSROOM
Appearance Counts

PROF: Hi, Dan, how did the interview go? Do you think you got the job?

DAN: Well, it didn't go well at all, and I don't think I'll get a job offer.

PROF: What happened?

DAN: Well, they were interviewing people in this huge hall. There must have been 30 or 40 other applicants. When my interviewer motioned for me to come over, I could see she was staring at me with this shocked look on her face. I figured it must have been the hat.

PROF: You were wearing a hat? What kind of hat?

DAN: My NY Yankees hat.

PROF: What? You wore a baseball hat to your job interview?

DAN: Well, yeah, but I took it off as soon as I saw her face. And I asked her if the hat bothered her. She said it didn't, but it just took her off balance. But I think it did bother her, because she was very short with me throughout the interview and didn't really seem interested in my portfolio or what I had to say. I can't believe that wearing a hat can make so much of a difference.

INTERVIEW CHECKLIST

☑ ***Research your interviewer:*** Get background information on the school district, the school, and the position. Use your resources to identify the interviewer (probably a principal) so that you are informed about his or her expectations of new teachers. Also check for his or her publications, program initiatives, committee work, and educational philosophy.

☑ ***Research the school and district:*** Seek out brochures or other material on the mission and goals of the district. Educate yourself on the financial situation, academic reputation, number of schools, and latest initiatives. Go to the local library and look up newspaper reports on school board meetings that might tell you about the latest programs, problems, initiatives, or hiring practices.

☑ ***Prepare yourself:*** Prepare a list of answers to questions that you would expect in an interview for a teaching position. Obtain specific information on an initiative in the district or school so that you can speak knowledgeably on the topic.

☑ ***Dress appropriately:*** Casual dress is inappropriate. Business attire is pro forma for the interview process. For this event in your life, remove the jewelry from any noticeable pierced areas, with the possible exception of an earring or earrings.

☑ ***Greet the interviewer:*** Shake hands firmly and establish eye contact. Usually an interviewer will try to relax you with small talk. Try not to respond with remarks that will extend this portion of the interview. For example, comments on the weather should not be extended with a complete report of climatic conditions in your hometown.

☑ ***Ask your prepared questions:*** You should have a list of prepared questions that you may or may not use, such as "Will I be expected to take on an extracurricular activity?" and "Do you use a specified reading program?"

☑ ***Request materials:*** One good idea is to ask for brochures or reports that might help you get a better picture of the school and its policies. Doing so demonstrates your initiative and interest.

☑ ***Thank the interviewer:*** Thank the interviewer orally. Then, within an hour of the interview, write a thank-you note to the interviewer and post it that day. The contents of the note should be general and possibly refer to one item discussed; however, be brief.

Briefcase CD CH1-7—Interview Checklist Template

Interview Questions

As a future teacher, you should be aware of the importance of preparation. Interviewers will ask you a variety of questions. To prepare for such questions, you should research the following in advance:

- ☑ The history and facts about the city in which the school is located
- ☑ Facts about the district to which you are applying and the surrounding districts
- ☑ Outstanding initiatives within the district, such as the literacy program, character education, and health education
- ☑ The names of the district superintendent and possibly the school board president

The Interview questions will be organized around four main topic areas:

Briefcase CD CH1-8—Probable Interview Questions

- ☑ ***Credentials:*** Your teaching certificate, your bachelor's degree, your major or area of concentration, and any other certificates applicable to the position you are seeking
- ☑ ***Experience with children:*** Your student-teaching experiences, as well as any other work with children throughout your adolescent and adult life
- ☑ ***Professional knowledge:*** Your working knowledge of teaching strategies and theories, and your strategies relating to classroom management
- ☑ ***Specific skills:*** Your particular areas of expertise (e.g., social studies, art, music, math) and your skills in computer technology and any field that would relate to extracurricular activities
- ☑ ***Personal views:*** Your viewpoint on various subjects and your way of handling certain situations

LEGAL SIDEBAR

Laws That Govern Employment

- Title VII of the Civil Rights Act of 1964 (Title VII)
- Equal Pay Act of 1963 (EPA)
- Age Discrimination in Employment Act of 1967 (ADEA)
- Title I and Title V of the Americans with Disabilities Act of 1990 (ADA)
- Sections 501 and 505 of the Rehabilitation Act of 1973
- Civil Rights Act of 1991
- Immigration and Reform and Control Act of 1986

PROBABLE INTERVIEW QUESTIONS

Topic	Probable questions
Credentials: Questions on this topic set the tone of the interview and establish a communication link that is comfortable for you and the interviewer.	What teaching certificate do you have in hand at this time? What psychology courses did you complete in your undergraduate program? methods courses? Did you minor in a specific subject other than your major? In what clubs or activities did you participate that would be beneficial to your work with children here?
Experience with children: Questions on this topic give the interviewer an idea of your range of experience with children.	Did you work with children before college? In general, how much time have you spent in actual classroom contact with students? Did you work with children during the summers?
Professional knowledge: Questions on this topic will help the interviewer gauge your knowledge of the field and your ability to articulate an instructional strategy.	Can you describe your teaching experiences with children during your preparation program? Tell me about your most successful lesson taught during student teaching. What type of grading system did you use? Do you subscribe to Howard Gardner's multiple intelligences theory? Can you describe how you incorporated one of our state's learning standards into one of your lessons? How would you organize a unit in your subject area (secondary)? How would you integrate subject areas using a theme (elementary)?
Specific skills: Questions on this topic are used to identify your particular areas of expertise and your skills that would relate to extracurricular activities.	What sports have you coached? Do you have any experience or skills in organizing after-school programs that would involve students? Have you had any experiences that help develop programs for student enrichment?
Personal views: Questions on this topic are geared to ascertain your ability to think quickly and to assess your reaction time.	How would you manage an irate parent who interrupts your class? If you had the power, how would you change the current system of education for very young children? for adolescents? What are your views on character education?

Illegal Questions The interview is a routine factor in the hiring process that has a history of its own. Throughout the civil rights movement of the 1950s and 1960s, new legislation and a series of court rulings brought about a number of restrictions within the employment process; one is the line of questioning interviewers may use. For example, the interviewer cannot legally ask about your race or ethnic lineage, such as "Where are your parents from originally?"

Once an illegal question is asked, you are immediately faced with a dilemma. If you answer the question, you give the interviewer personal information that may have a detrimental effect not only on your hiring, but also on your future with the district or school. If you exercise your legal right and refuse to answer, you risk antagonizing the interviewer, which may also be to your detriment. The only logical response is to provide as little information as possible, and later to review the entire interview and rethink your decision to accept a position with the district or school. Taking any job that is offered may solve your short-term financial problems but may ultimately damage your career by placing you in a situation that is stressful and that might jeopardize your teaching record.

Questions asked by interviewers for jobs are guided by the following federal laws: Title VII of the Civil Rights Act, the Age Discrimination in Employment Act, the Equal Pay Act, the Immigration and Reform and Control Act, and the Americans with Disabilities Act.

Areas of questioning that your interviewer must legally avoid	Questions that *may* be asked
Your ancestry, race, ethnicity, or national origin, or that of your family	Are you a U.S. citizen and do you plan on remaining in the United States? Can you speak and write English fluently?
Your age, weight, height, physical disability, or physical condition	Are you physically able to do the job? Do you require some accommodation?
Your marital status	Will you be able to comply with the daily work schedule? Do you anticipate any long absences during the year?
Lengthy inquiries into where and how long you lived in residences of your past, and with whom you live	How long have you been residing at your current address?
Inquiries into your religion, your religious practices, or those of your family	No question on this topic is legal, but the employer must afford you accommodation for religious observances.
Type of discharge from the military	How can your experiences in the military assist you in your job as a teacher?
Questions on bankruptcy or your financial situation, lawsuits past or pending, the type of car you drive, or any medications you may be taking	Have you been convicted of a felony? Have you ever been arrested for child molestation or child abuse?

VOICES IN THE CLASSROOM
The Illegal Question

My first job interview for a third-grade position alerted me to a potential problem in my young teaching career. The principal, a male, opened the interview asking if I was married and had children. Not being aware of the guidelines established by Title VII of the 1964 Civil Rights Act, I had no idea that this was an illegal question. When I responded that I was married but had no children, he asked if I was pregnant. Sensing my discomfort, he explained that it would do no good to continue with the interview if I was pregnant, as they would need to replace me halfway through the year when I left to have the baby, and that this would be unfair to the school and my students.

I assured him that I was not pregnant and even went on to swear that I would not be getting pregnant, so eager was I to snag the job. However, the interview questioning became even more bizarre when he asked me about my political persuasions and whether or not I believed in gay parents having children. I guessed that he wanted me to answer in the negative, but I had already surrendered enough of my integrity on the pregnancy issue and replied that I supported the rights of gay and lesbian parents. The remainder of the interview went along with the usual questions of my thoughts on curriculum, homework, classroom management, and parental communication.

I did not receive an offer for the job, saving me an uncomfortable phone conversation in which I would have refused. I knew that if I had gotten the job, the probability of a conflict with the principal was very high.

—*Math teacher*

Briefcase CD CH1-9—Questions for the Interviewer

Questions for the Interviewer

At any interview, you should be prepared to ask the interviewer questions. One job-interview expert who surveyed more than 150 job coaches, interviewers, and managers, cited "Not asking questions" as the number one reason for the interviewer to lose confidence in the applicant's ability (Kador, 2002). However, during the interview, any applicant must be able to "read" the interviewer's reactions to the questions being asked. If you ask too many questions, you might be viewed as too forward and self-interested.

You should develop questions in two main areas:

- ☑ ***Professional issues:*** Ask questions about the field of teaching (e.g., literacy programs, textbooks, library and media or computer availability, room assignments).
- ☑ ***Personnel issues:*** Ask questions about retirement, health benefits, and union shop requirements.

PROSPECTS

Networking is an essential strategy in today's job market when you are searching for the position that fits your credentials and personal needs.

The Teacher Shortage

Does a teacher shortage exist? The short answer is yes and no. The National Governors Association (2002) reported that by 2012, more than 700,000 teachers will retire, which is approximately 28% of the entire public school teaching force. However, since 1984, the number of colleges and universities preparing teachers for U.S. schools has increased from 1,287 to 1,354, and the number of graduates receiving bachelor's and master's degrees jumped by 50% to 230,000 (National Commission on Teaching and America's Future, 2002). In addition, approximately 80,000 retired or former teachers are available to return to the classroom.

In 2000, an estimated 160,000 teachers graduated with certification from U.S. colleges and universities (National Commission, 2002). In 1999, only 85,000 graduates were needed to fill jobs. Yet, in 2002, New York City had more than 11,000 uncertified teachers in classrooms.

Where Are the Shortages? The shortage is real, but the glut is also real. The shortage is felt most sharply in urban centers, where dwindling tax dollars and rising social costs have had a huge detrimental impact on public schools. These areas are often not attractive to newly certified teachers, who seek positions in the more well-supported and progressive suburban schools. Accordingly, the number of applicants for a single elementary position in the Dublin, OH, school district will far exceed the number of applicants in most urban school districts for a like elementary position. Therefore, you must expect that job openings in suburban, affluent school districts will be fewer and more competitive than those in either distantly rural or large urban areas.

Job Availability

The specific area of your certification often determines your job prospects. Bilingual teachers, especially of Spanish, and special education teachers are at a premium and may find jobs more easily than will social studies or English teachers. Likewise, science teachers, especially those specializing in physics and chemistry, will find a more favorable market. Although this information is interesting, you should not become discouraged if, for example, you are certified for elementary-level teaching, an area with an oversupply of teachers. Teachers are constantly retiring, taking leaves of absence, or going on extended sick leave, which creates a dynamic cycle of job openings.

The American Association for Employment in Education (2003) reported some national trends in the hiring process:

- ☑ Mathematics, all sciences, and special education fields have "considerable shortages" of teachers.
- ☑ "Some shortage" exists in kindergarten and the primary and intermediate grades.
- ☑ A "considerable surplus" of teachers exists in the fields of art and visual education, and social studies.
- ☑ States implementing class-reduction initiatives have a rising need for teachers.
- ☑ San Francisco's high cost of living has discouraged teacher applicants.
- ☑ The high numbers of charter schools in Arizona have created some demand there.
- ☑ Secondary math and science teacher shortages will increase by 2006.

Fields of greatest need	Fields in surplus
Special education—all branches	Health education
Chemistry	Elementary—pre-K, primary, and intermediate
Physics	Social studies (secondary)
Mathematics	English (secondary)
Technology education	Physical education—elementary and secondary
Bilingual education	Performing and visual arts—theater, dance, art
English as a second language	

Teacher Recruitment Incentives

A number of school districts throughout the United States are experiencing sharply depleted teaching forces as a result of retirements and high job turnover rates. These districts are most commonly in urban areas with large numbers of students with special needs. States such as Nevada, North Carolina, and Florida are growing in population, and school districts are hard-pressed to staff their schools adequately. Therefore, these districts will often offer **teacher recruitment incentives** for qualified teachers. For example, some counties in North Carolina offer as much as $2,000 in signing bonuses and an additional stipend for teachers of math, science, technology, and foreign languages. Additional perks you might receive include relocation allowances, laptop computers, and free health, dental, and life insurance (http://teach4nc.org/salaries/incentives.html). Baltimore City Schools offers $1,000 toward relocation costs, as well as a $1,500 signing bonus for teachers who acquire a master's degree in critical subject areas (Baltimore City Public School System, 2005). San Francisco City Schools offers a $2,500 signing bonus for teachers in critical subject areas (http://portal.sfusd.edu). Nebraska has a variety of loan-forgiveness and incentive programs for teaching in high-need schools (www.nebraskateachereducation.org/loanscholar.htm).

These four examples are only a few of such incentives offered throughout the nation. If you are willing to accept the challenge of teaching in schools with large numbers of students with special needs, and to live in urban areas, you may find that not only will you make more money, but you may also reduce some of your college loan debt.

Briefcase CD CH1-10—Supply of and Demand for Teachers

What Is the Troops-to-Teachers Program? In 2005, the U.S. Department of Education released final regulations for a Troops-to-Teachers program as part of a provision under the No Child Left Behind Act (Innovation for Teacher Quality, 2005). According to the provisions of this program, armed-forces personnel may receive as much as $5,000 toward their education as qualified teachers. The provision also includes rules on assistance to find employment in high-need local education agencies or public charter schools as long as participants agree to teach for 3 years. These regulations went into effect on September 15, 2005.

Region Codes: 1—Northwest; 2—West; 3—Rocky Mountains; 4—Great Plains/Midwest; 5—South Central; 6—Southeast; 7—Great Lakes; 8—Middle Atlantic; 9—Northeast; 10—Alaska; 11—Hawaii
Demand Codes: 5.00–4.21 = Considerable Shortage; 4.20–3.41 = Some Shortage; 3.40–2.61 = Balanced; 2.60–1.81 = Some Surplus; 1.80–1.00 = Considerable Surplus

SUPPLY OF AND DEMAND FOR TEACHERS

	Region											
Field	**1**	**2**	**3**	**4**	**5**	**6**	**7**	**8**	**9**	**10**	**11**	**U.S.**
Art/visual ed.	2.29	2.18	2.67	2.88	2.79	2.75	2.61	2.53	2.91			2.68
Bilingual ed.	4.17	3.93	4.67	4	4.38	4.2	3.88	4	4.67			4.12
Business ed.	2.5	2.63	2.8	3.11	2.86	3	2.56	2.88	3		3	2.87
Pre-K	2.17	2.89	3.2	2.3	3.26	2.93	2.14	2.39	2.82		4	2.57
Kindergarten	2.11	2.65	3	2.29	3.27	3	2.13	2.34	2.6		4	2.51
Primary (1–3)	2.2	2.65	3.38	2.19	3	2.95	1.97	2.36	2.29		4	2.43
Intermed. (4–5)	2.33	2.63	3.67	2.35	3.14	3.1	2.32	2.58	2.54		4	2.63
Middle	2.38	2.82	4.2	2.88	3.48	3.47	2.74	3.03	2.58		4	3
Eng. sec. lang.	4	3.55	4.5	4	3.94	3.79	3.29	4.15	3.6			3.8
Health ed.	2.29	2.5	3.5	2.63	2.69	2.5	2.27	2.11	3			2.51
Home ec.	3	2.67	4	3.67	3.2	3	3	4	2			3.17
Class. lang.	3	3	3	3.4	2.67	3	2.83	3.6	3			3.11
French	2.71	2.8	3.67	3.28	3.2	3.46	3.12	3	2.75	3		3.14
German	2.57	2.88	2.33	3.12	3	3.57	3.1	3.24	2.33	3		3.11
Japanese	2.25	3	3	3	3.33	3.8	3.5	4	2	3		3.23
Spanish	3.38	3.33	4.5	3.85	4.22	4.09	3.77	3.94	3.56	3		3.86
Mathematics	3.78	4	4.43	3.98	4.28	4.3	4.15	4.26	4.71	5	5	4.19
Music instru.	3	3.1	3.67	3.63	3.04	2.9	3.04	2.93	2.83			3.15
Music gen.	2.71	2.83	4	3.46	2.76	2.86	2.96	2.78	2.86	3		3
Phys. ed.	2.43	2.15	2	2.37	2.52	2.33	2.17	2.1	2.71		3	2.32
Literacy	3	3.08	3	3.32	3.26	3.27	3	3.26	3.1	3	4	3.18
Biology	3	4.22	3.2	3.6	3.86	4	3.66	3.77	4.06		4.5	3.78
Chemistry	4	4.31	3.2	3.94	4.16	4.16	4.04	4.07	4.4		5	4.7
Earth/physical	3.5	3.79	3.4	3.62	3.74	3.84	3.71	3.78	4.29			3.73
Physics	4	4.24	3.2	4.18	4.29	4.27	4.23	4.27	4.57			4.22
General sci.	3.38	4.08	3.88	3.49	3.73	3.96	3.6	3.55	4	5	4	3.69
Social studies	2	2.18	2.83	2.54	2.53	2.66	2.15	2.09	2.77	3	3	2.37
Special ed.	4.17	4.83	5	3.96	3.9	4.53	4.08	4.42	4.88			4.3
Speech ed.	2.67	3.8	3	3.11	3.5	3.45	2.8	3.13				3.2

Note. From 2004 *Job Search Handbook for Educators* (p. 8), by the American Association for Employment in Education, 2003, Columbus, OH: Author. Copyright 2003 by the American Association for Employment in Education. Reprinted with permission.

DOS AND DON'TS

Don't	Do
Submit your portfolio with the application (unless asked)	Bring your portfolio to the interview
Expect your career placement office to send your folder automatically	Follow up with a call to your career placement office each time you request your folder to be submitted
Send your application everywhere without first informing yourself of the location, size, and particulars of the schools	Research all schools to which you intend to apply; go to Web sites or to state education departments for specific information; speak with someone who works at the school
Submit a four-page résumé with details on every job you have had	Submit a one- or two-page résumé that is concise but informative; place detailed information about your experiences in your portfolio
Write a cover letter that instructs the reader on education, that is too lengthy or detailed, or that overly glorifies your accomplishments	Write a cover letter that is succinct, adds a note about the district to which you are applying, and provides one clear reason why you should be hired
Design an electronic portfolio that is too flashy and "busy" with graphics and animations	Design an electronic portfolio that is user friendly, is easy to navigate, and highlights your strong points with clarity and taste
Conduct a telephone interview in a public place or where you will be disrupted	Conduct a telephone interview with the following at hand: your portfolio, information on the district to which you are applying, and a notepad for notes
Arrive at an interview tardy, in casual dress, or unprepared for the questions to be asked	Arrive 10 minutes early, wearing business attire, prepared for questions that may relate to the school to which you are applying, and with questions for the interviewer
Forget to thank the interviewer for his or her time	Send a thank-you note to the interviewer

WEB SITES OF INTEREST

http://www.teachersatwork.com
This site provides help with résumé and job searches. It has an up-to-date listing of available jobs throughout the United States, and the search function is fast.

http://www.abcteachingjobs.com
This commercial site has 26,555 public and private institutions registered with it to find qualified teachers.

http://students.usask.ca/support/employment/tools/teaching
This site has a comprehensive list of probable interview questions.

http://www.totaljobs.com/education-jobs.html
This site posts teaching jobs in the United Kingdom and provides additional services such as checking your résumé for accuracy.

http://www.southernteachers.com/Teachers.htm
This site claims to be the nation's oldest teacher-placement service. It lists job openings in the Southeast, as well as in Virginia, North Carolina, and Maryland.

http://www.fapeonline.org/job_bank.htm
This site lists job openings in special education. It provides specific descriptions of the jobs and their locations.

http://nces.ed.gov/surveys/SASS/tables/table_01.asp
This site lists job availability by type of school (urban, rural, suburban) and school enrollment.

http://www.bls.gov/oco/ocos069.htm
This U.S. Department of Labor site lists job availability for all teacher positions, from preschool through high school.

http://www.aft.org/salary
This American Federation of Teachers Web site lists salary trends for all teachers. These statistics are the most readily available and comprehensive on teachers' salaries.

http://www.teach-now.org
This site details the alternative routes to certification in all 50 states and Washington, DC.

http://teach4nc.org/salaries/incentives.html
This site displays a sample of the types of incentives some school districts are offering to recruit new teachers.

http://portal.sfusd.edu
This site provides an example of a district offering a signing bonus for new teachers.

http://www.nebraskateachereducation.org/loan_scholar.htm
This site provides an example of a recruitment incentive.

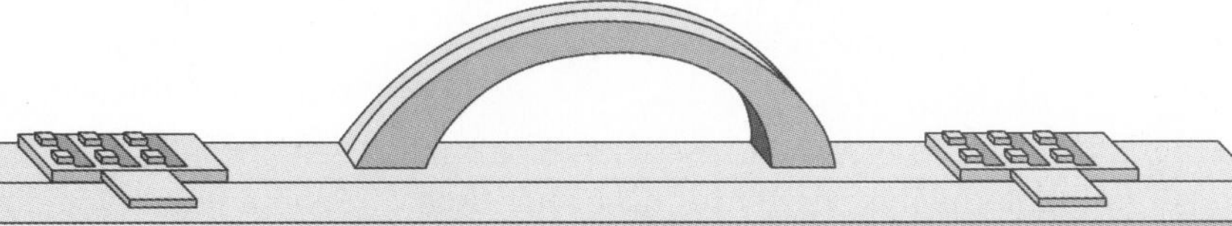

For Your Briefcase

To Do

- Identify your teaching preference.
- Prepare your résumé and cover letter.
- Prepare your portfolios—binder and electronic.
- Prepare for the interview—create a list of questions.

Resources on Your Briefcase CD

Samples

- Résumé Sample
- Cover Letter Sample

Templates

- Résumé Template
- Cover Letter Template
- Interview Checklist Template

Tables

- Portfolio Binder Format
- Electronic Portfolio Format
- Probable Interview Questions
- Questions for the Interviewer
- Supply of and Demand for Teachers

REFERENCES

American Association for Employment in Education. (2003). *2004 Job search handbook for educators.* Columbus, OH: Author.

Baltimore City Public School System. (2005). *BCPSS teacher stipends.* Baltimore: Author. Retrieved March 28, 2005, from http://www.bcps.k12.md.us/Careers/PDF/Stipend_Flyer.pdf

Innovation for Teacher Quality, 34 C.F.R. pt. 230 (2005).

Kador, J. (2002). *201 Best questions to ask on your interview.* New York: McGraw-Hill.

National Commission on Teaching and America's Future. (2002). *Unraveling the "teacher shortage" problem: Teacher retention is the key.* Washington, DC: Author.

National Governors Association Center for Best Practices. (2002, December 9). *Improving teacher evaluation to improve teaching quality.* Washington, DC: Author. Available from http://www.nga.org/portal/site/nga/menuitem.9123e83a1f6786440ddcbeeb501010a0/?vgnextoid=34b2303cb0b32010VgnVCM1000001a01010aRCRD&vgnextchannel=4b18f074f0d9ff00VgnVCM1000001a01010aRCRD

Roden, J. K., & Cardina, C. E. (1996). Factors which contribute to school administrators' hiring decisions. *Education, 117*(2), 262–267.

Wirt, J., Choy, S., Provasnik, S., Rooney, P., Sen, A., & Tobin, R. (2003). *The condition of education 2003.* Washington, DC: National Center for Education Statistics. (NCES No. 2003–067)

Chapter 2

Navigating the Education System

The universal brotherhood of
man is our most precious
possession. . . .
—*Mark Twain (1898)*

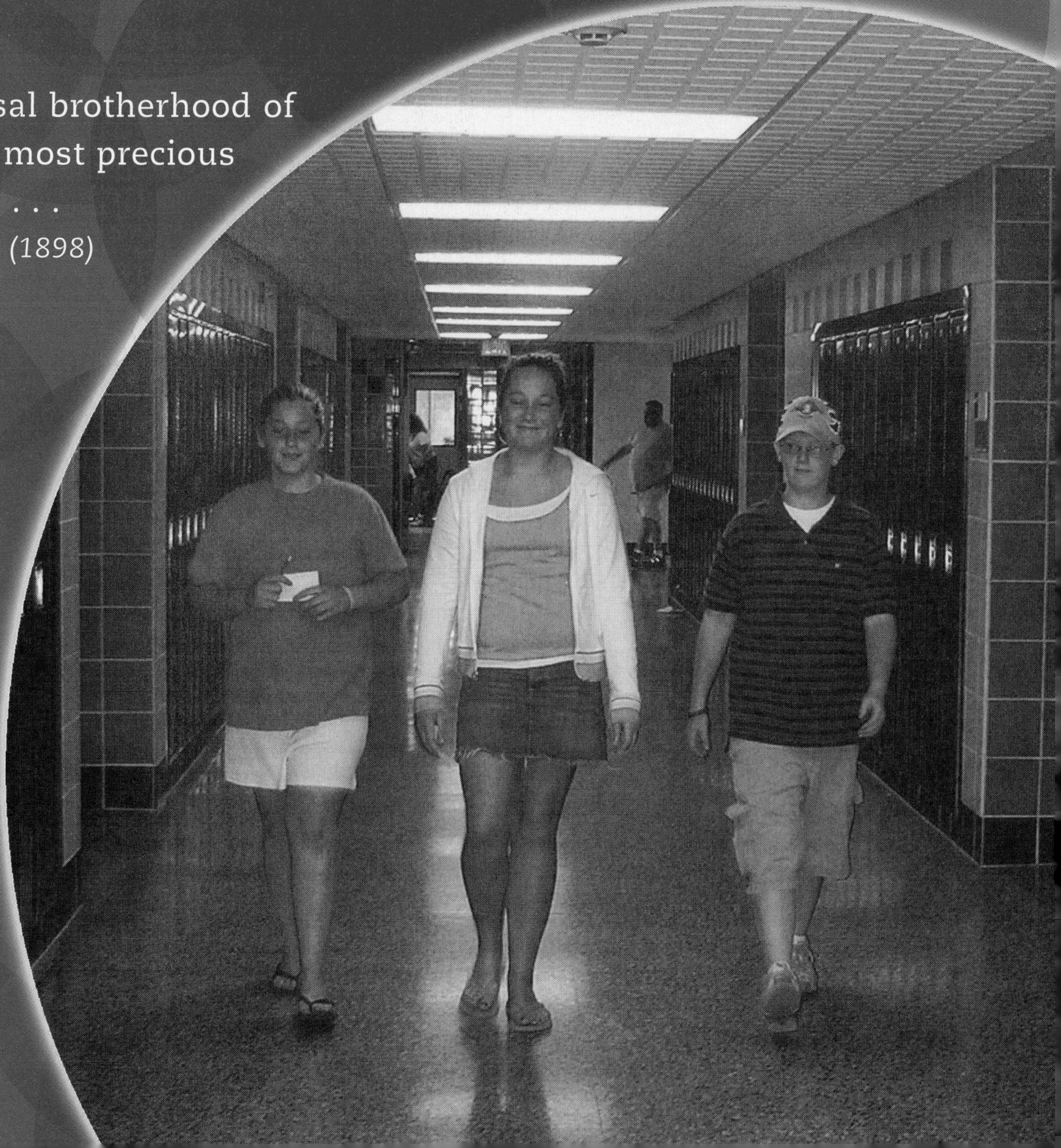

THE CHAIN OF COMMAND

ADMINISTRATIVE HIERARCHY

- ☑ *State board of education:* Commissioners or chancellors
- ☑ *School board:* Elected
- ☑ *Superintendent:* Hired by school board
- ☑ *District assistant superintendents:* Hired by superintendent
- ☑ *Principals:* Hired by superintendent
- ☑ *Vice-principals:* Hired by superintendent
- ☑ *Department chairs:* Selected and hired by superintendent

School systems are organized structures whose purpose is "to promote the intellectual growth and development of young people" (Kauchak, Eggen, & Carter, 2002, p. 215). They are not isolated entities but extensions of a vast system that has grown more complex and more integrated than Horace Mann would have ever imagined. They are organized around the business or corporation model:

- ☑ The board of education is like a board of trustees.
- ☑ The superintendent is the chief executive officer.
- ☑ Principals are similar to plant managers.

The School Board

FUNCTIONS OF THE SCHOOL BOARD

- ☑ Employs all staff
- ☑ Administers student services
- ☑ Organizes educational programs, instruction, and assessment
- ☑ Oversees attendance
- ☑ Coordinates communication within the district
- ☑ Maintains the physical plant
- ☑ Oversees all financial operations
- ☑ Acts as a liaison between the local and state governments of the district
- ☑ Represents the taxpayers and parents
- ☑ Advocates for the student in matters of education and safety
- ☑ Implements federal and state regulations and policies

School boards manage, regulate, and oversee the maintenance of all schools within their jurisdiction. Accordingly, they affect the lives of students, teachers, support personnel, administrators, and parents by the decisions they make.

School board membership ranges from 5 to 12 people who serve terms of office from 1 to 5 years. Teachers are not allowed to serve on school boards in the districts where they are employed.

State and federal guidelines, state commissioners, and departments of education guide the duties of a school board. However, a local board does have considerable power over the management of its district.

How the School Board Affects Your Teaching Program Although the particular influence of the school board on students and teachers is large, it is also somewhat aloof. Teachers are informed of the school board's decisions and mandates by means of the superintendent through his or her principals. Subsequently, the principal enforces these policies. The school board's decisions affect you through the following:

- ☑ Mandates relating to student behavior
- ☑ Mandates instituting new instructional initiatives (e.g., literacy programs)
- ☑ Mandates on grading and record keeping
- ☑ Hiring and dismissal procedures
- ☑ Decisions about teachers' employment relating to health, retirement, salary, and working conditions
- ☑ Decisions about school closings and layoffs

The Superintendent of Schools

Probably no person in the system defines the purpose and mission of a school district more than the superintendent does. Some people might even say that the district takes on the personality of the superintendent as he or she begins initiatives to improve the overall instructional and financial efficiency of the organization.

STATING THE FACTS:

On school size: Of the 14,310 school districts in the United States, most have 5,000 to 24,000 students (National Center for Education Statistics, 2004).

For the teacher, the superintendent and his or her job are distant from the daily routine, and the superintendent's influence is felt only through the overall educational program relayed through the principal's voice. As you will see from the following Voices in the Classroom section, superintendents are looking at the larger picture, much the way a CEO manages a corporation.

In Real Time: The Superintendent's Role

The superintendent's job is to make things happen. Thus, initiatives will flow from his or her office that will have a direct effect on the classroom teacher and staff. No single person is in a better position to initiate change and improve the effectiveness of the mission of the system than is the superintendent.

The District Office

Before blaming or criticizing supervisors, remember that they are looking at the broader picture.

To all school employees, teachers, administrative staff, custodial staff, aides, monitors, and security personnel, the central office is where employment begins and ends, and in the interim, it is the place where the record of employment is filed and maintained. No individual is bigger than the central office, not even the superintendent of schools. The district office is where the following occurs:

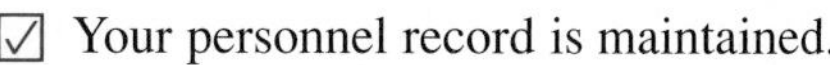

- ☑ Your personnel record is maintained.
- ☑ You inquire about health benefits or report problems with health insurance.
- ☑ You designate 10- or 12-month paychecks.
- ☑ Curriculum is written and revised.
- ☑ Final examinations are written in concert with other schools in the district.
- ☑ All district supervisors are headquartered, including those for special education, athletics, transportation, curriculum, the gifted and talented program, and literacy instruction.

In Real Time: Your Paycheck

Paychecks reflect a great deal of information and are often difficult to decipher. As a novice teacher, you should consult a veteran teacher on how to read the information accompanying your check (known as the pay stub*). You should then adopt the habit of identifying all the deductions on each payday to monitor the accuracy of your pay, because accounting systems can make mistakes.*

Assistant Superintendents and Departments

School districts are organized according to various structures, but most follow the simple bureaucratic pattern of managers or supervisors at each functional level. Each manager is generally known as an *assistant superintendent,* who answers directly to the superintendent. By looking at these managers' jobs in terms of the responsibilities and obstacles these individuals face, you may better appreciate why an organization does not always run as smoothly as many people would like.

VOICES IN THE CLASSROOM
The Role of the Superintendent

Failing to communicate

The school board had hired a new superintendent, who came to our district promising to improve instruction and overhaul the entire organizational structure. This was during the school-based management experiments, when sharing the governance of each school with teachers was believed to be the best way to get schools to run more democratically and with less conflict.

One of the first things this guy did was to ask all teachers to join committees and generate ideas on how to improve the schools. So some of us took him seriously and submitted our ideas—such as hire more monitors for the halls and cafeteria, fix the dozen or so leaks in classrooms and hallways, get additional counselors so that kids could actually be counseled, and a list of other, expensive items. Many of the elementary teachers asked for what they've always asked for—a planning period during the day to give them time to organize for their classes. The art teachers wanted rooms instead of carts, and the music and language teachers wanted fewer schools to cover during the day.

After less than a month on the job, the guy announced that we needed to build a new high school and that all of our energies needed to be focused on that. He then spoke almost exclusively on this building-of-the-high-school thing. Our requests were ignored; building-planning committees met and made decisions that were largely ignored because the district was being geared to get the community to buy into the building of a new high school.

So then we knew. The guy was hired to achieve this one goal, the pet project of a majority of school board members. But everyone had underestimated the stingy taxpayer. Within 18 months, the school board had four new anti–high school–building members, and the new superintendent was looking for another job. He lasted 2 years. A record for our district.

—A veteran teacher

Perspective on the job

Being a superintendent is a good job to have, I think, because you get to meet a wide variety of interesting people. Of course, it's also the worst job you can have because you get to meet a wide variety of very angry, misguided, and often vindictive people.

I think it's the chaos theory that says just a little difference in one area can make a huge difference in behaviors in another area over a period of time. Superintendents are always trying to make those differences; the problem is, we don't have a lot of time. School boards expect results, and parents want the big three for their children: Keep them safe, teach them well, and make sure they get recognized.

The superintendent has to juggle the needs of students, the instruction program, the maintenance of the physical plant, and the demands of his teachers. Sometimes these things all pull at you simultaneously and that usually means something has to give. You can't promise taxpayers *not* to raise taxes while negotiating a pay raise for teachers or upgrading your computer technology program. But most important, the superintendent has to protect the district from frivolous or not-so-frivolous lawsuits stemming from violations of legislative mandates, sexual harassment charges, or teacher personnel issues. This barely leaves time for checking on the instructional program. What I hate most about being a superintendent is that I rarely get to see kids; and when I do, they're usually in such bad trouble that I need to make a decision that might place great hardship on them and their families. Also, when I am invited to see student performances, they are so painstakingly rehearsed and directed that I rarely see some spontaneous educational activity.

Still, I wouldn't want it any other way. Superintendents can sometimes make huge changes quickly, and have the power to redirect teaching and learning to more positive outcomes. I don't think any other position in education gives you more flexibility to be able to effect change, really make things happen, and, who knows, maybe even make it better.

—A superintendent

DYNAMICS OF ADMINISTRATION

Department and responsibilities	Obstacles to goals
Buildings and grounds: Maintains all school buildings and property; engages in daily cleanings, repair, and upkeep	Insufficient staff, theft of materials, unpredictable events of nature, unknown equipment failures, insufficient funds, lack of cooperation from students and teachers
Transportation: Arranges for the daily transport of all students to and from schools; maintains all district vehicles; arranges for student transport to special events and field trips	Insufficient number of vehicles, mechanical breakdowns, rigid time schedules not coordinated between schools, erratic schedules of teachers and administrators
Personnel: Is responsible for all personnel records of every district employee; manages health plans for all employees; coordinates mandates from state and federal governments on the rights and responsibilities of employees	Many personnel changes of address, marital status, and family structure; attrition of personnel through retirement or other reasons (requires documentation and is often complicated)
Finance and payroll: Pays district bills, including the payroll; maintains employment records; manages health insurance premiums and sometimes negotiates claims; manages investments	Large number of employees at various ranks and steps, miscommunication by the liaison between the health insurance server and the employee, continuous upgrading and maintenance of finance software, complexity of laws governing finances
Special education: Is accountable for implementing the statutes of public laws regarding special needs; manages all special needs testing; provides information and guidance for parents of children with special needs	Complex and continuously changing federal and state regulations, litigation by unsatisfied parents, depletion of staff time and district funds as a result of litigation, regular classroom teacher resistance to modifications and accommodations for children with special needs
Instruction: Organizes and manages elementary and secondary instruction; initiates programs to improve instruction; coordinates instruction among the teaching staff; aligns instruction vis-á-vis the mission and goals of the district; organizes staff development programs	State-mandated testing programs that may dictate the instructional strategy; misalignment of the instructional program with individual teaching styles; variable teaching schedules, which preclude smooth planning of staff development; lack of appropriate instructional materials

The Principal

No other person is more poignantly visible in the life of a new teacher than the building principal. In fact, this person can make or break your teaching career by virtue of a few minor decisions. In most cases (but not all), the principal ultimately hires the teachers for his or her building. In this respect, he or she has an enormous impact on your life because he or she has chosen you to join the team. From the principal's viewpoint, you have already displayed some kind of excellence or made some type of impression that has caused him or her to choose you.

HOW THE PRINCIPAL AFFECTS YOUR PROFESSIONAL LIFE

- ☑ Does the actual hiring, or approves of hiring
- ☑ Assigns duties that relate to your position
- ☑ Approves or disapproves initiatives such as taking your class on a field trip
- ☑ Fields complaints (if any) from parents about your performance
- ☑ Assists you in your lesson planning and designing of the syllabus
- ☑ Is responsible for the enforcement of federal, state, and local laws and mandates
- ☑ Observes your classes and writes the official evaluation of your performance
- ☑ Has the most influence on the decision to grant tenure

The Principal as Supervisor Chief among the principal's duties is the role of supervisor. He or she will observe and evaluate your performance and ultimately make the final decision as to your continued employment. Accordingly, your actions and professional demeanor reflect on his or her leadership abilities as they are viewed and evaluated by *his or her* supervisor, usually the superintendent. Thus, although the principal is chiefly concerned about your overall effectiveness as a teacher, he or she also has a personal stake in your success.

The Principal as Manager of Instruction The principal must oversee the instructional program by ensuring that each teacher is using approved textbooks; is following state, federal and local laws; is obeying safety and security measures as outlined by the board; and is completing certification requirements. Therefore, the principal will be a visible or represented force in the new teacher's daily life. Within the scope of supervision, the principal may also be as intrusive or unobtrusive as desired. In many schools, the principal has an instructional vision that he or she wants teachers to follow. For instance, in one elementary school in Pennsylvania, the principal wanted his elementary teachers to use Gardner's multiple intelligences theory as their instructional technique (personal communication, July 2002). He required all teachers to craft their lesson plans with activities that aligned around the intelligences.

Briefcase CD CH2-1—Framework for Teacher Evaluation: Professionalism Checklist

The principal, the chief executive of the school, is responsible for both the welfare of the students and the effectiveness of the academic program.

The Principal's Evaluation Your principal, or his or her designee, will observe and evaluate you at least twice a year while you are untenured. Although such observation is only one of several indicators of your performance as a teacher and a professional, it is the strongest and, consequently, the most stressful. The following teacher evaluation frameworks will give you an overview of the criteria most principals use during their observation of your teaching performance.

The pattern that is usually followed is as follows: preconference, observation, write-up, response, postconference. You will be told that these observations are a time to get help if you are having problems and that their purpose is not to find fault but to help you improve. Most evaluators give a teacher some latitude and consideration with regard to inexperience and may overlook miscues. However, as with any important event in your life, the key to success is preparation, preparation, preparation.

FRAMEWORK FOR TEACHER EVALUATION: PROFESSIONALISM CHECKLIST

Category	Checklist
Classroom administration	☐ Maintains visible and current attendance records and lesson plans ☐ Submits required reports on time ☐ Complies with all safety, security, and general regulations ☐ Shows evidence of parental communication
Institutional and collegial participation	☐ Attends all faculty meetings ☐ Participates in committee or project work ☐ Attends school events ☐ Demonstrates an attitude of service to students and the mission of the school
Professional development	☐ Participates in seminars or workshops on learning and instruction ☐ Is active in professional initiatives on improving the instructional program

In Real Time: **Your First-Year Evaluation**

Being evaluated in your first year of teaching is a rite of passage that may be described as an ordeal. Being successful is tied directly to your sense of practicality in that you assess the situation and perform accordingly. Therefore, be sure to do the following:

- ☑ *Know your evaluator.*
- ☑ *Know your students.*
- ☑ *Prepare your lesson with great care.*
- ☑ *Be prepared for the unexpected.*

FRAMEWORK FOR TEACHER EVALUATION: CLASSROOM OBSERVATION CHECKLIST

Category	Checklist

Lesson planning and preparation	☐ The lesson plan reflects the following:
	  ☐ Local and state learning standards
	  ☐ Clear goals and objectives
	  ☐ Procedures reflective of all learners
	  ☐ Dependent and independent activities
	  ☐ Assessments aligned with goals and objectives
	☐ Worksheets and project descriptions are clear, concise, and commensurate with the goals and objectives of the lesson.

Classroom environment	☐ Classroom furniture is arranged for productive instruction and learning. ☐ Student work is displayed. ☐ Schedules and class rules are visible. ☐ Students demonstrate respect for the teacher and one another. ☐ An expectation of achievement pervades the room. ☐ The teacher is aware of all students' behavior.
Instruction	☐ Directions and instructions are clearly communicated. ☐ The teacher allows students to ask questions and responds to their concerns, providing ample feedback. ☐ Students participate well. ☐ Students have opportunities for both dependent and independent practice. ☐ The instructional pace is aligned with students' needs. ☐ Transitions between subjects or topics are seamless, with little loss of instructional time. ☐ Varying levels of cognition are being addressed.

—Cont.

Category	Checklist
	☐ The focus of instruction reaches all students. ☐ The lesson is flexible to account for directional changes predicated on students' responses.
Assessment	☐ Teacher feedback reflects an understanding of student comprehension. ☐ Assignments are aligned with the day's lesson and are connected to previous material covered. ☐ Multiple assessment instruments are used.

Briefcase CD CH2-2—Framework for Teacher Evaluation: Classroom Observation Checklist

The following guidelines will help you prepare for these important evaluations:

- ☑ Carefully prepare a lesson on a topic that is most likely to engage your students.
- ☑ Choose at least two modes of instruction besides your own presentation: that is, students in groups or dyads, discussion, class problem solving, an audiovisual aid, and so forth.
- ☑ In the preobservation conference, fully explain the material that led to the lesson.
- ☑ Prepare the evaluator with knowledge of specific student behaviors, the time of day, and the overall general progress of the class.
- ☑ At the beginning of the lesson, acknowledge, but do not overemphasize, the evaluator's presence.
- ☑ Teach to the students, not the evaluator.
- ☑ Be prepared for dead time; pace the lesson to use the entire time period.
- ☑ Be sure to review the lesson at the end, for closure.

The evaluations resulting from classroom observations will indicate a rating for your performance. The three possible ratings are usually *commendable, satisfactory,* and *needs improvement.* Often, first-year teachers receive a *satisfactory* evaluation for their first observation because many evaluators believe a pure novice cannot attain a *commendable* rating. In addition, your rating could be affected by the principal's expectations. Principals often base ratings on their personal concepts of how material should be taught or the classroom should be managed. Consider the following dialogue with a third-grade teacher (personal communication, August 2003):

TEACHER: I was being observed by my principal, who was known to be a stickler for classroom control. The lesson I chose was a fairly straightforward vocabulary drill where the kids would respond to clues I supplied from the stories we had read that week. The class became very excited about some of the clues I was reading, and some students responded more enthusiastically than others. Before you knew it, they were getting very excited and shouting out answers and—frankly—thoroughly enjoying themselves.

INTERVIEWER: Well, it sounds as though the class was caught up in the lesson. What did your principal think?

TEACHER: She jumped up to the front of the room. Shouted for the class to become silent. When everyone was pin-dropping quiet, she turned to me and said: "Now, Mrs. Voorhees can get on with her lesson." She resumed her seat in the back of the room and the kids then quietly answered my questions.

INTERVIEWER: How did you do on your observation report?

TEACHER: She killed me. I got checks in *needs improvement* under Classroom Management and *satisfactory* in Instruction.

The Principal as Mentor As with all supervisors, principals have a number of leadership styles, but generally these styles fall into two distinct categories: democratic and autocratic. The most recent and popular is Michael Fullan's (2001) *learning community model,* which is having a tremendous impact on educational leadership. Fullan believes that a school principal can be an agent of change or a blocker of change, and that he or she has the opportunity to establish a "learning-enriched" school, also known as an *interactive community of practice*. Fullan's view is that the teacher must be intricately involved in the leadership process by being allowed to invest in his or her views, skills, and ideas. A principal following the Fullan model, or any model that is democratic and sensitive to the contributional potential of the teachers, will also serve as mentor.

As a mentor, the principal can be a great source of help and solace to the first-year teacher. Providing assistance, advice, and comfort during times of struggle and frustration can alleviate the feelings of alienation that often accompany the initial steps into the profession. The mentoring principal is, according to Fullan (2003), a person who will fight to prevent fragmentation among his or her staff and will generate a sense of harmony through open communication and support of ideas and initiative.

Respect for the Power of the Office No one should underestimate the principal's impact on the new teacher's future. As supervisor, mentor, or evaluator, the principal exercises enormous influence and can be of great help toward your growth and development as a professional. However, he or she can also be the person who roadblocks your career at the onset. The new teacher's awareness of his or her environment means knowledge of his or her supervisor's personality and goals. You should not ignore the principal's instructions or rules, or undermine his or her leadership through complaints and stubbornness. Veteran teachers often wax angrily about the principal's methods or governance, and, all too often, new teachers, in an effort to win favor with these seasoned colleagues, engage in their complaint sessions without thinking.

The Vice-Principal

Some elementary schools; most middle, or junior high, schools; and most high schools have a vice-principal or an assistant principal. Although the description for this job is framed in administrative language, ultimately the vice-principal becomes the school's disciplinarian. Therefore, you will undoubtedly work with this person regularly. The job of vice-principal is thankless and stressful because this person is in daily conflict with students who routinely break school rules and run afoul of teachers, aides, and monitors. The vice-principal seldom has the opportunity to interact with students who are achieving, working, and partaking in the educational program.

The vice-principal can be a teacher's chief source of support and assistance.

All teachers work with the vice-principal on discipline in one fashion or

How can the vice-principal help me with classroom management problems?

The vice-principal is in a position to view the larger picture of student behavior. He or she knows which students pose problems for all teachers and which students cannot adjust to specific teachers or teaching situations. He or she has access to a spectrum of agencies and support people who can help you solve some of your classroom problems. Never hesitate to get in contact with the vice-principal not only for help with classroom management problems, but also for advice on instruction.

another, but the new teacher should welcome his or her assistance and learn to abide by his or her system of maintaining order. The toughest aspect of maintaining orderly discipline throughout the school is cooperation among teachers. Often, some teachers resent and defy the rules outlined by the vice-principal regarding disciplining students. This defiance results because rules do not always wash evenly over all classrooms. Note the following account:

> I ran into trouble with our assistant principal one day on the topic of gum chewing. There was a general school rule that kids weren't allowed to chew gum. It was an almost impossible rule to enforce as gum is an integral part of the teenager's life. So, some teachers rigidly enforced it in their classrooms by giving out detentions and minor punishments, and others, like me, ignored it as being too trivial to worry about, and I wasn't suffering any disrespect or lack of control because of it.
>
> One day a curmudgeon of a math teacher yammered angrily to the vice-principal that he saw no reason to enforce school rules if some teachers, namely me, were going to be allowed to flaunt them. Within minutes I had an irate vice-principal berating me for allowing kids to chew gum, and that because I was still a probationary teacher, this could adversely affect my employment status.
>
> It was a no-brainer—there was no more gum chewing in my classroom.
>
> —*A fifth-year English teacher (who* did *get tenure)*

The vice-principal can also be a mentor to the new teacher and would certainly welcome the opportunity to work with students who are participating in the educational program. His or her guidance in areas other than discipline can be invaluable, because a vice-principal can offer a perspective from outside the classroom that may enhance your overall instructional style and management. However, specifically in the area of discipline, the vice-principal is the point person for solving your students' most egregious behavior problems in the classroom. He or she may have data on the student who is most insufferable and causing you to be distracted from your teaching. Seeking the vice-principal's help is not a sign that you are unable to handle your students' disciplinary problems, but rather an indicator of your willingness to work with the team to solve problems.

In Real Time: Calling for Help

The teacher who reaches for the telephone each time a student is disruptive, and who makes no attempt to deal with the problem within the classroom environment, is quickly labeled as a questionable manager. Before you seek help outside the classroom, the vice-principal will want to know what measures you have taken to manage the problem.

INTERSTATE NEW TEACHER ASSESSMENT AND SUPPORT CONSORTIUM (INTASC) STANDARDS

1. ***Content pedagogy:*** The teacher understands the central concepts, tools of inquiry, and structures of the discipline(s) he or she teaches and can create learning experiences that make these aspects of subject matter meaningful for students.
2. ***Student development:*** The teacher understands how children learn and develop, and can provide learning opportunities that support a child's intellectual, social, and personal development.
3. ***Diverse learners:*** The teacher understands how students differ in their approaches to learning and creates instructional opportunities that are adapted to diverse learners.
4. ***Multiple instructional strategies:*** The teacher understands and uses a variety of instructional strategies to encourage students' development of critical-thinking, problem-solving, and performance skills.
5. ***Motivation and management:*** The teacher uses an understanding of individual and group motivation and behavior to create a learning environment that encourages positive social interaction, active engagement in learning, and self-motivation.
6. ***Communication and technology:*** The teacher uses knowledge of effective verbal, nonverbal, and media communication techniques to foster active inquiry, collaboration, and supportive interaction in the classroom.
7. ***Planning:*** The teacher plans instruction based upon knowledge of subject matter, students, the community, and curriculum goals.
8. ***Assessment:*** The teacher understands and uses formal and informal assessment strategies to evaluate and ensure the continuous intellectual, social, and physical development of the learner.
9. ***Reflective practice—Professional growth:*** The teacher is a reflective practitioner who continually evaluates the effects of his or her choices and actions on others (students, parents, and other professionals in the learning community) and who actively seeks out opportunities to grow professionally.
10. ***School and community involvement:*** The teacher fosters relationships with school colleagues, parents, and agencies in the larger community to support students' learning and well-being.

Note. The Interstate New Teacher Assessment and Support Consortium (INTASC) standards were developed by the Council of Chief State School Officers and member states. Copies may be downloaded from the Council's Web site at http://www.ccsso.org.

Council of Chief State School Officers. (1992). *Model standards for beginning teacher licensing, assessment, and development: A resource for state dialogue.* Washington, DC: Author. http://www.ccsso.org/content/pdfs/corestrd.pdf. Reprinted with permission.

TENURE

Briefcase CD CH2-3—Interstate New Teacher Assessment and Support Consortium (INTASC) Standards

In the field of teaching, the probationary period is generally about 3 years, although this time period varies from state to state and district to district. What probation means is that although you interviewed well, and your references and résumé are superb, the real test is how you function in the field daily. Many promising candidates have fallen hard and out during the first year. Others have struggled through to the third year only to be refused tenure, whereas many—fully one third—determine that this profession is not for them.

The criteria for gaining tenure also vary from district to district, but they generally follow those established by the Interstate New Teacher Assessment and Support Consortium (INTASC). These standards are considered those by which all teachers' performance is measured. Not only should you become familiar with them in general, but they should also be reflected in your formal lesson plan design.

***In Real Time:* What Is Tenure?**

Although believed to be a protective shield preventing administrators from firing incompetent teachers, tenure is a professional status that affords teachers security in their jobs. Because of the nature of teaching, without this security a teacher may be fired for disagreeing with the political views of his or her employers or parents or students. Tenure grants him or her the freedom to provide an open forum of all ideas without fear of recrimination.

Your Rights as a Probationary Teacher

For the nontenured teacher in his or her probationary period, the process for dismissal is practically automatic. In the first year of a teacher's contract, a teacher may be dismissed at the will of the board of education on a principal's recommendation. Unless specific language in the contract between the teachers' union and the district provides for a review-and-appeal process, a school board may dismiss probationary teachers simply by notifying them that their contract is not being renewed or that they are being terminated effective immediately. The history of litigation on tenure leans heavily on the side of school boards having the right to terminate probationary teachers (Scott, 1986).

Stating the Facts:

On tenure: "When deciding whether to renew the contract of a probationary teacher (a teacher who does not yet have tenure), a school board's powers are almost unlimited. In most such instances, the situation of the probationary teacher up for renewal is virtually the reverse of the situation of the tenured teacher. The burden of proof is on the teacher to establish that the board is acting in an arbitrary or capricious manner, has failed to live up to its side of a contract, or has violated the teacher's constitutional rights. In addition, the courts have traditionally been extremely reluctant to intervene when a school board has chosen not to renew the contract of a probationary teacher" (Scott, 1986).

Each district, in fact each state, treats tenure differently. Some districts provide for an appeal process for all probationary teachers regardless of time in service, but in general the rule of thumb is that first-year teachers can expect no job protection beyond that provided by the laws against discrimination. In most districts, a specific time period is allotted for notification of teachers that their contracts will not be renewed, usually sometime between March 30 and June 30.

THE TENURE DEBATE

Pro	Con
Tenure protects against dismissal for non-education-related reasons, such as political preference, religious orientation, teaching style, age, gender, or lifestyle.	A teacher's personal beliefs can affect his or her performance and influence on students (e.g., belonging to a political party advocating anarchy or anti-American ideals).
Tenure protects the right to teach the curriculum in an individual style without structures from administrators who seek a collective teaching style.	A teacher should conform to the administration's wishes about instructional initiatives. Teachers are employees of the school board, which appoints administrators, and need to follow guidelines established by them.
Tenure allows a teacher to provide instruction on sensitive issues such as religion and evolution without the threat of dismissal.	Tenure can protect teachers who are expounding views and beliefs that are contrary to the wishes of the community.

—Cont.

Pro	Con
Teachers need the protection of an extensive review-and-appeal process to ensure that dismissal is not unreasonable and arbitrary. However, it does not protect incompetent teachers because the district has the option to engage in the dismissal process.	Tenure protects incompetent teachers because the review-and-appeal process is long, cumbersome, and expensive, which makes it essentially unworkable from the viewpoint of the school board and its administrators.
Teachers need protection from dismissal based on student performance. Low performance rates may be due to many reasons other than teacher incompetence (e.g., learning disabilities, family problems, emotional difficulties).	A district should have the right to consider a teacher's competence if his or her students continually perform below standards.

LEGAL SIDEBAR

Rulings on School Districts' Rights

The courts have consistently ruled in favor of school districts' use of measures to maintain order and safety, and have only occasionally found them excessively violating the rights of students and school personnel.

Court case	Finding
Melzer v. Board of Education of the City of New York (7/16/2003)	The Second Circuit U.S. Court of Appeals ruled that a teacher who belonged to a pedophile group could be terminated because his active involvement disrupted the board's educational mission.
Scott v. Savers Property and Casualty Insurance Company (agent for school district; 6/19/2003)	The Wisconsin Supreme Court ruled that the school district was not liable for a guidance counselor's advice regarding National Collegiate Athletic Association (NCAA) eligibility that caused a student to lose an athletic scholarship.
Reeves v. Rocklin Unified School District (6/10/2003)	A California appellate court ruled that a high school principal's actions preventing an antiabortion group from distributing leaflets was not a violation of that group's First Amendment rights.
Marble Falls School District v. Shell (4/3/2003)	A Texas appellate court ruled in favor of a school district's right to require random drug tests for students participating in extracurricular activities.
State v. Jones (7/16/2003)	The Iowa Supreme Court ruled in favor of school officials' search of a student's locker after he refused to participate in a general locker cleanout.
A. H. v. State (6/6/2003)	A Florida appellate court ruled a school official's search of a student's wallet unconstitutional.
Counts v. Cedarville School District (4/22/2003)	A federal district court ruled against a school district that restricted student access to J. K. Rowling's Harry Potter books in the school library.

DOS AND DON'TS

Don't	Do
Ignore the importance of school board members' impact on your daily work	Stay informed by attending school board meetings
Join in conversations denigrating the work of individuals in the district office	Ask to see your personnel folder at the completion of your first year to become familiar with what is being recorded about you
Blame maintenance staff for problems in your room or call them for small jobs that you can ignore or fix yourself	Respectfully request maintenance staff to repair or replace broken equipment
Order materials that you "might" use or an exorbitant number of textbooks	Order on time and with respect to the needs of your students and those of the school and district
Disregard the importance of the principal's influence on your job security	Respect the principal's authority and perform your duties in and out of the classroom according to his or her directives
Ignore the role of the principal as a facilitator and mentor for your success	Invite the principal to visit your classroom; to look at a lesson you think is engaging; and to seek his or her input on lessons, student behavior, and parental interaction
Miss faculty or committee meetings or fail to participate in school community programs	Attend all meetings, listen, and provide input when possible; volunteer to help with projects that affect the school community
Refer students who misbehave to the vice-principal without first exhausting all other means	Seek the vice-principal's advice on student behavior, lesson planning, or special projects

WEB SITES OF INTEREST

http://www.csmonitor.com/2003/0909/p12s01-lepr.html
This Web site has an article on the role of superintendents.

http://www.nsba.org
This site for the National School Boards Association is where you may find a great deal of information on governance, school structure, and the latest instructional initiatives.

http://www.ed.gov/teachers/landing.jhtml?src=fp
The U.S. Department of Education Web site provides information specifically related to teaching.

http://www.ed.gov/about/offices/list/ous/international/usnei/edlite-index.html
This site provides information on international schools of education.

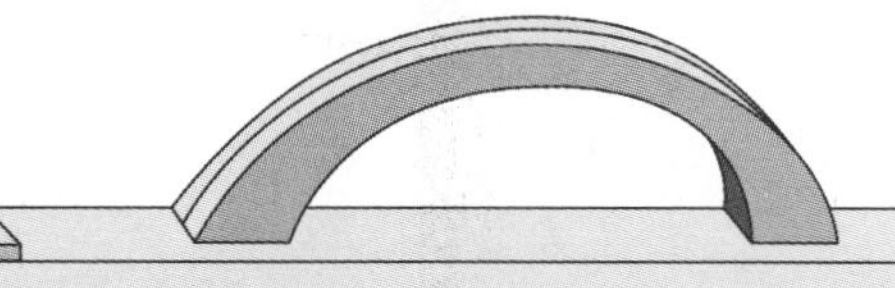

For Your Briefcase

To Do

- Learn the names of personnel at the district office who issue payroll checks and can explain health, retirement, and leave benefits.
- Familiarize yourself with the names of directors of major departments in your district.
- Speak with your principal about his or her plan for your observations. Do so early in the year.
- Familiarize yourself with the vice-principal's procedures and requirements relating to student disciplinary issues.
- Speak with your principal and your mentor about the district's probationary and tenure policy.

Resources on Your Briefcase CD

Templates

- Framework for Teacher Evaluation: Professionalism Checklist
- Framework for Teacher Evaluation: Classroom Observation Checklist

Tables

- Interstate New Teacher Assessment and Support Consortium (INTASC) Standards

REFERENCES

Fullan, M. (2001). *The new meaning of educational change.* Toronto, Ontario, Canada: Nelson Thomson Learning.

Fullan, M. (2003). *The moral imperative of school leadership.* Thousand Oaks, CA: Corwin Press.

Kauchak, D., Eggen, P., & Carter, C. (2002). *Introduction to teaching: Becoming a professional.* Upper Saddle River, NJ: Merrill/Prentice Hall.

National Center for Education Statistics. (2004, August 31). *The Schools and Staffing Survey (SASS): 2003–2004.* Washington, DC: Author.

Scott, J. (1986). *Teacher tenure.* Eugene, OR: ERIC Clearinghouse on Educational Management. (ERIC Document Reproduction Service No. ED282352)

Twain, M. (1898). *Following the equator: Part 3. A journey around the world* (Chap. 27). Hartford, CT: American Publishing Company. Retrieved from http://www.gutenberg.org/files/5810/5810-h/5810-h.htm

Learning the Teaching Process

Chapter 3

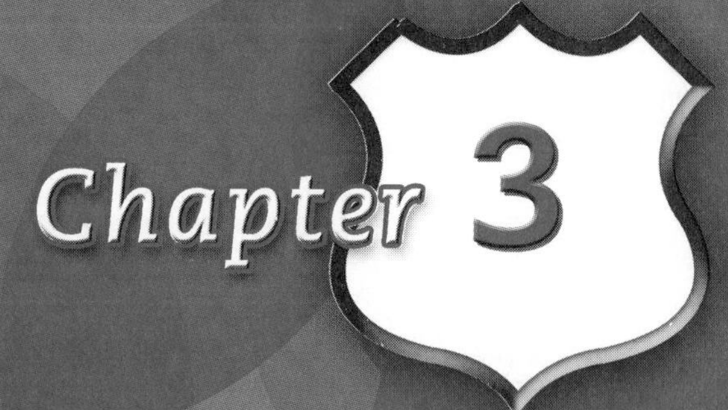

Getting Started: The First Year

The principal goal of education is to create men who are capable of doing new things, not simply of repeating what other generations have done.

—Jean Piaget (as cited in Duckworth, 1964)

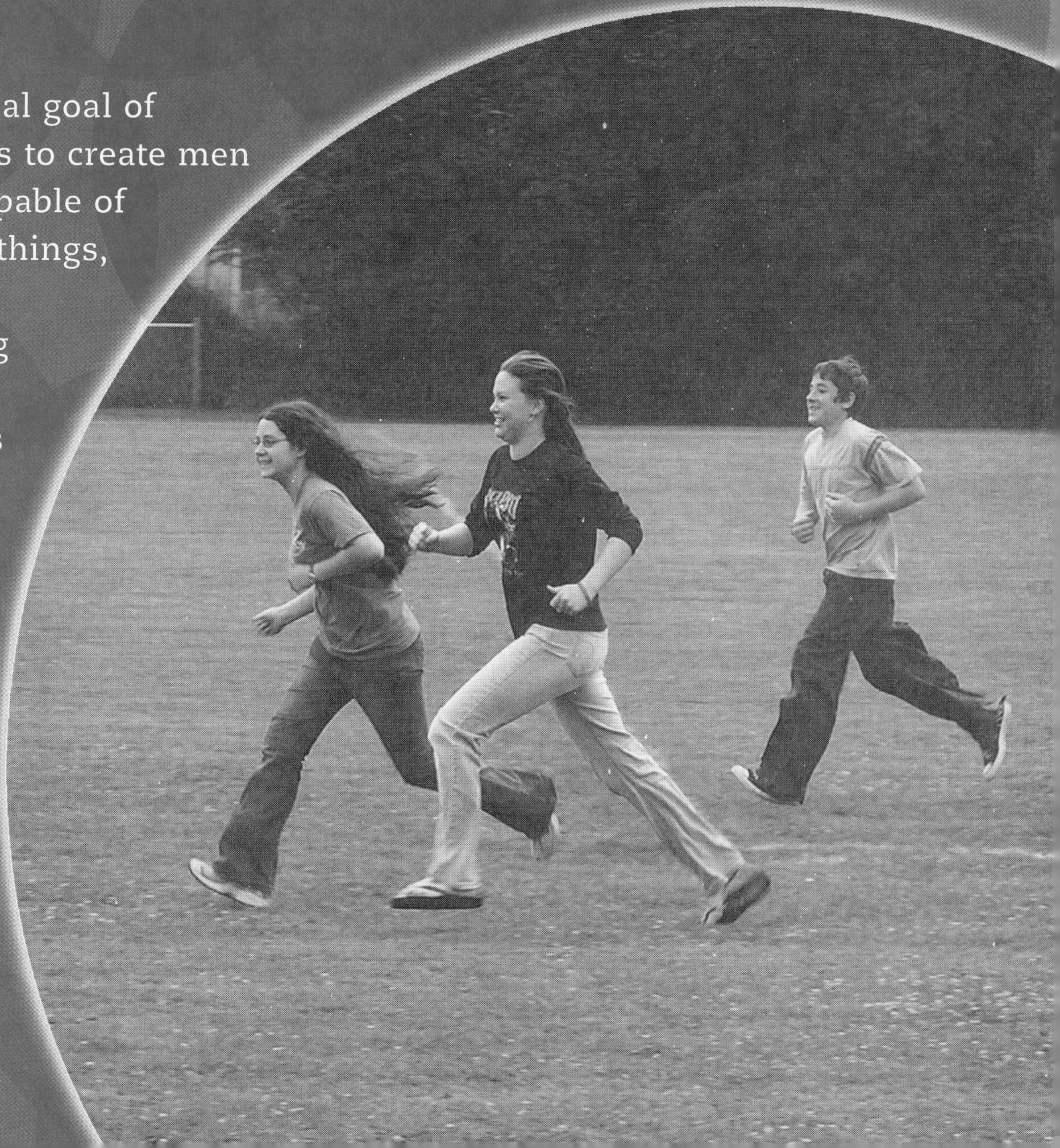

THE MONTH BEFORE SCHOOL STARTS

SUMMER CHECKLIST

- ☑ Visit the school.
- ☑ Gather supplies.
- ☑ Meet key people.
- ☑ Write lesson plans.

The first year of teaching begins 30 days before you walk into the classroom. The month before school starts is a time for preparation unlike any since your training as a teacher began. Such preparation is similar to staging a play or planning for an extended journey. Props must be found and organized; maps must be made.

Visiting the School

To be fully ready for the opening day of classes, you must first familiarize yourself with the physical plant. Visit the school as soon as possible. Locate your room and note its relation in the building to the administrative office, the auditorium, the gym, and the lavatories. Identify supply rooms, custodial offices, and support locations for special education, health, and counseling. Identify yourself to all personnel in the building, such as custodians, library–media specialists, health personnel, and secretaries.

Meeting Key People

In the few weeks before school begins, the newly hired teacher should become better acquainted with essential personnel (see Chapter 12 for more detail on the key people in your building). The following people will be of great help to you in the days prior to the first day of school.

The Principal As the key person in the building, the principal will provide the details of your responsibilities as a teacher and a member of his or her faculty. The principal will also give you the direction needed to begin your preparations for your teaching year.

Health Personnel The school will have a person responsible for the daily health care of the students. Usually a registered nurse, this individual will provide a great deal of support for your daily work with students. Most important, he or she will provide guidance on the sensitive issues of suspected child abuse and procedures for children with serious health concerns.

Department Head At the secondary level, the department head or department director can be of enormous help with the specifics of your job. His or her responsibilities include maintaining and ordering textbooks and supplies, as well as providing leadership on teaching initiatives in your subject area.

The School Counselor The counselor can give you specific information on your class load, your students' names, and procedures for organizing your roster. He or she will also inform you of the number of students assigned to you who have an **individualized education program (IEP;** see Chapter 10).

The Secretary A typical elementary school has at least one secretary who is akin to an executive manager. His or her role involves the following:

- ☑ Maintaining communication between the principal and the staff
- ☑ Monitoring the flow of supplies
- ☑ Acting as the first-line liaison between parents and teachers
- ☑ Providing guidance in the daily administration of the organization

During the first days of your teaching career, the secretary will be vital to you because he or she will have the information you will need regarding supplies, your room, the office, and building procedures.

INITIAL SCHOOL VISIT

Persons to meet	Possible questions
Principal	What is the school discipline policy? Is a schoolwide curriculum being used? What textbooks are required for my class? Do I have my own room, or will I be sharing it with someone? Other than teaching, what are my duties?
Health personnel	What do I do if a child gets sick in my room? Do I need to complete any health forms for my students? What is the procedure for suspected child abuse? What is the procedure for suspected drug abuse?
Department head (secondary school only)	Where do I get textbooks and teaching materials? What is the procedure for ordering materials? When are department meetings held? What duties will I have in addition to teaching?
School counselor	How many students will be enrolled in my class? What is the procedure for parent conferences? How many students with special needs are assigned to my class? What is the procedure for implementing a student's individualized education plan (IEP)?
Secretary	Do you have the class list? What is the procedure for procuring supplies? What is the procedure for taking student attendance? Is a particular grade or attendance book required? Do I need to complete any forms or reports? What are the telephone procedures? Does my room have a key?
Custodian	What, if anything, do I need to do to the room at the end of each day? How do I get into my room when it is locked? How do I get in contact with you if I have a mechanical problem?
Library–media specialist	Will an overhead projector (television, computer, opaque projector) be assigned to my room permanently? What are the library access hours? Do you have an information class with my students?

The Custodian The custodian is extremely important to your instructional program. He or she does the following:

- ☑ Cleans your room daily
- ☑ Makes minor repairs to keep your room in shape for use by you and your students
- ☑ Transports textbooks from storage to your room
- ☑ Is often called on to clean vomit or other unexpected unpleasantries in your room

STATING THE FACTS:

On supplies: A 1998 survey conducted by the National Supply and Equipment Association revealed that teachers pay for 77% of the school supplies needed in their classroom—an average of $448 per year (Magau, 2002).

Getting to know the custodian is not only wise, but also crucial to your being able to maintain a punctual and effective classroom environment.

The Library–Media Specialist The library–media specialist is in charge of all audiovisual equipment, print materials, and, in most school districts, computer laboratories. Introduce yourself to this important professional who will help you organize your materials for the coming year.

A teacher's supplies are essential to the success of his or her program.

Gathering Supplies

Gathering the materials needed to begin your first year of teaching takes both thought and initiative; it may also require a personal monetary contribution. Although districts usually provide a basic package of materials, teachers often spend hundreds of dollars a year to purchase supplies for their classes. When acquiring supplies, be sure to do the following:

- ☑ Label materials assigned to you with your name and room number.
- ☑ Gather materials you know you will need for the opening week of school.
- ☑ Check with the custodian about locks on your supply cabinet doors and to your room.
- ☑ Make sure you have a large store of pencils.
- ☑ Check your room for a pencil sharpener.

***In Real Time:* Buying Your Own Supplies**

School districts, always looking for ways to reduce operating costs, often target school supplies as a first budget cut. Copy paper, transparencies, art and craft materials, and supplemental texts are usually rationed throughout the school year. Copiers are frequently monitored by counters or completely restricted to an allocated number of copies for each teacher. Since the 2002 tax year, however, teachers have been permitted to deduct as much as $250 on their federal return, up front, for supplies purchased for use in the classroom.

Writing Lesson Plans

Most important in the month before school starts, write your lesson plans for the first days. (See Preparing for the First Lesson, which appears on page 46.)

THE FIRST DAYS OF SCHOOL

Your first day as a teacher is special, and you and those who share all the events in your life should celebrate it. It represents a crowning achievement for working hard, overcoming obstacles, and enduring and persevering, and it should be enjoyed.

SCHOOL SUPPLIES CHECKLIST

- ☑ ***Crayons, markers, and colored pencils:*** More is always better.
- ☑ ***Glue, paste, and glue sticks:*** These are a must for elementary classrooms.
- ☑ ***Cellophane and masking tape:*** At least four rolls of each will be necessary.
- ☑ ***Attendance book:*** This essential item will become a legal document. Some schools require all teachers to use the same book.
- ☑ ***Grade book (optional):*** You may want to use a computer or a notebook instead (see Chapter 8 for more on this topic).
- ☑ ***Three-ring binders:*** If your plan requires these, remember that some children's parents may not be able to afford them.
- ☑ ***Overhead projector:*** This item is more important for secondary classrooms.
- ☑ ***Computer:*** A computer is a necessity.
- ☑ ***Rolled paper:*** This is a must for elementary classrooms. It is sometimes available at home-supply stores.
- ☑ ***Construction paper:*** You will need all colors, but especially white, in both 8.5 × 11- and 11 × 17-inch sizes.
- ☑ ***Ruled paper:*** You will need at least 500 sheets for elementary students.
- ☑ ***Spiral notebooks:*** Again, if your plan requires these, some children's parents may not be able to afford them.
- ☑ ***Tissues:*** At least two boxes a month will be necessary.
- ☑ ***Scissors:*** Have at least 25 pairs—half that number for middle school students.
- ☑ ***Textbooks:*** Ensure that you have at least enough for an entire class. Secondary schools usually have a central book room; however, sometimes each discipline has a book room. Usually, the secretary or department coordinators keep the keys to these rooms.
- ☑ ***Pencils:*** Have no fewer than 50 on hand. By the end of the year, a middle school class will use four times that number—an elementary class, slightly less.
- ☑ ***Three-hole punch:*** This item is possibly a luxury but necessary if your plan requires three-ring binders.
- ☑ ***Yardstick:*** You may need one of these, depending on your plan.
- ☑ ***Rulers:*** Have at least a dozen on hand.
- ☑ ***Staplers:*** Two or more should suffice.
- ☑ ***Poster board:*** You will need 100–200 sheets in multiple colors.
- ☑ ***3 × 5-inch index cards:*** Keep a pack of these on hand.
- ☑ ***Liquid paper or correction fluid:*** You will need at least three boxes or bottles.
- ☑ ***Pencil sharpener:*** An electric pencil sharpener will save the class time.
- ☑ ***Paper towels:*** Always keep a steady supply in the room.

Briefcase CD CH3-1—Sample First-Day Icebreaker Activities

Briefcase CD CH3-2—Sample Welcome Letter—Third Grade

Briefcase CD CH3-3—Sample Opening-Day Letter—Sixth-Grade Math

To prepare for this special day, check what you will need and what you will need to do:

- ☑ ***Check your personal appearance:*** Are you dressed appropriately, practically, and comfortably?
- ☑ ***Ensure that your room is ready:*** Are your bulletin boards complete? Are the correct number of desks in place?
- ☑ ***Rehearse your greeting to the students:*** What will your first words be? What will your first command be?
- ☑ ***Have the daily lesson ready to begin:*** Think in terms of an engaging first assignment.
- ☑ ***Have a list of classroom rules pertaining to your expectations and students' behavior prepared in advance:*** Such a list is necessary before you begin writing your class contract, which you may not be able to finish until after the first busy week of classes.
- ☑ ***Have a prepared sheet (primary grades) or packet (intermediate grades and higher) that outlines your entire program:*** Include your personal philosophy relating to student learning, your goals for the year, and the daily rules applying to homework and classroom demeanor and behavior.

SAMPLE FIRST-DAY ICEBREAKER ACTIVITIES

Elementary school

Younger children really enjoy getting mail. It is very exciting to open the mailbox and see an envelope with their name on it. This activity can be completed in the first few days of school, with limitless possibilities for use throughout the school year. Begin by collecting shoeboxes or 12-pack soda boxes. Stop at a local shoe store or grocer to see if they will donate some boxes for your project. You will need at least one for every student, plus extras for replacements and additional students assigned throughout the year. Give each student a box and supply plenty of colored construction paper, glue and other materials (buttons, stickers, markers) that students may use to cover and decorate their boxes. Show students how a flap can be cut out of one end (keep it attached on one side) to make a "swinging door". Explain that students will need to include their name on the door and once completed, this box will become their personal mailbox. Designate an area of the classroom as the Post Office. Here, mail can be sorted by 2-3 students and a mailboy or mailgirl to make deliveries to student mailboxes. Student workers can be rotated daily, weekly or any way you choose. This is an excellent way to interact with parents and grandparents. Encourage them to send mail to your school for their child. A pen-pal project with a local (or distant) school can also be created.

As the teacher, you can send notes home as often as you like. (Laurie Marchesani, Elmira City Schools)

Middle and high school

Middle school

It is important for students to feel comfortable on the first day of school, especially on the first day of middle school. One method that seems to work with the young adolescent is to begin the year by focusing on them. This activity is geared to invite the student to highlight his or her own interests and background.

Open the class with the question: "What do you like doing the most?"

The answers will vary, but the question leads you to talk about how students might organize their interests into a graphic biography. For at least 30 minutes, allow them to design a graphic autobiographical poster.

For homework students will create a poster, no smaller than 18×24 but as large as they like. The poster will consist of pictures of family, pets, personal photos, or drawings. Some students will append items to the poster depicting a favorite sport or hobby.

The posters are then attached to the walls of the classroom until the entire class is familiar with each student's graphic autobiography.

High school

The maturity and experience of the older student demands that icebreaker exercises be conducted with a certain level of reserve and respect for the age. A popular opener is to have students pair off and draw a Venn diagram of their likes and dislikes. The inner section of the diagram would be the similarities while the outer section highlights the dissimilarities.

These are shared with the class while two large circles are placed on the blackboard to track these categories as a class. By the end of the class period, there should be a reasonable atmosphere of comfort and collegiality.

HOW TO DRESS

When dressing for school, follow these simple, practical guidelines:

☑ ***Dress comfortably:***

- Wear flat, cushioned shoes. You will be on your feet most of the day.
- Avoid loosely fitting clothes that may snag on desks and children.

☑ ***Dress appropriately:***

- Do not wear clothes that bear prominent insignias or logos promoting your political views.
- Avoid provocative dress in any manner.
- Avoid overly relaxed outfits such as sweatpants or athletic gear.

Dressing Appropriately

Dress contributes majorly to your students' first and lasting impressions of you. It also has practical meaning. Check with your principal or his or her secretary about specific district or school dress codes. Whatever the requirements, try to dress with comfort in mind (e.g., well-cushioned shoes).

Creating a Welcoming Room Environment

A teacher's room arrangement supports the instructional program and classroom management.

Preparation for the first day begins with organizing your classroom; how you do this will depend on your teaching assignment. For elementary, music, and art teachers, room preparation is a key ingredient for the first class. Bulletin boards should reflect not only material that will be taught, but also the mood for learning. Empty and drab is not welcoming. The physical environment of the room will reflect not only how much you care for the children who will spend one third of their day within its walls, but also your attitude toward learning in general. A room that celebrates learning as mirrored by the symbols and colors on its walls makes a statement about the value of the learning process.

Take some time to think through how you will arrange your desks and tables. Where students sit and the physical position of classroom furniture will have an impact on students' first impressions. Most teachers

LEGAL SIDEBAR

Teachers' Freedom of Expression

The Pennsylvania federal district court ruled that a school district cannot prohibit teachers from wearing "subdued" religious emblems, dress, or insignias because doing so would violate the First Amendment right to free exercise of religion.

—*Nichol v. ARIN Intermediate Unit 28* (2003)

select an arrangement of rows in the early days because rows provide easy and quick attendance taking, but also limit group interaction before you want it. The seating arrangement is a matter of personal style, but in the beginning, choose a desk arrangement that will facilitate your initial duties as a teacher. Therefore, clear, symmetric alignments will probably serve you better during the first week.

Preparing for the First Lesson

When you are preparing for the first lesson, three considerations should guide you: your students' age, the content and implementation of the lesson, and your tone of delivery. Note the following:

☑ Your *tone* is important because it affects your students' first impression of you.

- ***Strike a balance:*** Being too friendly and laid back may give students the idea that you are lax on rules and discipline. Conversely, being too stern may generate fear and anxiety—ingredients that have a negative impact on learning.
- ***Communicate security:*** Your students should feel secure in your room and with your leadership, and your voice should communicate such security. Research reveals that emotions are directly tied to comprehension (Goleman, 1995).

☑ The *content* is important because it will establish a motivational level for your students.

- ***Begin with content that is familiar and invites them to learn more about the topic:*** Provide an interesting fact that will stimulate their curiosity, or ask them to tell you about their knowledge of the topic you are introducing.
- ***Set the structure of how your lessons will be conducted throughout the year:*** Routine generates comfort. The more familiar your students become with your teaching style and your technique on lesson openers, the better the rhythm between your instruction and their learning.

FIRST-DAY INTRODUCTION

Teacher A	Teacher B
TEACHER: On this first day of school, let's begin by finding out what you remember from last year. Billy, what number divided by 3 equals 6? BILLY: Uh . . . I . . . SALLY: 18! TEACHER: Very good, Sally. Well, Billy, it looks like the summer has cleaned out your brain. Now I'll find out how many more students have empty attics!	TEACHER: Good morning, class. Welcome to the first day of school. Let's talk about math a little. What can you tell me about math and what you've learned? JIMMY: I didn't like it. AMY: I loved it! TEACHER: Let's talk for a minute about what we do and don't like about it, and see if we can find some math topics that might help us in our learning.

In the preceding table, Teacher A is delivering a message of authority and control. He is obviously in command and has an agenda specific to his strategic plan (i.e., review and move forward). In addition, he is sending a signal to all students by his decided put-down of Billy; whether intentional or not, he has successfully inhibited a free exchange of student perspectives.

In contrast, Teacher B leaves the door of opportunity wide open for all the class members. By not responding negatively to Jimmy's comment or praising Amy's remark, she has remained neutral and accessible. Also, by using the word *we*, instead of *I*, she has included everyone in the learning process.

Teaching During the First Days of School

Veteran teachers know that concentrated instruction during the first days of school is futile because you will only need to repeat it later, when classes settle into a manageable routine. Thus, the first days should be the time when you do the following:

- ☑ Establish communication lines between you and your students:
  - Engage in activities through which you can learn the students' names and something about each student. Have the students share with one another their favorite games, television shows, places to visit, foods, pets, and so forth.
- ☑ Probe for cues to the students' learning styles:
  - Ask questions related to what the students have already learned on a given topic. Ask them either directly or through a written survey how they best like to acquire information (e.g., "Do you remember something better when the room is quiet or when music is playing in the background?")
- ☑ Develop the structure of your routine:
  - Inform your students about procedures for getting lavatory passes, moving around the room, and following other rules that you outlined in your information packet.
- ☑ Establish a consistent strain of reinforcement that helps your students learn about your style.

FIRST-DAY ISSUES TO ADDRESS

Issue	Elementary teacher	Secondary teacher
Room arrangement	Small groups of four desks or tables are preferable.	Rows of desks work best for both middle school and high school students during the first days of school.
Preparations	Place activity instructions and materials on each desk for immediate engagement.	Have students' names on 3 × 5-inch cards, and affix the cards to the desks for quick and accurate attendance taking.
Administrative tasks	Use creative means to take attendance (e.g., have students line up by birth date).	Taking attendance is a method of communication and interaction. It is a vehicle for first impressions. Use creative methods such as having each student repeat the names of other students in a particular pattern.
Contingencies	Expect interruptions. Keep your attention focused on the class. Defer problems for later attention.	Expect interruptions. Keep your attention focused on the class. Defer problems for later attention.
Recap	Take as many detailed notes as possible on this day.	Take as many detailed notes as possible on this day.

Briefcase CD CH3-4—Sample Opening-Day Letter to Students on a Middle School Team

Middle School Middle school students may require a different instructional approach in the first days. In this age group, more socializing and energetic interaction occurs. These children are entering their seventh, eighth, or ninth year of school and are knowledgeable about the machinery that moves them through the system. They are quick

to recognize ineptness or inexperience and will, by nature, take advantage of any situation that allows them to relax the formality of obedience and compliance. Hence, a fire drill in a middle school has all the earmarks of disaster if not well organized and controlled by the teaching staff.

Because these students are experienced in classroom management, they may become chaotic when an assignment is too complex or they are asked for knowledge not yet acquired. As a result, you should do the following:

- ☑ Present material that allows them success and engagement but does not curb their initiative and industry.
- ☑ Use icebreaker activities that allow some social interaction but introduce a level of structure.
- ☑ Give students a chance to be identified by you.

High School In the high school classroom, initial meetings are also sessions in which students and teacher are learning about one another and ascertaining expectations. At this level, the students are keenly aware of why they are there and are generally prepared for work. Some guidelines for the first days in high school are as follows:

- ☑ Give the students a syllabus similar to the kind you received in college. They will want to know exactly what you will require them to do.
- ☑ Give them an initial problem to solve that will segue into the lesson.
- ☑ As with the middle schoolers, allow them to identify themselves to you and their classmates.

Managing Noninstructional Events

The first days in the classroom establish the rhythm and pace for you and the class; however, as mentioned previously, they may be unlike those of the rest of the year. For most teachers, the first week of classes, and in particular the first 3 days, is usually fraught with interruptions and confusion. During these days, administrators are gathering enrollment information, establishing special education groups, identifying students with health needs, and generally complying with federal, state, and local mandates, such as fire drills, and bus evacuation procedures.

OPENING-WEEK NONINSTRUCTIONAL EVENTS

Events	Your actions
Necessary information gathering (forms)	Incorporate these events into your day, and complete the tasks as quickly as possible.
Fire drills	Prepare your students for these interruptions. Train them how to exit the room quietly. Always count your students upon exiting and returning. Always have a refocusing activity ready for when students return to the classroom.
Telephone calls	Do not react to these interruptions. Seamlessly answer the calls, but keep them short and call back later.
Students called away from class	Allow the students to leave, without comment. Keep notes to re-introduce them to the lesson. Prepare to redirect the lesson if five or six students are called from the room.
Students with special needs	Prepare to accommodate students with physical disabilities (e.g., front-of-room seating, frequent lavatory trips, trips to the nurse's office for medications).

THE FIRST MONTH OF SCHOOL

FIRST-MONTH CHECKLIST

- ☑ ***Resources:*** Meet the staff; learn their jobs and their support services.
- ☑ ***Clerical responsibilities:*** Learn the reporting procedures.
- ☑ ***Parents' Night:*** Prepare your presentation. Know the students' names.
- ☑ ***Substitute folder:*** Create a folder with materials and detailed instructions.
- ☑ ***Tutors:*** Create plans and prepare work for your students' tutors.

The first month of school is important, punctuated with small learning experiences that will eventually mold the teacher you will become. Many of these experiences will occur externally from your classroom and may have a great impact on your teaching strategy.

Locating Resources

Knowing where to look for help and support is often at the heart of your success in the classroom. From textbooks to markers, films to overheads, information to procedure, resources are an integral part of your instructional program, and lacking them may inhibit achievement of your goals. Acquiring the necessary supplies for your lessons is not always accomplished by simply asking for them or filling out a form; it sometimes requires tact and diplomacy.

IN-SCHOOL RESOURCES

Faculty and staff	Resources
Library–media staff	☐ Instruct students on using library materials and on researching ☐ Monitor and instruct students on computer use ☐ Disseminate films, videos, and equipment for classroom instruction
Guidance office staff	☐ Maintain student schedules ☐ Store and administer all schoolwide tests ☐ Maintain student personal and academic records ☐ Operate as liaisons between parents and teachers ☐ Often are the point personnel for intervention from other support professionals
Special education department faculty members	☐ Are your classroom resources for students with learning disabilities (LDs) ☐ Are often placed with classroom teachers during instruction ☐ Test students for LDs and students already diagnosed with LDs ☐ Are a great resource for strategies on how to teach classes comprising students with different ability levels ☐ Act as liaisons between parents of students with LDs and teachers
Psychosocial staff (e.g., psychologist, social worker)	☐ Are resources for children who are emotionally disturbed (ED) ☐ Work with children who are ED as liaisons between students and teachers ☐ Are the point people for children with neglected or deprived home situations ☐ Are the contact people for students displaying signs of depression or anxiety
Therapeutic staff	☐ Work with children who are speech or hearing impaired ☐ Work with children who have physical disabilities ☐ Provide support services for such children ☐ Act as liaisons between teachers and parents of students with physical disabilities
Nurse	☐ Provides first aid and emergency medical assistance for children ☐ Is a source of help with children who have personal hygiene problems ☐ Is the point person when child abuse is suspected

LEGAL SIDEBAR

The Right to Attend School

The federal Equal Educational Opportunities Act of 1974 provides that no state may deny equal educational opportunities to an individual because of his or her race, color, sex, or national origin. Therefore, every person has the right to attend school, unless his or her conduct violates valid rules and regulations.

—Equal Educational Opportunities Act (1974)

Performing Clerical Responsibilities

Teachers entering the profession in this era are burdened during the week with volumes of paperwork not known to their predecessors. Most of this paperwork deals with organizing the student within the regimen of the school and complying with reporting and categorizing mandates. Some of your clerical responsibilities will be as follows:

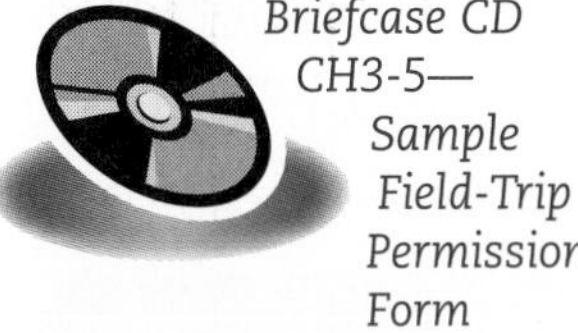

Briefcase CD CH3-5— Sample Field-Trip Permission Form

- ☑ Having students' parents complete free and reduced-price lunch program forms and, later in the year, field-trip permission forms
- ☑ Completing attendance forms for each child under your supervision
- ☑ Reviewing IEP forms for your students who require special education
- ☑ Completing various forms to verify students' residences, guardianship, and health status (e.g., vaccinations, immunizations)
- ☑ Filing and reviewing the list of children in your charge who have specific medical considerations that may need attention (e.g., bee sting allergy, asthma, hearing or sight loss)

Preparing for Parents' Night (Parents' Open House)

The main event of the first month of school, Parents' Open House, can be a source of discomfort for any teacher. Speaking before a group of parents is probably slightly less stressful than speaking before your peers. Parents' Night is a U.S. ritual that may have originated in February 1897, when the PTA was first organized to provide parental guidance to U.S. schools (National Parent Teacher Association, n.d.).

The turnout for Parents' Night varies among grade levels and schools. So many factors influence attendance that you should be prepared for the number of parents to range from a few to a great many.

Putting the event in perspective depends on what you teach. For the elementary teacher, the night is more personal and interactive, whereas for the junior or senior high teacher, it is usually a staid 15 minutes (or less), with roving groups of parents seeking their child's teachers and classrooms. For the art; music; physical education; and home, careers, and technology teachers, as well as the library–media specialists, the evening can be lonely. Parents are looking for the classroom teacher who spends the most time with their child, or the teacher most praised or most complained about at home. Whatever you teach, however, you would be wise to prepare a "lesson plan" for the night, just as you would for a class with your students.

PARENTS' NIGHT GUIDELINES

Elementary school	Middle and high school	Unified arts
Know all your students' first and last names.	Knowing names is understandably unlikely, although impressive.	Knowing names is understandably unlikely, although impressive.

—Cont.

Elementary school	Middle and high school	Unified arts
Have samples of student work either on the bulletin boards or at individual desks.	Have samples of student work displayed or single pieces on an overhead.	Show student work samples as they apply to the discipline (e.g., not feasible for physical education).
Prepare an overhead or a PowerPoint presentation of your teaching regimen. Include homework and assessments requirements.	Prepare an overhead or a PowerPoint presentation of your teaching regimen. Include clear specifics on grading.	Prepare an overhead or a PowerPoint presentation that outlines expectations and requirements, especially with regard to safety and health issues.
Provide contact information.	Provide contact information.	Provide contact information.
Have a question-and-answer period, but speak with parents about individual children after the session—never during.	Have a question-and-answer period. Ask parents to get in contact with the guidance office for appointments to discuss their child individually.	Have a question-and-answer period. Ask parents to get in contact with the guidance office for appointments to discuss their child individually.

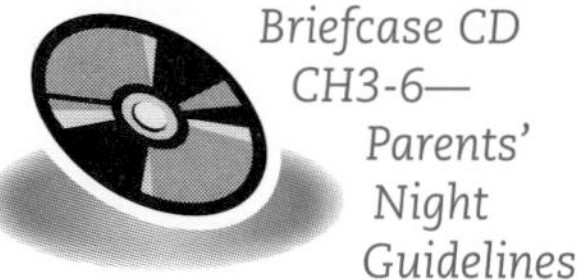

Briefcase CD CH3-6—Parents' Night Guidelines

Some of the realities of Parents' Night are as follows:

- ☑ *What* you say is almost as important as *how* you say it.
- ☑ Parents want to hear your views about their children, not a sermon or proclamation.
- ☑ Parents want to know how their children will be treated.
- ☑ Parents want to know exactly what you will be teaching their children.
- ☑ Parents want to know about your homework and behavior policies.
- ☑ Parents simply want assurance.

Briefcase CD CH3-7—Parents' Night Checklist

Creating the Substitute Folder

Being absent from work for a teacher is more complicated than for most other professions. You cannot simply call in sick and go back to bed. For teachers, their responsibility to their

VOICES IN THE CLASSROOM
Parents' Night Lecture: Not!

Hello. Welcome to Thomas Jefferson Junior High School. I am Mrs. Swarthout, your children's math teacher. I know you'd rather be home watching the playoffs; so would I, but it's Back-to-School Night, so here we are. This class is a pretty good one, because it's second period and the students are still a little sleepy. But, after a few minutes, I have them wide awake.

As you know, I require all students to have a notebook and it to be signed by you every night. If your child doesn't get the notebook signed to confirm that he or she did his or her homework, I assign a zero. So, if he or she gets the zero, it's partly your fault too. I believe in accountability, and if kids are going to learn math, they have to be responsible.

I give a quiz every Friday without fail. Students not "getting" the material may come to my room after school for extra help. I'm here every day till 4 o'clock. The taxpayers get their money's worth out of me.

I don't believe that math is too difficult for anyone. Some students just have to work harder than others. I don't tolerate any funny business because we don't have time. Other teachers like to entertain their students. I'm not in show business; I'm in the teaching business, and if you're going to get ahead in this world, you have to work hard and study.

Any questions?

Stating the Facts:

On substitute teachers: Each day, on average, a substitute teacher is teaching 10% of all U.S. classes. According to the results of a national survey, 89% of the substitutes received little or no training, and 69% did not undergo evaluation of their work (Tannenbaum, 2000).

students extends into the sick room. Although requirements for teachers regarding absences vary, the common rule is that lesson plans must be available for the substitute teacher. Because you seldom have 24 hours' notice that you will be sick, you must keep on your desk, in plain sight, a folder with contingency lesson plans for your class. *The last act before you leave your room each night should be to place this folder in the center of your desk.* In fact, some school districts require this folder to be on your desk in plain sight at all times.

The Plans You Should Leave for the Substitute A dilemma for most teachers is whether to have the substitute teacher continue with the lesson or lessons in progress, or to have the substitute teach an alternative lesson, marking time until you return. The problem with marking time is that it disrupts the rhythm of instruction, especially if you are in the middle of a project that is moving sequentially through specific steps. Likewise, having a person who is unfamiliar with the material, and your methodology, instructing or directing your class may cause confusion and require you to spend precious time sorting out the situation when you return. For most teachers, the wise choice is to provide a lesson that is more than just busywork but does not advance new material. Therefore, you should prepare a lesson that *reinforces* concepts or details you have already taught.

Dealing with the Tutored Student

Briefcase CD CH3-8—Substitute Folder Checklist

The absent student may not be physically in your classroom, but the district and you are responsible for ensuring that he or she receives ongoing instruction. This task is sometimes accomplished through home or after-school tutoring. In either case, you are responsible for providing an outline of the material that the tutor needs to cover. In addition, you will need to make sure the student takes any tests or quizzes that you have administered in his or her absence. In many cases, teachers postpone dealing with these tasks, then have to rush to amass the material that the student has missed and will miss. The wise teacher deals with such tasks expediently.

Who Should Be the Student's Tutor You will most likely be offered the chance to tutor the absent child. Deciding whether to do so is a difficult decision to make during

SUBSTITUTE FOLDER CHECKLIST

- ☑ An updated roster of all the students
- ☑ The schedule for the day, with room numbers for each class (if applicable)
- ☑ Keys or the location of keys to the room
- ☑ The room number for audiovisual equipment and the name of the contact person
- ☑ The lesson plan,
  - ☑ Typed
  - ☑ With explicit instructions
  - ☑ Including a sponge activity
  - ☑ With either an assessment or an activity to close the lesson
- ☑ Fire-drill instructions (e.g., the location of the exit and where the students line up outside)
- ☑ Step-by-step procedures for managing unruly students (e.g., detention, office, time-out room)
- ☑ Specific instructions about where completed papers are to be left
- ☑ A request for a brief narrative on the lesson and events of the day from the substitute

your first year. Tutoring will mean additional planning time, extra hours after school, and, sometimes, travel to distant parts of the city or county, although it is an avenue for extra revenue. Be sure to think through the advantages and disadvantages before accepting the job.

Common Facts About Tutoring Whether you are the tutor or tutoring is assigned to someone else, some common facts about tutoring follow:

- ☑ The person assigned as the tutor may be a teacher who is not certified in your subject area, or a person who has a degree but is not certified.
- ☑ Frequently, the material you leave for the tutor is not given to him or her, or because of failed communications, it is not retrieved by the tutor. In this case, the student will not complete the work you have assigned.
- ☑ You will need to adapt class lesson plans to those for the individual student.
- ☑ Group projects, especially those requiring several stages, are neither effective nor productive for tutored students.
- ☑ Upon the student's return, you may find that he or she is behind not only in completion of the material you sent home, but, more important, in comprehension.
- ☑ Prepare to give the returning tutored student some personal time to explain what he or she has missed, as well as extra time to complete past assignments.

ALSO IN YOUR FIRST YEAR OF SCHOOL

OTHER ACTIVITIES CHECKLIST

- ☑ Considering participation in extracurricular activities
- ☑ Being involved in a mentoring (induction) program
- ☑ Reflecting and planning for the second year

During your first year of teaching, you may supervise one or more extracurricular activities. You may also be required to participate in a mentoring, or induction, program to gain useful knowledge from a more experienced teacher. Finally, at the end of the year, you will need to reflect on the year and plan accordingly for your second year of teaching.

Supervising Extracurricular Activities

Successfully getting hired as a teacher may hinge on your expertise and interest in one or more extracurricular activities. Principals who need to staff intramural programs value any experience a potential employee may have as a sports team coach or supervisor of recreational activities. Typical extracurricular activities include the following:

- ☑ Extended-day programs, such as developmental and enrichment reading groups
- ☑ Individual clubs, such as the environmental club, the chess club, theater groups, and physical fitness programs
- ☑ Remediation classes in math, literacy, and social studies
- ☑ Gifted and talented programs
- ☑ All sports programs, including soccer, basketball, lacrosse, volleyball, football, swimming, baseball, softball, track, bowling, wrestling, and field hockey

The Balancing Act For the new teacher, whether to participate in initiatives after school and in the evening may depend on the stage at which you are with your graduate schooling. Working on a master's degree, meeting the demands of graduate study, and preparing for each work day in your first year of teaching may prove to be burden enough. However, if the principal or other school officials clearly encourage your participation, you would be wise to accede to their wishes.

VOICES IN THE CLASSROOM
A Role Model

When I think of "good" teachers, I think of Dick Baker. He was a science teacher who wore all the earmarks of that stereotype—flannel shirt, thick hiking boots, pocket protector, and white lab coat. Dick had an enthusiasm for the job that was so infectious that even the mid-1970s hippie-wannabes couldn't help but follow the guy through his projects.

He believed that the classroom should be alive with references to what he was teaching. So, it wasn't unusual to see him standing amid his eighth graders in the driving rain measuring rainfall and temperatures. Later, he had one of his classes construct a makeshift rooftop weather station. On field trips, which he scheduled often, his students could be found sitting cross-legged with their clipboards, listing several varieties of fauna and flora or scraping samples of rocks.

When not engaged in the sciences, he was working with his colleagues, attempting to bring science into their subject areas. He worked closely with the social studies teacher to bring the history of New York State's geophysical development into his lessons on glaciers and rock formations.

My most vivid memory of Dick, however, was the after-school projects he did with his students, or any students who wanted to join. One of the projects was a drill team. Who can help but wonder at the magic of teachers like Dick Baker, who could gather 25 to 30 adolescent girls and boys and get them to march in straight, disciplined, rhythmic lines?

—*A retired teacher*

One great benefit of working with students outside the classroom is that you gain a clearer perspective of their needs. More important, children of all school ages need adult role models outside the classroom who will provide the guidance and support they need to navigate the developmental waters.

The Liability Issue One matter of concern for all teachers should be the liability factor when they are working with students outside the classroom. One stipulation in the **No Child Left Behind Act (NCLB;** chap. C, subpart 5, § 2361), entitled the *Paul D. Coverdell Teacher Protection Act of 2001,* provides liability protection for teachers when they are working with children as long as they are within the legal definitions of supervising children on school-sanctioned property and within the prescribed descriptions of a school-sponsored event (No Child Left Behind Act, 2002). Despite these and other legal protections afforded teachers, you will be cautioned by both your district and your union representatives to follow some general rules relative to working with children in and out of the classroom. Among such rules are the following:

- ☑ Never transport students in your personal vehicle without parental consent.
- ☑ Acquire parental consent if a student will be working with you at your home.
- ☑ Always work with students in the appropriately provided area (e.g., ball field, gymnasium, auditorium).
- ☑ Never touch a student beyond what is called for in the activity.
- ☑ Never banter with your students using risqué language or telling profane jokes.
- ☑ If money is involved, make sure that a student representative is part of the accountability process, and always deposit funds with the school secretary or treasurer.
- ☑ Never leave a child unattended or without transport when the event concludes.

VOICES IN THE CLASSROOM
Mentoring and First-Year Mistakes

In my first year of teaching, a veteran science teacher, Mr. Pemberton [alias], decided that he would be my self-appointed mentor. He went out of his way to give me advice about how to handle the kids. I remember the first thing he told me: "Don't smile until Thanksgiving." This was his strategy to keep students under control.

Pemberton was known for his rigid application of school rules. He believed that if everyone followed the rules, students and teachers alike, we would have fewer behavior problems. He was known for his organized teaching. Students knew that they would have homework every night and a quiz on Friday. He did not seem to be well liked by them, but he was the hard-nosed pedagogue whom students bragged about years later as being strict—but fair. If caught chewing gum in his class, a student could expect detention—no argument given.

He made himself my mentor and would stand outside my classroom and listen; then, at lunch, he would give me advice on what I was doing wrong. Pemberton was what we call a *traditionalist.* His instructions to me were always laced with mottoes and phrases about duty, work, and responsibility. He believed in a set moral code and that it could be taught to and learned by every student who wanted it. The day of our parting came when I had committed the unforgivable sin—harboring a student who was a fugitive from class. He was a bright boy who had a different idea about education. Suffice it to say that he was not a traditional learner. He came to my study hall in a panic because he was supposed to be in Pemberton's science class but got held up in the library and didn't want to go to class late because he would get detention. I took pity on him and gave him a pass explaining that we were discussing homework.

During lunch, Pemberton questioned me about the boy. He knew that the boy wasn't my student and wanted to know why I would be discussing homework with a student who wasn't mine. I respectfully told him I thought that every student who needed help was in effect "my student." He then informed me that I had collaborated with the student in breaking school rules and that it was his duty to inform the principal.

Although nothing more serious than a mild oral reprimand from the principal resulted from this incident, it made me aware of the nuances of collegiality. From then until the remainder of my probationary period, I kept my door and my mouth closed.

—*A junior high school teacher*

Participating in Mentoring, or Induction, Programs

Prompted by the high attrition rate of new teachers, mentoring programs, more recently named **induction programs,** have grown in popularity throughout the United States (Darling-Hammond & Sykes, 1999). At last report, 30 states had instituted mandatory mentoring programs in which veteran teachers are placed with first-year teachers to provide a range of support from logistical to emotional. Although considered an effective method of assisting the new teacher with the many obstacles he or she faces during the first year, mentoring has been only cautiously supported by qualitative research.

One problem continuously cited is the high probability that the veteran teacher will impose his or her personal—often more traditional—educational philosophy onto the rookie (Darling-Hammond, Berry, Haselkorn, & Fideler, 1999). As most teacher preparation programs in U.S. colleges and universities adopt more student-centered teaching strategies that have been validated by extensive research, the new teacher is placed in a dilemma: Follow the mentor's advice and instruction, or abide by the training and education attained from many years of grueling and expensive education. Resolution of this dilemma requires common sense: Assess the context of the situation, determine what is best for the student, and trust your instincts.

Reflecting and Planning for the Second Year

As a teacher, you will learn quickly; this fact is a truism of the profession. Because the job has so many variables, teachers who hesitate may find themselves lost in a sea of noise, a bedlam of confusion, and a volume of backlog. As your first year comes to a close, the following may be true for you:

- ☑ You will have found systems and strategies, and tactics and resources all necessary for you to function with success.
- ☑ Despite this year of experiential education, you know you would be foolish to think you have found the perfect method for teaching.
- ☑ You will be concerned about the material you did *not* cover, as well as the effectiveness of your teaching.
- ☑ You will note numerous obstacles that prevented you from doing your job effectively (e.g., classroom control, difficulty of the material, classroom interruptions).
- ☑ You will recall that you developed a number of coping mechanisms that helped you survive the first year.
- ☑ You will begin to formulate new strategies and think of new ideas to help you become more effective.

Briefcase CD CH3-9—End-of-Year Checklist

Before the start of the second year, strategic plans must be designed with an eye on your missteps of the past year. Doing so is *reflective teaching*—when you think about your actions relative to students, parents, colleagues, administrators, and other school personnel.

END-OF-YEAR CHECKLIST

- ☑ Did my strategic teaching plan align with state and district standards?
- ☑ Was my class behavior plan effective?
  - ☑ What about it needs to be changed?
  - ☑ To whom may I speak about making improvements?
- ☑ Was my room arrangement serviceable during the entire year?
  - ☑ Should I look for a different furniture style?
  - ☑ Should I change the physical layout of the room with additional or less furniture?
- ☑ What materials did I lack that would have helped me have a more successful teaching year overall?
  - ☑ Do I need more audiovisual materials?
  - ☑ Are workbooks available that would support my program?
  - ☑ Do I need more art and craft materials?
- ☑ How can I better communicate with my students' parents? (See Parental Communication table in Chapter 11.)
- ☑ Which staff members can I consider true sources of help and support?
- ☑ Which staff members should I engage for more support?
- ☑ How can I improve student participation in the learning process?
  - ☑ Should I change my teaching style?
  - ☑ Are my assessments effective?
  - ☑ Can I find a more engaging way to present the material?
  - ☑ What outside help can I get to improve my instruction?
  - ☑ What can I do this summer to prepare myself for next August–September?
- ☑ What books can I read this summer to help me improve professionally?

DOS AND DON'TS

Don't	Do
Wait until the contract-required date to visit the school building and your classroom	Contact your principal or supervisor as early as you can after securing your job
Ignore the working staff in the building	Introduce yourself to all staff members
Fail to get needed materials if they are not supplied by the school	Get the materials you will need from the school or on your own, if you can afford them
Ignore your students' fears and uneasiness on the first day	Prepare icebreaking activities so that you can learn your students' names
Leave policies and rules to chance	Provide complete policy and rule descriptions during the first or second class meeting
Introduce difficult lesson material during the first days of school	Design lessons for the first days that transition students into new-grade material
Treat secretaries or support staff with condescension	Treat all support staff with deference, and respect the difficulty of their jobs, especially during the first days
Allow students to take attendance without your complete supervision	Make sure attendance procedures are followed and materials are secured during the day
Preach to parents during Open House about how to be better parents or scold them in advance about homework monitoring	Present parents with a brief summary of your philosophy, an outline of the instructional program, and your expectations for their children
Call in sick without having clear instructions for your substitute available on your desk	Prepare a substitute folder complete with seating plan, attendance sheets, and clear instructions
Ignore students from your class who are being tutored simply because they are not present	Provide the tutors with complete instructions and lessons so that the students will be kept current
Give long tests or quizzes on days when you will be observed by the principal or supervisor	Prepare a lesson for observation that will engage students and highlight your teaching skills
Become an 8:00 to 3:30 teacher who ignores the chance to work with students outside the classroom	Volunteer for supervising extracurricular activities
Forget the events of the year that may help you the following year	Keep a daily journal of events and reflections that will help you better direct your style for next year

WEB SITES OF INTEREST

http://teachersnetwork.org/ntol
New Teachers Online is a site that provides resources and information for new teachers.

http://www.teachermentors.com/MCenter%20Site/Mknowl.html
This site provides basic information on mentoring, including some assumptions new teachers often hold.

http://www.ed.gov/pubs/FirstYear/ch3.html
This site, from the U.S. Department of Education, provides tips and strategies for the first-year teacher.

http://www.teachingtips.com/articles/Droomenvironment1.htm
This excellent site provides tips on how to arrange your room before the first day of classes.

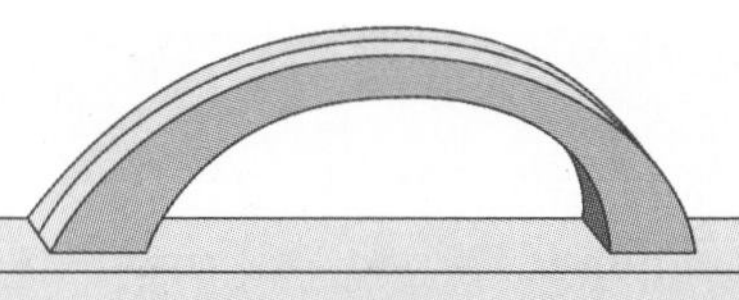

For Your Briefcase

To Do

- Visit your school.
- Meet the principal and key people.
- Survey your room and gather pertinent information (e.g., the supply request format).
- Prepare your bulletin boards.
- Gather your supplies and textbooks.
- Arrange your room for the first day.
- Prepare the opening-day lesson.
- Have 3 × 5-inch cards (or a facsimile) available on which to gather student information.
- Prepare the opening-week lesson plans.
- Prepare the Parents' Night talk.
- Gather plans and create a substitute folder.

Resources on Your Briefcase CD

Samples

- Sample First-Day Icebreaker Activities
- Sample Welcome Letter—Third Grade
- Sample Opening-Day Letter—Sixth-Grade Math
- Sample Opening-Day Letter to Students on a Middle School Team
- Sample Field-Trip Permission Form

Templates

- Parents' Night Checklist
- Substitute Folder Checklist
- End-of-Year Checklist

Tables

- Parents' Night Guidelines

REFERENCES

Darling-Hammond, L., Berry, B. T., Haselkorn, D., & Fideler, E. (1999). Teacher recruitment, selection, and induction: Policy influences on the supply and quality of teachers. In L. Darling-Hammond & G. Sykes (Eds.), *Teaching as the learning profession: Handbook of policy and practice* (pp. 183–232). San Francisco: Jossey-Bass.

Darling-Hammond, L., & Sykes, G. (Eds.) (1999). *Teaching as the learning profession: Handbook of policy and practice.* San Francisco: Jossey-Bass.

Duckworth, E. (1964). Piaget rediscovered. In R. E. Ripple & V. N. Rockcastle (Eds.), *Piaget rediscovered: A report on the Conference on Cognitive Studies and Curriculum Development* (p. 5). Ithaca, NY: Cornell University.

Equal Educational Opportunities Act, 20 U.S.C. § 1703 (1974).

Goleman, D. (1995). *Emotional intelligence: Why it can matter more than IQ.* New York: Bantam.

Magau, T. (2002, July). *Teacher buying behaviors.* Paper presented at Quality Education Data's Education Marketers' Forum, Washington, DC.

Nichol v. ARIN Intermediate Unit 28, 268 F. Supp. 2d 536 (W.D. Pa. 2003).

No Child Left Behind Act of 2001, Pub. L. No. 107-110, § 2361, 115 Stat. 1425 (2002).

National Parent Teacher Association (PTA). (n.d.). *Our history: 1897–1899.* Chicago: Author. Retrieved March 8, 2006, from http://www.pta.org/ap_our_history_decade_1117143473593.html

Tannenbaum, M. D. (2000, May). No substitute for quality. *Educational Leadership, 57*(8), 70–72.

Planning and Organizing

By failing to prepare, you are preparing to fail.
—*Benjamin Franklin*

PLANNING TO TEACH

THE INSTRUCTIONAL PROGRAM

- ☑ District curricular plan
- ☑ Yearly plan
- ☑ Unit plan
- ☑ Lesson plan

Arranging your room into stations will aid your instructional program.

The Plan

An effective teacher is prepared, has a plan, and knows how to implement it. No factor in the teaching profession is more indicative of a teacher's success than the organization of his or her instructional plan. This plan encompasses both the long-range (yearly) and the immediate (daily) blueprints for the teaching program. Mandates on what a teacher must teach originate from the state, the district, and the school curricular plan. The overall plan generally comprises **learning standards,** which are organized by skill and grade level and are often accompanied by suggestions for instruction.

What to Teach

The *what* of teaching is taken from the learning standards developed from both traditional and contemporary sources. Traditionally, reading, writing, and numeracy have formed the basis of the *need to know* for every child since the establishment of education in society. Contemporary sources are national organizations such as the National Council of Teachers of English, National Science Teachers Association, American Music Conference, National Council of Teachers of Mathematics, International Reading Association, and others.

SAMPLE NATIONAL LEARNING STANDARD

National history standard: K–4	Student outcomes
Topic 1: Living and Working Together in Families and Communities, Now and Long Ago	Students investigate a family history for at least two generations, identifying various members and their connections in order to construct a time line.
Specific lessons: Range in depth depending on grade level	Students interview family members, conduct interviews, design a time line, and write a report.
Assessments: Range in level of difficulty depending on grade level	Students are evaluated on grammar and usage in their written interview report.
	Students present an analysis that contrasts family lifestyles and the influences that bring about change in family and social structures.

Note. From *National Standards for History:* K–4 (Exp. ed.), by National Center for History in the Schools, 1994, Los Angeles: Author. Copyright 1994 by National Center for History in the Schools. Adapted with permission. Retrieved March 15, 2006, from http://nchs.ucla.edu

Learning Standards and the Teacher

Learning, or content, standards are the benchmarks by which school officials, parents, and legislators can determine the progress of their schools. For this reason, only an extremely rare school does not align its instructional program with the standards and encourage, if not mandate, their teachers to align their daily lessons with the standards framework. As you prepare your unit plan and daily plans, be sure to place the state standards within sight or to design a checklist that you can easily reference. Be prepared to demonstrate the alignment of your plans with the standards. They are broad enough so that you should be able to devise activities and instructional strategies that can be used to develop lessons promoting student comprehension under the general categories mandated by school officials.

From a teacher's viewpoint, learning standards and the specific benchmarks are an excellent source of direction and support during construction of the unit plan and daily lesson plans. Following the standards allows you to use the textbook as a tool, not as the curriculum itself, and provides you with a wide range of ideas in specific areas. The sample learning standards from *Texas Essential Knowledge and Skills,* and New York's learning standards, exemplify the type of structure and content that states across the nation are developing as curricular guides for teachers. Notice that the topics in each set of standards are fairly broad and can be applied by using any number of strategies.

SAMPLE LEARNING STANDARDS

Texas Essential Knowledge and Skills: Fifth grade	New York learning standards: Primary to sixth grade
History *Students* • Explain causes and effects of European colonization • Summarize how conflict between the American colonies and Great Britain led to American independence • Describe events that led to the creation of the U.S. Constitution • Identify important social changes of the 19th century, including the Industrial Revolution, westward expansion, and the Civil War • Describe important issues, events, and individuals of the 20th century	**Social Studies** *Learning Standard 1* The study of New York State and United States history requires an analysis of the development of American culture, its diversity and multicultural context, and the ways people are unified by many values, practices, and traditions. *Students* • Know the roots of American culture, its development from many different traditions, and the ways many people from a variety of groups and backgrounds played a role in creating it • Understand the basic ideals of American democracy as explained in the Declaration of Independence and the Constitution and other important documents • Explain those values, practices, and traditions that unite all Americans
Mathematics Numbers, Operations, and Quantitative Reasoning *Students* • Read, write, compare, and order whole numbers through billions • Read, write, compare, and order decimals through thousandths • Generate equivalent fractions	**Mathematics** *Learning Standard 1* Abstraction and symbolic representation are used to communicate mathematically. *Students* • Use special mathematical notation and symbolism to communicate in mathematics and to compare and describe quantities, express relationships, and relate mathematics to their immediate environments

—*Cont.*

Texas Essential Knowledge and Skills: Fifth grade	New York learning standards: Primary to sixth grade
• Compare fractions in a variety of ways • Relate decimals to fractions using models to the thousandths • Add, subtract, multiply, and divide whole numbers • Add and subtract decimals • Identify prime and common factors • Model adding and subtracting fractions with like denominators • Round whole numbers and decimals to tenths • Estimate to solve problems	

Note. (*Left column*) From *Texas Essential Knowledge and Skills,* by Texas Education Agency, 1998, Austin: Author. Copyright © Texas Education Agency. All rights reserved. Reprinted with permission. Retrieved from http://www.tea.state.tx.us/teks/teksls.pdf. (*Right column*) From *Core Subjects/Learning Standards,* by Elementary, Middle, Secondary, and Continuing Education (EMSC), New York State Education Department, 1996, Albany: Author. Copyright 1996 by the New York State Education Department. Reprinted with permission. Retrieved from http://www.emsc.nysed.gov/deputy/Documents/learnstandards.htm

SAMPLE LESSON ALIGNED WITH LEARNING STANDARDS	
Texas history standard	Identify important social changes of the 19th century, including the Industrial Revolution
Objectives	Students will ✓ Identify the major social changes that occurred during the late 19th century ✓ Identify the technological changes that occurred during this time ✓ Explain the impact of these changes on urban society
Focusing activity	✓ The class will view a 23-minute film entitled *The Industrial Revolution: Great Britain 1750–1850*, by Anne Roerkohl.
Instructional activities	✓ The class will discuss the film, focusing on the images presented.
Dependent activity	✓ The class will connect the film images to life in Great Britain during this time and discuss how it compares with the life of modern-day factory workers. ✓ In groups of four, students will compile a list of factors that composed the *Industrial Revolution.* ✓ Students will present their findings to the class in general.
Independent activity	✓ Students will find one primary document that reflects the life of workers during the Industrial Revolution and summarize the document in an essay. ✓ In the same essay, students will demonstrate how the living conditions were the cause of reactions leading to social change.
Assessment	✓ Students will include their study on the Industrial Revolution as part of their portfolios on historical events that shaped 20th-century political and social life.

Curriculum Basics

Presenting third graders with transparencies of new material on the symbiotic relationship between plant life and animal life will leave them bleary eyed and confused. However, the same lesson presented in a concrete format, with examples taken from their daily lives, could be engaging. For example, ask your students if they have ever observed the movements of spiders, bees, flies, or ants. Then ask them about their observations of plant life. Tie their data to the lesson, and complete it with visual aids that verify their experiences.

Briefcase CD CH4-1—Key Elements of Curriculum Preparation

Clearly, the two most important concepts of curriculum preparation are as follows:

1. Know your content.
2. Know your students.

KEY ELEMENTS OF CURRICULUM PREPARATION

Element	What it is	What to do
Content	Material mandated by state or school district standards, plus supplemental material	Organize material in sequence by chronology or theme.
Sources for instructional materials	Textbooks, electronic media, library, students	Gather interesting facts and notes from many sources to support the main curriculum.
Audience	Students	Consider whom you are teaching (age, gender, ability group) and find age- and gender-appropriate supplemental material.
School environment	Scheduling and daily routine	Plan according to the schedule of your school. Carefully select which subject is taught relative to the movement of the class's daily routine. Consider the flow of other school activities (e.g., days when pictures are taken, physicals are given, and assemblies are held; holidays).

As you have learned, the curriculum is a course of study organized in a sequential manner to achieve specified learning outcomes. Curricular material may be arranged by mastery level, as in math, or chronologically, as in social studies. The teacher's job is to place the material into a plan that is mindful of the following factors:

- ***The student***
  - Developmental age
  - Skill levels
  - Special needs
- ***The material***
  - Sequenced by either chronology or formula
  - Aligned with state and district standards
- ***The skills***
  - Appropriate for the students' level of accomplishment
  - Congruent with state and district standards
  - Congruent with expectations of achievement specific to the students' age

In the real world of teaching, curriculum comprises three basic domains: *content, sequence,* and *scope.* Content is *what* you teach, sequence is the *skill level* of instruction, and scope is the *breadth* and *depth* of the material taught.

THE BASICS OF CURRICULUM	
Content	*What* is taught (e.g., studying the drafting and ratification of the U.S. Constitution; studying the food chain; studying the literary devices used in poetry and prose; studying the congruency of right triangles).
Sequence	The *arrangement* of material based on *skill* or *mastery* levels (e.g., math begins with fundamentals and progresses to complex equations, whereas social studies expands from knowledge-level to evaluation-level skills).
Scope	The *breadth* and *depth* of the material you teach (e.g., in second grade, you may introduce multiplication of double-digit numbers across a wide range of applications, from money to weight to widgets). Scope is completely in the teacher's hands.

ENGAGING IN THE PLANNING PROCESS

Planning begins long before the bell rings in August or September, and it becomes an ongoing process that constantly changes depending on a variety of factors. The basic process is as follows.

Step 1: Become Informed of the Specific Curriculum

Acquire the curricular plan and syllabi of your district and school. They can be obtained from your principal or directly from the curriculum development office, which is generally located at the central offices of the school board.

Step 2: Develop a Yearly Plan

A yearly plan is necessary to maintain continuity and to increase your ability to manage your instructional plan. Making a yearly plan provides an opportunity to do the following:

- ☑ Create an overall picture of what you will teach throughout the year
- ☑ Align state and local standards with your lesson objectives
- ☑ Generate your unit plan and daily lesson plans in an orderly manner
- ☑ Gather resources and materials for your lessons
- ☑ Notify potential speakers and visitors
- ☑ Set up tickets, travel, and housing arrangements for field trips

THE YEARLY PLAN

- Acquire the curricular plan of the district.
- Acquire an accurate school calendar listing all attendance days.
- Arrange major topic or thematic areas to be covered during the year.
- Create a list of resources and materials needed to facilitate the lessons.
- Highlight dates for state-mandated tests when students will not be in class.
- Highlight probable major unit tests.
- Compile a list of possible class visitors.
- Determine places and dates of probable field trips.

THE UNIT PLAN

- Determine the main topics of your subject area by aligning material from textbooks and other sources with state and district standards.
- Establish a set of objectives (what you expect students to learn) for the unit.
- Block off the unit in time segments.
- Blueprint assessments throughout the unit.
- Prepare a culminating project to synthesize the unit.
- Note the scope and type of final test to be given on the unit.

Briefcase CD CH4-2—Yearly Plan Checklist

Briefcase CD CH4-3—Thematic Unit and Unit Plan Checklist

Step 3: Develop a Unit Plan

A unit plan should separate the year into parts by either theme or topic. For the elementary school curriculum, unit planning is an opportunity to incorporate an *interdisciplinary* format that enhances student comprehension (National Center for History in the Schools, 1994).

Although interdisciplinary instruction (a) is more difficult to schedule, (b) is often resisted by teachers comfortable with their own instructional style, and (c) requires more

THE THEMATIC UNIT

- Determine the main topics of your subject area by aligning material from textbooks and other sources with state and district standards.
- Establish a set of objectives (what you expect students to learn) for the unit.
- Find a common theme that might tie in the general idea of the topic.
- Block off the unit in time segments.
- Blueprint assessments throughout the unit.
- Prepare a culminating project to synthesize the unit.
- Note the scope and type of final test to be given on the unit.

specific coordination regarding alignment of standards with content, it allows students to see connections between subject areas and creates schemata that will help them comprehend the material taught (Brooks & Brooks, 1993). The *thematic unit* is a tool you can use to implement interdisciplinary teaching by forming the lesson around a theme or concept that easily reaches to topics in other subjects. Seemingly, math and history, by the nature of their content, indicate sequential and chronological arrangement, whereas music, art, technology, and foreign languages provide abundant opportunities for the thematic approach. However, with the increasing prevalence of **cooperative learning** techniques, teachers are incorporating the thematic approach in all subjects.

Briefcase CD CH4-4—Sample Unit Plan

Examples of Thematic Unit Ideas

Science
- Saving the planet
- Global warming
- Ecology
- Recycling

History
- Westward expansion
- Exploring the world (nation)
- Conflict for change
- Populist influence

Math
- Measurement
- Probability
- Shapes and sizes

English
- Antiheroes
- Man vs. nature
- Self-identification
- Literature as history

Art
- Portraiture
- Expressionism
- Modern art
- Changing patterns

Foreign Language
- Traveling
- Preparing a meal
- Starting a business

Music
- Tonality
- Genres
- Instrumentation
- Orchestration

Technology
- Privacy and computers
- Technical Internet machinery
- Databases

Home and Careers
- Finding a job
- Organizing the home and its finances
- Having a nutritional lifestyle

Guidepost

How many weeks should a unit plan run?
The length depends on the content and the subject area, but most units are about 3–4 weeks long.

Should all unit plans have a project?
No. Some units of instruction establish a specific skill or introduce a general topic that will be covered in other units. These units are usually shorter and structured more around a direct instruction teaching mode.

Should all unit plans have a theme?
No. Thematic units are not always feasible because some plans introduce or sharpen skills or content that will be incorporated into later units. For example, in math, the unit plan will follow a topic associated with a skill, such as measurement and computation of areas of shapes.

In Real Time: What to Teach

Covering the material has a separate meaning from learning the material. Every teacher must make choices as to which part or parts of the curriculum receive more or less attention than others. Giving them equal emphasis and finishing the required syllabus never happens. You, the teacher, must make choices based on knowledge of the content, your students' specific learning needs, and the time allotted to you.

Briefcase CD CH4-5—Sample Daily Lesson Plan

Step 4: Develop a Daily Lesson Plan Format

The daily lesson plan format should work for you and your particular subject but be flexible enough to accommodate various teaching strategies. Lesson plans are blueprints to guide you and your students through the material; however, rigid adherence to a plan can preclude the chance for creative student input.

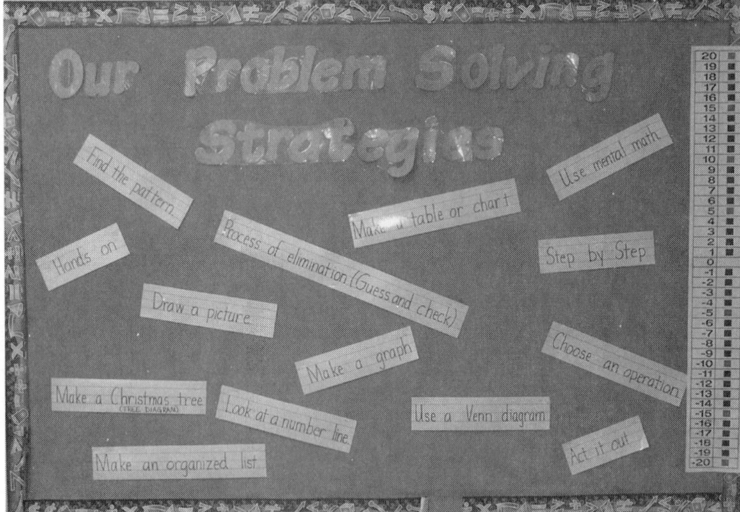

Bulletin boards can be excellent communicators and often give students ready reminders of their goals and work deadlines.

The basic lesson plan should contain the following information:

- ☑ ***Goals and objectives:*** The purpose and aims of your lesson
- ☑ ***Content:*** *What* you are teaching
- ☑ ***Instructional activities:*** The activities that will achieve your goals and objectives
- ☑ ***Dependent and independent practice:*** Working with the material in class; working with it independently at home or at the library
- ☑ ***Assessment:*** Determining the extent of student comprehension
- ☑ ***Reflection:*** Evaluating the events of the lesson and taking notes to cue the next lesson

LESSON PLAN TIPS

- ☑ ***Keep a journal or notebook on your desk:*** Use it to jot down notes on the lesson of the day, such as where you left off, who needed extra help, who was or was not working on task, and what additional materials you will need for the next day. Also use the journal or notebook to record ideas about changes to make the next time you teach the lesson plan.
- ☑ ***Always plan for more activities than you will probably need:*** Determining exactly how much time a particular class will take to respond to a lesson is sometimes difficult.
- ☑ ***Get into the habit of looking over the daily lesson plan before class begins:*** Doing so in the early morning will ensure that you still have time to gather any needed materials before class starts.
- ☑ ***Understand that reflecting on the lesson and taking notes are essential:*** They ensure the continuity of your entire teaching program. Without notes—unless you have a stupendous memory—you will find that on the following day, the details of the previous day become cloudy during the rush to pick up where you left off. Jot down notes on ideas to expand upon, on any additional materials needed, and on student performance (for future reference during evaluations).

SAMPLE DAILY LESSON PLAN

Lesson Topic: Comparing the original text of *Romeo and Juliet* with an artistic (cinematic) representation and gaining insight into the creative process

Goals: To promote student awareness of artistic tone and design through an application of critical analysis and evaluation; to generate recognition of the social, historical, and cultural features of the text.
(New York State Language Art Standard 2.1 and 3.1—Intermediate)

Main Objective of Instruction: To demonstrate the constancy of artistic design across social, cultural, and historical contexts and how each context depends on the human drives of survival, community, and love

Objectives:

- Students will be able to write a critical review of the 1996 movie *Romeo and Juliet,* using the original text as a frame of reference.
- Students will formulate a comparison framework, identifying the dramatic points presented by the original text and the attempted effect of the film.
- Students will orally discuss and provide conclusions on the characterizations of the original text and those of the film.
- Students will articulate the cultural aspects of the Elizabethan Age as expressed in the play and the cultural aspects of the modern age as expressed in the film.
- Students will articulate, through written response, the social factors affecting the theme of the play and the film.

Materials:

Films: *Romeo and Juliet* (1996); *Romeo and Juliet* (1969) (Zeffirelli)
Text: Folger Shakespeare Library's *Romeo and Juliet*
Overhead projector
Markers and paper for group presentations

Procedure: *NOTE: This lesson follows the completed reading of the entire play.*
Focusing Activity: Students will view the opening scene of the 1969 film version of *Romeo and Juliet*, then view the opening scene of the 1996 version.

1. The viewings will be followed by open discussion on points of similarities and dissimilarities:
   - What did you find most different between the two movies?
   - What was the effect of using guns as opposed to swords?
   - Why was that effect used?
   - What did you notice about the character of Tybalt in the modern film?
   - How does his character as a Hispanic man play to diversity?
   - How did the director of the modern film attempt to sustain Shakespeare's original tone?
   - How can we describe tone when speaking of films?
   - Which film had the greater dramatic effect?

During the discussion, students' comments and critical points will be placed on an overhead for them to copy to their notes.

2. The opening scene will be read aloud, with students participating as characters. The same questions will be asked relative to the original text and the two films.
3. Students view the remainder of the 1996 film.
4. Students view portions of the Zeffirelli film.
5. *Dependent practice:*
   a. Students write the opening paragraph of a film critic's review of the 1996 version of the film and share it with the class.
   b. Students work in cooperative groups to formulate criticism of the play and the film and prepare comparison charts.
6. *Independent practice:*
   a. Students complete the review of the film.
   b. Students complete handouts on Shakespearean theater.

—Cont.

c. Students complete handouts on the textual differences between modern and Shakespearean language.
d. Students write an editorial on teenage suicide.

Assessment:

1. Students write a comparative essay, choosing a single character from the play, and demonstrate the characterizations in the film and in the original play.
2. Students complete short essay answers on the application of terms such as *tone, mood,* and *dramatic irony* as they are used in both the film and the original play.
3. Students present oral arguments as to whether or not the film captured the essence of Shakespeare's intent and purpose. This exercise is accomplished in teams of three.
4. Students present their research on the Elizabethan Age through a written analysis of how aspects of that age are woven into the context of the play.
5. Students present a critical analysis, in written form, on the social and cultural aspects of the film and what impact they had on the artistic expression of the play as intended by Shakespeare.
6. Students present oral arguments as to the mores and values present during the Elizabethan Age and the modern age and how they were depicted in both the play and the film.
7. Students create a speculative work (newspaper, magazine, play, radio play, television show, videotape) that demonstrates a single theme or plot out of context (e.g., Shakespeare doing a television sitcom; Mark Twain conducting a talk show; Longfellow writing a poem about a space shuttle mission, etc.).
8. *Culminating activity!* Students submit their final analysis as to the motives of the characters in the play and analyze the relative impact of context and sociocultural influence on these motives.

In Real Time: Instructional Activities

One of the pivotal points that marks the difference between being a good teacher and an effective one is the choice and execution of your instructional activities. The more thought, care, and preparation that go into designing these activities, the more likely you will teach an engaging and productive lesson.

Briefcase CD CH4-6— Lesson Plan Checklist

Assessment is a key element in the teaching process. In fact, when designing a lesson plan, the effective teacher knows that assessment is the most essential tool for successful learning. Chapter 8 provides examples and procedures for a variety of assessment techniques. Linda Darling-Hammond (1999), a well-respected researcher in the area of assessment, noted that assessments can provide equity and stimulate learning opportunities by "informing teachers more fully about how their students think and learn" (p. 1).

VOICES IN THE CLASSROOM
Experience in Planning

My mentor teacher called me at home during the last week of August and asked me to drop by his house. He showed me into his family room, where he had taped up about 15 feet of newspaper stock. Scattered on the table were history texts, maps, books, and lists.

"We're planning out the year," he said. "Grab a beer and a marker."

We spent 3 hours sketching the entire school year around four basic themes and then attached lists of needed materials. Afterward, he gave me a shopping list of materials to get, books to read, and assignments to type.

"You don't go into battle without a plan, enough ammunition, supplies and a time line. Otherwise they'll cream ya," he said.

That was 20 years ago. It's now a tradition in my house; every August I tape up 15 feet of newspaper stock and plan out my year. It's become such a ritual that my wife celebrates the event with a special dinner.

—*A social studies teacher*

LEGAL SIDEBAR

A Teacher's Right to Teach

In Cupertino, CA, Steven J. Williams contended that his free speech rights were violated when he was required to submit class handouts to be screened by the principal for inappropriate religious content. He filed suit, and the case is currently in the courts (Murphy, 2004).

Step 5: Acquire Teaching Materials

Gather teaching materials that you will need to execute the lesson effectively. This step in the planning process is crucial; any inattention to gathering materials can completely disassemble your best laid plans. For example, forgetting to copy work sheets, to obtain a VCR, to order the video, or to collect the correct number of markers, pieces of poster board, pairs of scissors, and so forth could stall the lesson and provide students with an opportunity to begin occupying themselves in unproductive ways.

Many materials are available for your use in executing lessons, but their effectiveness depends on how well they relate to the context of the lesson. For example, the textbook is an invaluable tool for background knowledge and reference, but it will not generate comprehension without some form of interaction between the material and the learner. Therefore, using the textbook exclusively may not be the most effective mode of teaching.

Textbooks Unquestionably, for most subjects, the textbook is the most powerful tool in your classroom and has great influence over your instructional method. Some subject areas (e.g., math, science, and social studies) rely more on a single textbook, while other areas (such as reading, literature, foreign language, art, and music) require a variety of texts.

Some research has shown that textbooks tend to approach the material on the literal and interpretative level of learning and that the main focus is on terms and definitions (Tyson-Bernstein, 1988). In reality, the use of textbooks is necessary, but the effective teacher should be aware of the degree of his or her reliance on the text and balance it with use of other materials.

Work Sheets and Workbooks Work sheets are the backbone of a teacher's repertoire of tools and when used judiciously, they can be an effective teaching mechanism. However, like textbooks, work sheets and workbooks can also become a type of security

Guidepost

To what extent should I use the textbook?
You should consider the textbook as a guide that may be the best tool to keep your lessons balanced and organized. How much you use the book in your lesson will depend on the development of your plan for the particular topic.

What aspects of the textbook are most productive for me as a teacher?
Most textbooks provide a variety of activities and assessments at the end of each chapter. They are applicable only if you have covered all the material in the chapter. However, this section of the textbook is an excellent place to begin to gather ideas for developing activities for your class.

What solutions do I have when students forget their books, or when the school does not allow the textbook to leave the building?
Using textbooks in class can also be an asset to your teaching program.

- Devote a few minutes from each period or lesson to working on activities outlined in the text.
- Excerpt activities onto work sheets for homework or class work.
- Outline the chapters before class and put them on the overhead projector.

WATCH OUT Caution: Disadvantages of Overusing Textbooks and Work Sheets

Some teachers rely too heavily on textbooks and work sheets, which curbs their creativity and spontaneity with their students. Exclusive use of the textbook adheres you to the entire content of the chapters, which may not be part of what your state or district requires (or desires) you to teach. Work sheets can do the following:

- Create a perceived sense of accomplishment without allowing students to achieve in-depth comprehension
- Become a teacher's guide to student achievement that is only partly accurate
- Lend themselves to a level of student cooperation that is nothing more than copying material from each other

blanket for the unsure or inexperienced teacher. Overuse of this medium can produce a numbing effect that will be detrimental to student comprehension.

The many advantages of using work sheets and workbooks are as follows:

- ☑ When used as graphic organizers or Venn diagrams, they can engage students reflectively on the material and provide them with an avenue of expression leading them to deeper comprehension of the lesson.
- ☑ They are excellent tools for reinforcement and focus, especially when the material is particularly complex or difficult to grasp.
- ☑ They can be easily designed and reproduced with any word-processing program on a computer, or even freehand.
- ☑ Numerous commercialized work sheets and workbooks are available at economical prices.
- ☑ Many sites on the Internet allow you to download reproducible work sheets for free.

WORK SHEET USE

Ineffective Use	Effective Use
The work sheet is used for repetitive drills without challenging the student to a higher level of achievement.	The material is presented at increasing levels of challenge.
The material on the work sheet is crowded—difficult to read or unorganized.	The material is structured in an orderly, sequential manner with clear directions.
Work sheets are given routinely at the end of each lesson presentation, or for homework, or repeatedly throughout the week, so that they become an end in itself.	Work sheet use is pertinent to the lesson goals and objectives and is related directly to the material. Work sheets are a means to the goal of learning.
The work sheet lacks challenge and is only partially related to the lesson.	Work sheets offer an opportunity for students to design their own expressions related to the lesson and are open ended to stimulate student initiative.
Grading work sheets produces large numbers of scores for term reporting of grades.	Work sheets should be evaluated, not necessarily given a numeric grade, but assessed for improvement.
Often work sheets are only checked, which affords less expenditure of time on actual grading.	All students' work should be evaluated, or noted; feedback is a key element to effective instruction.

In Real Time: Work Sheet Misperception

A class of students quietly working away at filling up blank lines on a work sheet give the casual observer, the student, the parent, and even you, the teacher, a sense that real learning is happening because of the appearance of engagement. However, learning and comprehension occur through active engagement with the text, with the self, and with one another.

The computer is as common to modern-day students as the ink bottle was to our great-grandparents.

Multimedia In this millennial world of teaching, multimedia may be considered equivalent to what blackboard and chalk was for Emma Willard in 1829. The powerful influence of the computer and digital technology on most of today's youth underscores the necessity of tapping this valuable resource. The availability of multimedia materials greatly depends on the financial resources of your district and school. In the modern classroom, one CD-ROM has the capacity of an entire set of encyclopedias, and placed in a computer attached to a high-definition projector, it treats students to colorful, sound-enhanced images of history, scientific experiments, or mathematical wonders. Moreover, interactive media such as the software program A.D.A.M. The Inside Story (A.D.A.M., Inc., Atlanta, GA)—a three-dimensional layered graphic of human anatomy—engage students in a total and automatic learning experience.

MULTIMEDIA AND ITS USES

Media	Use
Televisions	For use with a VCR or DVD player. Televisions can also be used to view instructional programs usually broadcast by public radio stations. Most schools are equipped with cable television systems.
DVDs (require a DVD player)	For showing excerpts of movies. DVDs are inexpensive and easily connected to most televisions.
CD-ROMs (require a computer)	For providing extensive databases of information from statistical to enriching.
Overhead projectors	For providing instructions and notes. Most printers can now produce transparencies; however, supplies for making them are usually short because they are expensive.
Digital projectors	For projecting images from your computer onto a screen or clear wall surface.

In addition, the technically proficient teacher can have students take photos or videos of one another at work or play and, using a movie-editing program, embed them into a

STRATEGIES FOR COMPUTER LABS

- ☑ Have the assignment preloaded onto the network so that all students may access instructions when they are ready.
- ☑ Have a sheet that provides explicit step-by-step procedures, from turning the computer on to accessing the programs being studied.
- ☑ If possible, arrange your students so that you can see most of the screens at one glance.
- ☑ Set off-limit areas (e.g., the Web, other programs, the font or color menus).
- ☑ Arrange the lesson so that students more adept with computers may work ahead.
- ☑ Have more-skilled students sit with students who are struggling.
- ☑ At the outset of the lesson, be sure to train students how to save documents.

PowerPoint presentation or another document. Each class could design and construct its own Web site that could be lofted to the Internet by using the domain name of the district or one of the many free domain servers such as GeoCities or Angelfire.

Using the Computer Depending on your skill level, the computer is a valuable tool for both instruction and record keeping. Use computer technology for the following:

- ☑ To create databases with student identification information
- ☑ To create spreadsheets for grade keeping and tracking student progress
- ☑ To create work sheets and class work and homework assignments
- ☑ To access the Internet for momentary examples of material you are teaching
- ☑ To check facts, dates, and events related to your lessons
- ☑ To run software that quickly generates crossword puzzles, graphic organizers, and ready-made work sheets
- ☑ To organize your notes into clearly labeled slides
- ☑ To establish a Web site for your class or school from which parents might glean information about your teaching program and the agenda for your classes
- ☑ To link you with your colleagues in other districts or schools, through e-mail and listservs, and keep you informed

If you are fortunate enough to have one or more computers in your room, they are excellent workstations for students engaged in project work or inquiry-based learning. Computers may also be used for students to complete lessons or project work missed as a result of absences, or to work independently and complete their assignments.

Using Computer Labs In addition to helping teachers with managing their work, computers are valuable when used in computer labs, where each student works at a station. This use of computer technology is more common but is only as effective as your preparation. A number of issues are associated with computer lab use that the effective teacher needs to consider, including the following:

- ☑ Is the number of computers sufficient to accommodate the entire class?
- ☑ Is the computer program related to the lesson content?
- ☑ Are the students sufficiently skilled to navigate and achieve the goals of the program?
- ☑ Are media personnel available to fix omnipresent glitches in accessing the program?
- ☑ Does the program assess student work?

TAKING PREPARATION SERIOUSLY

Being a teacher is a job that entails more than just the 6 or 7 hours spent in school with the students. No teacher who is true to his or her profession, or who aspires to be an effective educator, can walk into a classroom on any morning without having spent a reasonable amount of time the night before in preparation. Preparation for the lessons of each day is the core of teaching. Although some teachers' spontaneity and charisma might capture and then enrapture a class within minutes, in time, if they do not prepare well, their lack of preparation will begin to show. Direction and clarity come only with preparation.

DOS AND DON'TS

Don't	Do
Begin any lesson without first knowing your expected learning outcomes	Prepare lessons that develop specific goals and objectives
Fail to consider the developmental age of your students	Provide instruction that communicates to *all* your students
Teach the state or local learning standards	Teach *to* the state or local learning standards by aligning them with your instructional content and strategies
Organize your curriculum content without considering both the scope and the sequence of the material	Develop lesson plans that take students from the knowledge level of understanding to the evaluation level
Begin a school year without having some idea of *when* you will be teaching *what*	Organize your entire school year in some time, topic, or mastery sequence
Design narrow lesson plans that address just the topic you are studying	Design lesson plans that encourage the integration of all subject disciplines
Write lesson plans that simply reflect page numbers and topic headings	Write lesson plans that list a series of questions you expect to ask your students to stimulate their engagement
Teach to the test or violate the integrity of giving your students a complete learning experience	Teach material that will assist your students on out-of-class mandated tests, but integrate it into the instructional content of the lesson
Teach solely from the textbook—chapter by chapter	Use the textbook as one of many resource tools to support your instructional plan
Overly rely on work sheets for dependent and independent practice of the material	Balance the use of work sheets with that of other activities that will engage the student in the material taught
Use multimedia resources for the sake of offering flashy but thinly layered lessons	Use multimedia resources to enhance the lesson and provide students with an alternative method of expression
Use the computer lab until you have made detailed preparations	Consult with the library–media specialist before using the computer lab; prepare lesson plans that allow for off-task time resulting from technical difficulties
Design your lessons so rigidly close to the learning standards that you are not spontaneous and responsive to your students' interests	Use the standards as a guide for directing your lesson planning
Overlook the importance of post-lesson notes as part of the lesson plan procedure	Keep a daily journal of notes on the progress of each lesson, on students, and on where to begin the next day

WEB SITES OF INTEREST

http://www.mcrel.org/compendium/browse.asp
This site is a link to the standards outlined in *Content Knowledge: A Compendium of Standards and Benchmarks for K–12 Education* (4th ed.), by Mid-continent Research for Education and Learning (McREL).

http://www.education-world.com/standards
This site provides the national content standards for all subjects.

http://www.ed.gov/G2K/standard.html
This site provides a complete listing of all standards.

http://w-w-c.org
The What Works Clearinghouse (WWC) Web site—cosponsored by the U.S. Department of Education, the American Institutes for Research, and the Campbell Collaboration—offers analyses of programs that have proved to work well in the classroom.

http://edstandards.org/Standards.html
This site provides links to the learning standards for each state and the District of Columbia.

http://www.socialstudies.org/standards
At this National Council for the Social Studies (NCSS) site, you will find the national curriculum standards for social studies.

http://www.artsedge.kennedy-center.org
This site includes a link to the fine arts learning standards.

http://www.nctm.org/standards
This National Council of the Teachers of Mathematics (NCTM) site has links to the national learning standards for mathematics.

http://www.nap.edu/readingroom/books/nses/html/6a.html
This link leads you to the *National Science Education Standards (NSES)* content standards for science.

http://www.aahperd.org
Through this site, by the American Alliance for Health, Physical Education, Recreation and Dance (AAHPERD), you can access the National Association for Sport and Physical Education (NASPE) national learning standards.

http://www.ncte.org
The national learning standards for English can be found at this Web site, by the National Council of Teachers of English (NCTE).

http://cnets.iste.org/sitemap.html
This National Educational Technology Standards (NETS) site provides the links to the national learning standards for technology.

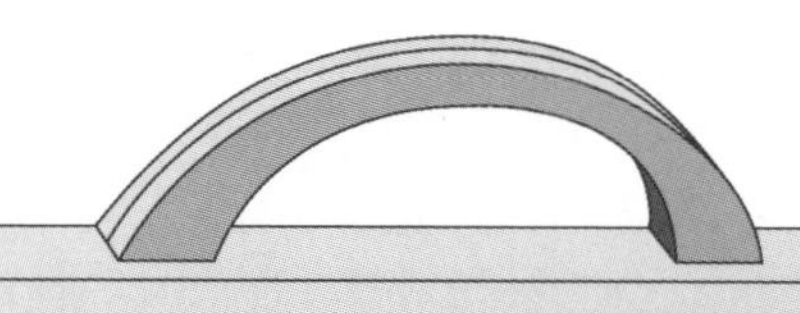

For Your Briefcase

To Do

- Write a year-long blueprint for the curriculum you will be expected to teach, in a content, sequence, and scope format.
- Segment the curriculum into unit or thematic unit plans.
- Review the entire textbook you are required to use.
- Design work sheets for use in the first month of teaching.
- Contact the media specialist to order equipment you will need for instruction.
- Scope out the computer lab for viability in your lessons.

Resources on Your Briefcase CD

Samples

- Sample Unit Plan
- Sample Daily Lesson Plan

Templates

- Yearly Plan Checklist
- Thematic Unit and Unit Plan Checklist
- Lesson Plan Checklist

Tables

- Key Elements of Curriculum Preparation

REFERENCES

Brooks, J., & Brooks, M. (1993). *In search of understanding: The case for constructivist classrooms.* Alexandria, VA: Association for Supervision and Curriculum Development.

Champagne, A. B., & Hornig, L. E. (Eds.). (1987). *The science curriculum: The Report of the 1986 National Forum for School Science.* Washington, DC: American Association for the Advancement of Science.

Darling-Hammond, L. (1999, August). *Developing a professional model of accountability for our schools.* Speech given to the British Columbia Teacher Federation, Victoria, BC.

Elementary, Middle, Secondary, and Continuing Education (EMSC), New York State Education Department. (1996). *Core subjects/learning standards.* Albany: Author.

Murphy, D. (2004, December 5). The nation, God, American history, and a fifth-grade class. *The New York Times,* p. 4.

National Center for History in the Schools. (1994). *National standards for history: K–4* (Exp. ed.). Los Angeles: Author. Retrieved July 18, 2005, from http://nchs.ucla.edu/standards/standardsk-4-1.html

Texas Education Agency. (1998). *Texas essential knowledge and skills.* Austin: Author.

Tyson-Bernstein, H. (1988). *A conspiracy of good intentions: America's textbook fiasco.* Washington, DC: Council for Basic Education.

Chapter 5

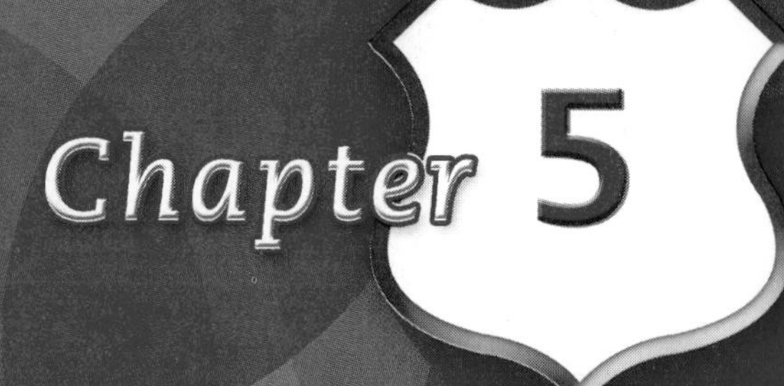

Managing Your Classroom

Nothing is more despicable than respect based on fear.
—*Albert Camus*

If a man does not
know to what port
he is steering,
no wind is
favorable
to him.
—*Seneca*

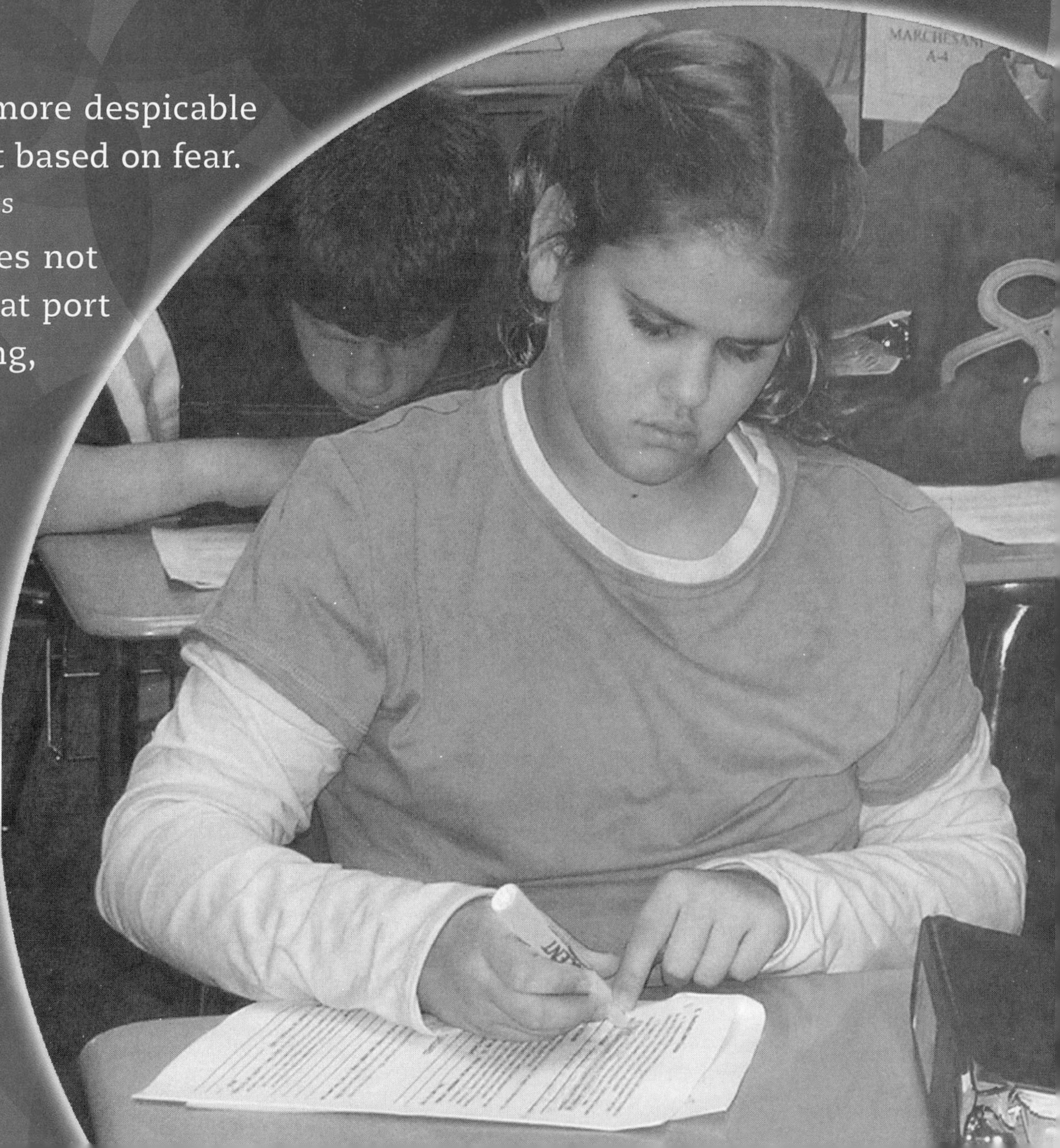

Nothing supports a successful classroom management plan better than meticulous and careful preparation. The effective teacher's management plan has numerous ideas, is as flexible as the school day, and always has alternative measures noted in the margins.

DEFINING CLASSROOM MANAGEMENT

Components of Classroom Management

Classroom management refers not only to behavior or student discipline, but also to the elements that compose your instructional organization. Some of these elements are as follows:

- ☑ Strategies for instruction
- ☑ Homework policy
- ☑ Grading policy
- ☑ Behavior policy
- ☑ Physical setup of the room
- ☑ Plan for parent communication
- ☑ Contingencies for other school activities affecting your instruction

Four Principles of Classroom Management

Teachers who are effective classroom managers keep four principles in mind at all times:

1. ***Send a positive message for learning:*** Handouts with rules and requirements should be written from a positive perspective. The classroom should be set up to be physically welcoming.
2. ***Understand that your students are all different:*** Be aware of your students' diverse backgrounds and needs. Consider their stages of physical, emotional, and cognitive development. Let this awareness and these considerations guide your words and actions.
3. ***Do not bring your personal life, attitudes, feelings, and biases into the classroom:*** Tolerance of all members of the classroom community is essential to a harmonious atmosphere for learning. As a teacher, you are responsible for presenting your subject material objectively.
4. ***Maximize the quality of your instruction:*** More than anything else, the organization and the execution of your lessons will determine how effective your classroom management plan will work. If you want to minimize behavior problems, you must maximize your instruction.

EFFECTIVE CLASSROOM MANAGEMENT

You must know the following:

- ☑ Your students' developmental level
- ☑ The political composition of the school
- ☑ The principal's and vice-principal's leadership styles
- ☑ The physical environment of the school
- ☑ Your colleagues' teaching and management styles
- ☑ Your beliefs about behavior management

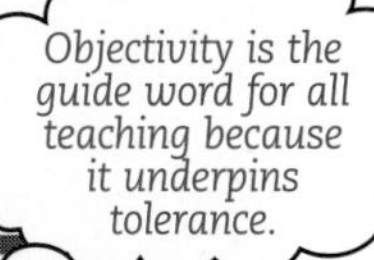

Importance of Classroom Management and Your Plan

The classroom management plan is not only a document; it is a blueprint for success—yours and your students'. *Bored students are potentially misbehaving and disruptive students.* Therefore, the key to effective classroom management is the care and effort you put into your plan, followed by the precision and skill of your implementation. In other words, it is all about how you organize and teach your lessons.

If you visit the classroom of a teacher whose students have only minor discipline problems and are always engaged in the learning process, you will find a hard-working teacher plying his or her craft with a great deal of planning supported by a diversified teaching style. You will find students helping one another on challenging problem-solving projects and seeking to learn more about the topics being presented to them. You will see a teacher who is fluid in movement around the room and who facilitates the learning process by giving one-on-one assistance to his or her students.

In the effective classroom, you will also find a stable and clearly defined management plan that is a dynamic document able to be modified as it fits the needs of the students it serves. Rigidity of management can spell disaster for a teacher. You must be prepared to make exceptions, review rules, and respond to the needs of the individual student.

DESIGNING YOUR MANAGEMENT PLAN: SIX STEPS

Briefcase CD CH 5-1—Six-Step Classroom Management Plan Checklist

Step 1: Creating the Classroom Environment

The classroom is your workplace, but it does not belong to you. You hear teachers making statements such as "When you're in my room, you should not chew gum," or "In my room, books are never on the floor." In fact, to a greater degree the room belongs to the students. Especially in the elementary class, the room is where a child spends half of his or her waking hours. Therefore, you should ensure the following:

- The classroom is welcoming, warm, and friendly, and has an atmosphere conducive to learning and investigation, with the promise of adventure in discovery.
- Students are comfortable but responsible for the upkeep of its function. Somehow they must own a piece of your room. For the elementary teacher, accomplishing such ownership is standard and workable (Figure 5-1). For the secondary teacher, doing so requires ingenuity and space control.

PHYSICAL LAYOUT OF YOUR CLASSROOM

Begin with a simple arrangement that promotes learning your students' names quickly:

- Alphabetically by first name or by last name
- By favorite food, pet, television show, or the like
- By their drawings or personally developed identity tags

Step 2: Organizing Your Instruction

The objective of teaching is to keep your eye on the prize: learning. Organizing your instruction to accomplish this goal is crucial. Following are some guidelines for doing so:

INSTRUCTIONAL ORGANIZATION

- Be sure of *what* you are teaching every day.
- Have the resources for the lesson in the room.
- Have a backup plan for when the video fails, or the projector bulb blows, or a fire drill is called.
- Outline homework and class work requirements.
- Outline the grading policy.

☑ ***Design your instructional objectives to align with state and district standards.***

- Make an outline of the general areas to be taught as described in your state and district syllabus (e.g., for math: fractions, measurements, and percentages).

☑ ***Construct a list of general materials you will need for your instructional program.***

- The list should be a general resource inventory (e.g., staplers, poster board, markers, glue, tape, textbooks), not a materials list for specific lessons.

☑ ***Develop a plan for on-task procedures.***

- Inform your students on the first day of school that they must check the front board (or bulletin board) every day, at the beginning of each period, to learn the opening assignment for each subject.
- Provide a fire-drill procedure. What should students do when they reenter the classroom?
- Include a procedure for end-of-class wrap-up (e.g., **exit slips**—"What are two or three facts you learned today?").

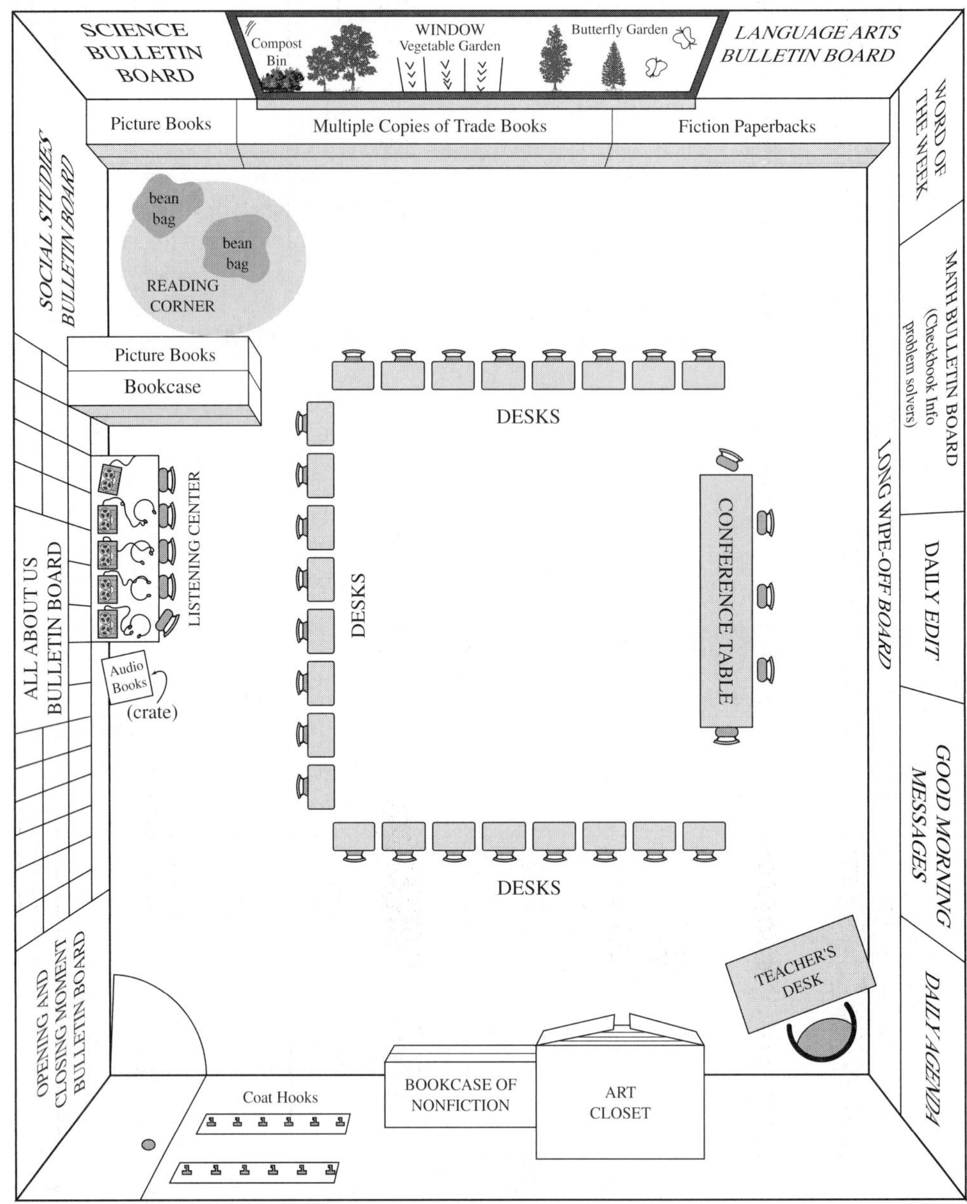

Figure 5-1. *Sample elementary classroom layout*
Reprinted with permission from Dr. Suzanne Kaback.

☑ ***Outline homework procedures.***

- Provide students with the rules for homework.
  - ***Examples:*** "All homework must be submitted on the next day of class. If you do not have the homework, you will lose 10 points for each day it is late. If you are absent, the homework is expected when you return, with no penalty."
  - "All homework is checked. If it is complete, you will automatically receive a 100% grade."
  - "You or your parents may contact me by e-mail at rjm@yahoo.com if you have questions about your homework assignment."

☑ ***Outline the grading policy.***

- ***Example of rules for in-class work:***
  - "All work completed in class is given a grade or mark of completion at 15% of your report card grade. If you are absent, you must make up the work within 2 days of your return."

- ***Example of rules for quizzes and tests:***
  - "All quizzes are 25% of your report card grade; all tests are 30%. All tests with grades less than 60% can be retaken after school. Being absent the day before a test does not excuse you from taking it on the day it is scheduled."
- ***Example of rules for project work:***
  - "Major projects are worth 20% of your report card grade. Projects are graded according to the chart given with each project."
- ***Example of rules for class participation:***
  - "Class participation is worth 10% of your report card grade. This grade is made up of participation in class discussions, respect for your classmates when they are giving answers, and your contributions to class work."

In Real Time: **Effective Instruction and Behavior**

To maintain a harmonious classroom environment that is relatively free of behavioral interruptions, put great effort into the teaching program and develop engaging, fulfilling lessons.

Step 3: Setting the Tempo of Instruction

The most essential element of the classroom management plan is how effectively you implement your instructional program. Simply put, *bored students are potentially misbehaving students*. Quality teaching that is dynamically delivered, that challenges each student, and that establishes and maintains excitement for learning is the single best way to prevent unpleasant classroom disruption. *How you teach affects how students behave.*

INSTRUCTIONAL TEMPO

- Develop a routine.
- Create teaching intervals.
- Respond to class signals.
- Diversify instructional modes.
- Make material relevant to students' experiences.

Your success at keeping students engaged depends on the tempo, or pace, of your instruction. Your instructional tempo will reflect how well you incorporate routine, interval teaching, and curriculum linkages into your program.

Briefcase CD CH5-2—Classroom Organization Checklist

Routine Establish a constant, but flexible classroom routine. Students who know what to do as soon as they come into the room will have a sense of direction and purpose that contributes to learning engagement. Research has shown that students respond to routine and organization because it gives them a sense of security and comfort regarding their duties and performance (Beattie & Olley, 1977). Your classroom organization should be visible on a wall or bulletin board and kept current.

LEGAL SIDEBAR

Dress Codes

Dress codes have consistently been upheld by the courts as long as they adhere to the four-pronged rules provided in *United States v. O'Brien*, 391 U.S. 367 (1968):

1. The rule refers only to the matter of dress.
2. The rule furthers the role of the government establishment (i.e., the school).
3. The restrictions on free speech are explicitly explained and clear.
4. The rule does not intentionally seek to limit free expression.

CLASSROOM ORGANIZATION CHECKLIST

Attendance taking	☑ Follow a routine for each day or class. Some standard ideas are as follows: • Students complete a 3 × 5-inch card each day or class and deposit it in a box. • One student is assigned to take attendance each week. • Students sign in on a whiteboard each day or class.
Sponge, or focusing, activity	☑ Begin each class or subject period with an activity that is always on the board or bulletin board and that students know must be completed as they begin the day or class.
Testing procedure	☑ Establish a set of rules for testing periods that differs from the regular classroom routine. For example, students may sit in different seats or must know what the rules are about disruption or interruption during testing times.
Reflection time	☑ Set aside a time period for students to reflect on what is being taught. They may use an exit slip or a journal entry to do so.
Routine and home base identification	☑ Set up routines that help establish a sense of security. Students need to know that the room belongs to them as well. For example, • Each Friday is coloring or puzzle day. Students may work on creative projects. • One day a week is dress-differently day. Students are allowed to wear one piece of clothing with a specific emblem or color. • Each student has his or her picture displayed with his or her favorite "things" mentioned. • Students bring in a bandanna or T-shirt that says something about who they are.
Policies	☑ Students should be aware of policies and logistics regarding homework, grading, and personal issues. Examples follow: • "Homework is always placed in the 'homework' folder." • "Makeup tests are always completed during lunch, during study hall periods, or after school." • "Wet boots must be removed and replaced with shoes." • "Desks and lockers are cleaned every other Thursday." • "Only the student clerk-for-the-day is allowed to answer the telephone and take attendance." • "Lavatory passes are given only between subject periods or in case of an emergency. Each student must have a signed pass before leaving the room."

Example of Interval Spacing in Teaching

Subject and Grade: Math; Grade 4 **Topic:** Percentages

Opening Presentation (10 min):
- Where in our lives do we use percentages?
- Show graphic examples of merchandise, such as newspaper ads, with percentages.

Explanation (10 min):
- Show the definition on an overhead, with numerical examples.
- Leave the overhead on during the entire period for reference.

Dependent Practice (15 min):
- Give students a work sheet or hands-on activity to use to practice computing percentages.
- Manipulatives work better and will stimulate a longer focus time.

Recapitulation (5–15 min):
- If you want a longer class period, ask students to share what they have done.
- If you want a shorter period, simply review the lesson and proceed to assigning homework.

Independent Practice—Homework Assignment (5–7 min):
- Using the whiteboard, an overhead, or posters, explain the homework assignment.
- Answer students' questions and ask students questions to stimulate clarity.

Transition (elementary only; 5–6 min):
- Give students time to transfer to the next subject. Let them move around the room and stretch.
- If you fear chaos, organize a 2- or 3-minute exercise session led by one of the students (e.g., stretching or running in place).

Briefcase CD CH5-3—Example of Interval Spacing in Teaching

Interval Teaching To manage the tempo of your instruction, teach in segmented time periods. Doing so will contribute to student engagement. Interval teaching involves short, organized intervals of instructional time and is geared to allow students to transition from listening to doing, then to reflecting, and, finally, to practicing. To accomplish interval teaching effectively, you must be keenly aware of the time, even perhaps assigning a student to be the timekeeper.

The single drawback to staggering instructional times is the possible loss of continuity if you adhere too closely to the schedule. One element of effective teaching is to know when to abandon the plan to seize the "teachable moment" or to allow student interest and thought to flow according to the need.

Briefcase CD CH5-4—Examples of Linking the Curriculum

Curriculum Linkage The instructional tempo is also influenced by how well the lesson being taught links to other aspects of your students' learning program. At the elementary level, when most subjects are taught by a single classroom teacher, the opportunity for across-curriculum linkages is almost natural. The work of the class is visible in the room, and the teacher of math is also the teacher of science, who can speak directly to the lessons of yesterday as they connect to the lessons of today.

At the middle and high school levels, curriculum linkage requires a more determined effort because students are programmed to think "math" in math class and "English" in English class. However, research strongly supports the notion that when children see relationships among concepts and subject areas, they achieve higher comprehension levels (Martinez, 1992).

Linking the curriculum requires little more than a mind-set on the teacher's part. While designing the lessons of the week or day, consider the many possible links that may be made to any other subject.

Examples of Linking the Curriculum

Writing

Write letters to
- Local or state legislatures
- Mayors of other cities
- Students in other schools
- Members of Congress

Math

Solve real problems:
- Amount of water available for the city, given its dimensions
- Net profit from selling a box of cereal, after production and marketing costs
- Distances within the city, the school, or the state
- Probability based on real statistics

English
- Write and produce a morality play.
- Rewrite a Shakespearean play in modern language.
- Develop skits for short stories or poems.
- Create a rap song for a novel, short story, or poem.

Social Studies
- Develop a real bill to introduce to Congress.
- Debate an issue of social importance.
- Research campaign finance.
- Research primary historical records.

Foreign Language
- Label every object in sight in the room.
- Write letters to foreign dignitaries or ambassadors.
- Create travel brochures.
- Design a mock trip to a foreign land.

Science
- Explore plant life and the life cycle by using herb gardens in class.
- Develop weather stations in school.
- Analyze the nutrient content of a variety of common foods.
- Use the Internet and other sources to find science kits, procedures, and programs promoting hands-on activities.

Music
- Using electronic pianos, compose individual works.
- Write music for the recorder.
- Compare rock-and-roll music with jazz, classical, and country.
- Trace melodies from the classics to modern.
- Write a rap song for an advertisement.
- Create a commercial jingle.

Physical Education
- Develop personal fitness agendas.
- Challenge students to exceed their personal records of excellence.
- Play down competition and promote cooperative exercising.
- Have students keep journals of their achievements.

Art
- Create posters for environmental issues.
- Sculpt heads using papier-mâché.
- Paint or draw self-portraits.
- Design and paint a mural on the classroom wall.

Briefcase CD CH5-5—Example of Class Contract Criteria

Briefcase CD CH5-6—Sample Class Contract—Elementary School

SAMPLE CLASS CONTRACT—ELEMENTARY SCHOOL

Class Contract

We promise to help and care for one another.

We will always use kind words such as *please* and *thank you* and *excuse me.*

We will remember that each of us has a job to do here at school.

In our class, everyone will have a chance to speak.

In our class, everyone will listen when someone else is speaking.

In our class, we will not fight, shout, throw things, or say unkind words to others.

We all promise to

- Try to be on time for school every day
- Keep our desks neat
- Care for one another's property
- Care for school property
- Try as hard as we can to complete our assignments

When we have a problem, we will

- Try to work it out ourselves
- Then ask for help from the teacher or another adult

We know that when we are not cooperating with one another or the teacher, we may lose free time or privileges or be sent to speak with the principal.

THE BEHAVIOR PLAN

- Should be designed mutually with your students
- Should be brief and simply worded
- Should reflect consequences
- Should be posted for easy reference

Briefcase CD CH5-7—Sample Class Contract—Middle or High School

Step 4: Designing the Behavior Plan

The Class Contract Design your behavior plan *with your students;* doing so ensures that the agreement is among all members of your learning community, not just between you as the teacher and the class as a whole.

Post the plan on a wall in clear view, where you and the class can refer to it when needed. *Remember:* What goes into the plan at the beginning affects classroom actions throughout the year. Careful construction at the beginning will prevent unexpected outcomes later.

Giving your students ownership of their behavior helps them establish a sense of responsibility for what happens in the room. Doing so also sends a message from you that their views and concerns are valuable.

TECHNIQUES TO USE TO PREVENT DISRUPTION

- ☑ Pace the instruction to your students' attention span.
- ☑ Provide frequent breaks to allow for processing of the material taught.
- ☑ Avoid lengthy presentations without visual aids.
- ☑ Encourage student participation in the discussions.
- ☑ Use video and sound clips to highlight the lesson.

Briefcase CD CH5-8—Strategies to Manage Disruption

How to Manage Student Misbehavior Most student misbehavior stems from the dynamic of where students are and what is expected of them. Some students will exhibit model behavior in science class but become amazingly juvenile in art class. Others will be silly and rude throughout the entire day with every teacher in every situation. However, *the activities on which students are working have a direct connection to how they behave.*

For young children, remaining focused for long periods is difficult if not almost impossible. Their young minds are growing and processing new and unfamiliar information, while their bodies are in a variety of developmental stages (Santrock, 2000, p. 542). Accordingly, they become restless quickly, especially when their interest is not being stimulated.

SAMPLE CLASS CONTRACT—MIDDLE OR HIGH SCHOOL

Class Contract

We are an equal opportunity classroom.

Everyone in this room gives and receives respect.

The teacher and students begin each class prepared to work together.

Everyone gets a chance to explain his or her behavior.

We all agree to

- Be on time for class each day
- Respect and care for one another's and school property
- Complete the tasks assigned—teacher and student

Disagreements

- Are settled by one another first, then by the teacher (your name)
- Are concerns for everyone, not just the individuals who are directly involved

Violations of this contract by the student result in

- One warning
- A visit to the principal's office
- A telephone conversation with parents

Violations of this contract by the teacher result in

- A class majority that informs the teacher
- A note from the class to the teacher

In Real Time: Assigning Consequences

Do not box yourself into a corner by doing or saying something that leaves you with nothing but bad choices. If you tell a student to be quiet or you will do something to him or her, you will probably have to do something to him or her. Never make a promise you cannot keep.

Diversify instruction by using visual aids to support your lesson.

TEACHER ATTITUDE CHECKLIST

What Is Your Attitude?

1. ☐ Yes ☐ Neutral ☐ No Do you think teachers are also performers?
2. ☐ Yes ☐ Neutral ☐ No Are you passionate about the subject or subjects you teach?
3. ☐ Yes ☐ Neutral ☐ No Overall, are you a serious person who dislikes comedy in the classroom?
4. ☐ Yes ☐ Neutral ☐ No Can you say that you take rejection well?
5. ☐ Yes ☐ Neutral ☐ No Are you open minded about body jewelry, hair color or style, and so forth?
6. ☐ Yes ☐ Neutral ☐ No Do you believe in no tolerance with regard to misbehavior?
7. ☐ Yes ☐ Neutral ☐ No Are you completely nonbiased with regard to race, religion, and ethnicity?

If you answered yes to questions 1, 2, 3, 4, and 7, your attitude appears to be positive in view of the behavioral dynamics related to children. If you answered no to these questions, your attitude about classroom management may call for a more structured and formatted behavior program.

ROLE MODEL TRAITS OF EFFECTIVE TEACHERS

Teachers who are good role models

☑ ***Are confident:*** They have clear ideas about their decisions.
☑ ***Understand human behavior:*** They understand the dynamics of behavior.
☑ ***Are organized:*** They are prepared for class and have clear plan for teaching the curriculum.
☑ ***Are reasonable:*** They create instructional plans that meet the students' needs.
☑ ***Are flexible:*** They know when to re-create the plan to conform to their students' needs.
☑ ***Are enthusiastic:*** They are passionate about their subjects and about teaching them.

In Real Time: **Ineffective Instruction and Behavior**

Behavior problems are directly related to instructional effectiveness. Students who are bored and not engaged in the learning program will often misbehave. Even adults become restless and surly when sitting through disorganized or poorly presented seminars or workshops.

Briefcase CD CH5-9—Teacher Attitude Checklist

Step 5: Knowing Yourself

Teacher Attitude Classroom management is tied closely to the teacher's attitude and demeanor. Knowing yourself helps you know your students.

Guidepost

Teacher Attitude

Ask yourself the following questions:

- What are your expectations of the students when you walk into a classroom?
- What is your personal definition of *reasonable behavior?*
- Think back to when you were a student. Who were your teachers with the best classroom management style? Whom might you identify as a role model?
- Which of your former teachers received the most respect, and how did he or she earn such respect?
- Which class had a learning atmosphere in which students cooperated, worked together, and developed respect for one another?

VOICES IN THE CLASSROOM
Of Not Having a Plan

I learned how *not* to manage a classroom from a young seventh-grade math teacher whose idea of getting control was through war. He declared war on all his classes, insisting on absolute obedience to his rules. His third-period class was the remedial group, a bunch of tough customers known more for their misbehavior than their low achievement.

After 2 weeks of this militaristic teaching, the third-period class began to resist. They renamed the teacher *Igor,* then demonstrated a unity, determination, and drive that, if used positively, might have made them an honors class.

The same students formed my fourth-period class, and each day they had their recap meeting in my room, congratulating one another on their triumphs and grieving over their losses. Then, they would plan for the next day. Although I discouraged them from what they were doing, and tried to get them to conform to the rules, they scoffed at me for not understanding the problem. "He started it," they reasoned, "and he was only getting what he asked for." So, third period for Igor was 45 minutes of paper airplanes and spitballs, dropped books and chairs, and lots of noise. For their efforts, they were hauled from their seats, pushed against the blackboard, and thrown into the hallway lockers. Still, they fought on. I even approached the teacher and suggested he declare a truce or at least try something different. He smirked and shook his head as though I couldn't possibly understand.

The end came abruptly the day before Thanksgiving vacation. The young martinet quit the field without as much as a salute. He never returned the following Monday and went straight into the insurance business, where he made a decent living.

Third period surprised me by not gloating or even cheering. They spoke of Igor affectionately and said they'd miss him and their daily battles. School once again became boring.

—*A retired teacher*

How Your Students "See" You How your students perceive you may shape how and to what extent they cooperate with you. Each teacher must make a personal decision about his or her attitude in the classroom and working with students.

A Teacher Who . . .

- Is obviously passionate about what he or she is teaching,
- Genuinely displays a liking for children and teaching,
- Has a cheery demeanor exuding confidence and pride in what his or her students are doing,
- Leaves personal problems at home, and
- Communicates a true desire for spending time with the students

. . . has established an environment for learning.

A Teacher Who . . .

- Enters class with a chip on his or her shoulder regarding student behavior,
- Assumes that all children misbehave, and
- Demands that all students "earn" his or her respect before he or she can give it

. . . has established a battleground mentality.

(Voices in the Classroom, see above.)

WORDS OF ENCOURAGEMENT TO USE

Following are some quotations you might hear teachers utter that reflect caring and concern:

- "Let's see how far we can travel today and find some wonders we never knew were there."
- "Let's make sure all of us will go outside for recess; please work together."
- "If you're confused, go to the beginning and find the first thing that you really understand."
- "You seem tired today. Why don't we all just take a few moments to close our eyes and relax?"
- "I hear what you're saying and wonder if there's a way to say it so that everyone can understand what you mean."
- "Getting it right isn't as important as working on it and doing your best."
- "Respecting others in the class has to begin with respecting yourself."
- "Sometimes we say things that are unkind; it doesn't mean we're hurtful or bad, just that we're human."

WORDS THAT SHOULD NEVER HAVE BEEN SPOKEN

Following are paraphrases of actual utterances spoken in both public and private schools:

- "I'm the adult in this room and you're the child; guess who's gonna win?"
- "Do you think you're being smart by talking like that? I guess not. Then you must be stupid."
- "I'll bet your mother and father are proud to have a kid who can't even sit up straight for more than a minute."
- "I want you people to understand that this is not a democracy—it's my way or the highway."
- "Who dressed you this morning?"
- "Bad little boys don't get to go out at recess time."
- "Some of the things you people do make me sick."
- "I don't want to hear your problems; I'm not your personal psychiatrist."
- "I'm not afraid of you—or your father."
- "I don't have to take the test; you're the one who's got to worry about getting this stuff."
- "Hey! I'm getting paid to be here. I can wait all day for you to settle down."
- "Did you leave your brain at home today?"
- "You know, the way you're behaving says something about how your parents raised you."

—Interviews with students, teachers, and administrators

Step 6: Knowing Your Students

How Knowledge of Your Students Affects Classroom Management

Knowing your students is a key to any classroom management plan. You should be aware of not only your students' developmental needs, but also the differences in their values, culture, interests, and specific problems as they change from year to year.

WATCH OUT Caution: Common Traits of Students Who Are Reluctant Learners

- They saunter into class when they feel like it.
- They never do their homework.
- They slump at their desks and either sleep or doodle.
- They never volunteer an answer and when called on, respond with either a disrespectful remark or a negative jibe.
- Some class members look up to them and support their antiauthoritarian behavior by also becoming disruptive and disrespectful.
- When they are absent, the class is noticeably more harmonious.

The Student Who Is a Reluctant Learner

Children who are picked on by others may be *reluctant learners*, or *oppressed students*. Other children pick on them to deflect attention from their own differences, peculiarities, or low self-esteem.

How to Manage Students Who Are Reluctant Learners

STEP 1 ***Call for an immediate halt to the teasing or badgering:*** However, do not linger or lecture on the incident.

STEP 2 ***Insist on a policy of equity in your classroom:*** Communicate your intolerance for bullying behavior.

VOICES IN THE CLASSROOM
Personal Remarks

One day in my fourth-grade class, I was beginning a new lesson on trees and plant life. Melinda, in the back of the room, raised her hand and asked, "Do you like that skirt you're wearing today?" At first I was put off and somewhat irritated that she had distracted my lesson and referred to my personal appearance. Then, the inner teacher took control.

"Why, yes, I do, Melinda. I chose it especially for today because I knew we were going to talk about plants and trees and I wanted to wear something with flowers on it. Do you know that trees also wear skirts?"

"What!" the class exclaimed.

"Yes," I said. "The bark is a covering that protects them from the weather. Can you think of other ways that bark helps trees?"

From that point on, we had a discussion about the elements of a tree. Then I segued into my lesson. I could have been stern with Melinda and told her that her question was inappropriate, but I believe a child's curiosity needs to be nurtured and that as an adult, I should be able to turn students' questions into teachable moments.

—Ms. S., a wise and caring teacher

Teasing among students occurs at all grade levels. Students who are reluctant learners can be in any grade.

STEP 3 ***Gain knowledge of the student's background and home environment:***

a. Check with the school psychologist or guidance counselor for background information on the student. What is his or her background and home environment?

b. Check with the principal or vice-principal about the student's discipline record.

c. If the student has learning disabilities, check with the special education teacher about what is being done to help the student.

STEP 4 ***Seek the advice of veteran teachers in your school.***

STEP 5 ***If the child is doing poorly academically, speak with the parents about possible problems and offer support.***

STEP 6 ***Be fair and consistent:*** If a student who is the object of ridicule makes foolish and provocative remarks, your response should be even, firm, and consistent with the standing equity policy in the classroom.

STEP 7 ***Encourage all students to participate in class activities, discussions, and projects:*** However, do not do the following:

a. Coerce, cajole, or embarrass a student to participate if he or she does not want to

b. Judge or communicate a value judgment on students' behavior, views, or actions simply because they are different

In Real Time: **Being the Voice of Reason**

Getting drawn into juvenile behavior is not difficult when you are confronting the emotional and childish behavior of some students. As a teacher and an adult, you must always maintain an even temperament and seek realistic solutions to the problems presented to you.

The Student Who Is Violent Although violence in schools is not nearly as troublesome as the media would have you believe, it is a reality that disrupts the learning environment and causes many children to fear coming to school.

STATING THE FACTS:

On bullying:

- According to the results of a National Institute of Child Health and Human Development (2001) study, 30% of students in Grades 6–10 reported being bullies, victims, or both.
- In a Kaiser Family Foundation study, 8- to 15-year-olds reported that they feared bullying more than drugs, alcohol, and AIDS (Fox, Elliott, Kerlikowske, Newman, & Christeson, 2003).
- According to the Centers for Disease Control and Prevention, 60% of bullies have criminal records by the time they are in their 20s (Fleming & Towey, 2002).
- The National Center for Victims of Crime (n.d.) reported that 1 in 12 students who stay home from school stay home because they fear going to school.

Bullying Chief among violence problems is bullying. Its prevalence seems to be growing, and its prevention continues to elude school officials. Research shows that former bullies were often victims and that socioeconomic status, aggressive parenting styles, and violence in the home are the contributing factors to the acts of violence these children perpetrate in school (Olweus, 1979).

Antibullying Programs Most schools have antibullying programs designed to reduce violence on school grounds. However, they are less effective immediately before and after school.

A number of programs address the issue of student violence. For example, the North Central Regional Educational Laboratory (NCREL; 1995) supports a program entitled *Violence Prevention Curriculum for Adolescents,* which uses a series of lessons on conflict resolution.

Managing the student who is violent should never be the job of any one teacher, but a group effort, with school administrators providing leadership. The administration must develop and implement systemic strategies, such as the following, to manage violence in the school:

- Outreach programs to the parents and families of students known to be violent
- In-school initiatives that directly address violent behavior

How to manage the student who is violent As a teacher, what is your role in managing violence in the school? Because bullying is a schoolwide problem that requires a systemic effort, your role should be supportive and cooperative. Following are some guidelines for safely managing violent situations:

- ***Be informed; be prepared:*** Learn the procedures to follow if you are ever confronted with a student who is violent.
- ***Find help:*** If you encounter bullying behavior in the classroom, or witness it on the way to or from school, enlist the help of school officials such as the vice-principal, the school nurse, the psychologist, and security personnel. *The situation is not one to confront on your own.* Figure 5-2 reflects the number of violent crimes committed against

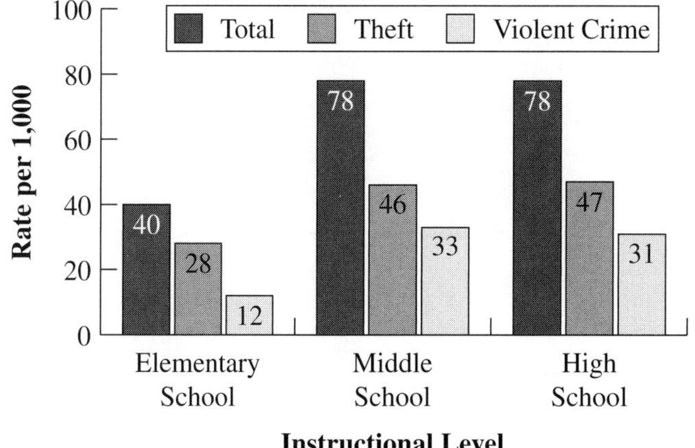

Figure 5-2. *Crime rate against teachers according to instructional level: 1997–2001*

From Indicators of School Crime and Safety: 2003 (Pub. Nos. NCES 2004–004/NCJ 201257), by J. F. DeVoe, K. Peter, P. Kaufman, S. A. Ruddy, A. K. Miller, M. Planty, et al., 2003, Washington, DC: U.S. Departments of Education and Justice.

LEGAL SIDEBAR

Fourth Amendment Application to Students in Schools

The Supreme Court ruled in *New Jersey v. T.L.O.* (1985) that although the Fourth Amendment also applies to students in public schools, the school environment is such that school officials do not need probable cause or a warrant to search students.

STATING THE FACTS:

On school violence: Eighty-three percent of students surveyed by CBS in 2000 reported feeling safe at school. School violence has declined steadily since 1997. However, 2.7 million crimes were reported in 2000, including 22 deaths, down from a high of 53 in 1992–1993 (Polling Report, Inc., 2000).

teachers in U.S. schools from 1997 to 2001. Of the 1.3 million crimes reported, 473,000 involved rape, sexual assault, aggravated assault, and simple assault (DeVoe et al., 2003).

- ***Remain calm and proceed slowly:*** For the immediate confrontation between teacher and student, the strategy is always to remain calm and proceed slowly.
- ***Students who are violent must be removed immediately:*** Students who become violent in the classroom, the hallways, the cafeteria, or wherever the education program is being conducted must be removed immediately. No teacher should have to endure the threat of personal harm or be injured while working with children on school property in school-sanctioned programs.

Students engaged in the learning process contribute to classroom harmony.

TABLE 5-1 STRATEGIES FOR MANAGING STUDENTS WHO ARE VIOLENT

Schoolwide intervention	Individual teacher strategies
The curriculum and instruction should reflect depth that is engaging and attentive to all students.	Establish a classroom management plan that reflects tolerance for all students.
The school environment should be inviting and nonchallenging.	Avoid "playing into" antisocial behaviors by consistently challenging students about their nonconformity.
Students who are troubled should be identified and provided with regular counseling.	Do not "back yourself into a corner" by making threats you know you cannot carry out.
Law enforcement personnel should be visible as instructors and sources of help.	Never remain alone in a closed room with a student who is potentially violent.
Punitive measures should be direct and swift but always accompanied by follow-up with psychological personnel.	In a confrontation, remain calm. Do not shout or become agitated. Get help at once. Always protect other children who may be in harm's way.

Table 5-1 provides a list of strategies that address how student violence can be managed both systemically and by the individual teacher.

VOICES IN THE CLASSROOM
Kids May Not Be What They Seem

In my second year of teaching, I learned how powerful a teacher's influence could be. Danny, an 11-year-old in fifth grade, was the biggest boy in the class, whom I pegged as my problem child by the second week. He would not sit still, keep quiet, or even try to listen to me when I spoke. When he wasn't disrupting, he was sullen and angry.

I tried getting angry, taking him out in the hall for a good talking to, sending him to the principal's office, and calling his mom, but he still interrupted, still refused to do his work, and kept up his antics. Then, in about the third week of the year, I hit a button that sounded an alarm. He refused to do a simple work sheet in social studies. As I tried to coax him into putting forth an effort, he slammed down his pen and pulled back in his chair, moaning, "I can't do this stuff. I'm too stupid. I'm too dumb to do any of this stuff."

My anger was immediate. I bore down on him in a furious rage. "Don't you ever say that!" I shouted. "You are *not* dumb. Don't you ever say that about yourself. It's the worst thing you can ever say or think. It isn't true!" I can't say whether it was the anger or the passion of what I was feeling, but a rush of tears came to my eyes.

The effect on Danny was astounding. He sat shocked and stunned, but quietly began to work on the assignment. The next day, and for every day after, he was quiet, cooperative, and incredibly industrious in his work. When he did have lapses, I would just go up to him and firmly ask him to settle down—and he did.

A few days after this incident, I overheard him telling another student, "Don't ever tell Mrs. M. you're stupid. She hates that." It occurred to me then that he was a young boy who needed to hear from someone who cared that he was worth something, that he was not a failure, and in believing it, he came from one place to another.

Danny made it through school—not as an honors student, but undefeated. After high school, he left the hometown and followed his fate; whatever that is, I know he's a success.

—Mrs. M., who is still teaching

USING COMMERCIAL BEHAVIOR MANAGEMENT PROGRAMS

Briefcase CD CH5-10—Commercial Behavior Management Program Summaries

A number of behavior management programs have been designed by researchers, principals, psychologists, and classroom teachers. The four most widely known and instituted by a large number of schools throughout the United States are described next. Some school districts mandate their use and provide staff development and materials to implement them. Although they are distinctively packaged as complete programs for managing student behavior, all four have similar traits that the classroom teacher may adopt entirely or in part.

Assertive Discipline

One of the most popular behavior management programs that arose in the 1980s was Lee Canter's **assertive discipline,** also called *cooperative discipline* (Canter & Canter, 1999). This behaviorist system proscribes tactics including measured responses to student misbehavior. The student recognizes and takes ownership of his or her inappropriate behavior, as well as the expectation of appropriate behavior.

Characteristics of Assertive Discipline

Briefcase CD CH5-11—Teacher Views on Classroom Behavior

- The behavior plan is exclusively in the teacher's control. It is nonnegotiable—not open to student interpretation.
- The teacher informs students that he or she has the right to teach and they have the right to learn.
- The teacher recognizes that students' behavior patterns are different and may require separate strategies to control their behavior.
- Students must be aware of the parameters of behavior and that consequences will be invoked for violating the standards.

CLASSROOM IDEAS FOR ASSERTIVE DISCIPLINE

1. ***Have a hierarchy of punishments:*** Develop a clear line of increasingly uncomfortable responses. A child who misbehaves should first be given a warning. However, if the misbehavior continues, the stakes must increase. Following are examples of such stakes:
   a. Name on the board
   b. Separation from others
   c. Loss of a privilege
   d. Removal to the office
   e. Parent contact
   f. In-school suspension
2. ***Clearly post the rules:*** Post the rewards for appropriate behavior and the consequences for inappropriate behavior.
3. ***Use behavior thermometers:*** Behavior thermometers allow the class as a whole to gauge its cooperation. Examples are as follows:
   a. Fill a jar with M&Ms, marbles, peas, or jellybeans to note proper behavior. Each time you note appropriate behavior, put a specific number of items in the jar. Whenever you note misbehavior, remove items from the jar. You determine the number to be inserted and removed in accordance with the behavior.
   b. Make a chart listing the names of children who misbehaved. This chart serves as a warning to the children not to repeat the misbehavior. This graphic depiction of behavior is a clear and constant reminder of the hierarchy of punishments, and it sends a message to children who are in compliance as well as those who are not.
4. ***Always note appropriate behavior and reinforce it.***
5. ***Always note violations of the rules and enforce the consequences:*** Never ignore inappropriate behavior. Be firm and unmoving, but never hostile or confrontational.

CLASSROOM IDEAS FOR CHOICE THEORY

1. ***Explore the wants and needs of each student:*** Use role-playing and simulation exercises to do so. Spend time with students to examine their basic needs and help them see how they expend energies in attaining them.
2. ***Discuss behaviors and choices with your class:*** Talk about the difference between good and bad choices.
3. ***Make a chart with your students that describes their respective jobs:*** Describe what the jobs do and do not entail.
4. ***Incorporate what Glasser calls SESIR:***
   a. ***Show:*** Students show their work and share it with the class.
   b. ***Explain:*** Students explain how they accomplished their work.
   c. ***Self-evaluate:*** Students evaluate their work according to a rubric.
   d. ***Improve:*** Students discuss with the class how to improve their work.
   e. ***Repeat:*** Students repeat this process until they are satisfied with good-quality work.

***In Real Time:* Popularity and Teaching**

Teaching is not a popularity contest. If you need your students to like you above all other teachers, you are setting yourself up for disappointment. Rejection by the young and youthful is a daily occurrence that has nothing to do with your personality or the quality of your character, but everything to do with the developmental dynamic of the child.

Choice Theory

Unlike the behaviorist assertive discipline program, William Glasser's **choice theory** is a humanist approach based on the innate rationality of the human psyche. Teachers must understand that all children have basic needs: survival, love and belonging, power, freedom, and fun. Glasser (1992, pp. 74–97) believes that disunity from these needs causes erratic and inappropriate behavior, and that children can be taught to control their behaviors by understanding more about their own relationships not only with these basic needs, but also with their peers.

Characteristics of Choice Theory

- In choice theory, children are asked to look at how they act by forcing them to view behavior in general from others' perspectives, which therefore generates a rationale for them to control their own behavior.
- Teachers need to help students make good choices and understand the elements of good behavior.
- Each student is responsible for his or her behavior; each must accept the consequences that result from that behavior.
- A nonconfrontational approach is used. The actions are separate from the student; teachers should use verbs that condemn the behavior, not the child.
- Students learn about the four components of behavior:
  - ***Acting:*** Doing something
  - ***Feeling:*** What you are feeling while you are doing it
  - ***Thinking:*** What you are thinking during the activity
  - ***Physically reacting:*** How your physical body reacts during the activity
- Students learn about controlling these components.

Positive Discipline

Fred Jones's **positive discipline** program is a behaviorist plan similar to Canter's assertive discipline, with some nuances.

CLASSROOM IDEAS FOR POSITIVE DISCIPLINE

1. ***Offer individual help to students struggling with behavior or work.***
2. ***Develop a behavior plan with consequences:*** Be sure to inform students of this plan.
3. ***Use body language to note inappropriate behavior in your class:*** Eye contact, facial expressions, posture, gestures, and physical proximity are all effective.
4. ***Use extensive incentive systems for proper and improper behaviors:***
   a. Awards, badges, certificates, and other tangible rewards
   b. Preferred-activity time (PAT) for off-task enjoyment
   c. Points for good behavior

Characteristics of Positive Discipline

- The teacher records students' behaviors to establish a baseline. Then, the teacher can use it to devise strategies to encourage appropriate behavior.
- The teacher must implement a management program that is not integrated with, but parallel to, instruction (Jones, 1987, p. 211).
- The teacher should offer rewards for appropriate behavior and follow through with punishments for inappropriate behavior. These reinforcers must be potent enough to be effective.
- Motivation is integrated with classroom management.

Congruent Communication

Haim Ginott may be considered a founding father in the area of behavior management because his books *Between Parent and Child* (1965), *Between Parent and Teenager* (1969), and *Teacher and Child* (1971) were hugely popular. He is noted for the following quotation:

> What counts most in adult–child communication is the quality of the process. A child is entitled to sane messages from an adult. How parents and teachers talk tells a child how they feel about him. (Ginott, 1971, p. 122)

This type of communication is called **congruent communication.**

Characteristics of Congruent Communication

- The teacher's behavior is a model for students.
- The student's misbehavior, not the student him- or herself, is addressed.
- The student's misbehavior is identified with the student's feelings and thoughts.
- Teacher anger is expressed, but sanely.
- Student actions, not the student him- or herself, is praised.
- The teacher helps students bolster their self-esteem and trust in themselves.

CLASSROOM IDEAS FOR CONGRUENT COMMUNICATION

1. Establish classroom decorum that student misbehavior is a result of poor decisions.
2. Avoid overcomplimenting students on their behavior, but praise their cooperation and positive actions.
3. Avoid using labels, and do not tolerate student use of labels.
4. Invite students' opinions and encourage their experiences as a focus on current behavior.
5. Create simple rules for your class that reflect a total tolerance of personal beliefs and rights.

DOS AND DON'TS

Don't	Do
Think you can begin the school year without a management plan	Design a carefully planned and well-documented management plan
Overly apply your experiences with classroom discipline to those of your students	Consider that children change from generation to generation but behavior is fundamentally the same
Forget that you are a role model for your students	Remember to think about your dress, actions, and words
Discount your own beliefs, feelings, and biases when designing your classroom management plan	Remember that personal biases and beliefs may not match your students'
Rely on a single teaching style without considering that each class and each student are different and learn differently	Reflect and examine your personal style of teaching
Have unrealistic expectations of children's behavior without studying their humanistic side	Provide a deportment that tells students you are concerned about them as people
Challenge or provide a battlefield for the student who is violent	Approach students who are violent with caution, and never provoke them
Ignore students who are reluctant or oppressed learners because they want to be ignored	Involve all your students equally, and emphasize their strengths
Choose any single plan and follow its precepts exclusively	Consider that all students are different—no matter how much they look and act alike
Create a hostile environment	Create an environment that tells students they are welcome, needed, and valued
Attempt to teach on any day without your objectives in line and your goals prepared	Build flexibility into your management plan
Ignore your teaching pace as a major contributor to class disruption	Pace your instruction to your students' needs
Box yourself into a corner by making threats you cannot implement	Remember that you are the adult who should be demonstrating reason and calm in every stressful situation
Put your students in harm's way by allowing a student who is violent to harass them	Make yourself aware of school and district policy regarding student misbehavior
Forget that the students are children	Remember that the students are children

WEB SITES OF INTEREST

http://maxweber.hunter.cuny.edu/pub/eres/EDSPC715_MCINTYRE/AssertiveDiscipline.html
This site provides an overview, with samples and narratives, on the use of Canter's assertive discipline.

http://www.fredjones.com/Positive_Discipline/Discipline_Intro.html
This site provides details on Jones's program on positive discipline. It is Jones's personal site, with detail from his text on positive discipline.

http://www.eqi.org/ginott.htm
This site provides highlights of Ginott's views and prescriptions on discipline in general.

http://www.nea.org/tips/manage/index.html
This site by the National Education Association provides a wide range of tips on classroom management techniques.

http://www.theteachersguide.com/ClassManagement.htm
This comprehensive site on classroom management includes a list of books and other resources to assist you in managing your class.

http://www.ez2bsaved.com/Quality_Schools/index-qs.htm
This site provides a graphic summary and highlights of Glasser's choice theory. A complete program on the implementation of choice theory can be found at this Web site.

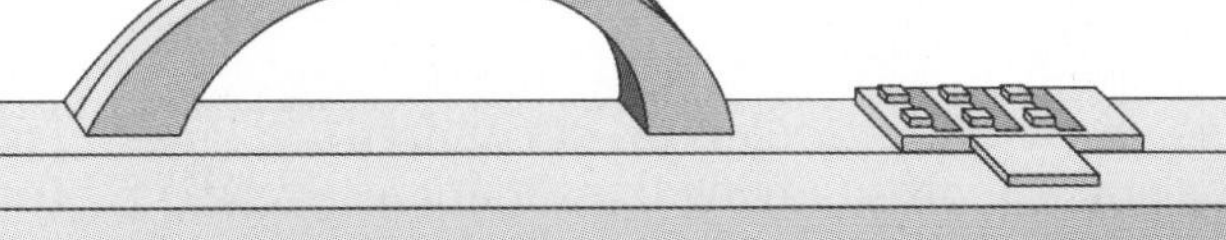

For Your Briefcase

To Do

- Experiment with a classroom furniture arrangement that best fits your class's needs.
- Design your homework, grading, attendance, and tardiness policies.
- Design the tempo of your instruction by varying the time use of each class period.
- Be aware of ways to link the curriculum to other subject areas.
- Write your class behavior contract with the class.
- Prepare strategies for students who are reluctant learners.
- Develop a contingency plan to deal with the student who is violent or bullying.
- Review commercial behavior programs to find ideas for your classroom.

Resources on Your Briefcase CD

Samples
- Example of Interval Spacing in Teaching
- Examples of Linking the Curriculum
- Example of Class Contract Criteria
- Sample Class Contract—Elementary School
- Sample Class Contract—Middle or High School
- Teacher Views on Classroom Behavior

Templates
- Six-Step Classroom Management Plan Checklist
- Classroom Organization Checklist
- Teacher Attitude Checklist

Tables
- Strategies to Manage Disruption
- Commercial Behavior Management Program Summaries

REFERENCES

Beattie, I., & Olley, P. G. (1977, Winter). Non-instructional factors relating to classroom climate: An exploratory study. *Education, 98*(2), 183.

Canter, L., & Canter, M. (1993). *Succeeding with difficult students: New strategies for reaching your most challenging students.* Santa Monica, CA: Canter Associates.

DeVoe, J. F., Peter, K., Kaufman, P., Ruddy, S. A., Miller, A. K., Planty, M., et al. (2003). *Indicators of school crime and safety: 2003.* (Pub. Nos. NCES 2004–004/NCJ 201257). Washington, DC: U.S. Departments of Education and Justice.

Fleming, M., & Towey, K. (Eds.). (2002, May). *Educational Forum on Adolescent Health: Youth Bullying.* Chicago: American Medical Association. Retrieved July 8, 2005, from http://www.ama-assn.org/ama1/pub/upload/mm/39/youthbullying.pdf

Fox, J., Elliott, D., Kerlikowske, G., Newman, S., & Christeson, W. (2003). *Bullying prevention is crime prevention.* Washington, DC: Fight Crime: Invest in Kids.

Ginott, H. (1971). *A book for parents and teachers.* New York: Avon Books.

Glasser, W. (1992). *The quality school: Managing students without coercion.* New York: Harper Collins.

Jones, F. H. (1987). *Positive classroom instruction.* New York: McGraw-Hill.

Martinez, R. (1992). Sparking interest in academics: Welding class helps students improve English, math grades. *Vocational Education Journal, 67*(8), 34–37.

National Center for Victims of Crime. (n.d.). *Bullying and harassment.* Washington, DC: Author. Retrieved July 8, 2005, from http://www.ncvc.org/tvp/main.aspx?dbName=Bullying

National Institute of Child Health and Human Development. (2001, April 24). *Bullying widespread in U.S., survey finds.* Rockville, MD: Author. Retrieved August 24, 2004, from http://www.nichd.nih.gov/new/releases/bullying.cfm

North Central Regional Educational Laboratory. (1995). *Violence Prevention Curriculum for Adolescents.* Newton, MA: Author.

Olweus, D. (1979). Stability of aggressive reaction patterns in males: A review. *Psychological Bulletin, 86,* 852–875.

Polling Report, Inc. (2000). *Education: Problems facing schools.* Retrieved July 8, 2005, from http://www.pollingreport.com/educ2.htm

Santrock, J. W. (2000). *Children* (7th ed.). Boston: McGraw-Hill.

Chapter 6

Teaching for Success: Methods and Models

Education is not the filling of a pail, but the lighting of a fire.

—*W. B. Yeats*

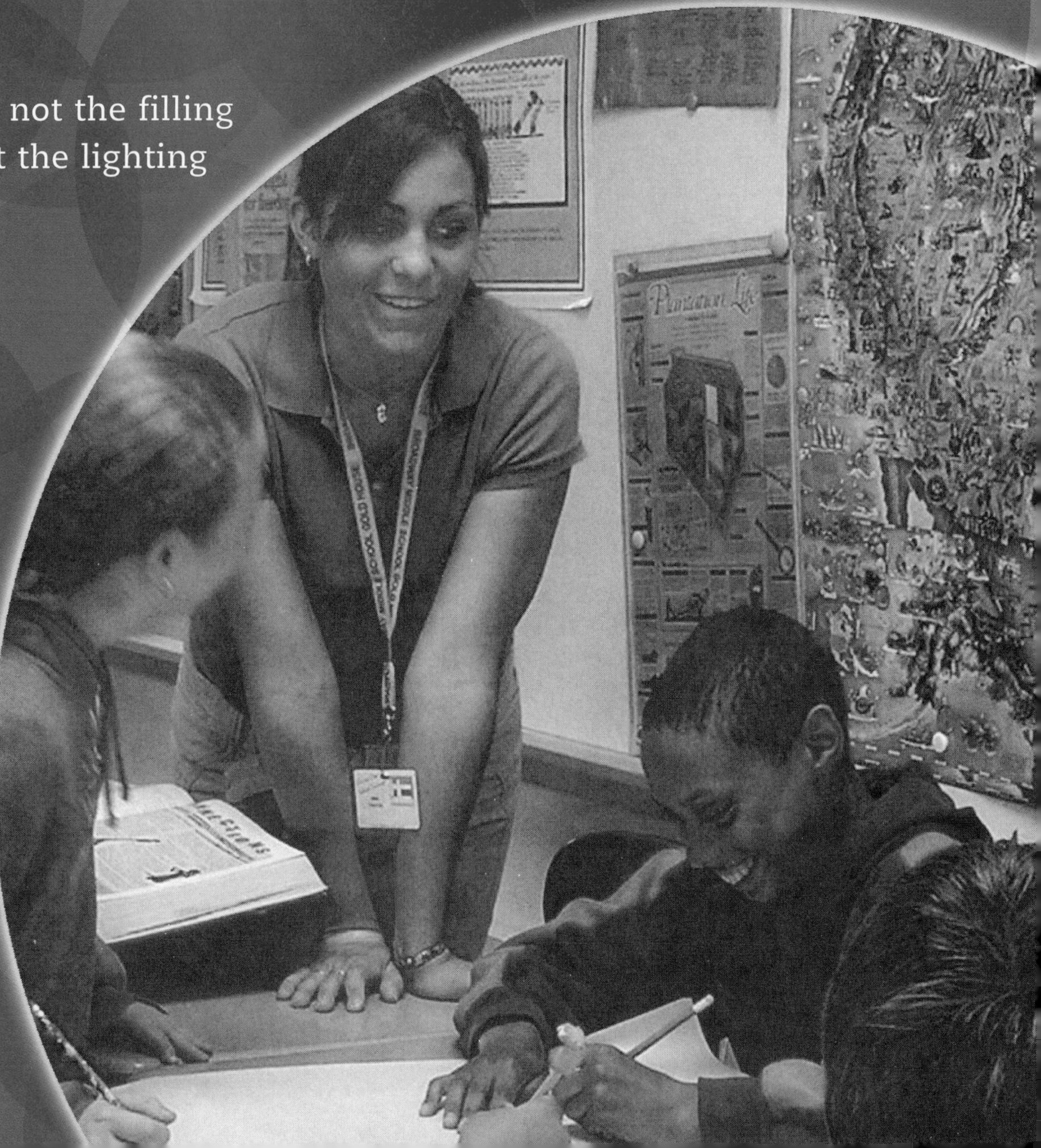

BEING THE TEACHER

Influences on Your Teaching

STATING THE FACTS:

On teacher effectiveness:

- Teachers with a broad background in education course work are more successful than teachers with little or none (Darling-Hammond, 2000).
- Teachers who expect more from their students will have higher success rates than those of teachers who communicate low expectations (Darling-Hammond, 2000).

The *how* of teaching is influenced by a number of factors, but the two main influences are *you—the teacher*—and *the learner.* The factors that affect you, the teacher, begin with the following:

- Your background in the subject you will teach
- Your understanding of the learners' developmental stages
- Your preparation for each day of teaching
- Your teaching strategy, or *how you organize and deliver your teaching plan*

Traits of an Effective Teacher

Experienced and successful educators know that the teachers whose students perform at exceptional levels and who receive high praise from parents and supervisors are those with the following traits:

- ☑ They are *excited* about what they are teaching, and show it.
- ☑ They treat their students with *fairness.*
- ☑ They have a *positive attitude* about teaching, learning, and being with their students.
- ☑ They are *prepared* for each lesson, each day.
- ☑ They are *sincere* in their motives and actions and acknowledge that they might make mistakes.
- ☑ They have *high expectations* for their students and *challenge* them daily.

RELATING YOUR TEACHING TO THE LEARNER

Factors Influencing Student Success

Even the most experienced teacher can be daunted by a learner who is not responding to instruction for reasons that may or may not be under the student's control. Some of the factors that influence student success are as follows:

- ☑ Cultural background
- ☑ Language
- ☑ Learning disabilities
- ☑ Age
- ☑ Gender
- ☑ Ability level
- ☑ Socioeconomic status
- ☑ Peer relationships
- ☑ Religion
- ☑ Parenting style
- ☑ Temperament

Ways to Balance Factors Influencing Student Learning

Each factor affecting students calls for a separate solution, and sometimes each student requires individual attention. However, some general guidelines can provide you with direction:

- ☑ ***Instruction should be sensitive to the students' diverse needs:*** Consider that your students may not have a place to study at home or may not be able to afford materials other students take for granted. Also, avoid references to *Mom* or *Dad.* Always remain objective.

STATING THE FACTS:

On factors affecting student learning:

- Children of low socioeconomic status are more likely to be exposed to prenatal drug use and AIDS and to be victims of violence and abuse; they are in a perpetual cycle of failure (Arnold & Doctoroff, 2003).
- A student who was classified as difficult, slow to warm, or easy as an infant can show behaviors consistent with these descriptions in your classroom (Chess & Thomas, 1977).

☑ ***Make great efforts to relate the material to students' lives in any way possible:*** Always begin instruction in concrete, visual terms and then move to the abstract after you think your students are grasping the meaning of the lesson. (Use Bloom's taxonomy and carefully design your lessons to move from the knowledge level to the evaluation level of cognition.)

☑ ***Consistency is the key to cohesive classroom instruction:*** Be diligent about instructions on work sheets and projects and be consistent in the application of the rules for all students. Provide additional help to those who are struggling, and always work with the special education teacher to fulfill modifications listed on a student's individualized education program (IEP).

☑ ***Rely on the support services available to you:*** The school nurse, the social service worker, the school psychologist, the special education director, veteran teachers, guidance counselors, the principal, and the vice-principal are all people from whom you should seek help when you are confronted with a child's problems that are adversely affecting the learning process. These professionals are trained and equipped to assist you in the classroom.

USING DIRECT INSTRUCTION TEACHING METHODS

A third factor in the *how* of teaching is the *method.* There are many ways to teach, but the method you choose will depend on you—specifically your skills and ability—as well as on your students and the numerous factors affecting them.

The two fundamental categories of teaching methods are direct and indirect teaching. How can you make these methods work for you, and when should you use each? The following discussion should be of help.

Briefcase CD CH6-1—Direct Instruction Procedure Checklist

Because all instruction must begin with the basic elements of **direct instruction,** it is a teaching method you will use to deliver much of your curriculum. The basic elements are *presentation of material*, *explanation*, and *reinforcement*. These elements are an inherent part of the teaching regimen, even for the most student-directed lessons.

Direct instruction is a model for teaching that comprises several structured and sequential steps. The best example is the Madeline Hunter model (see your Briefcase CD for a lesson plan template and checklist). The following elements generally compose the direct instruction model:

Briefcase CD CH6-2—Lesson Plan Template for the Universal Model

☑ ***Introduction and review:*** The teacher introduces the lesson by reviewing what was previously taught on the subject, then segues into the current lesson.

☑ ***Presentation and demonstration:*** The topic of the lesson is presented on an overhead, on a poster, in a lecture, or through multimedia. Guidelines are provided on the work required, teacher expectations, grading, and so forth. The teacher gives some type of demonstration that models what is expected of the students.

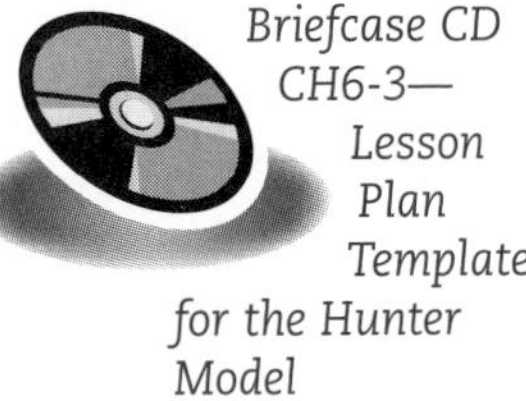

Briefcase CD CH6-3—Lesson Plan Template for the Hunter Model

☑ ***Questioning:*** Questioning provides the teacher with feedback on student comprehension and serves as a platform from which to expand student knowledge of and skill with the material being taught.

☑ ***Dependent practice:*** Through a dependent-practice exercise (work sheet, board work, oral presentation), students work with the material presented, with strong teacher input. This exercise also helps the teacher to ascertain what the students have not understood or misunderstood and to provide feedback.

LESSON PLAN TEMPLATE FOR THE HUNTER MODEL

Lesson topic:

☑ **Anticipatory set:** [The "hook" to grab your students' attention and get them to relate to the new material]

☑ **Objectives:** [These are set before the lesson and guide you through the entire lesson]

☑ **Teaching:** [Your presentation of the new knowledge or skill by using a lecture and possibly one of the following: a film, a tape, overheads, the blackboard, or pictures]

☑ **Modeling:** [Examples of what you expect the students to produce as a result of the knowledge or skill taught]

☑ **Guided practice:** [An exercise given to the students to help them practice what you have taught]

☑ **Checking for understanding:** [Revisitation of the concepts and assessment of whether the students comprehend the material; questioning strategies are essential]

☑ **Independent practice:** [Homework, group work, or individual practice that allows students to practice, on their own, what they have learned; should challenge students to achieve at a higher level than that of the guided practice]

☑ **Closure:** [Summary of the material and responses to cues from the students that may indicate confusion or ambivalence; clarification and reteaching of concepts that may have been misunderstood; reflection on the holistic concept and its applications]

Briefcase CD CH6-4—Hunter Model Lesson Plan Checklist

☑ ***Independent practice:*** Independent practice allows students to work on the lesson material on their own. It also serves as a reinforcement of what was taught and is usually completed at home or during quiet time in class.

☑ ***Final review and reinforcement:*** The material is summarized and rechecked for accuracy in the form of a review whereby the teacher then provides feedback and further clarification.

In Real Time: Homework

The best reinforcement for a daily lesson is the homework assignment. However, you must grade or check homework as quickly as possible. Homework should always be included as part of the student's grade.

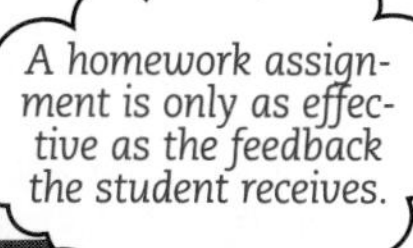

What Makes Direct Instruction Successful? The key elements of success for the direct instruction model are as follows:

☑ A *well-organized lesson plan* with a great deal of material that provides clear examples and depth of information

☑ A *demonstration* accompanying the lesson, *with clear and readable graphics* on an overhead, the whiteboard, or the computer

☑ A *questioning* period in which students get feedback on the lesson (student responses inform how you will clarify ambiguities)

☑ A *dependent practice* with examples that are incremental from least difficult to most difficult so that students can gauge their success with the material presented

☑ An *independent practice* to help students work with the material on their own, which gives them a sense of what they understand

☑ A *review* or summary of the material taught to provide further feedback for clarification or reteaching

☑ *Smaller classes* and *sessions of 40 minutes or less* depending on the students' age

Stating the Facts:

On direct instruction:

- In an extensive analysis of 29 comprehensive school reform models, direct instruction was one of only three models found to have the "strongest evidence of effectiveness" (Center for Research on the Education of Students at Risk, 2002).
- Project Follow Through researchers found direct instruction to be superior to more than 19 other instructional models when they were measuring basic skills achievement and self-concept (Watkins, 1988).

How Is Direct Instruction Effective?
Teaching a lesson by using direct instruction is thought to be effective for a number of reasons. Among them are the following:

- ☑ Direct instruction helps both the teacher and the student to stay on task and on schedule. Students know exactly what is expected of them because they see the lesson presented in a linear and clear manner.
- ☑ Direct instruction enables the teacher to present one or two clear examples to explain the concept being taught and to frequently review how the examples apply.
- ☑ Direct instruction focuses student attention on the specific information being taught.
- ☑ Direct instruction provides students with a sense of organization and direction.

When Should I Use Direct Instruction? Direct instruction is a valuable instructional tool for almost all lessons, and elements of it will be used in most lessons. However, the step-by-step direct instructional method is best used when your students need to grasp the initial concepts of a topic. Therefore, literacy, math, and science teachers usually favor direct instruction. It is also recommended for teaching higher order thinking skills because it presents critical-thinking steps in sequence and reinforces the concepts through student dependent and independent practice (Adams & Englemann, 1996). In short, direct instruction should be used *to introduce material, for review,* and *to transition to other topics and concepts.*

What Are the Disadvantages of Using Direct Instruction? Some instructors would say that direct instruction has no disadvantages (see the Association for Direct Instruction Web site, listed at the end of this chapter). However, one general criticism is that direct instruction can stifle teacher creativity because it is so formulaic. Likewise, direct instruction is structured and sequential, which can inhibit excursions into other areas if a student raises an interesting point that is off topic. In addition, using direct instruction to develop higher order thinking skills requires a great deal of planning and expertise and general skill in using the Socratic method (discussed in the next section). Other possible disadvantages of using direct instruction are as follows:

- ☑ Lecturing quickly leads to student disconnection.
- ☑ Teachers who do not monitor themselves may use a great deal of class time in repetitious explanations.
- ☑ Direct instruction challenges a teacher's ability to maintain classroom order because it requires a high level of student attention.

Socratic Method

Briefcase CD CH6-5— Socratic Method Procedure Checklist

One of the most ancient teaching techniques originated with Socrates. According to Plato, who related the famous story of Meno, Socrates took a young man through a series of questions that ultimately led all listeners, including the student, to a higher understanding of a concept. The actual "method" was to ask a series of questions that built on each other until the student realized aspects of the concept by asking questions of his or her own (Elkind & Sweet, 1997).

A step-by-step tool for using the original **Socratic method** is not available. However, if the method is combined with standard questioning techniques, the following examples may provide you with some direction if you are unfamiliar with the process. Once the instructor presents the concept, he or she might begin with a series of questions:

- ☑ ***An establishing question*** (e.g., "What is *egalitarianism*?")
- ☑ ***An expanding question*** (e.g., "What does it mean to you?")
- ☑ ***An organizing or clarifying question*** (e.g., "Does equality apply to all people in every situation?")
- ☑ ***A probing question*** (e.g., "What would equality mean in that situation?")
- ☑ ***A relative question*** (e.g., "Does equality mean the same as *fairness* or *balanced*?")

What Makes the Socratic Method Successful and Effective? The greatest benefit of using the Socratic method is that it moves the lesson away from the teacher as holder of knowledge to the student as an individual given the power to think through the problem and gain ownership of his or her learning. Looking directly at a student, speaking his or her name, and asking for his or her input on the topic at hand is powerful. It signals your interest in the student as a learner and that you value his or her abilities and viewpoint. Skillful questioning is an effective tool for engendering true student engagement in the learning process. The Socratic method is effective because it does the following:

- ☑ Involves the student in the learning process
- ☑ Helps clarify difficult concepts
- ☑ Helps introduce new concepts or learning objectives
- ☑ Opens a wide range of perspectives encouraging higher order thinking

One major advantage of this method is that it requires little to no resources beyond time and energy. Therefore, the following are true:

- ☑ It can be initiated in any setting and skillfully sustained for as little or as much time as is available.
- ☑ It can help stimulate the student who is quieter to speak up when he or she hears a comment that strikes a chord of understanding or protest.
- ☑ It reminds students that their opinions are valued and therefore motivates them to participate.
- ☑ It is an ancient tool born in the perennialist spirit of education that appeals to teachers who want to inspire their students in the classical manner.

When Should I Use the Socratic Method? The Socratic method is always effective when you are introducing new concepts in all subject areas. It is also useful as a reinforcement tool to help students look at two perspectives of an issue. For example, you could stimulate student questions about how they would feel if they were Southerners prior to the Civil War or as a way to discover the motives of the antagonist and protagonist in a novel.

What Are the Disadvantages of Using the Socratic Method? The disadvantages of using the Socratic method are similar to those for any teaching method. Spending an entire period or 40 minutes on random questions to arrive at an understanding of a single concept is sufficient and, depending on the student's age, possibly extreme. The main disadvantage is that the time consumed by questioning may detract from student dependent practice or other explanations that may be necessary to clarify your topic. In the pre–Civil War example given in the preceding section, if too much time is spent trying to establish the Southerners' perspective, you may run out of time and be unable to provide specific dates, people, and events that are also necessary for a clear perspective. Other noted disadvantages of the Socratic method are as follows:

- ☑ ***The teacher may inadvertently ask questions that will elicit comical or off-task remarks:*** If by mistake you or one of the students stumbles onto a question that can be taken as off-color or inappropriate, do not linger or explain it. Move on.

- ☑ ***Some students may not be able to follow the train of thought created by the questions and will lose interest quickly:*** Speedy questioning may be attractive to some students, but it confuses and bores the individuals who have difficulty processing information. Ask questions slowly and be patient with students' responses.
- ☑ ***Some students may find this line of teaching too unstructured and seek to find the purpose of the questions:*** Undoubtedly, some students will want to know "where this is going." Try to craft your questions so that a direction is obvious to all your students. If they begin to become confused, simplify the questions or stop and give an explanation.
- ☑ ***The greatest asset of the method, being able to introduce new concepts, is also a liability if the questioning does not produce a clear explanation of the concept:*** Before using this method, know in advance where you want your students to conclude. Keep in mind that the concept being taught must be in clear focus at the end of the session.

USING INDIRECT INSTRUCTION TEACHING METHODS

Indirect instruction is not in itself an instructional technique as direct instruction is. Rather, the term *indirect instruction* has come to mean any method used in which the student is an *active* (rather than a *passive*) participant. Therefore, indirect instruction comprises a number of instructional techniques that encourage students to participate *actively* in their learning. Educator and researcher Linda Meyer (1984) provides a clear definition:

> Indirect instruction is an approach where the process of learning is inquiry, the result is discovery, and the learning context is specific to problem-solving. (p. 383)

In her definition, Meyer mentions two specific techniques: discovery and inquiry learning, and problem solving. Both methods invite students to become actively involved. What follows is an examination of the methods that compose indirect instruction.

Briefcase CD CH6-6—Discovery Learning Procedure Checklist

Discovery and Inquiry-Based Learning

Discovery and inquiry-based learning is a well-known method of teaching that gained popularity with the proliferation of computers and the Internet. Jerome Bruner (1983) is credited with introducing discovery learning, which is a teaching method whereby the student is encouraged to seek his or her own answers to problems or questions posed by the teacher. The student then works with the material discovered to form his or her own perspective relating to the material.

Students should be made a part of the instructional process.

What Makes Discovery Learning Successful and Effective?

Discovery learning is effective for the following reasons:

- ☑ It actively engages the learner in the discovery process.
- ☑ It stimulates student interest by directly relating learning to the student.
- ☑ It connects to the learner's prior knowledge.
- ☑ It enables students to reach new conclusions from what is discovered.

STATING THE FACTS:

On inquiry-based learning:
"Inquiry-oriented science teaching was shown to promote development of classification skills and oral communication skills among bilingual third graders" (Rodriguez & Bethel, 1983, p. 293).

Most important, discovery learning fosters initiative and student engagement. Providing students with the opportunity to seek answers to questions and to solve problems makes them an active part of the learning process.

Discovery learning does the following:

- ☑ Encourages student initiative and commitment, which is directly related to cognitive comprehension
- ☑ Creates an atmosphere of responsibility and therefore supports a student's accountability for his or her work
- ☑ Is a key avenue for developing problem-solving skills that encourage cooperation among peers
- ☑ Provides the teacher with a clear picture of how well the student is grasping the material and using it at the higher levels of cognition

When Should I Use Discovery Learning? Discovery learning is most appropriate for any lesson that seeks to involve students in an exploration of more ideas associated with the main theme. Therefore, this method works best at the expanding and refining stages of the teaching process. After an introduction is given through direct instruction or the Socratic method, discovery learning might be appropriate as students explore how the concept being taught permeates both the physical and the ideal world.

What Are the Disadvantages of Using Discovery Learning? The main disadvantage of using discovery learning is that it requires additional classroom management and supervision of your students. Discovery learning often takes students out of the classroom into different areas of the school (the library, the computer center, offices, etc.). It may also require them to work outdoors on the playing field, which necessitates additional supervision.

Therefore, the main disadvantages of using this method are as follows:

- ☑ Increased supervision of students who are working out of the classroom
  - Keep good records as to the whereabouts of all your students. Implement a sign-out system that is strictly enforced.
- ☑ Increased supervision of the students *in* the classroom who are working in dyads or groups
  - Circulate among the groups as they are working and move from group to group regularly.
- ☑ The possibility of parental involvement beyond what is best for the student
  - Advise your students about too much parental help on homework; encourage them to seek help from their parents, but put them on the honor system to do the work on their own.
- ☑ The high incidence of plagiarism from the Internet because students are unfamiliar with citing references
  - Advise your students on the illegal use of Internet-copied materials. Give them a lesson on plagiarism and its penalties. Cite some high-profile cases of famous authors who have lost millions of dollars or have damaged their careers. Show them what is correct and incorrect when they are gathering material from the Internet.
- ☑ Student confusion as a result of no specific framework or sequence of material being taught
  - Provide clear instructions from the outset, but be ready to revise the directions as the project ensues. Do not be afraid to make changes.

LESSON IDEA FOR DISCOVERY LEARNING

Document-Based Questions (DBQ) Strategy

Document-based questions are used as an instructional strategy primarily in the social studies or humanities classrooms. Students work with primary source materials such as news and magazine articles, diaries, and other documents found in the local library, as well as the Internet, to focus on a specific subject area in the curriculum. Teachers utilize a number of activities to implement these lessons: role-playing, compositions, reports, journals, class presentations, posters, dioramas, skits, short stories, or combinations of these.

DBQ Example

Subject area: *Diary of Anne Frank*

Focusing question: How do people manage to maintain normal, working relationships with others during war time or other times of great stress?

Primary source possibilities: Photocopies of the diary; the book *Diary of Anne Frank,* the play by the same name; interviews with Miep Gees, Mr. Frank (after the war), and other survivors of the Holocaust

Student activity: Students create posters and develop a presentation reflecting the source material they have found. The presentation gives both historical data and a possible answer to the focusing question.

Briefcase CD CH6-7—Sample Document-Based Question Lesson

What Are Some Possible Discovery Learning Projects? Discovery learning projects can be developed from virtually any lesson presented. However, the following types of projects lend themselves to discovery learning:

- ☑ Researching the Netherland's policy and actions toward Jews during World War II
- ☑ Finding as many ways as possible to determine how to mow a square piece of lawn beginning at the center
- ☑ Determining the temperature and precipitation levels of the Northeast during the past decade
- ☑ Finding architecture with characteristics similar to those in the world's largest cities
- ☑ Comparing the typical diets of people from Mexico, France, and Poland
- ☑ Finding the fat and carbohydrate content of typical meals at local fast-food restaurants

Project-Based and Problem-Based Learning

Briefcase CD CH6-8—Project-Based or Problem-Based Learning Procedure Checklist

Project-based learning and problem-based learning (PBL) are often seen as two teaching methods but overlap in principle; thus, they can be looked at simultaneously. The essential element of PBL is its use of real-world situations for which students must solve a problem by using observational and critical-thinking skills. This method, although seemingly new to modern educators, has its roots with John Dewey's experiential learning model (Aspy, Aspy, & Quimby, 1993). What makes this model of teaching so appealing is the high level of student interest in dealing with the real world.

Some features of PBL are the following:

- ☑ Students are given a problem to solve requiring them to gather information, often in teams or dyads.
- ☑ PBL is somewhat unstructured because the parameters for the students are expanded, which enables them to construct their own meaning of what they find when they are solving the problem.
- ☑ The problem is framed in a real-world situation, such as the following:
  - "We are building an A-frame house and need to know what size furnace and air-conditioner are required."

Stating the Facts:

On PBL:

Elementary school students in Dubuque, IA, demonstrated significant test score gains after a problem- or project-based learning program was incorporated in the schools. One school alone raised its scores from the 39th percentile to the 80th (Borman, Hewes, Overman, & Brown, 2002).

- "A specific species of fish is disappearing from a local river. What procedures or actions are necessary to rectify the situation? What obstacles might be encountered?"
- "The issue of gun control is emotional. How can this issue be resolved in a compromise that would satisfy people on both sides of the issue?"
- "We are going to depict a nature scene by using three artistic mediums: clay, metal, and canvas and paint. All three must be incorporated."

In each of the preceding examples, students must gather a substantial database of information and design a plan of action before solutions can be obtained. Most important, students must record the obstacles that they encountered, how they overcame these obstacles, and what effects the solutions have on other people or systems.

What Makes PBL Successful and Effective? The effectiveness of the PBL teaching method rests with the heightened student response to solving problems. The nature of this method stimulates curiosity and encourages engagement. However, the main reason PBL is effective is the student's use of higher order thinking skills on a natural level. Unlike simply solving a puzzle offered by the teacher, finding the answers to real-world problems has the additional factor of being gratifying in a sense that the student is making a contribution.

When Should I Use PBL? PBL is an excellent tool for helping your students extend and refine their learning of a concept. However, as with discovery learning, students must have some working knowledge of terms, facts, and statistics, as well as direction, before they can address the problem. Such working knowledge can be provided through lectures, or direct instruction. PBL is best used when you are seeking to help your students grasp the meaning of a larger concept through their own initiative and work. Therefore, use PBL at the point in your lesson when the student is expected to grasp the essential meaning of the concept being taught.

What Are the Disadvantages of Using PBL? Although no drawbacks to using PBL are readily apparent, a teacher should be cautious before launching a PBL lesson or unit. Some of the factors to be aware of are as follows:

- ☑ What materials and resources will be necessary to implement the lesson, and do I have the ability to get them ready on time?
  - Long-range planning can prevent this problem. Look at the project thoroughly and make a list of materials and resources needed.
- ☑ How well does PBL apply to this particular topic, and does it align with district and state standards?
  - When designing weekly or monthly lesson plans, align the state and district standards; do not wait for the day of the lesson.
- ☑ As in the cooperative learning method (discussed subsequently), team members often do not work well together and usually are in conflict over workloads.
  - Try to compose your teams of members who vary in interest, ability, and gender; always remember that diversity is a goal.
- ☑ Some students will have difficulty understanding the material or organizing themselves well enough to begin the project or problem solving.
  - Work closely with the special education teacher and aides; be sure to check with the guidance counselor about students who are struggling. The more informed you are, the better prepared you will be to help your students.

CH6-9—Sample Problem-Based Lesson

What Are Some Possible PBL Lessons? Each subject area presents ample opportunities for using PBL, but it is most effective when it is used to expand and refine material already presented. Following are some suggestions for lessons using PBL:

- ☑ "What is the *national debt* and how does it affect our economy?" (intermediate grades)
- ☑ "What is the pollution rate of European and Eastern European countries? How does it compare with that of the United States? What are the major pollutants?" (middle to high school)
- ☑ "As financial director of your athletic program, you must budget all monies for all sports at the school. Construct a formula that would give equal funding to all sports. Provide a credit and debit sheet of all materials and other costs." (middle school)
- ☑ "What type of books would you like to see in a private library in the classroom?" After a visit to the local library, students must compile a list of books by type, then by title and author. (primary grades)

SAMPLE PROBLEM-BASED LESSON

What if

In 1999, Robert Cowley published a book titled *What If? The World's Foremost Military Historians Imagine What Might Have Been.* It poses a series of questions about probable outcomes of history if different choices had been made. Using this concept as a theme for all subject areas, students can work on problems involving changed perspectives. This lesson provides an outside-the-box view of historical, factual, and biographical events that encourages students to think about the elements of the problem as they are, and as they could be. Following are some ideas about how you might use this problem-solving technique.

Problem solving using . . .	What if . . .
English language arts	The main character in our story did not succeed in overcoming her obstacle? The antagonist decided to become a protagonist? The story took place in modern times or ancient times?
Social studies	The British decided not to send troops to quell the revolution? America refused to join the French and English during World War I? The stock market crashed in 1939 instead of 1929?
Science	Nuclear reactors could supply all our energy needs? Our streams and rivers became polluted at a greater rate and threatened freshwater supplies? Weather patterns affected agricultural production?
Math	All schools gave first graders laptop computers? Retail store cash registers failed for an entire week? There were no prime numbers? We reduced everything you see in the room to one quarter its size?
Music	We wrote a song using only four notes? Beethoven had never lived? We could use only the bass clef? We combined rap music with classical music?
Art	We found a famous painting hanging in our library? We redecorated the entire school in a modern art design? Our nation's capital was redesigned by Frank Lloyd Wright?

Briefcase CD CH6-10—Cooperative Learning Procedure Checklist

Cooperative Learning

Probably the most popular teaching method, besides direct instruction, is cooperative learning. Because it so closely follows experiential learning, capitalizing on student experiences and cooperation among students, this method is considered the most valuable when you want students to comprehend the material being taught. In cooperative learning, a

Briefcase CD CH6-11—Types of Cooperative Learning

group of students is given a task related to the concept being taught. The effort may be directly related to meaning, as in PBL, or to refining concepts already discussed and grasped. This method requires each student to assume a portion of responsibility for the assignment and to report to his or her team members.

Many types of cooperative learning are used. However, the following seem to be most popular:

- ☑ ***Student teams achievement divisions (STAD)*** is a system in which each team is placed on an achievement level on the basis of scores on tests or quizzes the students give themselves. Team members form study groups in any way they want and test and quiz one another on the material. They then sum a team score to compare with other teams' scores. STAD is effective when teachers want students to master a specific skill, such as one in math, a foreign language, or science.
- ☑ ***Jigsaw*** is a similar team exercise, except each student on the team is responsible for a specific portion of the material to be learned. He or she then "teaches" it to the other team members. Finally, the teams present what they have learned to the other teams.
- ☑ ***Group investigation*** is a technique that more closely follows the PBL model. Each team must develop its own strategies for isolating the meaning of the topic, then develop subtopics, plot a method to find information on the topic, and finally organize the information into a formal presentation. Each team also evaluates itself at the completion of the project.
- ☑ ***Carousel feedback*** is a specific technique developed by Spencer and Laurie Kagan (2000).

Briefcase CD CH6-12—Carousel Feedback Technique

What Makes Cooperative Learning Successful and Effective? Extensive research has revealed that cooperative learning provides strong academic improvement, as well as overall positive benefits in student behavior, self-esteem, and motivation. (Slavin, 1995). Some of the key benefits of cooperative learning are as follows:

- ☑ It mirrors real-life work situations in which employees work together to solve problems.
- ☑ It engenders cooperative behaviors more so than whole-class teaching does.
- ☑ Students engage in social interactions that help foster cooperative behaviors.
- ☑ As a group, students can explore a broader perspective of the topic and approach it at higher levels of thinking.
- ☑ Groups can also help provide a routine in class work by assigning repetitive tasks to the group as a whole.

Stating the Facts:

On cooperative learning:

- The results of a study of first-grade readers revealed that collaborative literacy groups contributed to positive peer interactive relations and higher levels of self-confidence in reading (James, 2003).
- Research on third graders revealed that use of the Jigsaw method of cooperative learning, along with the use of graphic organizers, was significant in improving student self-esteem and the work ethic (Box & Little, 2003).

In Real Time: Success Using Cooperative Learning

Cooperative learning is only as effective as teacher organization, monitoring, and assessment. Students who are gifted can either promote or destroy the cooperative unit. They must be given clear guidelines and enough initiative to challenge their abilities. They also must be allowed the opportunity to lead as well as made to understand the integrity of the group dynamic and the benefits that derive from it.

Cooperative learning promotes peer cohesion.

When Should I Use Cooperative Learning? Cooperative learning is best used to generate student comprehension, generalization, and expansion of concepts that have been taught. It works best when students are solving a problem or seeking information on a topic.

Some teachers use cooperative learning almost exclusively; however, much depends on the subject being taught. For example, social studies lends itself to cooperative learning because students seek to explore the causes and effects of historical events, and reproduce, in real life, the dynamics of historical documents.

CAROUSEL FEEDBACK TECHNIQUE

Procedure	Description
• The class is divided into groups. Each group completes a project. For example, each team might devise a clean-air bill to present to Congress for passage. • The teams spread their projects around the room, and each team stands in front of its project. • They then rotate clockwise to the next project, where they observe and orally react to the others' projects. One person from each group records feedback. • The teams then rotate again, and observe, discuss, and give feedback on the next project in line. • A new recorder is selected for each round to write up feedback. • This process continues until each team reaches its project. • The feedback forms are then given to each team for reflection.	This model, summarized here, is one of many cooperative learning paradigms established by Dr. Spencer and Laurie Kagan (2000). Their approach gives teachers greater control over the process by offering dozens of methods with which to approach topics in a cooperative manner. Carousel Feedback promotes student participation and cooperation while exposing the entire class to the declarative knowledge of the topic. To overcome the main obstacle of cooperative learning—when stronger, more aggressive members of the group dominate—help them divide the tasks evenly so that everyone has some area of responsibility. Be sure to establish guidelines for accountability and to give weaker members the help they will need to be successful. Intervene in groups in which some members are "taking away the project" for themselves.

LEGAL SIDEBAR

Mandated Instruction Policy

Introduced by Senator Robert Byrd (D–WVA), the Consolidated Appropriations Act, 2005 (2004), implemented Constitution Day and Citizenship Day on September 17 of each year. On this day, schools are required to teach some aspect of the U.S. Constitution. Although such instruction is mandated, the application has a great deal of flexibility.

What Are the Disadvantages of Using Cooperative Learning? A teacher should not discount lightly the disadvantages of using cooperative learning, especially the potential of disrupting classroom harmony. In fact, many teachers avoid using this method because of the heavy potential for students to misbehave. However, such misbehavior need not be the case. Some of the disadvantages of using cooperative learning, and possible remedies, follow:

- ☑ Placing students in teams is welcoming a social interaction that leads to comedy, loud noise, and off-task behavior.
  - Before the beginning of the lesson, review the procedures to follow for the specific project. Discuss with your students the need for quiet and on-task behaviors, as well as respect for other teams and the class as a whole. Provide clear lines of accountability for students exhibiting disruptive and off-task behaviors. Keep active in the room, moving from group to group to present a physical presence that will help deter such behavior.
- ☑ In group work, one or two students may become the leaders and rush ahead to accomplish the tasks. Other members, who cannot keep up, then give up. Quicker members complain that they are doing all the work.
  - This serious flaw in the cooperative learning model can be remedied by assigning each student a specific task for which he or she is responsible. Also, provide clear evaluation rubrics that inform each member of how the final grade will be compiled.
- ☑ Sometimes the dynamic of the group simply is not working because of serious personality conflicts. This situation can inhibit the goals and work of the team.
  - Intervene immediately when disruptions occur because of personality conflicts. Try to resolve them through standard conflict management techniques (e.g., talk out the problem, and try to sway perspective). If this approach does not work, consider rearranging the team members.

COOPERATIVE LEARNING TEAM STRUCTURE

Team member	Duties
Recorder	Keeps records of the team's progress; keeps notes for the presentation
Reader	Reads directions and notices pertinent to the task
Manager or timer	Keeps the team on task and on schedule
Ambassador	Communicates with other teams and the teacher or other resource people such as the librarian
Researcher	Is responsible for acquiring information in addition to what the team has already found

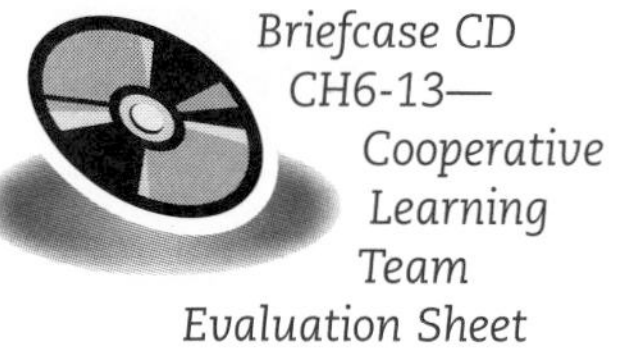

Briefcase CD CH6-13—Cooperative Learning Team Evaluation Sheet

☑ When in a cooperative group, students may strike bargains to share each other's work on a scale that leaves some members doing little.

- To prevent this situation, (a) provide a clear set of expectations for each group member (e.g., speaker, reporter, researcher) and (b) provide a rubric and an evaluation form that reveals grading levels.

What Are Some Possible Cooperative Learning Projects? There is no end to the use of cooperative learning groups in the classroom. Cooperative learning is conducive to all subject areas at all levels from K through 12. Following is an assortment of possible lessons for the cooperative learning mode:

History
Create a time line for a specific era in U.S. or world history. Each group is assigned a time period.

Reading
Use the concept of **Readers' Theater** or **Literature Circles.** Each team can read a book or story, following the Jigsaw method or the Carousel Feedback model. Each group then reports on its story or book.

Math
Have each group create a graph with an x and y axis to simulate a portion of a street map. Different groups may be assigned different cities. Museums, hotels, and restaurants can be plotted by using x and y indicators on the graph.

Biology
For a middle school or an intermediate lesson, students investigate the systems that function in the human body. Each group examines a system or a part of the system, with each member assigned a body organ.

VOICES IN THE CLASSROOM
Using Cooperative Learning

We were studying agriculture in my fifth-grade class. I had set up cooperative learning groups to explore all aspects of agricultural America. The culminating project was for the students to construct a physical representation of the concept of *agriculture*. Naturally, most of these representations were farms.

On the day of the presentations, I stood before five perfect projects, one as flashy and shiny as the other. In one particular project, at least 20 farm animals were made out of plaster, not plastic. I picked up the pig, and on the bottom was a price tag: $5.95. I calculated that those animals had cost almost $100. In fact, the entire farm was built with expensive wood, stained and varnished.

One of the students confessed that Jennifer's father had "helped" with most of the project, and he bought the animals. I was awestruck and speechless. How would I ever be able to grade this project—or the others for that matter?

Each of the projects demonstrated time, energy, creativity, and applicability to the theme. They all received a 100, but Jennifer thought theirs was worth more because it was obviously the best. I learned a valuable lesson that day about parental involvement and the wisdom of establishing a detailed rubric to be given to the students at the outset.

—*A wiser teacher*

COOPERATIVE LEARNING TEAM EVALUATION SHEET

Team Evaluation
(Complete this form individually.)

Members of your team: ______________________ ______________________
______________________ ______________________

Dates and times your team met: ______________________ ______________________

Names of your members who were absent: ______________________ ______________________
____

List at least three tasks that were accomplished during your meetings:

1. ____
2. ____
3. ____

List any obstacles you encountered while working on your project:

____
____
____

Explain, in your own words, the extent of your contribution to the team's work.

____
____
____

Explain, in your own words, how well you think the team worked together and how it could improve.

____
____
____

What grade do you think you deserve for your work? ______________________

What grade do you think your team deserves? ______________________

Your name: ____

Concept Teaching

Briefcase CD CH6-14—Concept Teaching Procedure Checklist

Concept teaching is a variation on thematic units, except it provides a broader application of topics. Using any concept that relates to your topic, such as *roads* in social studies, or *change* in science, or *relationships* in language, or a *triangle* in math, you can construct meaning that will expand to a broader and more comprehensive application of the material.

Another word for *concept* is *category*. By looking for ways to categorize topics in your lesson, students can begin to make connections that form a comprehensive "picture," which will increase the probability that they will be able to grasp the material you have taught.

Concept teaching does the following:

- ☑ It supports building relationships among categories and topics, which makes them easier to understand (Rosch, Mervis, Gray, Johnson, & Boyes-Baren, 1976). An example might be the triangle: In math it has three sides and a variety of uses; in social studies, the three branches of government form a triangle of balanced power. Examining all aspects of the direct and relational meanings of the concept helps take students to levels of thinking outside their normal scripts and opens opportunities for new concepts to be formed (Taba, 1967).

- ☑ It stimulates critical thinking as students begin to think in terms of definitions and applications. They may see not only what characterizes an idea, but also what characteristics are *not* present in its function. An example might be studying the concept of climatic aberrations in hurricanes or tornadoes, but also looking at damage caused by the same dynamics *not* classified as a hurricane or tornado.
- ☑ Concepts are generally assigned two attributes: critical and noncritical. *Critical* attributes define the concept and clearly separate it from other concepts. An example might be the attributes of a car—motion, fuel, speed, braking, and steering; they are necessary for a car to function. A *noncritical* attribute would be speed from 0 to 60, air-conditioning, or CD players. These attributes are not found in all cars and therefore affect the meaning of *car.*
- ☑ Teaching in concepts requires the use of **concept mapping.** Helping students brainstorm the many concepts composing the topics you teach is facilitated by the use of the concept map. The concept map is the same technique used in process writing that is known as *clustering* or *webbing.* Students make relational connections by using a graphic organizer. (*Note:* The Inspiration software program is an excellent tool for creating concept maps.)

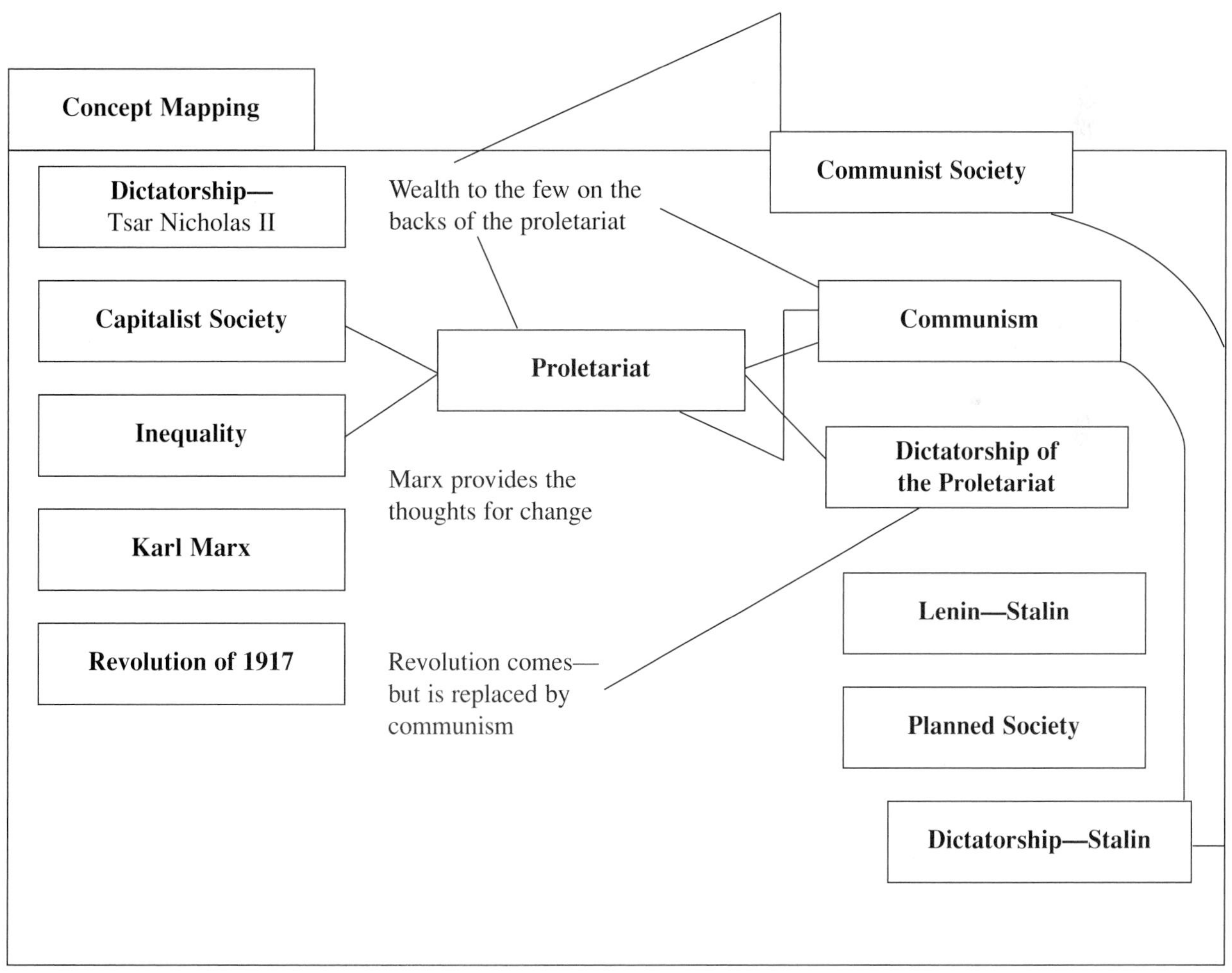

What Makes Concept Teaching Successful and Effective? The main reason concept teaching is effective is the wide spectrum of topics it provides, which enables students to see relationships among familiar ideas and apply them in novel ways.

Concept teaching promotes discussion and generates student-initiated learning. It is unquestionably a powerful method for stimulating higher order thinking about important concepts related to your curriculum.

The effectiveness of concept teaching is seen almost immediately as students grapple with their own definitions of such concepts as *liberty, probability, change, inertia* (scientific and social), *entropy, responsibility, sharing,* and *community.* These are just a few random concepts whose introduction will stimulate student discussion and help generate an understanding of more than a single perspective.

When Should I Use Concept Teaching? Concept teaching may be used from K through 12 (and beyond), in all subject areas. Every subject taught in school or curriculum (overt and hidden), is in some way associated with a single concept or group of concepts. Concept teaching is no more or less effective in math than in social studies, in foreign language or in art, in music or in health. Each of these subjects can be identified with a host of concepts that underpin their definition and function.

A most appropriate use of concept teaching is when you are using thematic units. Each theme may be explored for the concept or concepts that underlie the essence of the theme. For example, a fourth-grade class exploring the theme of *erosion* in science or social studies (or both) may also deal with the concept of *farming* and the differences between northeastern farms and western farms. Students begin to discover that farming techniques are suffused with the concepts of *growth, climate conditions,* and *marketing.* Soon, the concept of *economy* is introduced as an underlying cause affecting various ecological concepts.

Concept teaching is generally not as effective when you are attempting to teach a specific skill, such as factoring a polynomial. It focuses on ideas, not skills.

What Are the Disadvantages of Using Concept Teaching? Concept teaching has a few disadvantages beyond the most obvious. Because the concept lesson is carefully prepared in advance and is aligned with district and state standards, only teacher facilitation will adversely affect its effectiveness. Consider these potential problems:

- ☑ The single most obvious disadvantage of using concept teaching is the possibility that students who process information more slowly than others will become confused and eventually bored.
  - Use of a graphic organizer or a concept map will help decrease this problem. Students who can see the visual growth of the relational pieces of the concept will be more likely to participate.
- ☑ Because concept teaching focuses on ideas, not skills, it will not be effective for teaching a specific skill.
  - Use the concepts surrounding the teaching of the skill to help students grasp a broader view of the process. For example, the concept of *cause and effect* is pervasive throughout most subject areas.

What Are Some Possible Concept Teaching Lessons? Possibilities are endless when you are using concepts. Following are some of the concepts teachers have used effectively:

- ☑ Choose a historical character (e.g., George Washington; Martin Luther King, Jr.; or Susan B. Anthony) and create a concept map of his or her life. Then, identify one concept that can be further brainstormed, categorized, sorted, and prepared for research.
- ☑ The topic *cellular structure* can provide an excellent interdisciplinary lesson between science and social studies. Students brainstorm the word *cell* and find relational terms that support the definition. Through discussion, and possibly essays, students configure the functions of cells in a variety of venues.

- ☑ For a novel or short story, create a storyline map that focuses on the main theme of the work. Identify the key concepts that underlie the action or plot, and encourage students to find relational concepts that affect character motive.
- ☑ In the primary grades, for math, teaching students grouping of hundreds can be approached from both concrete and then abstract (or application-level) concepts. Students begin with concrete items such as stones or chips and then move to dollars and cents.

DOS AND DON'TS

Don't	Do
Begin the year with a lengthy lecture on the kind of teacher you are	Begin the year by becoming familiar with your students and allowing them to question you about your expectations
Create unreasonable rules for the class that immediately create obstacles between you and some of the class members.	Begin the year with clear, concise, and few rules that reflect the needs of the child as well as the need for order
Label your students by intelligence level	Avoid assigning stereotypes on the basis of a student's past record in either academics or behavior
Assume that all students hear, see, and process information equally	Allow for the many ways students learn, and accommodate their learning styles
Present your material too quickly or in large segments	Pace instruction to allow for reflection and downtime to process information
Assign homework that has no connection to the lesson or unit plan	Correct and remark on all homework assignments (a student's value for homework is closely associated with your value of it)
Use cooperative learning for any other reason than promoting the goals of the lesson	Use cooperative learning to promote comprehension of the material and greater engagement in the learning process
Settle on one teaching strategy for every topic or lesson	Vary your teaching techniques in accordance with the needs of your students, the topic being taught, and the environment in which you teach

WEB SITES OF INTEREST

http://www.humboldt.edu/~tha1/hunter-eei.html
This Web site provides a clear and functional example of the components of a direct instruction lesson.

http://www.adihome.org
This Association for Direct Instruction site provides clear and comprehensive information about the foundations of direct instruction and is a great resource for materials.

http://www.adihome.org/phpshop/faq/faq.php?username=
This link, on the official site for the Association for Direct Instruction, provides a host of answers to typical questions about direct instruction.

http://www.teach-nology.com/teachers/methods/models/direct
This site provides clear definitions of direct instruction as well as links to various other instructional resources.

http://www.teach-nology.com/currenttrends/cooperative_learning
This site provides links to sites that reflect a host of cooperative learning formats.

http://edtech.kennesaw.edu/intech/cooperativelearning.htm
A great in-depth resource for functional cooperative learning, this site provides clear, step-by-step procedures.

http://www.wilsonmar.com/1movies.htm#ReviewSites
This excellent site provides a complete list of movies that are appropriate for students in all grades. The movies are also categorized by ideology, movie types, themes, and reviews.

http://www.frsd.k12.nj.us/rfmslibrarylab/di/differentiated_instruction.htm
This site is a springboard to a large number of sites on differentiated instruction, including brain-based, cooperative, and inquiry-based learning, as well as on constructivism and performance assessment.

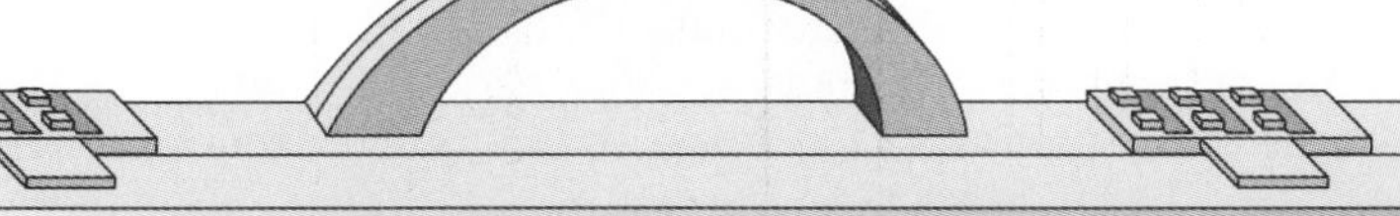

For Your Briefcase

To Do

- Review your curriculum to determine which type of instruction you will use (e.g., direct, indirect, project).
- Align your curriculum with a variety of teaching techniques.
- Gather materials for each unit.
- Create a time line for your instructional units.

Resources on Your Briefcase CD

Samples

- Sample Document-Based Question Lesson
- Sample Problem-Based Lesson

Templates

- Direct Instruction Procedure Checklist
- Lesson Plan Template for the Universal Model
- Lesson Plan Template for the Hunter Model
- Hunter Model Lesson Plan Checklist
- Socratic Method Procedure Checklist
- Discovery Learning Procedure Checklist
- Project-Based or Problem-Based Learning Procedure Checklist
- Cooperative Learning Procedure Checklist
- Cooperative Learning Team Evaluation Sheet
- Concept Teaching Procedure Checklist

Tables

- Types of Cooperative Learning
- Carousel Feedback Technique

REFERENCES

Adams, G. L., & Englemann, S. (1996). *Research on direct instruction: 25 years beyond DISTAR.* Seattle, WA: Educational Achievement Systems.

Arnold, D. H., & Doctoroff, G. L. (2003). The early education of socioeconomically disadvantaged children. *Annual Review of Psychology, 54,* 517–545.

Aspy, D. N., Aspy, C. B., & Quimby, P. M. (1993, March). What doctors can teach teachers about problem-based learning. *Educational Leadership, 50*(7), 22–24.

Borman, G. D., Hewes, G. M., Overman, L. T., & Brown, S. (2002, November). *Comprehensive school reform and student achievement: A meta-analysis.* Baltimore: Johns Hopkins University, CRESPAR.

Box, J. A., & Little, D. C. (2003, December). Cooperative *small*-group instruction combined with advanced organizers and their relationship to self-concept and social studies achievement of elementary school students. *Journal of Instructional Psychology, 30*(4), 285.

Bruner, J. (1983). Education as social invention. *Journal of Social Issues, 39,* 129–141.

Center for Research on the Education of Students at Risk (CRESPAR). (2002). *Comprehensive school reform and student achievement: A meta-analysis.* Retrieved July 28, 2004, from http://www.csos.jhu.edu

Chess, S., & Thomas, A. (1977). Temperamental individuality from childhood to adolescence. *Journal of Child Psychiatry, 16,* 218–220.

Consolidated Appropriations Act, 2005, Pub. L. 108-447, § 111, 118 Stat. 2809 (December 8, 2004).

Cowley, R. (Ed.). (1999). *What if? The world's foremost military historians imagine what might have been.* New York: Putnam.

Darling-Hammond, L. (2000, January 1). Teacher quality and student achievement: A review of state policy evidence. *Education Policy Analysis Archives, 8,* 1.

Elkind, D., & Sweet, F. (1997, May 6). The Socratic approach to character education. *Educational Leadership, 54.*

Jones, I. (2003). Collaborative writing and children's use of literate language: A sequential analysis of social interaction. *Journal of Early Childhood Literacy, 3*(2), 165–178.

Kagan, S., & Kagan, L. (2000). *Cooperative learning course workbook.* San Clemente, CA: Kagan.

Meyer, L. A. (1984). Long-term academic effects of the direct instruction Project Follow-Through model. *Elementary School Journal, 84*(4), 380–394.

Rodriguez, I., & Bethel, L. J. (1983, April). An inquiry approach to science and language teaching. *Journal of Research in Science Teaching, 20*(4), 291–296.

Rosch, E., Mervis, C. B., Gray, W. D., Johnson, D. M., & Boyes-Barem, P. (1976). Basic objects in natural categories. *Cognitive Psychology, 8,* 382–439.

Slavin, R. E. (1995). *Cooperative learning: Theory, research, and practice* (2nd ed.). Boston: Allyn & Bacon.

Taba, H. (1967). *Curriculum development: Theory and practice.* New York: Harcourt Brace & World.

Watkins, C. L. (1988). Project Follow Through: A story of the identification and neglect of effective instruction. *Youth Policy, 10*(7), 7–11.

Chapter 7

Getting Down to the Nuts and Bolts of Teaching: Instructional Activities

You cannot teach a man anything; you can only help him find it within himself.

—*Galileo*

SUCCEEDING AT TEACHING

The *act* of teaching—working day to day with students and applying the teaching methods—is the subject of this chapter. Many teaching techniques can be used for any subject, whereas others work best for just math, or social studies, or music. As most veteran teachers will tell you, grand schemes and dynamic creative lessons do not generate learning and teaching success; rather, the everyday contact, momentary decisions, and student-by-student interactions form the basis of successful teaching.

Teachers across the United States use endless types of instructional techniques. However, following is an overview of the fundamental teaching activities that help make a classroom dynamic:

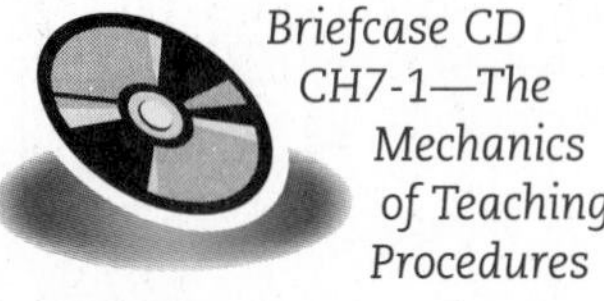

Briefcase CD CH7-1—The Mechanics of Teaching Procedures

- ☑ ***Pacing:*** Gearing the pace of your instruction to the appropriate age, developmental level, and interests of your students
- ☑ ***Sponge activities:*** Using introductory and concluding activities to provide solid transitions between lessons and classes
- ☑ ***Technology:*** Using the ever-increasing selection of electronic tools that generate organization or presentation and connections to the modern world of our students
- ☑ ***Diverse instruction:*** Teaching in a variety of modes (e.g., lecture, cooperative learning, discussion, and problem-based and project-based instruction).
- ☑ ***Learning modalities:*** Being attentive to the various ways in which children learn, such as the following:
  - Multiple Intelligences
  - Learning Styles
  - Brain-Based Learning

Pacing

One key element of teaching, regardless of strategy, is the **pacing** of the instruction. Instruction that is too fast paced can preclude the brain processing necessary for student comprehension. However, teachers are constantly under pressure to "cover the curriculum" or teach what will be tested. For this reason, knowing how to deliver instruction in a timely fashion is essential.

Effective teachers can "read" their students' participation level and know when they are moving too fast or when the class is becoming bored. These teachers know when to call a halt and divert to a physical activity. More than any specific strategy, knowledge of when to move forward and when to slow or stop must be acquired quickly, in your first months of teaching. No one can teach you how to do this; you have to learn to be aware of the cues each group of students gives you when the pace of the class is out of rhythm.

For the elementary classroom, simply moving on to another subject, adjourning to the reading corner, or reverting to work on projects may suffice. However, for the middle school or high school teacher, a time span must usually be filled. If student cues are telling you that the class is becoming disengaged, you must move to a new rhythm. Experienced teachers know that student attention will wane near the end of the period; therefore, they arrange for the lesson to complete 10 or 12 minutes early and end the period with a sponge activity. This change of pace keeps students engaged.

Student Cues A teacher is informed about his or her pacing by student cues. Ignoring these indicators can lead to student apathy or class disruption. As a classroom manager and instructor, consider the following cues relating to slow- or fast-paced teaching:

- ***Cues to slow-paced instruction:***
  - A rising noise level
  - An increase in the number of lavatory pass requests

- Increased body movement by more than one third of the class
- Dozing among four or more students
- Daydreaming among four or more students
- Silliness among four or more students

- ***Cues to fast-paced instruction:***
  - An increase in the number of student questions on content or procedures
  - Restlessness when independent study begins
  - Complaints from three or more students about not being able to keep up
  - Total silence—no questions or comments

In Real Time: Class Interruptions

A teacher's pacing can be adversely affected by outside interruptions such as telephone calls, fire drills, and visitors at the door. Attempting to refocus the class by using threats and punitive measures only lengthens the interruption. Try using the questioning techniques outlined in Chapter 6 to refocus on the lesson.

Sponge Activities

Briefcase CD CH7-2—Sponge Activity Types and Categories

The **sponge activity,** as its name reveals, "sponges" up the transitional time between subjects or topics. The name is a misnomer, however, because a sponge activity can also be used two other ways: to engage the student immediately and launch the topic of the day, and to summarize or conclude a lesson at the end of class. The Internet provides numerous examples of these start-up and complete activities (see Web Sites of Interest at the end of this chapter). However, if you take only a few moments to reflect on your lessons, you should be able to create your own specific sponges. You might want to think in terms of sponge activity types (e.g., written responses, oral responses, dialogue, monologue, group responses) and categories (e.g., lists for written responses, thinking challenges for group responses).

SPONGE ACTIVITY TYPES AND CATEGORIES

Type	Category
Written responses	Lists (e.g., types, styles, names, sizes, colors)
Oral responses (individual)	Facts (e.g., statistical, historical)
Oral responses (group, dyads)	Thinking challenges (e.g., unscrambling, finding, encoding, decoding)
Journal entries	Reflections on the lesson of the previous day or a key concept in the lesson for the current day
Dialogue	Discussion of a concept for the day
Drawing, painting	Depiction of a topic in the lesson of the day
Physical tasks	Arrangement of students in groups, or by alphabetization, age, height, telephone number, distance from school, etc.

Following are some specific sponge activities related to a variety of topics:

Social Studies

1. Write the word *liberty* on the board.
2. Have students write a paragraph on what liberty means to them.
3. Share and discuss their responses.

Language Arts and Foreign Languages

1. Write a sentence on the board that has glaring errors that alter its meaning: "The box of apples have holes in them big enough to fit earthworms."
2. Have students, alone or in groups of two, work out the errors and correct them.

Math

1. Write a problem on the board that goes beyond what students have already learned.
2. Give them time to arrive at an answer. Ask two or three students to work it out on the board.
3. Explain how it is done.

Science

Write a question on the board and ask students to answer it in their journals (e.g., "Why do some animals change colors?").

Music

Play short excerpts from various musical numbers (from classical through rock and roll) and ask your students to identify the time periods of these numbers.

Briefcase CD CH7-3— Sample WebQuest

SAMPLE WEBQUEST

Grade 6

Topic U.S. National Parks

Questions

1. How many U.S. national parks exist?
2. Where are they located?
3. What is unique about each?
4. What travel routes would we take to visit each of them?
5. What activities are available for tourists at the parks?
6. What restrictions does each park have?
7. What are some of the problems at each park?

Assignment

- ☑ Plan a journey to one of the parks. Create a complete travel package for three people. You are responsible for all details, including food, money, mileage, transportation, recreation, housing, and so forth.
- ☑ Check the price for flying on each of at least three airlines, and choose the most costly and the least costly.
- ☑ Design and present a travel brochure on your chosen park. Include a brief history of the park, activities, and facts.
- ☑ Acquire information from the park such as catalogs, brochures, and maps. (Include your letter to the park service in your packet.)
- ☑ Write a paper on the park, describing how and why it became a national park. Include the reasons for park conservation by the federal government, the names of key people who helped designate the park as national, and the cost to the government for maintaining the park.

Web Tracks For each step of this assignment, list the URL of each Web site you visit. Be sure to include links to these sites in each section of the assignment that you complete.

Note: Reprinted with permission from Jill Eagan, Broadway Middle School, Elmira, NY.

Technology

Technology—specifically computers and the Internet—is a curricular tool you can use to gain access to a rich variety of information that will quickly facilitate student engagement and learning. Probably one of the best examples of the use of technology in education is a **WebQuest.** During a WebQuest, students use Internet search engines to find a wide range of information on a given topic. Similar to concept teaching, a WebQuest begins with a brainstorming session on a given topic or concept. However, each connection to the main concept is framed in a question that sends the student on a "quest" to discover as much information as possible on the topic. Often, the WebQuest is done as a cooperative learning project in which students assign themselves specific topics to investigate. (See Web Sites of Interest at the end of this chapter for a link to the excellent Spartanburg County School District, Glendale, SC, WebQuest.)

Briefcase CD CH7-4—WebQuest Procedure Checklist

Another outcome of the WebQuest is that students often make connections on the Internet with other groups involved in quests. Sometimes students engage in separate activities to maintain communication with their acquaintances.

Diverse Instruction

Briefcase CD CH7-5—Instructional Methods

Although eventually your students will be able to identify you with a particular teaching style, you will probably not adopt a single method of instruction (e.g., lecture) and use it exclusively for the entire curriculum. Strategically designing a variety of instructional methods—**diverse instruction**—helps produce successful teaching.

Encourage student creativity.
Reprinted with permission from Mrs. Jana M. Wilcox Laufer on behalf of her daughter Farrah Laufer.

INSTRUCTIONAL METHODS

Method (when used)	Description	Purpose
Lecture (only as needed—for short periods)	Presenting material in an organized and coherent manner with or without visual aids	To introduce a new topic; to lay foundational knowledge; to explain concepts or systems *Examples:* What is the food chain? What is mercantilism? What are congruent angles?

—Cont.

INSTRUCTIONAL METHODS

Method (when used)	Description	Purpose
Discussion (in almost every lesson and almost every day)	Calling on students, using probing, focusing, and expanding questions	To follow up on a lecture; to assess student comprehension, attention level, and engagement; to precede a project or inquiry learning; to explore a concept or topic *Examples:* What other systems resemble a food chain? Do we engage in mercantilism today? What other geometric figures can be congruent?
Demonstration (as needed according to the nature of the topic and in place of a lecture if possible)	Using materials or visual aids to model a procedure that students can then duplicate	To provide a visual explanation of a system or concept; to provide a model for students to follow *Examples:* How does heat affect water molecules? How do you arrive at the value of pi? How did 18th-century legislators dress?
Grouping (four or more) (as needed according to the nature of the topic and at least once per unit)	Randomly selecting students to participate in groups to focus on a topic or problem	To engage students in project or inquiry work; to help students become involved in the process; to generate work on a large interdisciplinary project *Examples:* Exploring character motives in a novel; planning to follow the Oregon Trail in 1848; solving math problems relating to building construction
Grouping (dyads) (as needed according to the nature of the topic and frequently within a unit)	Grouping two students to work together on a problem or topic	To problem solve or to explore a topic in the short term *Examples:* Performing an experiment for which one student records the steps and observations; writing a piece of music with lyrics; creating lists and categories related to consumerism
Grouping (fishbowl) (as needed according to the nature of the topic and at least once per unit)	Having one group of students discuss or present material while the remainder of the class observes and comments	To help students work on issues or solve difficult problems (students outside the fishbowl observe and comment) *Examples:* How could Native Americans have been treated more fairly? Analyze the characters of Boxer and Squealer according to motive.
Role-playing (as needed according to the nature of the topic)	Having students assume a character role to demonstrate scope and depth	To engage students and help them with perspective *Examples:* Portray Patrick Henry as he gives his famous speech. Portray Anne Frank as a modern historian of World War II. Portray a CEO defending the rights of his or her business to manufacture without expensive antipollution devices.

—*Cont.*

Method (when used)	Description	Purpose
Think, pair, share (as needed according to the nature of the topic)	Having students work on a problem individually, then work with another student, then share their findings with the class	To problem solve or examine a concept, a topic, or an idea *Examples:* How much time and money would it take to walk from New York City to Los Angeles? What do illegal immigrants do for and against the overall health of our country?
Peer tutoring and assessment (as needed according to the nature of the topic)	Having students who understand the material work with those who are struggling	To aid in any lesson involving skill or concept acquisition

Note. See the Briefcase CD accompanying this text for the following instructional examples:

Briefcase CD CH7-6—Lesson Tips for a Civil War Unit (Grade 8)

- Lesson Tips for a Civil War Unit (Grade 8)

Briefcase CD CH7-7—Newspaper Project for Social Studies (Variable Grades)

- Newspaper Project for Social Studies (Variable Grades)

Briefcase CD CH7-8—Pictograph Lesson (Variable Grades)

- Pictograph Lesson (Variable Grades)

Briefcase CD CH7-9—Rubric for Pictograph Lesson (Variable Grades)

- Rubric for Pictograph Lesson (Variable Grades)

Briefcase CD CH7-10—Unit Exam in Social Studies (Grade 8)

- Unit Exam in Social Studies (Grade 8)

Briefcase CD CH7-11—Instructional Schemata with Examples

All the various instructional methods may be fitted to your particular students' grade level, the subject area, and the school environment. Each can be modified through the use of schemata that will help shape the direction of your instruction and guide your students' learning.

INSTRUCTIONAL SCHEMATA WITH EXAMPLES

Schema	Description	Example
Inquiry	Present the class with a problem that has many answers and can be viewed from different perspectives.	If you have two different groups of numbers, how can they have the same mean (average)?
The big question	Encourage class members to contribute their views on a topic by asking probing and expanding questions.	Why do hurricanes always lose speed once they hit land, and what gives them their speed and ferocity?
Concept mapping	Using whiteboards, posters, or computers, have students web relational ideas centered on a specific topic or concept.	Central concept: Treaties. Possible relational ideas that students might find: Relationships—negotiations—bargaining—voting—trade—currency.
Cloze	Provide a summary or key paragraph relating to the material you are presenting, but with words or phrases missing. Students may fill in the spaces according to their perspectives. Correct and incorrect answers are relative to the student's perspective; therefore, this exercise is not a test.	"Still the Americans had certain _______. They had every reason to _____because they were defending their own ____, ____, and ____. Reuben Stebbings was ____ of many soldiers" (Davidson & Stoff, 1998). Students may have varied answers.
Estimation	Ask your students to make a guess or an approximation from information given.	Can you predict what will happen to the balance of nature during a drought? Which animals and plants are more affected? How do you think it will affect people living 1,000 miles away?
Abstraction	Help your students construct a model that exemplifies a concept you are teaching.	Create a constitution for a new club you are organizing whose purpose is to improve the ecological environment of your city. The club must raise its own funds and develop an action plan to achieve its goals.
Generalizing	Provide situations in which your students can generalize material being taught to a different audience or venue.	Using the formulas for finding the area of a circle, square, and rectangle, conduct a physical measurement of large areas in the city that are in those three shapes.
Discrimination	Provide categories within the concept you are teaching that allow your students to discriminate particular attributes.	When measuring this room, find two ways to describe the length and width.
Discrepant facts	Provide your class with a list of discrepant facts—facts that are seemingly false or unbelievable.	If the earth is spinning at 1,100 miles per hour, why is my hair still in place? How many men actually signed the Declaration of Independence on July 4?

TEACHING THE MULTIABILITY CLASS

Although ability grouping and tracking are still prevalent in most schools, a movement toward the heterogeneous classroom is gaining momentum (Hayward, Brandes, Kirst, & Mazzeo, 1997). However, even in schools in which students are stringently tracked by their ability levels, large numbers of students classed as middle level have abilities that vary beyond the parameters of their ability group. Thus, every teacher must be prepared to deliver lessons that account for this ability range. The effective teacher uses a few standard measures to help deliver comprehensive instruction to students with a wide range of abilities. These measures include using **graphic organizers** and taking into account the students' **learning modalities.**

Examples of Graphic Organizers

Venn Diagram In a **Venn diagram,** you write concepts, ideas, names, facts, and dates inside circles that overlap, providing students with an immediate visual picture of the material in your lesson.

Briefcase CD CH7-12—Examples of Graphic Organizers

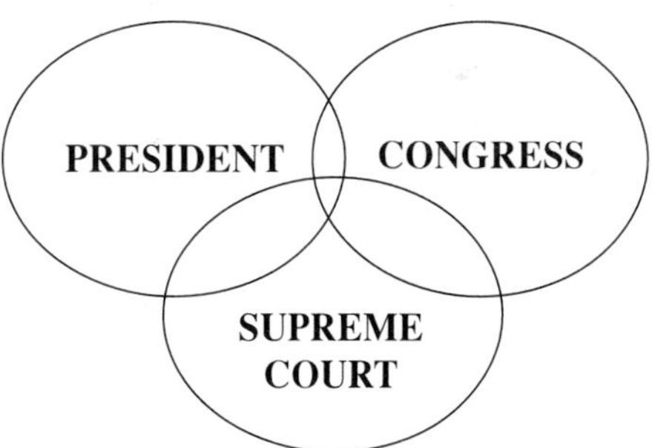

K-W-L In **K-W-L** (*K*now, *W*ant to know, *L*earned), you focus students' attention on the topic by having them review what they already know, where they want to go with the topic, and what they learn as the lesson unfolds. Usually, this organizer is presented in a tabular format.

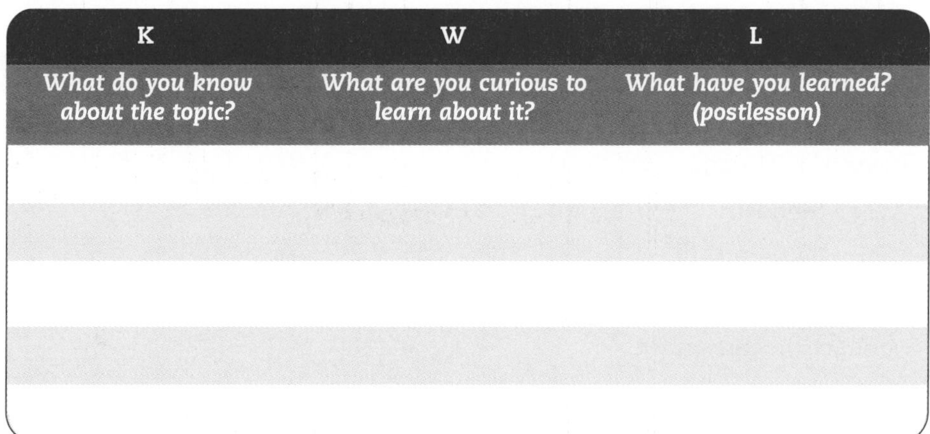

K	W	L
What do you know about the topic?	*What are you curious to learn about it?*	*What have you learned? (postlesson)*

Webbing **Webbing** is similar to concept mapping in that they are both brainstorming techniques in which a graphic is used to record students' responses. One format is to use a large oval in the middle with the main concept listed inside, then write subtopics in smaller ovals around the large oval.

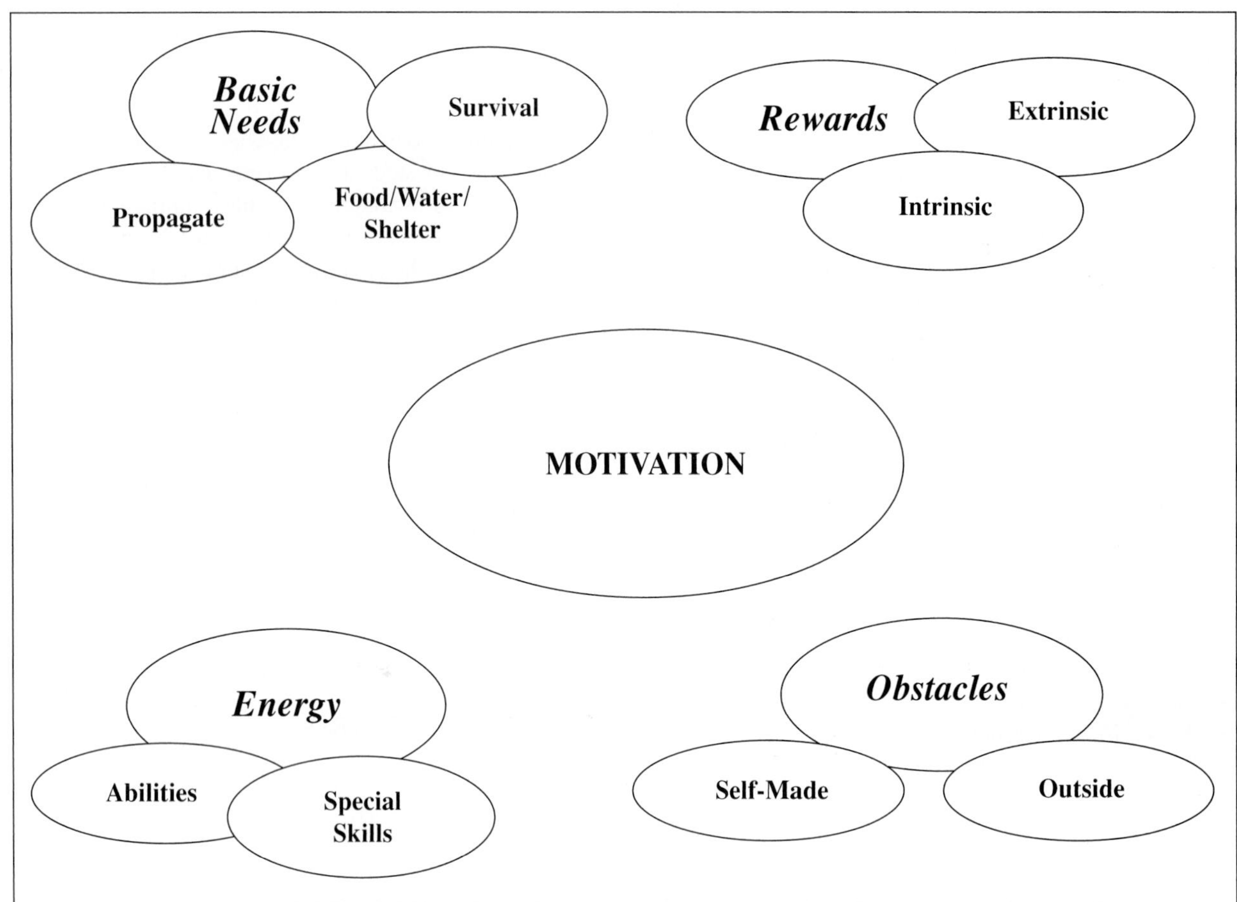

Compare–Compare Grid An excellent visual aid for presenting a quick overview of the facts relating to a topic, the **compare–compare grid** is also useful as a K-W-L tool.

Trait	New York City	London, England
Population		
Geographic location		
When founded		
Type of government		
Major religion		
Products manufactured		
Languages spoken		

Storyboard A **storyboard** is used to help students review what was read, in a structured order that allows them to present their interpretation and understanding of the material. A storyboard may be drawn in any number of graphic forms.

Title: ______________________________

Author: ______________________________

Character 1: (description) ______________________________

Character 2: (description) ______________________________

Setting: ______________________________

Conflict: ______________________________

____

____

Events in the Story:

____

____

____

____

____

Resolution:

____

____

Title: *Animal Farm*

Author: George Orwell

Character 1: *Snowball:* The wisest of the pigs, who had most of the ideas. He gave the pigs direction and vision as to what should happen when Jones was first overthrown.
Character 2: *Napoleon:* The shrewdest of the pigs, who wanted to have all the power himself and knew that violence was the way to get it.
Character 3: *Boxer:* He is representative of all the animals who work hard, are loyal to the original ideas set forth by Old Major, and trust the pigs because of their brain power.

Setting: Although set in England, it could be anywhere.

Conflict: The animals are first set against Jones, who is a tyrant. Later, the main conflict is between the animals and the pigs. However, skirmishes with neighboring farms and struggles among themselves add further conflicts. Man versus Man.

Events in the Story:

1. Animals overthrow Jones.
2. Animals empower pigs to run the farm, with Napoleon and Snowball as leaders.
3. The Seven Commandments are written and published.
4. Snowball is expelled.
5. Animals begin construction of a giant windmill.
6. Commandments continually undergo changes but become fewer each time.
7. Some animals are executed.
8. The farm is invaded by Frederick.
9. The windmill is destroyed.
10. The pigs retain and increase their control and power.
11. The pigs return the name of the farm to its original name: Manor Farm.

Resolution: The conflict between the pigs and the animals is not resolved. Boxer's death only stirs the animals to more remorse and depression as they resolve themselves to their fate.

Briefcase CD CH7-13—Ideas for Multiple Intelligences

Briefcase CD CH7-14—Sample Multiple Intelligence Lesson

Learning Modalities

Multiple Intelligences-Refer Howard Gardner's (1983) theory of **multiple intelligences** contends that a person does not possess a single quantitatively known entity called *intelligence* but has a range of intelligences reflecting his or her abilities. Many schools have adopted his methodology of presenting lessons through these intelligences, which thus gives each child a chance to excel across a spectrum of skills. By capitalizing on a child's strengths in learning, the effective teacher can help that child realize his or her potential.

IDEAS FOR MULTIPLE INTELLIGENCES

Intelligence	Idea
Verbal–linguistic	Read material on the topic.
Logical–mathematical	Create Venn diagrams or cluster maps, or do cubing.
Visual–spatial	Create dioramas, posters, mobiles, drawings, or paintings, or work with clay.
Bodily–kinesthetic	Role-play, or act out skits or scenes on the topic.
Musical	Listen to period music relating to the topic; compose music.
Interpersonal	Work in groups; interview others.
Intrapersonal	Do journal writing, compile personal reflections, or create artistic expressions.
Naturalist	Discuss environmental factors or geography.

SAMPLE MULTIPLE INTELLIGENCE LESSON

Topic: Zimbabwe	
Verbal–linguistic	Find historical information on Zimbabwe and present it to the class. Write a report of your findings.
Logical–mathematical	Collect vital statistics on Zimbabwe and write a report, giving details about the population, agriculture, and markets.
Visual–spatial	Create a tactile map of Zimbabwe and the continent of Africa.
Bodily–kinesthetic	Role-play an interview with Nelson Mandela or other African leaders about the future of their country.
Musical	Listen to African music. Discuss the differences between it and American folk music.
Interpersonal	Locate a recent immigrant from Africa and interview him or her for a report to the class, or interview a person who is an expert on African affairs.
Intrapersonal	Write a personal reflection on the struggles of African nations in the modern world.
Naturalist	Write a report or give an oral report on the environment of Zimbabwe and how it influences the work of the people and their lifestyle.

Briefcase CD CH7-15—Learning Styles Defined

Learning Styles Separate, but not mutually exclusive, from the multiple intelligences theory is the notion that each child has a different mode of learning and therefore processes information accordingly (Taylor, 1997). The three general learning styles are as follows:

1. ***Auditory:*** Students with an auditory learning style learn best through oral communication—by hearing instructions and listening to material being read or discussed.
2. ***Visual:*** Students with a visual learning style learn best when presented material graphically—through pictures, forms, and multimedia.
3. ***Kinesthetic:*** Students with a kinesthetic learning style learn best through hands-on activities and when allowed to move physically in project and group work.

Other learning style factors are the following:

- Room temperature and outdoor temperature
- Solitary or group work
- Noise levels
- Eating patterns
- Sleep patterns

Briefcase CD CH7-16—Gregoric's Cognition Model

Cognitive Factors Affecting Learning How a child processes information is also considered a major learning style of which teachers should be aware. According to Anthony Gregoric's highly accepted theory on cognitive processing, a student processes information through two of four basic ways: concrete (according to the five senses), sequential (step by step), abstract (intuitively), random (holistically). Any given student will approach learning as one of the following types of thinkers:

- ***Concrete–sequential thinker:*** Is practical and approaches learning in a step-by-step fashion
- ***Abstract–random thinker:*** Looks for the rationale behind what is being taught in a global sense
- ***Concrete–random thinker:*** Seeks the bottom line
- ***Abstract–sequential thinker:*** Wants to know the *why* of a topic in specific terms

According to **Gregoric's cognition model,** successful teachers design their lessons with the various types of student cognitive processing in mind.

LEARNING STYLES DEFINED

Auditory	Visual	Kinesthetic
Is eager to discuss or debate ideas and concepts	Needs material presented in graphs, charts, maps, and pictures	Needs to move around the room
Enjoys speaking and giving presentations	Needs to have a clear view of the teacher's body language and facial expressions	Responds to manipulatives and other hands-on activities
Responds to musical cues to aid in learning	May want to illustrate personal understanding of stories or the material presented	Can focus while moving, such as exercising
Is verbal throughout the learning process	Will respond to the use of computers and other multimedia equipment	Likes an overview of material before focusing on specifics

Gregoric's Cognition Model

Concrete	Sequential	Abstract	Random
Thinks in terms of the five senses—tends to live in the moment	Follows a logical, step-by-step pattern when solving problems	Thinks through ideas and tends to use intuition over direction	Solves problems by looking at all information holistically or in "chunks"

Abstract–Sequential

Student	*Teacher*
Will seek the *why* of the topic and look at the many ways it influences other events or ideas	Should structure lessons to contain full explanations and background information, allowing the student to provide input

Concrete–Sequential

Student	*Teacher*
Will probably function in a practical manner, taking each point of the lesson step by step	Should structure, number, and fully explain the instructions for the lesson

Abstract–Random

Student	*Teacher*
Will look for the rationale behind what is being taught	Should design specific instructions with an open-ended element that allows for the natural expansion of thought

Concrete–Random

Student	*Teacher*
Will attack the problem quickly, seeking the bottom line; will also want a solid solution or a clear picture to appear at the end of the lesson	Should design lessons to be open ended to allow for extended analysis, prediction, and exploration of creative ideas

Stating the Facts:

On how children integrate information:

"Students who learn information in one room and are tested in another room score lower than students who are taught and tested in the same room" (Sprenger, 1999, p. 84).

Brain-Based Instructional Techniques Research on the brain has revealed significant discoveries about how children integrate information and to what extent external forces affect their learning. For example, the brain processes 6 times more information than the visual or audio input it is receiving (Caine & Caine, 1994). Therefore, the child can become easily confused if his or her stored information is in conflict with what you are presenting or if his or her brain is processing

Briefcase CD CH7-17—Brain-Based Instructional Procedure and Suggestions

both stored and incoming information more slowly than you are transmitting it. The basic tenets of **brain-based learning** are as follows:

- ☑ The brain needs time to process information from short-term memory to long-term memory.
- ☑ The brain processes information more efficiently when interaction with others is involved.
- ☑ The brain responds to items it recognizes and can make connections to previously learned material.
- ☑ Emotion is an integral element of brain processing, and stress can negatively affect the learning process.

BRAIN-BASED INSTRUCTIONAL PROCEDURE AND SUGGESTIONS

Procedure	Suggestions
Presentation of material	Present your lessons in short chunks of information and with graphics when feasible.
Period of reflection	Allow a period for reflection and questioning following the presentation of new material.
Student interaction	Allow students to explore the material presented through student-to-student interaction such as discussion or problem solving.
Stress-free environment	As much as possible, work to maintain a harmonious and nonthreatening classroom environment.
Challenge	Provide your students with challenging tasks that require them to think beyond their current comprehension level.
Associations	Present lesson material with ample associations to other topics, even other subject areas.
Multiple instructional modes	Present material through a combination of lecture, discussion, group work, and multimedia instruction.

STATING THE FACTS:

- **On the brain and teenagers:** The frontal lobe of the brain, which controls planning and judgment, remains immature during the teen years. The prefrontal cortex, which is responsible for complex thinking, organization, working memory, and impulse control, is the largest section of the brain and the slowest to develop during adolescence (Caskey & Ruben, 2003).
- **On the brain and music education:** Researchers found that young children who received music instruction scored higher in spatial task ability than children who had not (Shaw et al., 1997). Additional research revealed that EEG scans of young children (aged 6–7 years) who were given music instruction registered more spatial efficiency (Flohr, Miller, & Persellin, 1996).

Howard Gardner's project work and his theory of multiple intelligences have informed teachers on more efficient ways to craft their instruction. When you associate Gardner's work with the ever-increasing knowledge on brain processing, you can see the importance of presenting your instructional material with these concepts in mind.

VOICES IN THE CLASSROOM
A Student-Centered Teacher

Mr. Randel was a social studies teacher who taught seventh and eighth graders. He believed in visuals in a big way. When you walked into his classroom, the first thing you noticed was chaos—a mess. It was chock full of equipment, rolls of paper, and boxes of materials. He had at least two overhead projectors as well as a permanent 16-mm film projector and two opaque projectors. In one corner, he had a ditto machine.

The walls were covered with white paper on which students had created huge posters reflecting lists, or drawings, or charts about what they were studying. Some of the paint and markers found their way off the paper onto the walls. The windows were segregated into rectangular panes, each of which contained a student's drawing or writings—in psychedelic colors. The room smelled of a mixture of markers, paint, and cleaning spirits.

The desks and chairs in his room were scattered all around as students either sat and worked or used them as makeshift tables on which to draw and color. Some students would cuddle on the floor near the sink, which was a designated area for study only. Often, some of his students would bleed out into the hall, where they would lay out longer pieces of paper for ever-bigger murals.

There was organization to this chaos, however. Each student had negotiated a contract to complete a study of some aspect of the curriculum. The painting and the posters were just one aspect of the job. Many of his students were in the library looking up information or at the typing room preparing it for submission.

All this occurred before anyone had ever heard of Howard Gardner and his eight intelligences. In some respects, Randel was ahead of his time, but to his colleagues and the administration, he was a major pain. His colleagues detested his teaching methods because the kids would come from his class to theirs still high from the freedom. Some students would chide other teachers to be more like Mr. Randel, who gave a kid a little respect. The administration hated the mess and the disorder and the lax application of rules. Not even all the kids were enamored of this style of teaching. Many students would try to get transferred out of his classes because they couldn't handle the disorder and wanted the traditional tell-me-what-to-do kind of teaching. As Randel was never given any honors students, he didn't have to contend with the aggressive upscale parent more interested in traditional instruction with high grades. No, Randel's kids were always the students who had low to middle ability and generally came from poorer homes where parents were difficult to find.

—*A former teacher*

LEGAL SIDEBAR

Academic Freedom

Part of being a successful teacher is being allowed the freedom to teach as you see fit. A federal court in Maine ruled that a teacher may proceed with his free-speech lawsuit claiming that he was directed to cease teaching non-Christian religions in his social studies class (National School Boards Association Legal Clips, 2005).

HANDLING INSTRUCTIONAL PROBLEMS

Successful teachers are able to navigate the many instructional problems that arise. Following are descriptions of some common problems and strategies for handling them.

The Unexpected

Each technique discussed in this chapter *may* be successful for you as a teacher. However, execution is crucial, and no matter how attractive the technique, without a thoughtful implementation of the material, a sharply prepared lesson can suddenly fall apart. You must be prepared for the unexpected and shift your mode of instruction accordingly when it happens. For example, consider the following scenarios:

- ***Student disruption:*** The class is generally listening, but two boys are giggling and throwing paper wads at each other.
- ***Student discomfort:*** A girl in the front row is openly listless and not interested. Her head is down on the desk, and she is completely disassociated from the lesson.
- ***Interruption—Door:*** A knock on the door interrupts your discussion, and the vice-principal or principal asks you to step into the hall for a short conference.
- ***Interruption—Telephone:*** The telephone rings during your introduction of new material or directions for a project.
- ***Student sick:*** A boy suddenly leaps up and vomits on the floor.
- ***Material shortage:*** The lesson begins, and you discover that you do not have enough texts, folders, markers, or other items.
- ***Outside event:*** On the day of one particular lesson, a tragedy involving one of the students who attends your school is obviously affecting your students.

Strategies for Handling the Unexpected Although unexpected events can be categorized and managed accordingly, in the real-life classroom, each is different because each student is different and each class is different. However, for the scenarios just indicated, the following strategies may be effective:

- ***Student disruption:*** Waste no time in defusing the situation by using your outlined discipline plan for the classroom (see Chapter 5). However, spend no more than 30 seconds on the matter so that it does not become a major distraction for the class.
- ***Student discomfort:*** Say nothing to the girl that would make her a focus of student attention (and possible derision). During the transition to the next activity, take her aside, speak with her privately, and consider referrals as per your management plan.
- ***Interruption—Door:*** Before stepping into the hall, ask your class to read or begin work on what you already gave them. Or, after listening to the message being given, ask if you might speak with the person after class. If you spend more than 5 minutes in the hall, on your return to class, change the mode of instruction.
- ***Interruption—Telephone:*** Take the message, but be brief and insist that you must return to your class. Make sure you pick up exactly where you left off, giving the interruption no time to develop into a withdrawal of the class's attention.
- ***Student sick:*** The lesson is blown for at least 15 minutes. Do what you would do for any sick person and then call the custodian immediately. Remove the class from the room to the hall and keep the students as quiet as you can until the area is cleaned. On return, change the mode of instruction.
- ***Material shortage:*** A material shortage can usually be avoided by ample preparation; however, it happens. Think in terms of pairing and sharing, and do not allow the lack of materials to prevent the lesson from going forward. Change instructional modes only if the material shortage is such that the lesson cannot be completed.
- ***Outside event:*** An outside event involves a situation that counselors and school officials usually address. In cases of death, students are generally allowed to seek counsel during the days immediately following the tragedy. Lessons should not be halted, but you should expect that this material will need to be revisited. You should also allow students to talk out their grief as appropriate.

Lack of Student Commitment or Understanding

When confronted with lack of student commitment or indications that the students are not "getting" the material, review both *what* you are teaching and *how* you are teaching it:

- ***Review the lesson plan:*** Are the objectives reasonable? Is the material too concentrated for them to understand? Can it be reduced in content or rearranged so that you can present it from a different perspective?

- ***Look at your instructional mode:*** Is the instructional mode you have chosen getting a response from the students? If it is a lecture, are they paying attention? If it is cooperative learning, are they disgruntled about the grouping, directions, or expected outcomes? Be prepared to change the mode on the spot. You can switch from lecture to discussion, or from cooperative learning to lecture instantly.
- ***Consider the class makeup:*** Do two or three students seem to be disrupting the class every day? Could they work on other material in another part of the room? Should you discipline them more frequently? Have you called the vice-principal or their parents? Does this class like to talk about the issues rather than write about them? Consider having them take more of a leadership role in the discussion.
- ***Incorporate the unusual:*** Sometimes infusing something unusual into the lesson sparks interest. Some teachers have students bake cookies in class, or institute a completely hands-on process with scissors, paste, markers, and so forth. Think in terms of stimulating their interest relative to the topic by asking them what they would like to do.
- ***Change the pace:*** If the students are not responding to your lesson, try slowing the pace by reducing the material into smaller pieces with more student involvement. Have movie clips available to restimulate their interest. Stop the lesson. Play a CD. Resume the lesson.

Frustration and Sense of Failure

Even the most effective teachers have days when nothing works. They also have classes or groups of students who refuse to respond to instruction, no matter how brilliantly planned and skillfully it is executed. Frustration is a by-product of teaching. The causes are numerous and elusive. Many factors influence students' learning and not only their overall comprehension level, but their daily lives in school.

You should remind yourself that you are teaching children—individuals—and not subjects or lessons. When teachers say they are "teaching a lesson" on economics or probability, what they really mean is that they are "providing instruction" to a group of children "about" a topic. These children are individuals who have different learning modalities and temperaments. Thus, inevitably, on any given day, one or more of them will be disgruntled, confused, unhappy, or uncooperative by virtue of their temperaments, their learning styles, or their home life.

DOS AND DON'TS

Don't	Do
Deliver your instruction in long sessions	Pace your instruction to the students' age, developmental level, and interests
Use a single instructional technique for all your lessons	Use a variety of techniques to explain the material to your students
Ignore obvious student cues about how you are teaching	Be alert to student cues so that you can modulate your instruction
Begin the lesson of the day by simply starting to tell your class what to do	Use sponge activities to bridge the previous lesson with the current lesson
Ignore your students' understanding and use of computer technology	Use the computer and its tools to enhance your instructional program
Teach all your material as if every child has the same comprehension level	Use graphic organizers and instructional techniques that serve children of all comprehension levels

—*Cont.*

Don't	Do
Teach all your material as if every child has a quantifiable intelligence level	Teach your material with the knowledge that all children and adults have a range of intelligence across a wide spectrum of skills
Ignore your students' various learning styles	Teach your material with awareness of the cognitive, emotional, and physical factors that affect learning
Expect to devise a foolproof instructional plan	Consider that some circumstances will arise that require instantaneous decisions about how you teach

WEB SITES OF INTEREST

http://www.henry.k12.tn.us/teachersworkshop/managemnt.html
This master site for classroom management has a link to many sponge activities.

http://k6educators.about.com/cs/classroommanageme2
This site has links to specific sponge activities and other class openers.

http://www.mtlakes.org/ww/tech/webtools/class.htm
This excellent site provides myriad classroom ideas and activities, including sponges.

http://education.nmsu.edu/webquest/examples.html
http://btc.montana.edu/ceres/html/EdActivities.html
Both these sites provide detail on WebQuests, with a variety of examples from teachers and students and in all subject areas.

http://www.davison.k12.mi.us/dhs/staff/hewitt/hewitt14.htm
http://www.coollessons.org/auroracourse99.html
These two sites are rich with lesson plan examples.

http://www.spa3.k12.sc.us/WebQuests.html
This site is for the Spartanburg County School District of Glendale, SC, WebQuest.

http://www.webquest.org
This site has specific information on WebQuests.

http://www.sctboces.org/isc/iss/trainings/webquesting
This site has a usable tutorial to help you and your students create a WebQuest. You may also get in contact with jeagen@elmiracityschools.com for further guidance on how to create a WebQuest with your class.

http://www.funderstanding.com/brain_based_learning.cfm
This site provides some rudimentary knowledge and excellent ideas related to brain-based instruction.

http://results.about.com/learning_styles
This excellent site is a springboard to other sites related to learning styles and instruction for the multiability classroom.

http://www.frsd.k12.nj.us/rfmslibrarylab/di/differentiated_instruction.htm
This site provides a host of links to a variety of teaching techniques that cater to diverse students.

http://www.gigglepotz.com/mireflect.htm
This Web page has a handy-to-use reflection sheet related to multiple intelligences instruction.

http://eduscapes.com/tap/topic73.htm
This site provides links to various graphic organizers that will be useful to you in the classroom.

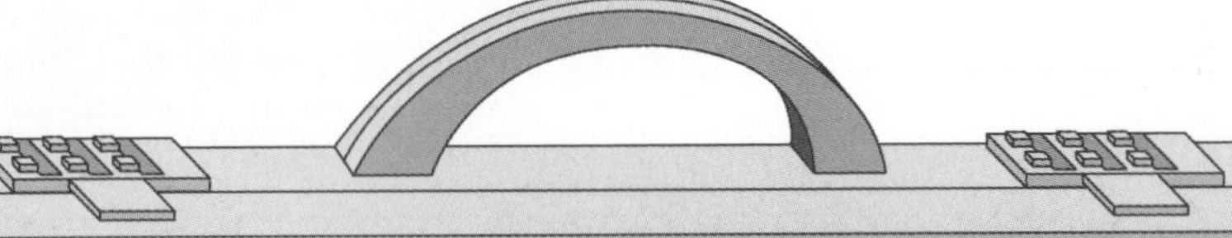

For Your Briefcase

To Do

- Create a list of sponge activities for everyday instruction.
- Look for ways to diversify your instruction for each unit.
- Create schemata of instruction for each unit.
- Develop graphic organizers to apply to your lessons.
- Find areas of instruction in which you might consider the multiple intelligences of your students.
- Identify your students' learning styles.
- Review your curriculum and lessons for brain-based learning applications.
- Develop a contingency plan for classroom interruptions.

Resources on Your Briefcase CD

Samples

- Sample WebQuest
- Lesson Tips for a Civil War Unit (Grade 8)
- Newspaper Project for Social Studies (Variable Grades)
- Pictograph Lesson (Variable Grades)
- Rubric for Pictograph Lesson (Variable Grades)
- Unit Exam in Social Studies (Grade 8)
- Examples of Graphic Organizers
- Sample Multiple Intelligence Lesson

Templates

- WebQuest Procedure Checklist

Tables

- The Mechanics of Teaching Procedures
- Sponge Activity Types and Categories
- Instructional Methods
- Instructional Schemata with Examples
- Ideas for Multiple Intelligences
- Learning Styles Defined
- Gregoric's Cognition Model
- Brain-Based Instructional Procedure and Suggestions

REFERENCES

Caine, R. N., & Caine, G. (1994). *Making connections: Teaching and the human brain.* New York: Addison-Wesley.

Caskey, M., & Ruben, B. (2003, December). Awakening adolescent brains: Middle matters. *Education Digest, 69*(4), 36–39.

Davidson, J. W., & Stoff, M. B. (1998). *The American nation.* Upper Saddle River, NJ: Prentice Hall.

Flohr, J., Miller, D., & Persellin, D. (1996, July). *Children's electrophysical responses to music.* Paper presented at the 22nd International Society for Music Education World Congress, Amsterdam, the Netherlands. (ERIC Document Reproduction Service No. EDPS025654)

Gardner, H. (1983). *Frames of mind: The theory of multiple intelligences.* New York: Basic Books.

Hayward, G. C., Brandes, B. G., Kirst, M. W., & Mazzeo, C. (1997, January). *Higher education outreach programs: A synthesis of evaluations.* Berkeley: Policy Analysis for California Education (PACE).

National School Boards Association Legal Clips. (2005, February 10). *Employment/curriculum.* Alexandria, VA: National School Boards Association. Retrieved June 25, 2005, from http://www.nsba.org/cosa

Shaw, G., Rauscher, F., Levine, L., Wright, E., Dennis, W., & Newcomb, R. (1997, February). Music training causes long-term enhancement of preschool children's spatial-temporal reasoning. *Neurological Research, 19*(1), 2–8.

Sprenger, M. (1999). *Learning and memory: The brain in action.* Alexandria, VA: Association for Supervision and Curriculum Development.

Taylor, M. (1997, Spring). Learning styles. *Inquiry, 1,* 45–48.

Chapter 8

Assessing and Grading

Never discourage anyone . . . who continually makes progress, no matter how slow.
—*Plato*

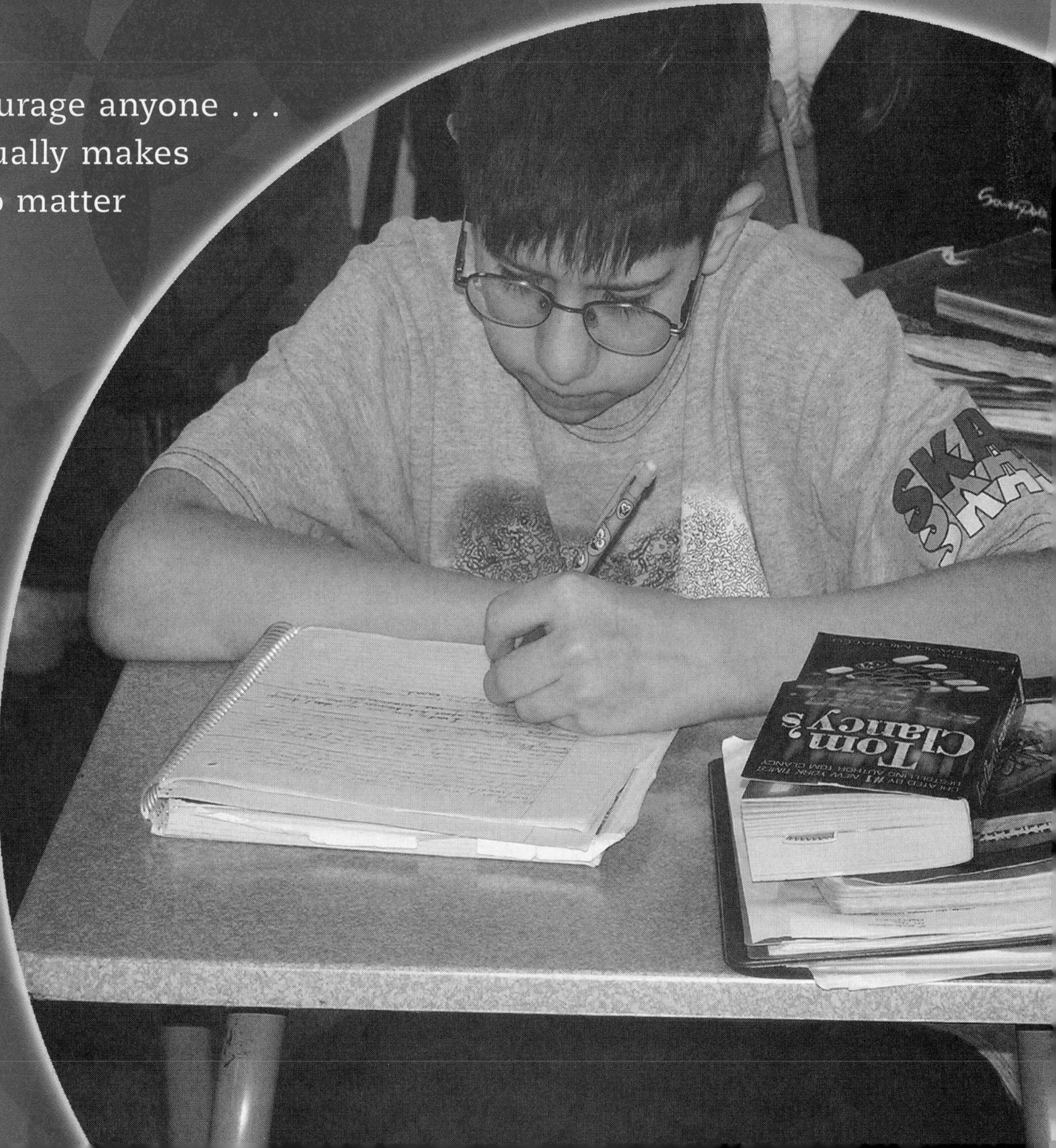

ASSESSMENT DEFINED

Assessment is a constant responsibility for all teachers as they attempt to determine exactly what their students are learning. Assessment *is* the following:

- ☑ A source of feedback to use to shape decisions about your instructional strategy
- ☑ A test of your students on the material taught that is used to determine the scope and depth of their understanding
- ☑ A gauge for the student to use to evaluate his or her progress

Assessment *is not* an end in itself.

Assessment can be performed during the teaching process to measure ongoing progress—**formative assessment**—and at the end of a lesson or unit to determine the extent of students' learning—**summative assessment.** Furthermore, two main types of assessment are currently used: **traditional assessment** and **authentic assessment.**

FOUNDATIONS OF ASSESSMENT

	Type of assessment	
Factor	Formative	Summative
Purpose	To measure ongoing progress	To determine the extent of learning (given at the end of a unit or lesson)
Format	Diverse instruments from observation to pop quizzes	Usually a test
Ultimate function	A dynamic indicator of student understanding throughout the teaching process	A cumulative marker—a final grade or score—that is useful for tracking trends and long-range progress

TRADITIONAL ASSESSMENT

Veteran teachers refer to *traditional assessment* as the techniques used most frequently in the long history of education. Plato would not have used a multiple-choice test to assess whether his students understood his teachings; he would have simply asked them. However, in the 20th century, traditional testing came to mean standardized, or machine-designed, tests that enable educators to test large numbers of students and score the results quickly while also discovering trends in student responses (Moon, Callahan, & Tomlinson, 2003). Following is a discussion of the measurement tests that are the most popular and most used in the U.S. school system.

Multiple-Choice Test

The **multiple-choice test** is a staple in the education world and is debatably the assessment tool most used in education (Ballantyne, 2003).

Advantages of the Multiple-Choice Test The three main advantages of using the multiple-choice test are as follows:

1. It can be designed and administered with relative ease.
2. It can be corrected fairly rapidly.
3. Numerous professional materials are available for creating the test, including "factory-made" multiple-choice test questions.

Disadvantages of the Multiple-Choice Test The two main drawbacks to using the multiple-choice test are the following:

1. Designing unambiguous questions and responses is difficult.
2. Some students are more efficient than others in learning how to arrive at correct answers without actually knowing the material.

Effective Multiple-Choice Questions Effective multiple-choice test questions have these qualities:

Briefcase CD CH8-1—Examples of Effective and Ineffective Multiple-Choice Questions

- ☑ Are phrased clearly, accurately, and straightforwardly
- ☑ Include only material that was taught
- ☑ Do not contain either word cues that point to the correct answer or confusing phraseology
- ☑ Do not purposefully attempt to mislead the test taker through word manipulation
- ☑ Have no misspelled words or incorrect usage
- ☑ Seldom have the word *not* in the responses
- ☑ Do not include responses that refer to other responses, such as *a & b, b only, c & not d*

EXAMPLES OF EFFECTIVE AND INEFFECTIVE MULTIPLE-CHOICE QUESTIONS

Effective	Ineffective
Which of the following is an example of positive correlation? Researchers have found a relationship between a. *Students who eat fast food more than two times a week and obesity* b. Students who exercise less than 2 hours per week and high body-fat measurements c. Students who take vitamins every day and fewer doctor visits	Which of the following is *not* an example of positive correlation? Researchers have found a relationship between a. Students who eat fast food more than two times a week and obesity b. *Students who exercise less than 2 hours per week and high body-fat measurements* c. Students who eat high-sugar-content foods and high body-fat measurements
In 1998, the death rate per 100,000 population in the age group 1–20 years was due to a. Respiratory disease b. Cancer c. *Accidents* d. Rheumatic heart disease	In 1998, the death rate from unintentional injuries of all types per 100,000 population in the age group 1–20 years was a. 47.5% b. 39.1% c. 110.2% d. 15.9%
Pluto is a planet that a. Is closer to the sun than Neptune is b. Has a shorter orbit around the sun than that of Earth c. *Is the farthest confirmed planet from the sun* d. Orbits around the sun in fewer than 365 days	Pluto is a. A moon orbiting Saturn b. Donald Duck's pet c. *The farthest confirmed planet from the sun* d. None of the above
The main reason for the American Revolution was a. *The colonists wanted representation in government* b. The tea tax was affecting commerce c. British troops invaded Boston d. The Northern colonies wanted to end slavery	The main reason for the American Revolution was a. *The colonists did not want government without representation* b. The colonists wanted freedom of religion c. a and b d. a only

When to Use Multiple-Choice Tests Multiple-choice tests are effective when they are used in appropriate situations. In other instances, they are not. The following table provides guidelines as to when to use or not use multiple-choice tests:

EXAMPLES OF WHEN TO USE AND NOT USE MULTIPLE-CHOICE TESTS

Use to	Do not use to
Measure knowledge of facts, statistics, names, dates, and events	Measure higher levels of cognition
Reinforce the material taught	Provide conclusive data for final grades
Stimulate student discussion on the material taught	Gauge complete student comprehension of the material taught
Track trends in student acquisition of basic knowledge	Test a student's opinion or creative ability
Increase student knowledge of the material	Test students if the test may adversely affect a student's culture or ethnicity

WATCH OUT

Caution: Pitfalls to Avoid When Using Multiple-Choice Tests

- Avoid using the word *not* because it emphasizes the test, not the content.
- Avoid too many questions that simply ask for information recall.
- Avoid nonsense responses because they trivialize the purpose of the test.
- Do not use *a and b only*–type questions, again because they focus on the test, not the content.

Briefcase CD CH8-2—Checklist for Writing Multiple-Choice Questions

Writing Multiple-Choice Test Questions When constructing multiple-choice test questions, you should follow certain guidelines to ensure both the accuracy and the efficiency of the test:

STEP 1 ***Align the test items with the standards:*** Before writing the test items, quickly sketch a draft of the content that will make up the test. Check it against the learning standards of your state or district. Doing so provides a quick validation of what you have been teaching against what is required to be taught.

STEP 2 ***Write items requiring an answer to a question or completion of a statement:*** These formats are the most straightforward and leave little room for misinterpretation. You simply ask a question and provide three distractors besides the correct answer:

Which of the following is a prime number?

a. 2
b. 1
c. 14
d. 16

In completion questions, students choose from four answers to complete the sentence:

a. The president of the Confederacy during the Civil War was
b. General Robert E. Lee
c. Henry Clay
d. Jefferson Davis
e. Dred Scott

STEP 3 ***Write accurate information:*** Do so for the incorrect responses as well as the correct answers. That is, the incorrect responses should be accurate in their facts but simply inapplicable to the particular question. Students can learn from the incorrect responses and may be misled if the information is inaccurate. The correct responses should be accurately matched to the question, without room for misinterpretation. Students cannot give an accurate response to an inaccurate question.

STEP 4 ***Provide complete information:*** Each question should include a great deal of lead information to provide a wide scope of reference. Give ample descriptions of events, people, or locations to prevent misinterpretation.

STEP 5 ***Provide only pertinent information:*** Do not give information that will distract the student from the point being asked. When writing the responses, avoid using completely unrelated information (e.g., "Pluto is Mickey Mouse's dog"). It can distract the students and trivialize the test.

STEP 6 ***Avoid tricks:*** Do not write tricky questions that use a play on words or correct responses that are distinguished from incorrect responses by a single word, such as *wouldn't* for *couldn't,* or *force* in lieu of *fierce*. Tricky questions test more than the material taught; they also test the students' puzzle-solving abilities—which is not fair to all students.

STEP 7 ***Avoid using* none of *or* all of:** The responses *None of the above* and *All of the above* trivialize the question and distract the student from the material, instead focusing his or her attention on the construction of the question. Also, responses that refer to other responses (e.g., *a and d only*) confuse students who are visual learners.

Multiple-Choice Tests

Ask yourself the following questions:

How difficult should the test be?
A multiple-choice test that is too difficult will discourage students who are slower achieving and cause students who are high achievers to question your responses.

Are multiple-choice tests appropriate for the grade level I teach?
This form of test effectively identifies your students' foundational knowledge of a topic, especially in the intermediate grades and in middle school.

Are multiple-choice tests appropriate for the subject I teach?
Multiple-choice tests are flexible and can be used for any subject, at least for the knowledge level. However, they do not assess the students' wider perspectives on the material taught.

Do I have enough time in my schedule to create a good multiple-choice test?
The best aspect of multiple-choice tests is that they save you time correcting papers. However, you must allow time to design a reliable and valid test. Remember, also, to allow time for photocopying: These tests must be duplicated and usually require two or more sheets of paper.

True–False Test

The **true–false test** is an old, time-honored assessment tool that truly takes the "value" out of evaluation. Other than having one possible advantage, the true–false test is generally used to reduce the teacher's workload while falsely reflecting student comprehension.

Advantage of the True–False Test The true–false test has one dubiously positive use: When comprising 20–30 questions or more, it can cover a wide expanse of material that was taught and at least familiarize students with the content.

Disadvantages of the True–False Test Following are the two main disadvantages of using the true–false test:

1. The student has a 50% chance of answering each question correctly regardless of knowledge of content.
2. True–false questions have a strong chance of being misinterpreted as a result of ambiguous wording.

Therefore, this assessment tool will not inform you about what or if students have learned.

Effective True–False Questions At their best, true–false questions have these characteristics:

- ☑ Are worded carefully, clearly, and straightforwardly
- ☑ Do not contain confusing phraseology or ambiguity
- ☑ Do not purposefully attempt to mislead the test taker through word manipulation
- ☑ Have no misspelled words or incorrect usage
- ☑ Seldom have the word *not* in the responses

EXAMPLES OF EFFECTIVE AND INEFFECTIVE TRUE–FALSE QUESTIONS

Effective	Ineffective
Sacagawea was the only female Native American member of Lewis and Clark's expedition.	Sacagawea was not the only female Native American member of Lewis and Clark's expedition.

Caution: Disadvantages of Using True–False Tests

- True–false questions can easily be misinterpreted because of students' variable perspectives. Word the questions carefully, being especially judicious in the use of adjectives and verbs.
- These tests may give the teacher a false-positive reading of student comprehension.
- True–false tests are not effective for assessing high levels of cognition.

When to Use True–False Tests True–false tests can be appropriate when used as part of objective testing and when worded carefully to avoid ambiguity. However, like multiple-choice tests, they should not be used to arrive at final grades for either a report period, a semester, or an entire year.

Writing True–False Test Questions When composing true–false questions, make them clear and free of ambiguity. Compare the effective and ineffective sample true–false questions in the preceding table.

Guidepost

True–False Tests

Ask yourself the following questions:

Are my test questions well designed?
True–false tests are usually well received by students and therefore can be used to help them achieve a level of success and security with the material taught. However, poorly designed true–false questions will easily confuse students who are low achieving and cause students who are high achievers to question the wording and meaning.

Are true–false tests appropriate for the grade level I teach?
This form of assessment is suitable for all grade levels and is most effective when used to determine your students' overall familiarity with the material taught.

Are true–false tests appropriate for the subject I teach?
True–false questions are suitable for all subject areas.

Do I have enough time in my schedule to create a good true–false test?
As with multiple-choice tests, true–false tests can be relatively easy to conceive and design and are quickly corrected. Nevertheless, writing clear, well-phrased questions will take some time.

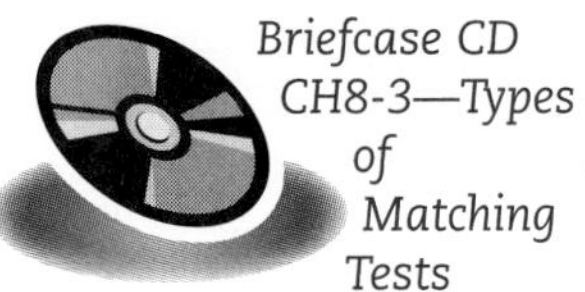
Briefcase CD CH8-3—Types of Matching Tests

Matching Test

The **matching test** is a favorite test tool among teachers and has many creative applications. Some of the types most frequently used are word searches, crossword puzzles, location maps, and straight matching columns.

Advantages of the Matching Test The four main benefits of using the matching test are as follows:

1. It assesses student understanding on a literal cognition level by presenting comparisons or contrasts among concepts, categories, events, geographic locations, problems, or people in history.
2. It is compact, which allows you to measure a large amount of related factual material in a relatively short time.
3. It is well suited to measuring associations.
4. It reduces the effects of guessing.

Disadvantages of the Matching Test The matching test has these two main disadvantages:

1. It encourages rote learning.
2. It can contain irrelevant clues.

TYPES OF MATCHING TESTS

Test	Uses	Where to Find
Word search	Provides a drill for recognition of terms Encourages students to concentrate on solving a puzzle	Ready-made tests in workbooks or on the Internet Computer software programs that automatically construct word searches Internet locations at which you can create them online: http://puzzlemaker.school.discovery.com/CrissCrossSetupForm.html
Crossword puzzle	Challenges students to create connections between words and terms while keeping the organization of numbers and clues consistent within the integrity of the puzzle Requires students to decide where to place words on the basis of their relationship to other words and the theme of the puzzle *Example:* Have your students create a crossword puzzle, from diagram to clues. Doing so calls for higher level thinking skills.	Computer software programs that automatically construct puzzles Internet locations at which you can create them online: www.puzzle-maker.com/CW and http://puzzlemaker.school.discovery.com/CrissCrossSetupForm.html
Location maps, diagrams, and straight matching columns	Can be used in all subject areas Especially effective when diagrams and visual aids are used abundantly *Examples:* Geographic identification, identification or categorization of pieces of information by using diagrams or blueprints	www.washburn.edu/cas/history/stucker/AHA2002.html

—*Cont.*

Test	Uses	Where to Find
Carbo Reading Styles Program (Carbo, Dunn, & Dunn, 1994)	Provides creative ways to stimulate student interest in choosing the correct answer; in one involving a battery-operated light board labeled with names, dates, places, concepts, and so forth, the student answers by touching a wand to a metal clip; if the answer is correct, a light shines Engages the student kinesthetically Provides a handy tool for reinforcement	www.kentuckyliteracy.org/CARBO.doc

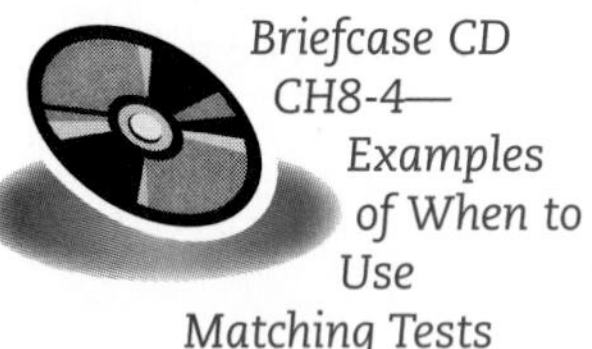

Briefcase CD CH8-4—Examples of When to Use Matching Tests

When to Use Matching Tests Use matching tests to assess student recall of literal-level material. The typical matching test is limited to measuring factual information on simple associations. When learning outcomes emphasize the ability to identify the relationship between two things, a matching exercise may be appropriate.

Writing Matching Test Questions Designing matching test questions depends on the purpose of the assessment. For example, word searches do not assess student comprehension of the material but instead simply familiarize students with the terms being studied. In contrast, a matching test with terms and concepts in opposite columns may challenge students to make the correct associations by engaging in higher level thought processes.

Matching test questions should therefore be written with the purpose of assessment in mind. Following are tips on how to write clear and purposeful matching tests:

- ☑ Always use material that was taught within the lesson content.
- ☑ If you use sentences in the matchup, be sure they are clear, unambiguous, and specific to the lesson content.

WATCH OUT

Caution: Pitfalls to Avoid When Using Matching Tests

- Excessive use of matching tests reflects an overemphasis on literal-level material. Restrict the use of matching tests as much as possible. Try to create challenging identifiers for each term.
- Word searches measure only the student's recognition of terms. Use these types of tests only for drill and identification of terms.
- Do not rely on matching tests to measure student comprehension because they have an inherent "guess" factor.

EXAMPLES OF WHEN TO USE MATCHING TESTS

Subject area	Use
English and foreign languages	Vocabulary, story facts, literary techniques, quotations, usage, writing mechanics
Social studies	Dates, events, notable persons, concepts, geography
Mathematics	Math facts, math concepts, systems, simple word problems
Science	Terms, procedures, names, systems
Music	Terms, historical events, notable composers and musicians
Art	Terms, techniques, historical events, works of art, notable artists
Careers and technology	Terms, techniques, occupations, statistics
Physical education and health	Terms, statistics

- ☑ Write clear directions for the test, making sure to highlight unusual aspects (e.g., "Some items in column b are not used").
- ☑ To prevent student frustration and confusion, do not cram too much material onto one page; use double spacing.
- ☑ When using map identification matching questions, provide clearly drawn diagrams that allow students to discern the differences between ocean and land.

Matching Tests

Ask yourself the following questions:

Would matching tests be effective for my students?
Matching tests may be the best method of assessment for students who struggle with testing in general. However, such tests seldom challenge the student who is higher achieving.

Are matching tests appropriate for the grade level I teach?
Matching tests are appropriate for all grade levels because of the many types that are available.

Are matching tests appropriate for the subject I teach?
Although matching tests can be used for all subjects, they are better suited for those with much content, such as social studies and science.

Do I have enough time in my schedule to create a good matching test?
Matching tests are time friendly: They are easy both to construct and to correct.

Essay Test

The **essay test** is one of the oldest forms of assessment. It integrates the skill of written expression with what the student has learned about the topic.

Advantages of the Essay Test The essay test has the following three main advantages:

1. It provides a more accurate indication of student learning than that of some of the other assessment types.
2. It promotes critical-thinking skills.
3. It allows students to express themselves in their own words.

Disadvantages of the Essay Test Despite the advantages of the essay test, it also has four main disadvantages:

1. Grading it objectively can be a challenge.
2. It is time consuming to score.
3. Less content can be sampled.
4. It can be more challenging for students with English as a second language.

Effective Essay Questions The effective essay question prompts the student to respond by providing a reflection of his or her complete understanding of the material taught. Effective essay questions do the following:

- ☑ Give clear, specific directions
- ☑ Specify the length of the answer (number of paragraphs or pages the student should write; note that length stipulated in *words* may cause students to write exactly that number, which will inhibit the cohesion of the essay, whereas length stipulated in *paragraphs* helps direct students toward an organized essay)
- ☑ State which elements will be graded
- ☑ Always include a rubric

In the following examples of essay questions, notice the specifics given as a prompt. Always provide a brief introduction and as many specifics as possible.

CH8-5—Checklist for Writing Essay Questions

When to Use Essay Tests

A wise practice is to assign essays relatively sparingly, for specific connections to your unit, unless you are an English teacher. (In English, writing tasks are a regular part of the instructional day.)

Writing Essay Test Questions

Students automatically look for two elements in essay assignments: clear directions and the amount they need to write. Students are often fearful of essays because these tests are open ended and somewhat nonspecific. You can ease students' concerns by providing a good deal of direction and communicating your expectations:

STEP 1 ***Give clear instructions:*** Provide one to three sentences of explanation. Give examples of elements you want to see expressed.

STEP 2 ***Provide a rubric:*** Give a list or scale of the mechanical points you will be grading (e.g., spelling, usage, sentence structure, cohesiveness, organization, vocabulary). Provide specifics as to what content you expect.

STEP 3 ***Provide a checklist:*** Give your students a checklist of the elements you expect in their essays.

WATCH OUT

Caution: Pitfalls to Avoid When Using Essay Tests

- Reading and grading essay questions can take a great deal of time. Set aside a set time for correcting essays, and stick to it.
- Without using a specific rubric, assessing essays can be subjective. Use a rubric (see the discussion on rubrics later in this chapter).
- Learners who have difficulty expressing themselves find essays frustrating and often become easily discouraged. Take learning styles into consideration when correcting essays.

EXAMPLES OF EFFECTIVE AND INEFFECTIVE ESSAY QUESTIONS

Effective	Ineffective
Intermediate grades	
Each autumn, the leaves on almost every tree slowly turn color and then fall to the ground. Explain how the changing seasonal climate affects leaves on most trees in autumn. Be sure to check your paper for incomplete or run-on sentences and grammatical and spelling errors. Organize your essay clearly, providing details and examples.	Write an essay explaining why leaves change color in autumn. Your paper must contain no spelling errors, must have complete sentences, and must be clearly written with no grammatical mistakes.
Length: At least two paragraphs	*Length:* 150 words
High school grades	
Many people question the reasoning that allows an 18-year-old to serve and die for his or her country but does not allow him or her to drink alcohol. Write a persuasive essay that explores the question of whether to lower the drinking age to 18. Be sure to provide complete arguments on both sides of the issue. Your paper must be free of spelling and grammatical errors and must follow a specific and organized pattern of argument.	Write a persuasive essay defending your position on why the drinking age should be lowered to age 18. Spelling and grammar count.
Length: Five paragraphs	*Length:* 200 words

SAMPLE PERSUASIVE ESSAY AND RUBRIC (GRADE 7, 8, OR 9)

Scientists report that the earth's mean temperature is rising. Many of them believe this warming is due to the burning of fossil fuels. Present your position on the causes of global warming and what can and should be done to prevent a future ecological disaster.

Rating	Rubric
Outstanding	No grammatical and spelling errors have been made. Sentences are complete, balanced, and specific to the topic. Transitional words and phrases are used properly to provide cohesion. The argument is presented in an organized manner with examples, definitions, and details. The conclusion states, in summary form, the high point of the argument.
Excellent	Few grammatical and spelling errors have been made. Sentences are generally complete, balanced, and specific to the topic. Transitional words and phrases are seldom used. The argument is presented in an organized manner but needs a few more definitions, details, or examples. The conclusion does not effectively restate the high point of the argument.
Good	Many grammatical and spelling errors have been made. Some sentences are run on and not balanced. Transitional words and phrases are not used. Some details are provided, but no examples or definitions are given. Support for the argument is generally poor.
Poor	Many grammatical and spelling errors have been made. The structure is poorly organized, with many run-on and fragmented sentences. The points of the argument are unclear and presented in a disorganized manner. No conclusion is stated.

PERSUASIVE ESSAY CHECKLIST

- ☑ The opening sentence introduces my topic or argument.
- ☑ My opening sentences attract the reader to my topic or argument.
- ☑ The first paragraph presents details or gives examples to identify and then support my topic or argument.
- ☑ The middle paragraphs expand on my position on the topic or argument and include possible solutions.
- ☑ The concluding paragraph restates the topic or argument.
- ☑ No spelling errors have been made.
- ☑ No usage errors (*their–there; they're–there; to–too–two,* etc.) have been made.
- ☑ Transitional words connect each paragraph.
- ☑ My sentences are balanced in length and meaning.

Note. Checklists for creative writing assignments and for expository writing assignments must be geared to respective modalities of writing.

Essay Tests

Ask yourself the following questions:

Would essay tests be effective for my students?
Essay tests are excellent for ascertaining general student comprehension of material taught. However, students who struggle with the writing process will have difficulty responding to the writing prompt because of anxiety over the physical and mental demands of writing. Provide additional help for these students and give them structured guidelines, such as writing outlines.

Are essay tests appropriate for the grade level I teach?
The essay test is a flexible assessment tool because it can be applied to any topic or subject. However, its appropriateness must be weighed against the students' development level. Students in the early stages of cognitive development may become frustrated if they have to try to express themselves clearly in an essay.

Are essay tests appropriate for the subject I teach?
Essay questions are appropriate for all subject areas except math. However, written explanations of math word problems are an excellent means of assessing comprehension.

Do I have enough time in my schedule to create a good essay test?
Essay tests take time to design, reproduce, and grade. Grading essays can take 3–20 minutes per paper. Remember, though, that *students deserve comments on what they write;* only putting a grade on the paper shows a lack of sincerity about the importance of the assignment.

AUTHENTIC ASSESSMENT

With authentic assessment, students must *show* what they have learned. They are presented with tasks that mirror the priorities and challenges found in the best instructional activities and that are related to real-life situations and problems. Strategies include researching, writing, analyzing, collaborating, and presenting (Wiggins, 1990).

Chief among this type of assessment is **performance assessment,** in which students can present and explain their comprehension of what was taught through demonstrations, project work, or presentations. Another widely used technique is **portfolio assessment,** in which students place their work in **portfolios** during a particular time period. These collections of work usually reveal a growth in students' comprehension of the material during the time period. Finally, other components of authentic assessment are **preinstructional techniques,** which measure students' prior knowledge, and **rubrics,** which are standards or guidelines by which students can measure their performance on assignments or tests.

ADVANTAGES AND DISADVANTAGES OF AUTHENTIC ASSESSMENT COMPONENTS

Component	Advantages	Disadvantages
Performance assessment	Allows students to integrate tasks and ideas	Is time consuming (complicated to fit into your schedule)
	Gives a holistic picture of student comprehension	Allows little control over outside help on assignments
	Does not create a competition between teacher and student	Results in students' perceiving that they have not learned the material
		Is resisted by students who normally do well on objective tests

—Cont.

Component	Advantages	Disadvantages
Portfolio assessment	Gives an adequate picture of student achievement and comprehension Creates a high degree of student motivation Allows students to have time to reflect on and review finished work	Creates the need for more physical space for storing the portfolios Is time intensive for the teacher (students expect comments on their work) Requires verification that students are doing the work themselves
Preinstructional techniques	Provide the teacher with insight into what students already know Engage students in the lesson immediately	Are time intensive for the teacher
Rubrics	Provide an objective standard for grading Allow students to know exactly what is expected of them to receive a specific grade	Can frame students' expectations too much Create the need to police students to use the rubrics

Comparison of Traditional and Authentic Methods

Authentic assessment is a more accurate and comprehensive indicator of student learning than is traditional assessment. However, despite extensive research supporting the use of authentic assessment, it is not commonly used. The reasons for this lack of use are time and money. Administering authentic assessments requiring manipulatives can be expensive. The expense and time needed to evaluate these assessments can make them administratively ineffective. In contrast, standardized tests are considerably less expensive, can be administered with minimum materials and organization, and are scored in minutes locally, or within weeks commercially.

Use of Both Traditional and Authentic Assessment

Despite the differences between traditional and authentic assessment, you can successfully integrate the two. For example, you can ask multiple-choice questions that call for more than one response *and* for an *explanation* of the response. Note in the following two examples how each requires the student to think about his or her answer beyond the boundaries of the question.

ASSESSMENT TYPES

Traditional assessment	Authentic assessment
The student selects a response from choices.	The student performs a task.
The choices are usually theoretical.	The choices are usually real-life related.
It tends to test the recall level of knowledge.	It more often asks students to apply and analyze.
Responses are related to the topic.	Responses refer directly to the topic.
It is mostly teacher designed.	It is designed by the student.

EXAMPLES OF INTEGRATED TEST QUESTIONS

Question 1

Prior to the French and Indian War, the Iroquois traded almost exclusively with the French. From the following reasons given, choose two that best explain why the Iroquois began to trade with the English.

a. The English were more powerful and had better weapons.
b. The English paid more for furs and charged less for food and goods.
c. The French were cruel to the Iroquois and angered many tribes.
d. The English trader William Johnson won the Iroquois' respect.

In the space below, explain how the information in the two answers you chose became causes for the French and Indian War:

____
____
____
____
____

Question 2

The place where a plant or an animal lives is called a

a. Food cycle
b. Carnivore
c. Habitat
d. Prey

After you choose your answer, tell why you think your answer is correct.

____
____
____
____
____

Give an example of an animal and the place where it lives:

____
____

What is the name of the place where you live?

____

How is it the same or different from where animals live?

____

Performance Assessment

In performance assessment, students are asked to *demonstrate* their understanding of the material taught. They must integrate ideas and tasks, reflecting a more holistic picture of what they have learned, and engage in a process that requires a variety of skills. This approach gives them more opportunities to express what they have learned across the entire spectrum of their abilities.

Briefcase CD CH8-6—Performance Assessment Examples

For a performance assessment to be effective, the following must occur:

- ☑ Students must be given clear, specific instructions.
- ☑ The scoring rubric must be explained before the assignment begins.
- ☑ The students must be asked to incorporate *more than one* aspect of what they have learned.
- ☑ The students' presentations must last 5–7 minutes each.

PERFORMANCE ASSESSMENT EXAMPLES	
Subject area	**Example**
Science	Ninth graders are given vials of water (taken from various sources) and water-testing materials. Students must test for pH levels, hardness, and solids. They are evaluated on the accuracy of their report.
Mathematics	Fourth graders are given paper, scissors, and paste or elastic bands to construct two- and three-dimensional figures as they explore geometric patterns to identify simple closed curves, the vertex, concave, and convex. They are evaluated on the accuracy of their figures and the explanation of each.
Social studies	Seventh graders are asked to write a diary entry as young boys or girls traveling on the Oregon Trail who are seeing their first Native Americans. Students are evaluated on the extent and accuracy of what they have learned about life for pioneers and Native Americans, as well as geographic and historical data.
Language arts	Second graders are asked to prepare a poster that reflects ideas, facts, and characters of a book they just read. Students are evaluated on the accuracy and organization of the material.
Music	Fifth graders are asked to compile an arrangement of musical works to be put onto a CD reflecting a specific genre and time period of music. They must accurately identify the works, instruments, and time period. Students are evaluated on content and on historical and chronological accuracy.
Art	First graders are asked to paint their favorite outdoor scene using primary colors. They must paint at least one figure in each primary color and the remainder in a combination of colors. Students are evaluated on how well they follow instructions and their accuracy in completing the task.

Note the incorporative element in each example in the table above. No trickery or competition takes place between the test and the student, just serious inquiry as to what has been understood. Within this framework of assessment, the teacher can judge whether to move on or to review the topic.

WATCH OUT

Caution: Pitfalls to Avoid When Using Performance Assessment

- Performance assessment requires a great deal of class time because students must have equal amounts of time for their presentations. Restrict students to a set time (e.g., 5 minutes each).
- The class attention span will begin to wane quickly during presentations, which can promote class disruption. Try to involve class members by having them prepare questions for the presenters.

When to Use Performance Assessment Use performance assessment when you want to effectively gauge the extent of students' comprehension.

Portfolios

In a portfolio assessment, student work is cataloged throughout an extended lesson or a unit, or for the entire year. It provides a progressive record of student progress. The portfolio reflects the student's determination to do his or her best work and at least one example of a teacher-directed and -selected work. The portfolio contains not only the completed work, but also intermediate work along the way: checklists, rough drafts, sketches, and so forth.

Why is the portfolio an effective assessment tool? The portfolio is a comprehensive, challenging, and creative assessment tool that allows the student to engage in his or her own learning. It is also both a **reliable test** and a **valid test** of student comprehension (Koretz, Klein, McCaffrey, & Stecher, 1993). The portfolio does the following:

- ☑ Gives the teacher an accurate picture of each student's achievements and comprehension
- ☑ Demonstrates the developmental scale of how the student improved throughout the process

Performance Assessment

Ask yourself the following questions:

Would this type of assessment be effective for my students?
This method is an excellent mode of response for students who do not achieve well on traditional tests. It also helps reveal the depth and breadth of comprehension among these students. However, the repetition factor can lead to behavioral problems during the process. For this reason, you should keep presentations to a 5- or 7-minute limit and use performance-type assessment as a culmination of a unit or multiple lessons.

Is performance assessment appropriate for the subject I teach?
It is appropriate for all subject areas. However, it may not reveal the scope of students' grasp of basic skills or terminology. When this is the case, give traditional assessments to ascertain whether your students have learned the required information.

Do I have enough time in my schedule for performance assessment?
You need to set aside large chunks of class time for student presentations. However, you can save time on grading by rating the students' presentations as they give them.

- ☑ Provides for students' reflection and review of their work, which encourages intrinsic rewards
- ☑ Provides a running record of student work for parental, student, and teacher review
- ☑ Allows students to work at their own pace
- ☑ Challenges students to achieve at higher cognition levels
- ☑ Gives students a sense of ownership and pride in their accomplished work
- ☑ Gives students responsibility for their work and consequences for not meeting this responsibility

Briefcase CD CH8-7—Portfolio Checklist

The box entitled "Portfolio Contents" shows the array of items that can go into a portfolio. Some examples are as follows:

- ☑ An essay on a science concept such as *erosion* would be an ongoing assignment requiring collection of information from a variety of sources. The student would show his or her work throughout the process.
- ☑ In an English project on a biography, the portfolio would contain the data collected, including photos of the subject or artifacts the subject owned.
- ☑ For most writing assignments, a checklist of items must be completed before and after the actual writing.
- ☑ A mathematics portfolio would contain work sheets and extended problems that require a lengthy process (e.g., calculating the mean average stock prices during a 3-week period).
- ☑ A social studies portfolio might include summaries of case studies or research studies collected for a project on First and Fourth Amendment rights. The entire project would reflect the student's progress throughout the process.

PORTFOLIO CONTENTS

- ☑ All writing—narrative, persuasive, expository, and descriptive
- ☑ Reflections of work completed in and out of class
- ☑ Drawings, photographs, diagrams, charts, or graphics associated with the work, either completed or in progress
- ☑ Comment sheets from peers or teachers
- ☑ Handouts and instruction sheets related to class matters or associated with work completed or in progress
- ☑ Notes or journals related to work completed or in progress
- ☑ One piece that is teacher assigned
- ☑ One piece that is student selected
- ☑ One piece that challenges the student to perform at higher levels of thinking

Assessment of Portfolios When assessing the portfolio, you must establish a specific set of criteria that you share with your students. Assign a percentage to each criterion and affix this information as a chart to the front or back of the portfolio folder.

Portfolio assessment criteria may include the following:

- ☑ Progress from the beginning to the conclusion of the assignment, theme, or problem (5%)
- ☑ Student reflections on progress (10%)
- ☑ Accuracy of the information related to the assignment, theme, or problem (20%)
- ☑ Demonstration of thinking beyond the knowledge level (25%)
- ☑ Various materials in different genres related to the assignment, theme, or problem (20%)
- ☑ Overall completeness and organization of the materials, including deadline integrity (20%)

WATCH OUT

Caution: Possible Problems With Using Portfolios

- Portfolios occupy a great deal of classroom space. Ask your building principal for additional storage.
- Portfolios are not always effective with students who have difficulty being organized and adhering to time schedules. You will need to spend more time working with these students when using portfolios.

When to Use Portfolio Assessment Use portfolio assessment if you want students to recognize how they are developing and what steps they are taking to improve.

Preinstructional Techniques

Preinstructional techniques measure students' prior knowledge—their comprehension of the topic *before* you present your formal instruction. Researchers and educators agree that students' prior knowledge has a strong influence on their comprehension and engagement of the material (Ogle, 1986). The following strategies may assist you in this determination:

- ☑ ***K-W-L method:*** Donna Ogle (1986) developed the *K-W-L* teaching method for reading, and it is recommended for preinstructional use:

  K stands for *know:* What do I already *know* about this topic?

  W stands for *want*: What do I *want* to know about this topic?

  L stands for *learn*: What have I *learned* about this topic?

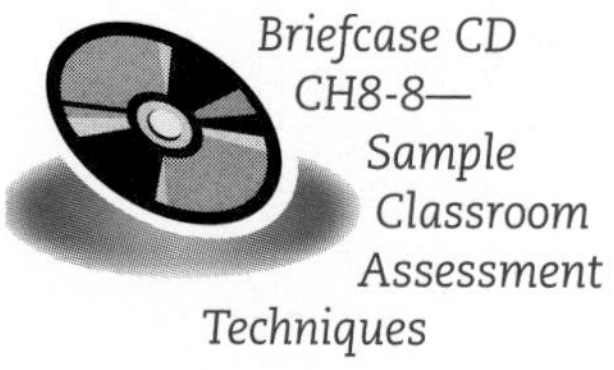

Briefcase CD CH8-8—Sample Classroom Assessment Techniques

- ☑ ***Classroom assessment techniques:*** Thomas Angelo and K. Patricia Cross (1993) developed the following six classroom assessment techniques:
  1. ***Focused listing:*** Before instruction, have students list several ideas or concepts related to the topic.
  2. ***Empty outlines:*** Give students an outline of the unit or lesson with blanks to be completed before, during, or after the unit or lesson.
  3. ***Memory matrix:*** Give students a table with categories listed vertically and horizontally. Students then fill in the rows and columns before, during, or after the lesson or unit.
  4. ***Minute paper:*** At the beginning of or during the lesson, students write on what they have learned for 1 minute (also a good sponge activity).
  5. ***Muddiest point:*** During the lesson, ask students to write or discuss the most ambivalent, or "muddiest," point of the topic.
  6. ***Knowledge probe:*** Students write a quick summary of their background knowledge of the topic.

Rubrics

A rubric is a standard or guideline by which the student can measure his or her response to what is being assigned. It is a set of expectations that provides the limitations for each

Portfolios

Ask yourself the following questions:

Would this type of assessment be effective for my students?
Portfolios are appropriate for all grades, from K through 12. However, they are not always effective with students who have difficulty being organized and maintaining time schedules. Also consider that some students may be getting a great deal of help from home. Some of the pieces in the portfolio should be spontaneous (or done during class) and labeled as such.

Is portfolio assessment appropriate for the subject I teach?
Portfolios are most closely associated with art and English language arts. However, they can be appropriate for any subject.

Do I have enough time in my schedule for portfolios?
Portfolio assessment requires a high degree of teacher commitment. You will need time to organize the portfolio assessment, keep records, review each folder regularly, and write comments about the student's progress.

Does my classroom have enough space for me to store portfolios?
You should keep portfolios in a convenient location so that you and your students can have easy and frequent access to them. To solve the space problem, you can use cardboard boxes, milk crates, a file cabinet, or art portfolio folders.

graded achievement level. You can use any numerical or verbal format for a rubric as long as it reflects achievement from the lowest level to the highest.

Students appreciate a rubric because it provides them with a detailed list of what they must do to achieve the desired grade. It also serves as a guide for the students to reflect on their work as they move through the assignment.

For teachers, the best feature of the rubric may be the fact that it prevents argument or discussion over the grade given for an assignment. The rubric frames all criteria for the assignment, and the student either does or does not conform to them.

The effective rubric

Briefcase CD CH8-9—Generic Rubric Examples

- ☑ Is written clearly and concisely
- ☑ Sets out the required items specifically
- ☑ Contains no more than four levels of proficiency
- ☑ Is accompanied by an evaluation of the proficiency levels (e.g., A, B, C, D; or Unsatisfactory, Satisfactory, Commendable).

Creation of a Rubric Consider the following steps when constructing a rubric:

STEP 1 ***Write down your assignment goals and expectations for your students.***

STEP 2 ***Separate the goals into categories of content expected to be learned:*** The following example is for a presentation on information gathered during an ecology assignment:

Delivery
Organization
Accuracy of information
Outside sources

WATCH OUT Caution: Pitfalls to Avoid When Using Rubrics

- Exclusive use of rubrics may curb student creativity because students may adhere too strongly to the frameworks. To prevent this problem, allow your students to negotiate changes in your rubric or to negotiate an entirely different set of guidelines for the project.
- Students tend to ignore rubrics. Remind them frequently to consult their rubric.

GENERIC RUBRIC EXAMPLES

Rubric 1		
Poor	**Satisfactory**	**Proficient**
The piece contains sentence fragments or run-on sentences.	The piece contains few sentence fragments or run-on sentences.	All sentences in the piece are grammatically constructed.
Sentences lack development of transitions.	Sentences are reasonably developed, with some transitions.	Sentences and paragraphs have transitions and are coherent.
More than five words are misspelled.	Only a few spelling errors are evident.	No spelling errors are evident.
The thoughts are not organized or consistent.	The thoughts are organized, are consistent, and follow a reasonable thought pattern.	The thoughts are well organized, with distinctive thought patterns.
The theme is incoherent.	The theme is coherent and supported.	The theme is well developed and has a conclusion.

Rubric 2		
Beginning	**Developing**	**Achieved**
The piece has simple but complete sentences.	The piece has some complex sentences reflecting similar ideas.	All sentences in the piece are grammatically constructed.
The thoughts extend from one sentence to another.	Sentences are showing transitions to more complex ideas.	The sentences support the paragraph, and the paragraphs support the theme.
Some words are misspelled.	Fewer words at this grade level are misspelled.	Spelling errors are made only for words above this grade level.
A thought related to the theme begins to develop.	The thoughts build on one another and are connected.	The thoughts show a direct causal link.
Ideas central to the theme begin to develop.	Theme transition is apparent as the student applies ideas to the theme.	The theme is supported with facts, examples, and comparisons.

STEP 3 ***Separate the categories into levels of proficiency:*** You can develop these levels as a numerical or letter scale or as Unsatisfactory, Satisfactory, and Commendable, for example:

1	2	3	4

Briefcase CD CH8-10—Sample Rubric

STEP 4 ***Develop descriptions for each category:*** Align them with the numbers or terms of proficiency see (page 163):

STEP 5 ***Include the rubric on the assignment sheet:*** Insist that your students attach the sheet to the final paper or submission. In the case of oral presentations, always require your students to submit summaries of their presentations.

Assessment of Rubric-Based Assignments When evaluating the project or assignment, use the rubric as a guide to determine each student's grade. When reviewing the work with the student, you will be able to point out exactly where points were lost and what the student needs to do to improve.

	Proficiency			
Category	**1**	**2**	**3**	**4**
Delivery	Spoke unclearly; was disorganized; read from notes	Spoke unclearly; was somewhat prepared; read from notes	Spoke clearly; was fairly well prepared; read from notes	Spoke clearly; looked at audience; did not read from notes
Organization	Incoherent	Somewhat organized; points followed consistently	Organized but with some unclear points	Extremely well organized and exceptionally clear
Accuracy of information	Little to no information related to the topic	Some information related to the topic but mostly off topic	Generally accurate information, with some miscues	Completely accurate information, with additional information included
Outside sources	None cited	One source cited	Two sources cited	Three or more sources cited

TESTING AND TEACHING

Testing is currently a popular topic in the United States because the mandates of the No Child Left Behind Act have caused somewhat of a testing craze. However, the tests given to large numbers of students for use by school officials to determine progress trends are distinct from those you give in your classroom. The word *immediate* comes to mind regarding the need for tests within teaching programs.

Teachers must have some indication of student progress as it relates to their daily lessons. In fact, the effectiveness of their lesson objectives is tied directly to student achievement on the tests teachers use to assess student learning. If the tests indicate a lack of achievement, teachers must reexamine their lesson plan as a first stage of developing effective instruction.

Teaching to the Test

Should you teach to the test? The only answer that makes sense is a firm "yes." Ignoring the reality that your students will be tested on material they are expected to have learned—and, by implication, what you were expected to have taught—would be foolish. If many of your students score at or below the mean on an end-of-year or a standardized test, the principal, the students' parents, and even many of your students may ask you what happened.

Also, *not* teaching to the test flies in the face of giving tests. The meaning of "teaching to the test" is not so much that you are selling out to the true spirit of education as it is that you are applying a practical tool to genuinely ascertain student progress. A well-designed teacher-made test complements a well-designed teacher-made lesson plan. A high level of student achievement is an indicator that you succeeded in your teaching objectives.

Guidelines for Teaching to the Test

An effective teacher can teach to the test—either standardized or final exam—without stilting his or her style or compromising the students' needs. To help your students succeed, throughout the year do the following:

- ☑ Embrace student-sensitive instructional strategies. (See the discussion on brain-based instruction and learning styles in Chapter 6.)

VOICES IN THE CLASSROOM
Teacher Accountability

I once knew a school board president who convinced the superintendent to give him all the test results for the past 3 years at the high school. He then ranked each teacher's test results to determine the "worst" and the "best" teachers.

At an executive session of the board, the president then labeled the teacher who led the list as *incompetent* and said he should be fired. Although the teacher was tenured and had been teaching math for 6 years, his students' test scores *were* generally the lowest. Somehow this information was leaked to the media, and although the teacher's name was withheld, the situation created some citizen reaction.

The board president had overlooked that this teacher was teaching all low-level classes. His students were all struggling in math, and although they did not score high on the end-of-year test, they did manage to get through the year because he was a persevering, caring teacher who worked hard to get them through.

—A former teacher

- ☑ Carefully design lesson plans that engage student learning. (See Chapters 6 and 7.)
- ☑ Have one eye on the *format* and *probable questions* that will appear on the final exam. If the final exam is a combination of multiple-choice, matching, and essay questions, some part of your instructional time must be spent reviewing test-taking techniques.
- ☑ Give your students guidance and direction on *probable content* areas that will appear on the exam. If you spent 12 weeks on the Civil War, and the final exam focuses on the American Revolution and the Industrial Age, your students may overlook the excellent field trips and projects they did and wish you had spent more time on what appeared on the exam.
- ☑ Give your students plenty of *feedback and reinforcement.* Organize your lessons so that each student is always aware of his or her grade and progress. Provide ample alternative assignments to reinforce what has been taught.
- ☑ Expect your principal to hold *strategy meetings* with you and other teachers to develop a plan to get higher results on standardized tests. Strategies may include holding after-school tutoring sessions, team teaching, reviewing copies of old tests, and administering practice tests.
- ☑ Adhere to the directives of your district, your school, and your principal. Often, districts will implement initiatives that require you to record progress on students who are low achieving and provide them with separate assignments to bring up their grades.
- ☑ Do the best you can under the circumstances, always keeping the individual student's needs in the foreground.

GRADING

Grading is the method used to give students an indication of their achievement level, or progress. Unfortunately, by association, grades are used to classify, categorize, and divide students into groups, a practice that sends positive messages to some and negative messages to a great many others. Alfie Kohn (2004) believes that the bumper sticker so often seen on cars that reads "My Son is an Honor Student at Podunk Middle School" should read "All Students Are Honored at Podunk Middle School."

LEGAL SIDEBAR

Giving Grades for Behavior

A federal circuit court ruled that giving a student a grade reduction because of nonacademic conduct is illegal. Teachers may not use grades to discipline a student.

—Smith v. School, City of Hobart (1993)

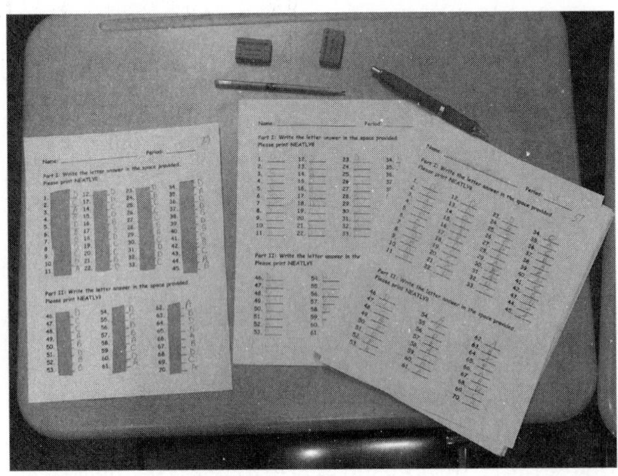

Much of a teacher's time is absorbed by correcting and evaluating student tests.

In the real world, however, grades *are* given. As a teacher, one of your primary responsibilities is to *give grades* for work accomplished. By definition, this term means that the work will be evaluated on a scale of excellence ranging from 100 to 0, or A (*Outstanding*) to F (*Failing*). No matter how excellent your creative talent at giving students grades without telling some that their work is less than that of others, you will fail to prevent some students from feeling badly. The best way to minimize the hurt that accompanies students' perceptions of their grades is to provide a system that is as fair as possible without compromising the goal of all grading: to indicate student performance.

Sensitivity to Students' Needs

No matter how objective you want to make grading, it will always be considered an evaluation of a person's achievement, and therefore of the person. Teachers must be aware of the sensitive nature of criticism and must remember that assigning a grade is a form of criticism. Giving a child an *N* for reading means that he or she is not working to his or her potential or grade-level expectation. This fact must be communicated to the student and to his or her parents with sensitivity and encouragement, and should be accompanied by a plan for improvement.

You are being sensitive to students' needs when grading their work by doing the following:

- ☑ Providing direction on how they can improve their grades
- ☑ Communicating to students and parents the general direction (an outline) of your teaching plan
- ☑ Communicating to parents your expectations and goals for the work assigned
- ☑ Providing a fair and flexible grading system

The Teacher's Role

The U.S. school system is built on the meritocratic system of rewards and punishments, and awards and certificates, which has made the student's report card grade a status symbol. Because of the evaluative nature of grading, teachers strive to design systems that are as objective as possible, removing the subjective elements that often leave them vulnerable to accusations of favoritism.

A child's interest in reading is often stimulated by teacher attitude.

Relating to grading, you are expected to do the following:

- ☑ Provide parents with detailed explanations of their child's progress
- ☑ Verify and validate the report card grade and the final average grade at year end
- ☑ Keep copious records of student achievement
- ☑ Be able to produce details of your grading system for parents, the principal, or other need-to-know professionals

Therefore, you must give serious thought to how you will maintain and configure your students' grades.

Organization of Your Grading System

Briefcase CD CH8-11—Grading Methods and Their Applications

Briefcase CD CH8-12—Letter Grading Formats

Grading Students in Elementary School For elementary school grading, the system has evolved to include a great deal more written, anecdotal information and limited use of symbols or numbers. Because anecdotal information is time consuming to record, you may want to develop a system of recording specific indicators of a child's progress. For example, using key words such as *daily progress, class participation, student-to-student relationships, responses to questions posed about material read, reading rate, reading understanding, vocabulary strength,* and *organizing skills* will help cue you when you write the anecdotal report.

Likewise, checklists are always helpful when you are gathering information on a student's overall progress. Whether you use a daily checklist to mark student participation and application to the lessons, or a weekly list, it will help you later organize your anecdotal report.

GRADING METHODS AND THEIR APPLICATIONS

Method	Steps	Applications
Point system	1. Give students points for each assignment and quiz. 2. Convert the points to percentages. 3. Average the percentages to get the final grade.	Project work Cooperative groups Open-ended assignments
Straight percentages	1. Give each assignment a percentage grade. 2. Average the percentages for the final grade.	Situations with few assignments of equal difficulty

—*Cont.*

Method	Steps	Applications
Weighted percentages (relative)	1. Give each assignment a percentage, weighted by importance or difficulty level. Following is an example: Homework is weighted ×1. Quizzes are weighted ×2. Unit tests are weighted ×3. 2. Configure the final grade to a straight percentage: Add all grades and configure them according to a base of 100%.	Subjects heavy in content and proficiency skills, such as math or science Any other subject with assignments of varying difficulty levels
Weighted category percentage (cumulative)	1. Average and weight each category. Following is an example: Homework = 25% of final grade Quizzes = 35% Unit test = 30% Class participation = 10% 2. Average the grades for each category. 3. Configure the averages by assigned percentages (e.g., 25%, 35%, 30%, 10%) to arrive at a final grade.	Subjects heavy in content, such as social studies, business, and science
Letter grade (holistic)	1. Give students a rubric whereby each letter grade denotes a general level of achievement. 2. Give students a final letter grade based on compliance with the rubric.	Subjects involving much creativity and possible subjectivity, such as literacy, literature, and language arts

LETTER GRADING FORMATS

Letter grades	Letter symbols
1. Give each assignment a letter grade relative to the student's level of achievement. 2. Convert the letters to numerical equivalents. 3. Average the numbers for a final grade.	1. Give each assignment a letter symbolizing the student's achievement level: S (*satisfactory*) I or N (*needs improvement*) P (*proficient*) 2. Write comments. Calculating a final average is unnecessary.

Grading Students in Middle and High School In middle and high school, multiple grading methods are used, all ultimately based on the number *100*. Whether you use a letter grade, a point system, the 4.0 system, weighted averages, or a straight count, the computer will spew out an average that ranges from passing at 65% or 70% to 100%, the highest grade possible.

Whichever method you choose, the essence of assigning a grade is universal: *A grade must be tied to the material taught, and it must reveal the extent of the student's compliance with your published targets.* For example, if you expect your students to be able to

GRADING GUIDELINES

- ☑ Provide students with detailed requirements for each assignment.
- ☑ Provide students with a numerical breakdown or a rubric for each assignment.
- ☑ When possible, provide remarks in addition to numerical or letter grades.
- ☑ Compile as many grades as possible before the end of the report period.
- ☑ Provide students with alternatives to improve grades or make up past work.

spell the words you chose correctly, the grade you assign will reflect the extent of each student's success in achieving this target.

Make your students aware of the criteria you are using to configure their grades. If report card grades are numerical and you are using letter grades, convert them to numerical equivalents before entering them in your grade book. Letter grades will stimulate questions from your students when they see the numerical grade on their report cards and wonder how the final grade was configured.

In Real Time: **Careful Grading**

Grading students' work is a criticism of their performance; therefore, as a teacher, you must be sensitive to your remarks and always be prepared to back up comments and grades with reasonable explanations. Also, never lose sight of the fact that the grade is merely a symbol of achievement: it is not learning itself.

Briefcase CD CH8-13—Grading on a Curve

Grading on a Curve

"Grading on a curve" means building students' grades around the scores that were attained. Essentially, three approaches can be taken to grading on a curve:

GRADING ON A CURVE

Approach	Grading format
1	Everyone's grade hinges on the lowest and highest student scores. For example, all the students' grades on a test are written on the board. The top 10% will receive As; the next highest 20%, Bs; the middle 40%, Cs; and so forth.
2	All scores are skewed to compensate for a factor relating to the test that inhibited the use of a straight percentage rating. The skewed grades more clearly reflect probable achievement *if the negative factor had not intervened.* Such factors might include the following: a. One or more questions were discovered to be invalid or unreliable. b. The test was simply too difficult for the student achievement potential at the time. The grades are then ranked higher by virtue of an arbitrary percentage, such as 25. For instance, if a student's original grade was 62%, then skewed by 25%, the new grade would be 78%.
3	An arbitrary number of points is added to each student's grade. This approach usually benefits students who scored at or above the average more than students who scored lowest.

From these three methods, you can deduce that *grading on a curve is unfair.* One student's achievement should not affect another student's. The establishment of grades should reflect achievement levels, not competitive levels of achievement. A well-designed rubric would solve this problem.

In Real Time: **The Special Education Teacher and Grading**

Your special education teacher is an excellent resource for designing and grading assessment systems. He or she is trained in developing strategies for students who have difficulty processing information. Techniques such as categorizing questions, using fewer distractors, and generating verbal cues can help students reduce the errors that stem from their inability to manipulate the information, providing them opportunities for success.

Extra Credit

As students progress through elementary school into middle and high school, their grade-consciousness becomes acute, and their expectation of fairness is foremost in their minds. Questions of fairness are far fewer when students know exactly how you are grading their work and how the final grade will be configured. In addition, most students will want alternatives to help improve their grades or erase poor grades. Sometimes termed *extra credit,* these alternative assignments are designed to give students an opportunity to demonstrate more effort. Giving extra credit is a teacher choice, but closing the door on an alternative to improve poor grades is also shutting out an opportunity for the student to engage in the learning process.

Integration of Extra Credit into Your Program If you plan to provide alternative assignments, reveal the complete grading and assignment formats at the beginning of the school year and review them at the beginning of each new unit. The less random these alternative assignments are, the fewer questions about your fairness will arise. Notice in the following example how the main assignment can be completed in class with few resources available. The alternative assignment requires a visit to the library and has more depth to the requirement.

Main assignment	Alternative assignment
Write out the First Amendment to the Constitution. What are the rights contained in this amendment? Give two examples of each right that apply to modern society.	Find one famous case for each freedom mentioned in the First Amendment and provide a summary.

What to Grade

What to Count In terms of academic performance, a good rule of thumb is that *everything counts.* When students submit papers in social studies, or science, or math with words that are misspelled, they should be held liable for these mistakes. Your students should understand that learning is holistic and integrated, and therefore subject to evaluation. However, they should also be given every opportunity to demonstrate their understanding of the material being taught.

What Not to Count Your grading system should always reflect academic performance, never behavior. Using grades to discipline students is not only illegal, but also contrary to the spirit and purpose of teaching. Instead, include a class participation element in your grading system. Doing so will ensure that you communicate your approval or disapproval of a student's classroom behavior. Students who disrupt the class cannot receive full credit for class participation because such behavior is not meaningful participation.

***In Real Time:* Do Not Grade Behavior**

Grades resulting from assessment are indicators of student achievement and progress; accordingly, they should not be used to punish or reward students, or as a barometer for student behavior.

Record Keeping

Briefcase CD CH8-14— Grade Book Example

As a teacher, you are responsible for maintaining and updating student achievement records. The more information on a student's progress you compile, the more efficient and complete your assessments of the student's achievement. At the elementary level, records of testing scores, comments, and assessments are all used to determine a child's passage to the next grade, the need for special education services, or recommendations for psychological reviews (Figure 8–1).

Note Taking

Chapter 4 covered keeping records such as a daily diary or journal. However, you should also record comments or notations that will give you additional information about the student's performance on each assignment. Most grade books do not provide ample space for note taking, so you should make these notations in your daily journal. When the time comes to configure the final grades for the report card or to sit in conference with a parent, this additional information will prove invaluable.

Attendance

Vigilantly keep a daily attendance record for each class you teach. For the teacher, maintaining attendance records is a legal obligation that is sometimes tested in the courts. As an employee of the school district, you are acting as a surrogate parent insofar as knowing the physical whereabouts of each child. You may be called on to verify that a child was in fact in your classroom for a specified period. For example, if a child is charged with committing a crime during the time he or she was supposed to be in your class, you may be asked to verify, in an official capacity, whether the child was in your classroom at that time. In such a case, you will have to produce your attendance book, which will then be entered into evidence as an official document. Thus, taking attendance is serious business.

Many teachers allow students to take attendance as part of their classroom citizenship. Although doing so is an excellent way to instill a sense of responsibility, it is also fraught with legal entanglements. Remember that you are solely and legally responsible for the official attendance records of your class. Any mistakes a student makes become your mistakes. Also, you may want to consider the dangers of a student's viewing your official records and sharing this information with peers. Err on the side of caution and take your own attendance.

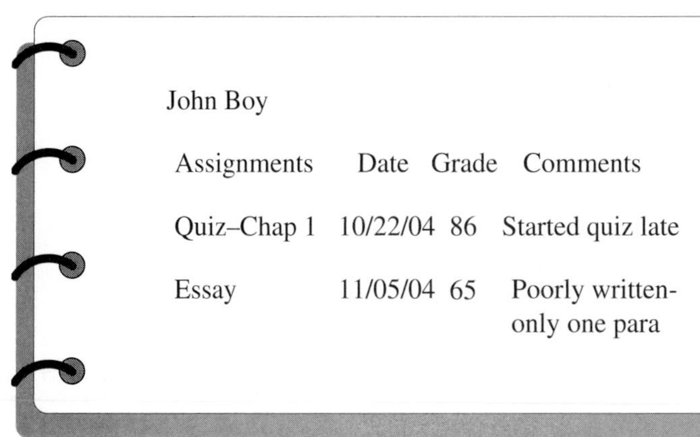

John Boy

Assignments	Date	Grade	Comments
Quiz–Chap 1	10/22/04	86	Started quiz late
Essay	11/05/04	65	Poorly written- only one para

Figure 8-1. *Sample entry in a teacher's grade book*

Records and Parents

As a result of the Family Educational Rights and Privacy Act (FERPA), also known as the *Buckley Amendment,* parents have the right to see any of their child's records kept by the school. They have a guaranteed right to view their child's records after a reasonable notice is given to the school or district. However, parents do not have right to look at your grade book or ask to see evaluations you write of their child's work because the act notes that records kept solely by you, the maker of the records, need not be disclosed to the parents or the student. Parents are only entitled to know their child's grades and be made aware of comments or insertions in the child's permanent school record.

DOS AND DON'TS

Don't	Do
Use commercially prepared multiple-choice questions without checking that their content is valid in relation to the material you taught	Refer to other sources for test material and incorporate it into your testing format
Use true–false questions as a valid or reliable assessment of student learning	Use true–false questions to reinforce the material taught or to stimulate discussion
Purposefully design multiple-choice questions to confuse or challenge your students' ability to solve the puzzle	Design test questions that are concise and directly related to the material taught
Rely on any single instrument to assess student learning Box yourself into a corner by stating that a student's final grade or report card grade is determined by a single test	Use a variety of instruments to compile a student's grade
Assume that students with languages other than English (LOTE) understand test questions or directions even if they do not ask for clarification	Provide students with languages other than English (LOTE) with additional help and direction before testing
Take a week or longer to correct written work	Return students' written work within 48 hours or other reasonable time margins
Fail to comment on written work	Return students' written work with ample comments on responses that are commendable and on those that need improvement
Give take-home tests constructed on the knowledge level of cognition	Construct take-home tests that require student thinking and reflection of material taught
Assign a project or an extensive paper without providing a rubric	Provide students with some form of rubric against which they may determine the level at which they are performing
Give a report card grade based on the grades of a few quizzes or assignments	Derive report card grades from a variety of assignments that reflect student achievement in detail
Use a student's behavior to influence the grade you assign for academic performance	Remember that grading a student's academic performance on the basis of his or her classroom behavior is illegal
Allow students to take attendance unless you supervise the process (remember that you are legally responsible for attendance records and that you cannot relegate this responsibility)	Design various methods of attendance taking that involve student participation but also provide accurate accounting data (students should never take attendance in an official capacity)
Keep a sloppy filing system or forget to record grades or other notations on a student's progress or achievement	Organize a filing system that is secure and organized for easy access

WEB SITES OF INTEREST

http://www.geocities.com/jnsteinke/ferpa/ferpa.htm
This site gives an excellent summary and interpretation of the Family Educational Rights and Privacy Act (FERPA).

http://school.discovery.com/schrockguide/assess.html
This excellent site has samples of rubrics.

http://www.tki.org.nz/r/assessment/atol_online/ppt/online_workshop_1.ppt
This site provides a PowerPoint presentation on both formative and summative assessment.

http://fcit.usf.edu/assessment/basic/basicc.html
This site provides practical information on the reliability and validity of tests.

http://course1.winona.edu/lgray/el626/Articlesonline/Popham.html
This site provides an article on teaching to the test.

http://www.teachermentors.com/RSOD%20Site/PerfAssmt/P.AssmtLinks.html
This site has numerous links to other sites on performance assessment.

http://fp.uni.edu/teachctr/cet_web/test.html
This site includes some interesting points on grading.

http://www.learner.org/resources/series93.html
This site is about assessment in math and science.

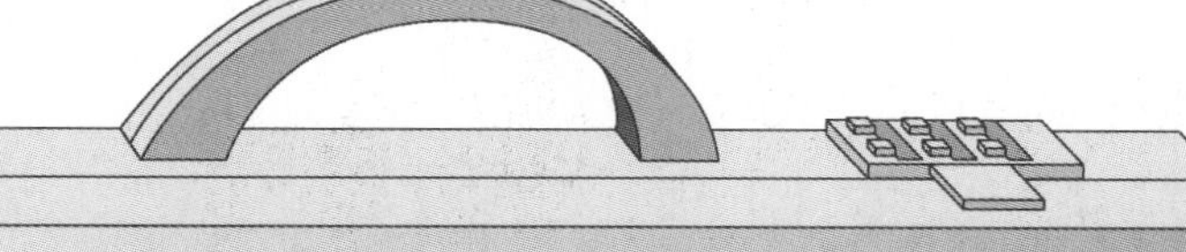

For Your Briefcase

To Do

- Examine your curriculum to determine which assessments will best reflect student comprehension.
- Develop rubrics for essays and projects.
- Develop a guideline sheet for students' portfolios.

Resources on Your Briefcase CD

Samples

- Examples of Effective and Ineffective Multiple-Choice Questions
- Examples of When to Use Matching Tests
- Performance Assessment Examples
- Sample Classroom Assessment Techniques
- Generic Rubric Examples
- Sample Rubric
- Grade Book Example

Templates

- Checklist for Writing Multiple-Choice Questions
- Checklist for Writing Essay Questions
- Portfolio Checklist

Tables

- Types of Matching Tests
- Grading Methods and Their Applications
- Letter Grading Formats
- Grading on a Curve

REFERENCES

Angelo, T. A., & Cross, K. P. (1993). *Classroom assessment techniques: A handbook for college teachers* (2nd ed.). San Francisco: Jossey-Bass.

Ballantyne, C. (2003). *Multiple choice tests.* Murdoch, Western Australia: Teaching and Learning Centre, Murdoch University. Retrieved June 29, 2004, from http://www.tlc.murdoch.edu.au/eddev/evaluation/mcq/mctests.html#constructing

Carbo, M., Dunn, K., & Dunn, R. (1994). *Teaching students to read through their individual learning styles*. Upper Saddle River, NJ: Prentice Hall.

Kohn, A. (2004, November 10). *Performance vs. learning.* Speech given at Gibson Theater, Elmira College, Elmira, NY.

Koretz, D., Klein, S., McCaffrey, D., & Stecher, B. (1993, December). *Interim report: The reliability of Vermont portfolio scores in the 1992–93 school year* (CSE Tech. Rep. No. 370). Los Angeles: University of California, National Center for Research on Evaluation, Standards, and Student Testing (CRESST).

Moon, T. R., Callahan, C. M., & Tomlinson, C. A. (2003, April 28). Effects of state testing programs on elementary schools with high concentrations of student poverty—Good news or bad news? *Current Issues in Education, 6*(8). Retrieved February 10, 2006, from http://cie.ed.asu.edu/volume6/number8/

Ogle, D. M. (1986, February). K-W-L: A teaching model that develops active reading of expository text. *The Reading Teacher, 39*(6), 564–570.

Smith v. School, City of Hobart, 811 F. Supp. 391 (N.D. Ind. 1993).

Wiggins, G. (1990). The case for authentic assessment. *Practical Assessment, Research & Evaluation, 2*(2). Retrieved July 4, 2004, from http://PAREonline.net/getvn.asp?v=2n=2

Becoming an Effective Teacher

Knowing Your Students

Children need adults who are convinced of the value of childhood. They need adults who will protect them from the ever-ready molders of their world. They need adults who can help them to develop their own healthy controls, who can encourage them to explore their own unique endowments, who can know the limits of their ego strengths and not allow programmers of any sort to infringe on those limits. Children need adults—in every walk of life—who care as much for children as they care for themselves.

—*Fred Rogers* (1994)

LEARNING WHO YOUR STUDENTS ARE

Briefcase CD CH9-1—*Characteristics of* Students

Children are the same and they are different. We as adults tend to think that the current generation of children is alike in every way with us when we were children, so we are surprised when we find this idea to be false. We hear our parents' refrain echoing in our mind: "Kids were different when I was your age." Some of us even believe this saying to be true, and, from a strictly scientific perspective, children *are* different.

The children you will teach will be relatively alike in their physical development, less alike in their emotional and cognitive development, and mostly different in personality. What makes them *who* they are is a combination of the following:

- Physical development
- Emotional development
- Cognitive development
- Social development
- Family composition
- Family socioeconomic status
- Family values

MORALS AND ETHICS—WHAT IS THE DIFFERENCE?

Aristotle defined *morals* as that which a society establishes as its behavioral norm, whereas *ethics* is how the individual responds to this moral code. Some people believe that we are all aware of what is right and what is wrong, and that simply applying the rule of universality provides us with a moral and ethical standard (Wood, 2001).

CHARACTERISTICS OF STUDENTS

Stage	Characteristics	Impact
Physical development	Students are either within the mean range of height and weight, or late or early maturing.	Students' physical development may affect their relationships with peers and their self-esteem.
Emotional development	Students may demonstrate maturity levels consistent or inconsistent with their age.	Emotional development may influence students' relationships with parents and other individuals in authority.
Cognitive development	Students will most likely demonstrate the cognitive competence reflected in Piaget's stages of development.	Cognitive development affects students' personal decision making and choices relating to their class work.
Social development	Students' social interaction will range from late to early maturing and is influenced by their physical, emotional, and cognitive development.	Social development has a significant impact on classroom behavior and the learning process.
Family composition	Families can be categorized as one of the following: two parent, single parent, other than parent, one parent with spouse, one parent with spouse and children from another family, or same-sex parents.	Family composition affects students' school performance and their relationships.
Family socioeconomic status	According to U.S. Census reports, a family's socioeconomic status will fall into a specific category: low income, low to middle income, middle income, high to middle income, or high income.	A family's socioeconomic status may have an enormous effect on the quality of a student's education.
Family values	Each family will either subscribe to a specific religion or political persuasion, or have no preference. Each family will also adhere to a personal code of ethical and moral behavior.	Students are influenced by their parents' religion and political beliefs.

VOICES IN THE CLASSROOM
Student Perspectives on Their Teachers

I was most influenced by my music teacher, Mr. Eric Blodgett. By loving his job, he made everyone else enjoy learning about all of the fundamentals of music. He alone taught me about having a good work ethic and striving for my dream. He believed in me like no one else and gave me every advantage to make all of my dreams success stories. He forced me to do things I never wanted to embark upon, but with the result that he taught me a lesson: By trying new things, you can build character and advance your limits. His class was anything but easy, and he took music very seriously. We practiced every other day, and taking our instrument home was not an option.

He made us believe that anything is possible when your heart is in it. If you watched his face when he taught us about Beethoven or Bach, you could tell that he started and finished each and every day with the same energy and enthusiasm as he had the day before.

Unfortunately, I was not given the chance to meet Mr. Berst until my senior year, when I took his government class in the fall. I could immediately tell that I would like him. His friendly appearance made his classroom a welcoming environment. He was eagerly willing to share insight on all different topics, and he was very easy to talk to. I felt as if I could tell him or ask him anything.

He told us made-up stories about how he was born in a scientific lab and said that he was more powerful than any other weapon. He told us these crazy stories and corny jokes to catch our attention and help pull us into a lecture.

One of the things that I liked most about his classes was the debates and discussions that he would start. Our class luckily fell during the election, so we had the chance to learn about all the different positions that the candidates held and debate about them.

I learned a great deal from Mr. Berst during that class. I loved the enthusiasm and excitement that he dedicated to the class. We felt like [his] priority while we listened to him teach.

Note. (*Left column*) Reprinted from the essay "The Worst and Best Teacher in My Education," by Jennifer Jenkins, with her permission. (*Right column*) Reprinted from the essay "The Worst and Best Teacher in My Education," by Ryan Thompson, with her permission.

STATING THE FACTS:

On teenagers:

- According to the results of a 1999 study, 71% of the general public believe teenagers are lazy, disrespectful, and wild (Duffett, Johnson, & Farkas, 1999).
- Teenage crime is at its lowest since 1967, and 47% of all teenagers volunteer in the community (Federal Bureau of Investigation, 2002).
- Drug abuse is down almost 30%, and pregnancy and abortion rates are down 50% (Federal Interagency Forum on Child and Family Statistics, 2003).

Each Generation by Name

Each person belongs to a generation that supposedly bears specific characteristics earning its members a stereotypical name: the Silent Generation, Baby Boomers, Generation X, Millennials, or, the latest, the Cyber Generation. If each generation did possess these characteristics, teachers' jobs would be much simpler. By examining the character traits of the so-called **Millennial Generation** (the children currently in the classroom), teachers could establish methods that would help them control, or at least understand, their students' behaviors.

The following profile of the Millennial Generation reflects the view of Neil Howe and William Strauss (2003), who believe that members of the United States can be categorized by virtue of their position in the time line:

CHARACTERISTICS OF MILLENNIAL CHILDREN

Born after 1979, Millennial children

- Are visual and often see concepts in terms of logos, brand names, and symbols (e.g., Nike)
- Are considered one of the most nurtured of all generations
- Have experienced, as a matter of course, school lockdowns, extreme safety measures, the presence of security guards in school, and expansive antidrug and antialcohol programs
- Have a good deal of self-assurance, self-confidence, and faith in the future
- Have confidence in their parents' decisions and believe in the family
- Are comfortable with technology and believe college is necessary

Differences Between Children in the Past and Today's Students

Briefcase CD CH9-2—Statistics on U.S. Children

The "Baby on Board" signs found on the bumpers and windows of the family vehicle introduced the Millennial Generation. These signs gave people the idea that these children were cared for as no other generation. Some people believe that these children were coddled, others that they were nurtured with the best ideals and materials (Howe & Strauss, 2003). The problem with attributing set traits to an entire group of children, or even adults, is that people are surprised when individuals in the group do not behave as expected.

Whether or not you believe in generational profiling, children's interests, activities, and lifestyles change every decade or so. However, teachers would be naive to think that all children will behave in accordance with a set standard by virtue of their generational status. The broader truth is that each student is an individual with specific needs and interests, albeit influenced by environment and family.

STATING THE FACTS:

On crime and violence among teens: Since 1993, the rates for serious violent crime committed by youths aged 12 to 17 dropped from 44 times per 1,000 to 18 times per 1,000 (Federal Interagency Forum on Child and Family Statistics, 2005).

STATISTICS ON U.S. CHILDREN

Factor	Statistic
Number (aged newborn to 18 years)	73,043,506
Percentage of total U.S. population	26%
By race and ethnicity as percentage of total U.S. population	Hispanic/Latino: 16% African American: 15% Asian/Pacific Islander: 4% American Indian/Alaskan: 1%
Limited English proficiency	3.5 million (4.7%)
Living with two parents	68.8% (38% African American; 65% Hispanic/Latino)
Living with only mother	23%
Living with only father	4%
Living with grandparents	6%
Population percentage considered married	59%
First marriages ending in divorce	50%
Total number divorcing each year	4.0 per 1,000 of population
Estimated number of children involved in divorce	1,075,000
Decrease in standard of living for females after divorce	45%
Women stalked by an ex-husband	380,000 per year
Men stalked by an ex-wife	52,000
Likelihood children of divorce will divorce	50%
Poor children in the United States	12,518,068 (17.2% of all children)
Children in families receiving food stamps	9,687,950 (13.2% of all children)
Children in school lunch program	29,600,000 (39.9% of all children)
Children who were victims of abuse or neglect (reported)	895,569 (1.23% of all children)

Factor	Statistic
Per-pupil expenditure in public schools (2003)	$8,073
Fourth graders' reading proficiency	73%
Fourth graders' math proficiency	80%
Average class size, public elementary schools	21.1
Average class size, public secondary schools	23.6
Children without health insurance coverage	9.3 million (12.7% of all children)
Children not fully immunized	25%
High school completion rate	85.7%
Juvenile violent crime	12% of all violent crime
Children and teens in correctional custody	100,510
Children (aged 1–18 years) killed by firearms (2003)	1,836
Religious composition (2001)	Protestant: 54% Roman Catholic: 25.9% Jewish: 1.4% Islamic: 0.6% No preference: 15.0% Various sects: 0.7%

Note. Data from *American Religious Identification Survey,* by The Graduate Center, The City University of New York, n.d., New York: Author (Retrieved March 2006 from http://www.gc.cuny.edu/faculty/research_briefs/aris/key_findings.htm); *Children Living Arrangements and Characteristics: March 2002* (Pub. No. P20-547), by U.S. Census Bureau, June 2003, Washington, DC: Author (Retrieved March 5, 2006, from http://www.census.gov/prod/2003pubs/p20-547.pdf); "A Decade of Effort," by L. Olson, January 5, 2006, *Education Week,* 25(17), pp. 8–10, 12, 14, 16, 18–21; *Digest of Education Statistics, 2000* (Pub. No. NCES 2001-034), by T. D. Snyder and C. Hoffman, 2001, Washington, DC: National Center for Education Statistics, U.S. Department of Education (Retrieved March 2006 from http://nces.ed.gov/pubsearch/pubsinfo.asp?pubid=2001034); *Divorce Statistics Collection,* by Americans for Divorce Reform, n.d., Arlington, VA: Author (Retrieved March 2006 from http://www.divorcereform.org/index.html); *Good News About Public Schools in Oregon,* by National Education Association, n.d., Washington, DC: Author (Retrieved March 5, 2006, from http://www.nea.org/goodnews/or01.html); *Health Insurance Coverage in the United States: 2002* (Pub. No. P60-223), by U.S. Census Bureau, September 2003, Washington, DC: Author (Retrieved March 5, 2006, from http://www.census.gov/prod/2003pubs/p60-223.pdf); *Juvenile Arrests 2003* (Bulletin No. NCJ 209735), by Office of Juvenile Justice and Delinquency Prevention, U.S. Department of Justice, August 2005, Washington, DC: Author (Retrieved March 2006 from http://www.ncjrs.gov/html/ojjdp/209735/contents.html); *Poverty: 2004 Highlights,* by U.S. Census Bureau, Housing and Household Economic Statistics Division, 2005, Washington, DC: Author (Retrieved March 5, 2006, from http://www.census.gov/hhes/www/poverty/poverty04/pov04hi.html); *Profile of State Prisoners Under Age 18, 1985–97* (Special Rep. No. NCJ 176989), by U.S. Department of Justice, Bureau of Justice Statistics, February 2000, Washington, DC: Author (Retrieved March 2006 from http://www.ojp.usdoj.gov/bjs/abstract/pspa1897.htm); *Program data: child nutrition tables,* by Food and Nutrition Service, U.S. Department of Agriculture, n.d., Alexandria, VA: Author (Retrieved March 5, 2006, from http://www.fns.usda.gov/pd/cnpmain.htm); *Public Education Finances: 2003,* by U.S. Census Bureau, March 2005, Washington, DC: Author (Retrieved March 5, 2006, from http://ftp2.census.gov/govs/school/03f33pub.pdf); *Welcome to WISQARS™,* by National Center for Injury Prevention and Control, Centers for Disease Control and Prevention, n.d., Atlanta, GA: Author (Retrieved March 2006 from http://www.cdc.gov/ncipc/wisqars).

Family Composition

The family unit has undergone drastic changes since the 1970s. Gone are the 1950s television-land families comprising a mom, a dad, and 2.5 children. Following is an overview of the modern U.S. family, in accordance with the U.S. Census Bureau (Fields, 2003):

- ☑ Of all family households, 68.8% have two live-in parents.
- ☑ Among the 111 million households, 57% have children younger than age 18 years.
- ☑ Of families with children, 27.7% have one parent.
- ☑ Twenty-three percent of children are living with a female parent.

STATING THE FACTS:

On stepfamilies:

- Stepparents and noncustodial parents are far less willing to lay out cash for college than are parents in intact marriages (Sandefur, McLanahan, & Wojtkiewicz, 1992).
- Living in a mother–stepfather family has as much of a negative effect as living in a mother-only family (Furstenberg & Cherlin, 1991).

☑ Among U.S. children, 4.3% are living with a relative other than their biological parents.

☑ Each year, more than 1 million children are added to the group known as "children of divorce."

☑ Fifty-eight percent of all divorced children live with one biological parent and his or her partner.

☑ Only 22.4% of families comprise one wage earner who is male.

☑ The percentage of same-sex female householders with children was reported as 17% in 1998.

In Real Time: Sensitivity to Family Composition

No other factor is more essential in the modern classroom than a teacher's sensitivity to his or her student's family composition. Many students will be without a live-in father or mother or will have a live-in stepfather or stepmother, whereas many others will be living with grandparents or other relatives. This fact should automatically prevent you from using the casual phrase "your moms and dads." Train yourself in the use of the word guardian, or the more commonly used caregiver. *Do not assume that a child is a member of the traditionally held concept of* the family.

Briefcase CD CH9-3—Quickstats on Socio-economic Status

Socioeconomic Status

The socioeconomic status of the students in your classes depends on the geographic location of your school and whether it is rural, urban, or suburban. Nevertheless, children of poverty seem to be prevalent in most schools, regardless of location or demographics.

QUICKSTATS ON SOCIOECONOMIC STATUS

Factor	Stat
Poverty line	$18,104 (31.7% of the population)
Total number of children in poverty	13 million
African American children at poverty level	22.7%
Hispanic children at poverty level	21.4%
Living on less than $25,000 a year	27.7% Caucasian 42.5% African American 37.2% Hispanic
Average income for female-only householder with children	$25,175

Note. Data from *America's Children: Key National Indicators of Well-Being 2003*, by Federal Interagency Forum on Child and Family Statistics, July 2003, Washington, DC: U.S. Government Printing Office. Retrieved March 20, 2006, from http://www.childstats.gov/index.asp

In Real Time: Sensitivity to Domestic Situations

A teacher must always be mindful of his or her students' home life as it pertains to socioeconomic status. Such consideration is essential when you are assigning your students project work that may require purchasing expensive materials or when you nonchalantly ask your class to bring in "something for the party tomorrow."

Religious Composition

The religious composition of the children in your classroom may follow the national pattern; however, a well-prepared teacher should be aware that each community shapes the religious makeup of its schools. Religious influence can be noticeable in some areas of the United States and may have an impact on the type of textbooks used, the scope of holiday celebrations, and the content of science instruction and some health classes on sexual awareness (Hoffman, Sable, Naum, & Gray, 2006).

U.S. RELIGIOUS COMPOSITION

Religion	Percentage of adult population
Catholic	25.9
Baptist	19.4
Methodist	8.0
Lutheran	5.2
Presbyterian	2.8
Jewish	1.8
Pentecostal	1.8
Episcopalian	1.7
Mormon	1.4
Churches of Christ	1.0
Jehovah's Witnesses	0.8
No preference	15.0
Undetermined	21.9

Note. Data from *America's Children: Key National Indicators of Well-Being 2003*, by Federal Interagency Forum on Child and Family Statistics, July 2003, Washington, DC: U.S. Government Printing Office. Retrieved March 20, 2006, from http://www.childstats.gov/index.asp

In Real Time: **Sensitivity to Religion**

Whether teaching 1st or 12th grade, any teacher must be constantly aware of the sensitivity of some students to the issue of religion. Teachers must take extra care when dealing with religious subjects, historical facts, events, or figures. They should always be referred to in the objective case and never personalized with religious beliefs or bias. Furthermore, assignments that skirt religious values should be avoided (e.g., the famous lifeboat exercise in which students form groups and decide who is or is not valuable in the face of life-threatening decisions).

Students with Special Needs

Approximately 13%, or 6.4 million, students are classified as learning disabled (Hoffman et al., 2006). Each year, more students are being included in regular education classrooms (formerly known as *mainstreaming*), and in most cases, these classrooms have been assigned a resource teacher to "push in" as support. One consequence of the laws governing special education is a coteaching configuration in which the classroom teacher is assigned a special education teacher and possibly a teacher's aide to work with students with special needs. As a novice teacher, you should be aware that the special considerations given classified students are mandated by federal law and are nonnegotiable. Denying a child who has been classified any of the considerations outlined in his or her plan is illegal. Although you are responsible for this child's grades and progress, the special education teacher can be of great assistance to you by working with the child individually.

BEING COGNIZANT OF STUDENTS' DEVELOPMENT

Briefcase CD CH9-4—Developmental Stages

As a teacher, you must know the developmental stages of the children you teach. Following is a synopsis of these stages to give you a quick reference and a reminder that physical, cognitive, and socioemotional development can affect student learning and motivation.

DEVELOPMENTAL STAGES

Early to middle childhood		
Physical	***Cognitive***	***Socioemotional***
Grows $2^1/_2$ inches in height each year Gains 5–7 pounds in weight each year Experiences refinement of gross- and fine-motor skills	Has brain growth from nine tenths of adult size to full size Has almost complete neuronic development, which is most intense during early childhood Is evolving from thinking concretely to thinking symbolically	Is more comfortable with strangers Seeks initiatives and experiments with autonomy
Middle childhood through adolescence		
Physical	***Cognitive***	***Socioemotional***
Experiences a growth spurt (awkward stage) Has a tremendous hormonal surge and development of sexual organs	Is completely aware of the symbolic Is egocentric in perspective Is in a period of fantasy and blatant generalization	Is establishing autonomy Is developing relationships Is formulating a self-identity

Early to Middle Childhood Development (Ages 5–11 Years)

Physical Development The physical body develops rapidly in early childhood. During this stage, the body experiences a refinement of fine- and gross-motor skills.

Strategies for You as a Teacher Children need to move their bodies during this time of life; therefore, be sure to do the following:

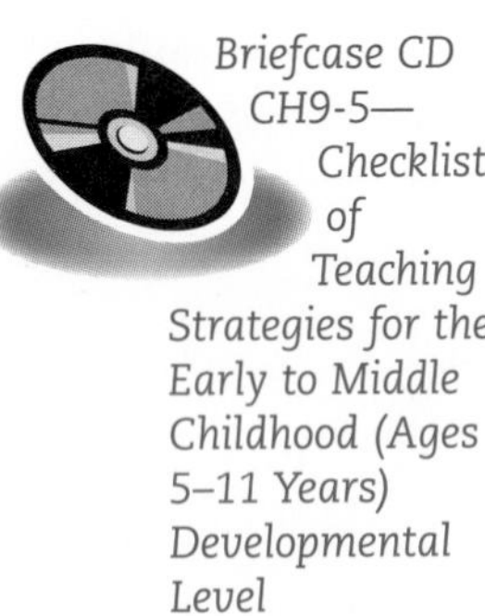

Briefcase CD CH9-5—Checklist of Teaching Strategies for the Early to Middle Childhood (Ages 5–11 Years) Developmental Level

☑ Plan to move your students around the room as you switch subjects, or arrange to move from one style of teaching to another (e.g., presentation format to group format).

☑ Fully use recess time, making sure all children take part in activities (outdoors if possible), or schedule midmorning and midafternoon exercise sessions of at least 5 minutes.

☑ Provide activities in which children use hand–eye coordination.

☑ Schedule lavatory visits at relatively the same times each morning and afternoon.

Cognitive Development Cognitive development is as rapid as physical development. The size of the brain is out of proportion to body size; at age 3 years, it is 75% of its adult size, and at age 5 years, a full nine tenths (Santrock, 2000). The brain is undergoing rapid neuronal growth, and during this time, cognitive stimulation is important for children in the learning process (Caine & Caine, 1994).

Strategies for You as a Teacher Children require connections and elaboration when learning new material. Therefore, keep these points in mind:

- ☑ When introducing a new topic, provide numerous comparisons to other items that you know relate to children's lives (e.g., pizza sizes when discussing fractions, the four seasons when discussing change, or comparison of the balance of power to that of a football or basketball game).
- ☑ Give your students an opportunity to reflect on the information provided (i.e., do not move on to a new concept on the same day that you introduce another concept).
- ☑ Be patient if the next day your students do not remember what you taught the previous day. The young brain needs reinforcement and connectivity before it makes permanent schemata that signal true comprehension.
- ☑ Do not institute punitive measures when a child is struggling to understand difficult concepts.
- ☑ Provide peer interactive activities to increase comprehension.

Socioemotional Development Socioemotionally, the young child is at what Erik Erikson calls the stage of *initiative versus guilt.* As children explore their world, initiative that is seen as mistakes that are punished could generate a flush of guilt that lowers self-esteem. Also, at this stage, children begin to feel the guilt of committing a crime against authority and punish themselves for simple transgressions (Santrock, 2000).

Strategies for You as a Teacher At this time, peer influence begins to gain strength as children see the value of cooperation and play with one another, so be sure to do the following:

- ☑ Allow your students time to talk with one another, either within the context of the lesson or casually.
- ☑ Capitalize on students' fascination with videos and the digital world by using animated software or showing film and television clips to enhance your lessons.
- ☑ Allow all students a chance to participate by giving each of them a classroom responsibility at which they can succeed.
- ☑ When engaged in organized projects, allow students to choose some direction and sequence for completion of the work.
- ☑ Always be prepared for some form of conflict resolution that is as nonintrusive as possible (i.e., that is not overwhelmingly authoritative, such as shouting or stopping all children's play to correct just one or two students).
- ☑ Have a recourse for children who do not play well with others or are bullying others (e.g., remove them from the room or recess area, engage them in a separate activity, encourage them to help with a task).

STATING THE FACTS:

On television viewing: The average American child spends 1,500 hours per year watching television but only 900 hours in school (Tashman, 1994).

Middle Childhood Through Adolescence (Ages 12–18 Years)

Physical Development The physical growth seen during this stage is most generally described by the words *awkward* and *sudden.* Most notable is the development of the body in preparation for sexual reproduction, which causes obvious bodily changes.

Strategies for You as a Teacher The middle school teacher must be sensitive to this awkward stage. Following are some tips:

- ☑ In your classroom management plan, insist on mutual respect that forbids name-calling and bullying.

Briefcase CD CH9-6—Checklist of Teaching Strategies for the Middle Childhood Through Adolescence (Ages 12–18 Years) Developmental Level

- ☑ Refrain from assigning boys seats in cramped corners or tight places that might highlight their awkwardness.
- ☑ Relax strict lavatory visitations for females and consider that their needs may differ from those of males at this time of their life.
- ☑ Refrain from comments directed at the body, either in jest or for use as examples.
- ☑ Be aware that teenage sleep patterns are affected at this stage of development and that being sleepy in the morning has more to do with changing circadian rhythms (Carskadon, Wolfson, Tzischinsky, & Acebo, 1995).

Cognitive Development Cognitively, the adolescent has reached Piaget's formal operational stage of development but is still egocentric in his or her thinking. At this time, the teenager engages in sweeping generalizations of thought characterized by either–or reasoning that is often devoid of sound logic and begins to understand hypothetical thinking.

Stating the Facts:

On the brain in adolescence: Scientists now believe that adolescence is when the final neuronal growth spurt occurs, sometime between ages 12 and 15, with active enlargement of the area in the frontal or occipital portions of the brain where speech centers are located (Sprenger, 1999).

Strategies for You as a Teacher This time in a child's life begs for teacher guidance and patience:

- ☑ Provide materials that challenge students' capabilities through problem-solving and extensive inquiry-based procedures.
- ☑ Invite student participation in the organization of materials to be used for instruction.
- ☑ Allow students to share their ideas with peers through nonthreatening dialogue, debate, or discussion.
- ☑ Capitalize on students' fantasy-driven writing and concepts to place curricular material in a context of their understanding.
- ☑ Encourage an environment of idea sharing as free as possible from value judgments by you or peers.

Socioemotional Development The teenager's socioemotional growth is a time for social experimentation and confrontation of issues relating to privacy, dating, and attachment. This crucial period can have lasting influences throughout a person's life, and teachers play an essential role as nurturers for their students.

Strategies for You as a Teacher As you teach adolescents, you will need to be firm. Following are some guidelines for dealing with teens in light of their socioemotional status:

Stating the Facts:

On teenagers' views of their role: Adolescence may also be a time when the teenager sees him- or herself in a heroic role or, more dangerously, in the role of victim (Santrock, 2000).

- ☑ Resist the pressure to place friends near friends during grouping situations.
- ☑ Draw attention away from the student considered different or nerdy by involving the student in gainful participation.
- ☑ Resist calling too frequently on the brightest, most alert students, which may inadvertently result in your being labeled a teacher who has favorites—and the students' being labeled as "teacher's pets."
- ☑ Consider that young teens are loud and expressive, which should preclude your need to have an absolutely quiet classroom.
- ☑ Consider that older teens are quiet, sometimes reclusive, and nonexpressive, which should preclude your judgment that they are not interested in what you are teaching.

LEGAL SIDEBAR

Corporal Punishment

Corporal punishment is less prevalent today. Twenty-seven states and the District of Columbia prohibit any type of corporal punishment in public schools. Twenty-three states permit it, but in most of these states, local districts are given latitude on its use (Center for Effective Discipline, n.d.)

TAKING THE STUDENTS' PERSPECTIVE INTO CONSIDERATION

Students come to school carrying a variety of interests and burdens.

The most important people in the school are the students. This fact should be evident; yet, abundant proof exists that the student is often the last consideration when programs, initiatives, and regulations are put into effect. Often the student is thought of as a collective entity who is the recipient of services the institution provides. Rules and regulations are created to prevent harm to all students, to encourage academic excellence, and to accommodate the daily needs of each member of the student body. However, at times, this ideal goal falls short in reality.

As you try to understand the students you teach, consider how they view the rules that govern their daily world. Having such an understanding will help you make informed decisions when you are dealing with the everyday issues that affect the learning process.

CONSIDERATION FOR THE STUDENT

Situation	Consideration
Sitting quietly for long periods is difficult.	Provide frequent breaks during which children may get up and stretch or walk around the room. This practice should apply to high school students as well.
Young people have opinions, and although naive at times, young people of all ages want to be heard.	Allow students to voice their opinions. Provide time for them to vocalize what they understand to be true, giving them an opportunity to test their theories.
Some children need more time to think ideas through. Most students need time to assimilate information and to reflect on difficult concepts.	Do not allow the few students who grasp concepts more quickly to set the pace of instruction. Be sure that all students are invited to participate at their own pace.

—*Cont.*

Situation	Consideration
Discipline is important, but not the reason for schooling.	Structure your classroom environment and teaching program around the academics, not the controlling influence of behavior codes. Remember that the codes are a means, not an end, in your program.
Silliness is part of being a child.	Children's silliness is part of growing and should be channeled within the teaching program. It provides an opportunity to instruct students on what is funny and when comedy is appropriate.
Children are vulnerable. A child can be easily manipulated by an adult, both parent and teacher.	Allow students opportunities to develop their individualism through experimentation and expression of their own views.

STATING THE FACTS:

On student discipline: A survey of 725 teachers revealed that 80% believed discipline problems stemmed from a few troublemakers and that unruly student behavior is the main problem that depresses them and is an incentive for them to leave the profession (Vogel, 2004).

Cafeteria and Total Silence

Need for the Rule Children are, by nature, active and kinesthetic. Lunchtime calls for a relaxation of the rules of order. Some children cannot control themselves and cause chaos through excessive noise and worse—throwing food. The rights of all children are being violated when a few disrupt this period, and in some cases this chaos can be dangerous to students' safety.

Students' Perspective Young growing bodies need exercise and release from hours of restrictive activity. Culturally, eating food is a natural time for interaction, talk, and spontaneity. Total silence shuts down this interaction and robs students of needed interaction and release from confinement and work.

Tardiness

Need for the Rule Rules against tardiness are geared to prevent the consistent laggardness of some students in getting to school or to class. Without these rules, students would be lingering in the halls or setting their own time schedules and disrupting the instructional program.

Students' Perspective Being late is often caused by unavoidable events in life such as having car trouble, oversleeping, being involved in small accidents, or forgetting books, homework, and so forth. Having a blanket rule that punishes all students for tardiness without allowing for the occasional mishap dismisses the student's individual needs.

Gum Chewing and Eating in Class

Need for the Rule Gum chewing and eating snacks in class only disrupt the student from his or her lessons. In addition, it creates a waste hazard and can destroy school materials through abuse.

Students' Perspective The need for sugar or quick energy is natural for the growing body, and unfortunately U.S. youths consume an enormous amount of sugared treats; for them it is a habit. Most difficult for students is the inconsistency in the application of the rule—when one teacher allows it and other teachers do not. Such inconsistency only confuses them, providing a rationale for not obeying the rule.

Homework

Need for the Rule Assigning homework generally begins as early as first or second grade, and its purpose is crucial to a teacher's instructional program, both as reinforcement of the material taught and as an assessment of the learning process. It also provides continuity of instruction from day to day.

Students' Perspective Homework is an intrusion into the personal, out-of-school part of students' lives. Often, homework assignments are a source of stress because they are ambiguous or require skills that have not yet been completely learned. In addition, forgotten homework, a natural occurrence in the lives of developing children, can cause distress resulting from punitive measures imposed by the teacher.

DEALING WITH PARENTAL PRESSURE ON STUDENTS

As just discussed, the life of a student can be daunting if you take the time to view it from his or her perspective. Besides dealing with the inherent stressors resulting from the school–child relationship, many students are caught in the achievement race perpetrated by highly motivated parents. Such students' grades are in the top 20%, and these students are usually intensively involved in one or more sports or activities. Their days are filled with going to practice, doing homework, and being shuttled to events.

STATING THE FACTS:

On students' schedules:

- "An estimated 38 million children between ages 5 and 18 participate in one or more organized sports programs in the United States—but every year, a third of them quit. Some switch to other sports, some pursue other interests, and some just burn out" (Creager, 1999, p. A1).
- "In just the past 20 years structured sports time has doubled, unstructured children's activities have gone down 50%, household conversations have become far less frequent, family dinners have declined 33%, and family vacations have decreased 28%. Kids have become talent to be groomed" (Rosenfeld & Wise, 2000, p. 179).

Rigor Versus Excess

Children who are the products of *hyper-parenting,* a word coined by Dr. Alvin Rosenfeld and Nicole Wise (2000), are known as *overscheduled children,* a technical term for the children of the moms and dads who are argumentatively aggressive for their children to achieve in a highly competitive world. The days beyond school hours for these children are crowded with lessons, games, and activities, all geared to prepare them for each level of schooling in the years ahead, and beyond to the workplace. To the parents' credit, ample research results indicate that extracurricular activities both improve academic success (Galley, 2000; Holloway, 1999–2000) and promote positive social ties among peers (Broh, 2002).

However, the stress that may occur as a result of overscheduling is clearly addressed by Erikson's psychosocial development theory of *identity versus role confusion* and *intimacy versus isolation.* During these stages, the preadolescent and adolescent struggle with their role within the social environment and with initiating and maintaining relationships (Erikson, 1968).

The Consequences

As the teen tries to deal with all these expectations, he or she may seek solace by pursuing activities that provide comfort and acceptance. Often, such activities include drug and alcohol use, naive experimentations with sex, and role diffusion, in which the bizarre is adopted as the norm. For the younger child, Erikson's (1968) stages of *initiative versus guilt* and *industry versus inferiority* spark the beginning of distrust and confusion when the child is dealing with adults.

VOICES IN THE CLASSROOM
Students Who Influence Our Lives

The kid was a real pain. I mean *pain* in the supreme sense of the word. He was 14 years old, but his demeanor, language, and understanding of adult life all said he was 21 and beyond. He wouldn't let me complete a sentence or make a statement without a comment.

If I told the students to take out last night's homework, he'd respond: "Take it out where? Here?" He said it so often the rest of the class began to recite it with him—and, of course, I was too unaware to keep the words from leaving my mouth in time. He sat in various seats throughout the room as I tried to keep him neutralized. But his loud voice and cackling laugh always managed to find its way from any location in the room. He was impervious to detentions or in-school suspensions. His glib tongue generally guided him through the system with limited prison time.

He could get me angry inside 30 seconds after the bell, and sometimes, I think he was doing it just to time himself on how quickly he could get to me. I limped through the entire year with this guy, and credited his antics with having deprived the class from receiving the education they deserved. I had given up on him and the class by March.

In late April, after the spring break, I was in the faculty lounge venting about my poor year. I mentioned my main source of excruciation. A music teacher, who seldom spoke to me, came over and said in a stern voice, "If you knew anything about that kid's life, you wouldn't be talking like that." I was embarrassed and curious at the same time. So I went down to the school nurse, who knew everything, and inquired about my boy.

What I found out left me stunned and shaken. He lived with his mother, a younger brother and sister, and a cousin in a squeezy apartment where no one would choose to live. His mother had been arrested for drug possession at least twice and lived on social services and leavings from her boyfriends. The kid worked part time in an auto junkyard, pulling old tires off cars and doing general labor. He babysat and got all three kids to school every morning. In essence, he was the father.

The next day when he came into my class with that wisecracking smirk and swaying way of his, I just looked at him in wonder. I didn't respond to his antics and I didn't do much of anything in class because I was so deeply ashamed of myself. As he left class that day, he stopped at my desk and said: "Hey, Teach, whatsamatter? Life gettin' too tough for ya? Ya look depressed today."

—*A teacher who had an epiphany*

When I think of the ideal student, I think of Michelle. She was in my honors English class and kept me on my toes as I tried to stay just one step ahead of her. I swear she had read every classic that I thought only English majors in college would read. It took a month of doubt on my part before I realized that she had actually read *Wuthering Heights* and not just seen the movie. When she wasn't doing science projects, she was rereading *Gone with the Wind*, "the ultimate book," she said. But it wasn't her intellectual acumen that I admired so much as her sensitivity to peers and adults. When the classroom became noisy, she would help me bring it back to order by asking a question or bringing the distracters back to the task. She had a genuine interest in what we were learning, and never approached the lesson from the perspective of grades or personal accolades. She was not an active competitor and often stepped aside or remained silent so as not to upstage those more eager to display their achievements. She was an unusual student.

I will always remember Michelle, not only for these attributes, but because the year she was in my class I had gone through a personal tragedy that all but did me in. Michelle tactfully enlisted a few members of the class, who came to my home, cheered me up, offered to help, and became good friends as well as good students.

Michelle went on to success and fame, as everyone knew she would. Our lives have been parted by time and distance, and although I do not know her whereabouts today, I am sure she is having a positive effect on all those who are working and living in her world.

—*A teacher reflecting on students in her life*

A child often needs time alone to reflect on what has been taught.

The Teacher's Role

As a teacher, you spend approximately 25–30 hours per week with the children in your class—a premium time when they are captivated and focused on specific tasks generated by your leadership. Therefore, consider the following:

- ☑ Be aware that your homework assignments may not be students' only obligations for the evening. Be prepared to give them more time to complete the work.
- ☑ Whenever possible, help your students manage their time wisely. Give them some direction on organizing and regulating their time schedules.
- ☑ Speak with the parents of the child who you believe is being overtaxed. Offer them some strategies to manage the child's schedule so that he or she may get more downtime.
- ☑ Seek advice from the professionals in your building who understand these issues. See the school psychologist, the guidance counselor, and the school nurse. Become informed.

DOS AND DON'TS

Don't	Do
Underestimate your students' intelligence, talent, or potential	Begin your teaching year with the perception that all students can achieve when they are challenged
Stereotype your students by race, ethnicity, or language ability	Consider the cultural and ethnic context of your students' lives
Ignore the socioeconomic status of your students when imposing rules and standards that may be beyond their means	Provide all your students with instruction free from stereotypes grounded on socioeconomic status
Disregard a student's religious convictions when they are exposed during a lesson	Give every consideration to each child's religious beliefs by avoiding judgments by word or body language
Regard students in special education with any difference than you would other students	Provide appropriate instructional and testing modifications with the input and guidance of the special education teacher
Keep your students seated for longer than 30 minutes without a break (Grades K–5)	Provide frequent exercise breaks by having students walk around the room or do calisthenics (Grades K–5)
Prevent students from relative freedom of movement within the classroom (Grades 6–12)	Respect older students' ability to be responsible for their own needs without direction (Grades 6–12)
Automatically consider emotional outbreaks as a sign of immaturity	Consider the many emotional crosscurrents that affect childhood and adolescent development
Assume that students of the same age will naturally engage instructional material at the same rate of comprehension	Provide a multitude of strategies to present instructional material in consideration of each child's developing cognitive level
Enforce class rules so rigidly that contingencies cannot be considered	Provide a flexible classroom management plan that affords student input and accommodates contingencies
Casually use the word *respect* without having your students consider its meaning	Encourage your students to take note of active demonstrations of respect between and among class members

WEB SITES OF INTEREST

http://www.cdipage.com
This site provides pertinent information on child development.

http://www.nacd.org
This National Association of Child Development site is mainly for parents who have concerns about their children's developmental pace.

http://fcd-us.org
This Foundation for Child Development site offers a great deal of statistical and pertinent information related to child development.

http://www.mc.maricopa.edu/dept/d46/psy/dev/Fall98/Theories/theories.html
This site provides a comprehensive list of developmental theories.

http://www.agts.edu/faculty/faculty_publications/articles/creps_generations_chart.pdf
This URL will take you to a PDF file that provides a clear picture of generational divisions.

http://www.futureofchildren.org/information2827/information_show.htm?doc_id=79339
This is an excellent link from *The Future of Children* journal, providing a descriptive explanation of the brain and its effects on learning and development.

http://www.futureofchildren.org/information2827/information_show.htm?doc_id=79338
Also generating from *The Future of Children* publication, this link has a discussion of personality and attachment.

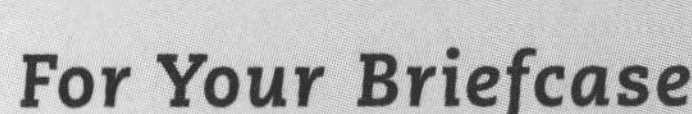

For Your Briefcase

To Do

- Review the developmental stages of your students as a class.
- Create a list of contingencies for which you should be prepared.

Resources on Your Briefcase CD

Templates

- Checklist of Teaching Strategies for the Early to Middle Childhood (Ages 5–11 Years) Developmental Level
- Checklist of Teaching Strategies for the Middle Childhood Through Adolescence (Ages 12–18 Years) Developmental Level

Tables

- Characteristics of Students
- Statistics on U.S. Children
- Quickstats on Socioeconomic Status
- Developmental Stages

REFERENCES

Americans for Divorce Reform. (n.d.). *Divorce statistics collection.* Arlington, VA: Author. Retrieved March 2006 from http://www.divorcereform.org/index.html

Broh, B. A. (2002). Linking extracurricular programming to academic achievement: Who benefits and why? *Sociology of Education, 75*(1), 69–91.

Caine, R. N., & Caine, G. (1994). *Making connections: Teaching and the human brain.* New York: Addison-Wesley.

Carskadon, M. A., Wolfson, A. R., Tzischinsky, O., & Acebo, C. (1995). Early school schedules modify adolescent sleepiness. *Sleep Research, 24*, 92.

Center for Effective Discipline. (n.d.). *U.S.: Statistics on corporal punishment by state and race.* Columbus, OH: Author. Retrieved March 5, 2006, from http://www.stophitting.com/disatschool/statesBanning.php

Creager, E. (1999, August 10). Played out: Why young athletes throw in the towel. *Detroit Free Press,* p. A1.

Duffett, A., Johnson, J., & Farkas, S. (1999). *Kids these days '99: What Americans really think about the next generation.* New York: Public Agenda.

Erikson, E. H. (1968). *Identity: Youth and crisis.* New York: Norton.

Federal Bureau of Investigation. (2002). *Uniform crime reporting index.* Washington, DC: Author.

Federal Interagency Forum on Child and Family Statistics. (2003, July). *America's children: Key national indicators of well-being 2003.* Washington, DC: U.S. Government Printing Office. Retrieved February 21, 2006, from http://childstats.ed.gov/index.asp

Federal Interagency Forum on Child and Family Statistics. (2005). *America's children: Key national indicators of well-being 2005.* Washington, DC: U.S. Government Printing Office. Retrieved February 21, 2006, from http://childstats.ed.gov/americas-children/beh4.asp

Fields, J. (2003). *America's families and living arrangements: 2003* (Current Population Rep. No. P20-553). Washington, DC: U.S. Census Bureau.

Food and Nutrition Service, U.S. Department of Agriculture. (n.d.). *Program data: Child nutrition tables.* Alexandria, VA: Author. Retrieved March 5, 2006, from http://www.fns.usda.gov/pd/cnpmain.htm

Furstenberg, F., & Cherlin, A. (1991). *Divided families: What happens to children when parents part.* Cambridge, MA: Harvard University Press.

Galley, M. (2000, October 18). Extra benefits tied to extracurriculars. *Education Week, 20*(7), 8.

The Graduate Center, The City University of New York. (n.d.). *American Religious Identification Survey.* New York: Author. Retrieved March 2006 from http://www.gc.cuny.edu/faculty/research_briefs/aris/key_findings.htm

Hoffman, L., Sable, J., Naum, J., & Gray, D. (2006). Public elementary and secondary students, staff, schools, and school districts: School year 2002–03. *Education Statistics Quarterly, 7*(1&2), 109–119.

Holloway, J. H. (1999–2000, December–January). Extracurricular activities: The path to academic success? *Educational Leadership, 57*(4), 87–88.

Howe, N., & Strauss, W. (2003). *Millennials go to college: Strategies for a new generation on campus.* Great Falls, VA: LifeCourse Associates and American Association of Collegiate Registrars and Admissions Officers (AACRAO).

National Center for Injury Prevention and Control, Centers for Disease Control and Prevention. (n.d.). *Welcome to WISQARS™.* Atlanta, GA: Author. Retrieved March 2006 from http://www.cdc.gov/ncipc/wisqars

National Education Association. (n.d.). *Good news about public schools in Oregon.* Washington, DC: Author. Retrieved March 5, 2006, from http://www.nea.org/goodnews/or01.html

Office of Juvenile Justice and Delinquency Prevention, U.S. Department of Justice (2005, August). *Juvenile arrests 2003* (Bulletin No. NCJ 209735). Washington, DC: Author. Retrieved March 2006 from http://www.ncjrs.gov/html/ojjdp/209735/contents.html

Olson, L. (2006, January 5). A decade of effort. *Education Week, 25*(17), 8–10, 12, 14, 16, 18–21.

Rogers, F. (1994). *You are special: Words of wisdom for all ages from a beloved neighbor.* New York: Penguin Books.

Rosenfeld, A., & Wise, N. (2000). *The over-scheduled child: Avoiding the hyper-parenting trap.* New York: St. Martin's Press.

Sandefur, G. D., McLanahan, S., & Wojtkiewicz, R. A. (1992). The effects of parental marital status during adolescence on high school graduation. *Social Forces, 71*(1), 103–122.

Santrock, J. W. (2000). *Children* (6th ed.). Boston: McGraw-Hill.

Snyder, T. D., & Hoffman, C. (2001). *Digest of education statistics, 2000* (Pub. No. NCES 2001-034). Washington, DC: National Center for Education Statistics, U.S. Department of Education. Retrieved March 2006 from http://nces.ed.gov/pubsearch/pubsinfo.asp?pubid=2001034

Sprenger, M. (1999). *Learning & memory: The brain in action.* Alexandria, VA: Association for Supervision and Curriculum Development (ASCD).

Tashman, B. (1994, November 12). Sorry Ernie, TV isn't teaching. *The New York Times,* p. D2.

U.S. Census Bureau. (2003, June). *Children living arrangements and characteristics: March 2002* (Pub. No. P20-547). Washington, DC: Author. Retrieved March 5, 2006, from http://www.census.gov/prod/2003pubs/p20-547.pdf

U.S. Census Bureau. (2003, September). *Health insurance coverage in the United States: 2002* (Pub. No. P60-223). Washington, DC: Author. Retrieved March 5, 2006, from http://www.census.gov/prod/2003pubs/p60-223.pdf

U.S. Census Bureau. (2005, March). *Public education finances: 2003.* Washington, DC: Author. Retrieved March 5, 2006, from http://ftp2.census.gov/govs/school/03f33pub.pdf

U.S. Census Bureau, Housing and Household Economic Statistics Division. (2005). *Poverty: 2004 highlights.* Washington, DC: Author. Retrieved March 5, 2006, from http://www.census.gov/hhes/www/poverty/poverty04/pov04hi.html

U.S. Department of Justice, Bureau of Justice Statistics. (2000, February). *Profile of state prisoners under age 18, 1985–97* (Special Rep. No. NCJ 176989), Washington, DC: Author. Retrieved March 2006 from http://www.ojp.usdoj.gov/bjs/abstract/pspa1897.htm

Vogel, S. (2004, May). *Teaching interrupted: Do discipline policies in today's public schools foster the common good?* New York: Public Agenda. Retrieved July 11, 2005, from http://www.publicagenda.org/research/research_reports_details.cfm?list=3

Wood, A. W. (Ed.). (2001). *Basic writings of Kant.* New York: Modern Library.

Chapter 10

Adapting for Special Needs and Diversity

American kids have no idea how lucky they are to have good teachers.
—*Linh, a Vietnamese refugee* (Pipher, 2002)

I like you just the way you are.
—*Fred Rogers* (1994)

I have a dream that my four little children will one day live in a nation where they will not be judged by the color of their skin, but by the content of their character.
—*Martin Luther King, Jr.* (1963)

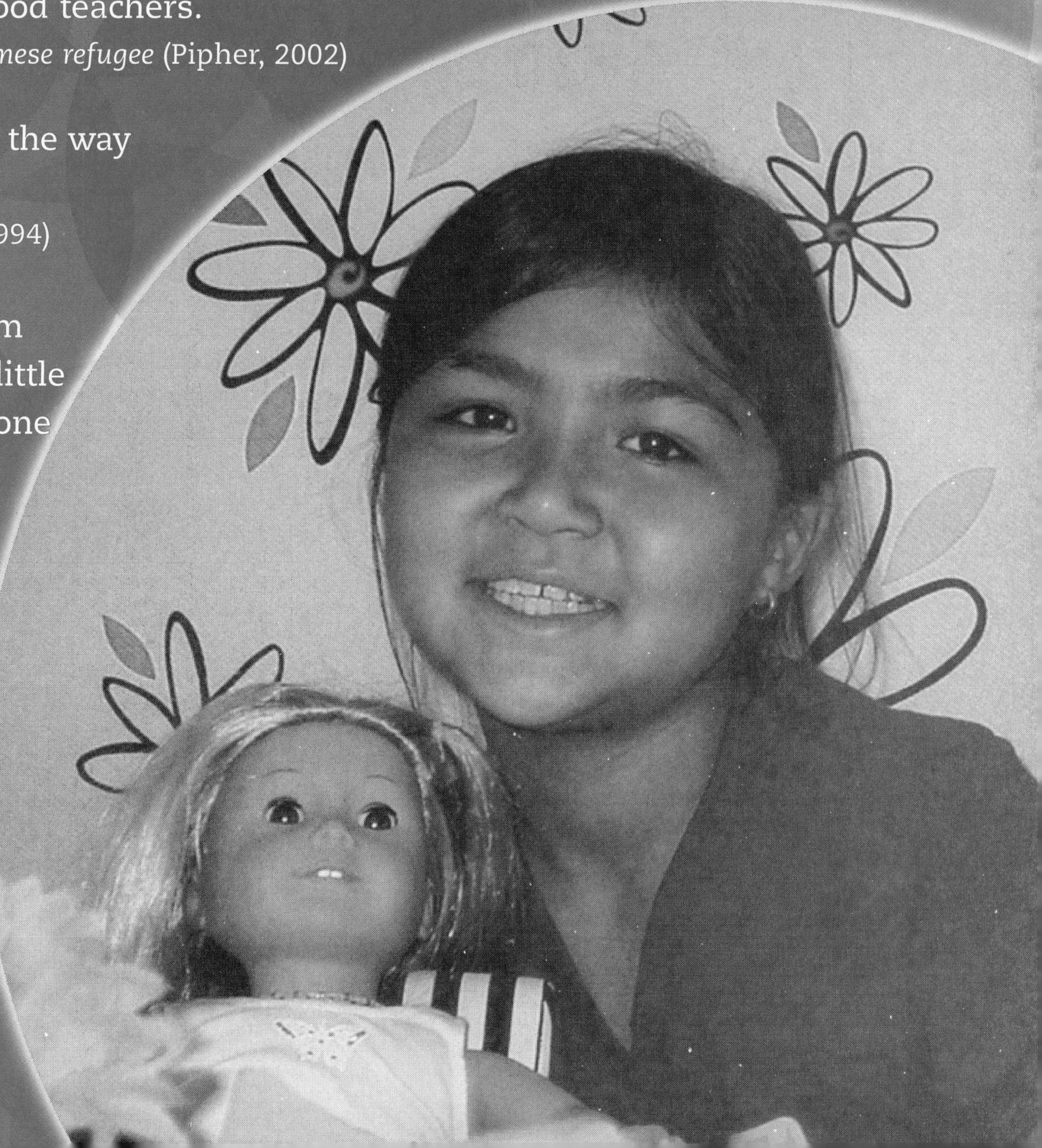

DEFINING DIVERSITY

This 1950s class is a metaphor for the lack of diversity in U.S. schools during that era.

When you look at a national magazine with a photograph of a typical 1950s U.S. classroom, you see no diversity among the students beyond height and weight differences. The word *diversity,* which, in the 1950s, simply meant "different," has come to mean "rich in culture, ethnicity, and much more." **Diversity** today includes gender, disabilities, body differences, religion, politics, and sexual preference. We, as U.S. residents, celebrate our differences and welcome them as an amalgam of what we call *American culture*.

The True Scope of Diversity

The 21st century is a time in human history when the differences that once separated people and culminated in hatred and violence are beginning to draw them together in productive harmony, albeit slowly. Nevertheless, racial and ethnic differences still strongly divide many groups of people. Cafeterias still reflect an awareness of racial differences as African American and White students segregate themselves, more often in middle and high school. Many classes of students are separated by ability, and many schools by socioeconomic status. Likewise, women have not achieved parity with men in salary and career success.

STATING THE FACTS:

On Hispanic and Latino population growth: The Hispanic and Latino population is the fastest growing segment in the United States, and by 2020, it will represent 17.8% of all Americans (Snyder & Hoffman, 2003).

The media continues to report on the academic separations between White people, and African Americans, Hispanics and Latinos, Asian Americans, Native Americans, and other minority groups. Yet, in fact, so little separates people along so-called racial lines. In 2002, Steve Olson wrote an article entitled "We Are All Related to Kevin Bacon." The truth is that, from a scientific standpoint, racial differences are extremely slight:

Briefcase CD CH10-1—Statistics on U.S. Minority Groups

> The relentless focus on differences also obscures our remarkable genetic unity. Geneticists have demonstrated that we are all descended from a small group of people, perhaps just a few thousand, who lived in eastern Africa about 6,000 generations ago. So if everyone in the world were to take their family trees back 6,000 generations, all of the names on those trees would be the same (p. B.02)

DIVERSITY DEFINED

The University of Maryland (n.d.) defines *diversity* as follows (boldface added):

> Diversity is **"otherness,"** or those human qualities that are different from our own and outside the groups to which we belong, yet are present in other individuals and groups. . . . Primary dimensions [of diversity] are the following: **age, ethnicity, gender, physical abilities/qualities, race** and **sexual orientation.** Secondary dimensions of diversity . . . include, but are not limited to: **educational background, geographic location, income, marital status, military experience, parental status, religious beliefs,** and **work experiences.**

LEGAL SIDEBAR

Race and College Admission Decisions

On June 23, 2003, the U.S. Supreme Court ruled that the University of Michigan may use race as a factor to create diversity in its law school as long as *race* is narrowly defined. This ruling emphasized the importance of having a diverse population in U.S. schools.

—*Gratz v. Bollinger* (2003) and *Grutter v. Bollinger* (2003)

In Real Time: **Teacher Sensitivity**

Believing in the limitations of a person's innate intelligence is at the foundation of racism and social prejudice. Teachers, more than any others, must be sensitive to and conscious of the potentiality of all their students regardless of race, nationality, ethnic background, religion, language, disability, gender, or physical condition.

UNITED NATIONS *DECLARATION ON RACE AND RACIAL PREJUDICE*

Article 1

- ☑ All human beings belong to a single species and are descended from a common stock. They are born equal in dignity and rights and all form an integral part of humanity. . . .
- ☑ All peoples of the world possess equal faculties for attaining the highest level in intellectual, technical, social, economic, cultural and political development.
- ☑ The differences between the achievements of the different peoples are entirely attributable to geographical, historical, political, economic, social and cultural factors. Such differences can in no case serve as a pretext for any rank-ordered classification of nations or peoples.

Note. From *Declaration on Race and Racial Prejudice,* by United Nations Educational, Scientific and Cultural Organization (UNESCO), 1978, Geneva, Switzerland: Author.

CHARACTERIZING THE DIVERSE CLASSROOM

A child is a single person in a multicultural society in which we as citizens strive to celebrate the values, beliefs, and religions of all peoples.

The term **multicultural** was popularized in the late 1980s and early 1990s but has given way to the more comprehensive term *diversity*. The reason for this change is natural because the diverse classroom includes not only a variety of cultures and languages, but also abilities, talents, levels of special needs, and genders. Also included may be differences of opinion regarding religion, social customs, or food preferences. The essential element for a teacher to consider is that the differences of all students should contribute to the overall learning experiences, not deter or burden them.

Sensitivity in Addressing Your Students' Ethnicity or Race

The teacher who is sensitive to student diversity will understand the appropriate terminology to use to refer to each class member. Following are some of the terms that should be used (and not used):

- ☑ *African American* is preferred to *Black* because the former term refers to the concept of culture rather than that of race. (*Note:* No hyphen is used in *African American* because *African* is considered an adjective.)

WHAT MAKES PEOPLE DIFFERENT

- ☑ Ethnic origin (or race)
- ☑ National origin
- ☑ Religion
- ☑ Sexual preference
- ☑ Physical features
- ☑ Individual life choices (dress, food, music, lifestyle)
- ☑ Cultural factors (dress, food, music, rituals, lifestyle)

- ☑ *Native Americans* should not be referred to as *Indians.* The former term denotes students whose culture is rooted in that of early America's indigenous peoples.
- ☑ The term *Chicanos* originally referred to urban Mexican Americans and had a political connotation as it became popular during the 1960s. The current preferred term is *Mexican Americans* (Trimble & Dickson, 2005).
- ☑ *Latino* refers to Spanish-speaking people who live in Latin America, which was named by explorer Francisco Balboa to distinguish it from the Americas in which Anglos lived (Spring, 2001).
- ☑ The term *Hispanic* is ambiguous to many people. However, most Spanish-speaking people who are *not* natives of Latin America or Mexico are considered Hispanic; in fact, the U.S. Census Bureau uses the term to encompass both Latino and Hispanic members. Some Latinos, however, are offended by the term *Hispanic* and prefer to be identified as American (i.e., Latin American; Mercurial, 2003).
- ☑ *Asian Americans* refers to people from any Asian country or Pacific Island; however, Pacific Islanders prefer to be referenced separately.
- ☑ *Filipinos* are from the Philippines and generally prefer to be called *Filipinos* in lieu of *Pilipinos* (Filipino, n.d.).
- ☑ *Alaskan Native Americans* mostly comprise Aleuts, Inuit, and Eskimos. In general, they prefer to be called *Alaska Natives* (Trimble & Dickson, 2005).

Briefcase CD CH10-2—Proper Ways to Address Students of Different Ethnicities and Races

STATING THE FACTS:

On the Origins of *Hispanic* and *Latino*:

- The word *Hispanic* originates from the Latin *Hispania,* which the Romans used to refer to the peoples from the Iberian Peninsula. The Anglo-Saxons are believed to have coined the term *Hispanics* (Trimble & Dickson, 2005).
- The word *Latino* refers to the Latins of ancient Rome, but currently, *Latino* is used to refer to a male person from a Latin American country such as Cuba, Puerto Rico, or Mexico (Trimble & Dickson, 2005). (The feminine form is *Latina.*)

Other Forms of Diversity

When you think of diversity in the millennial classroom, you must be aware of *all* differences among the students. Some of these differences tend to separate people along ideological lines, but for a teacher, the word *equality* carries the responsibility of tolerance.

Obesity Now considered to be at epidemic levels, obesity in preschool-age children through late adolescence is a problem that has become a focal point in U.S. schools. As budget cuts stimulate schools to make deals with beverage companies, health officials

HISPANIC OR LATINO?

The term *Hispanic*

- Is generally used in *formal* writing
- Is used to refer to people who hail from Spain or Portugal
- Is accepted by many Hispanic and Latino and Latina individuals as a form of reference (NASW Press, n.d.)

The term *Latino*

- Is generally used in *informal* writing
- Is used to refer to people from South America or Caribbean areas
- Is preferred by some Spanish-speaking peoples as a form of reference but is rejected by others (such as Mexican Americans; NASW Press, n.d.)

OFFICIAL U.S. GOVERNMENT CLASSIFICATION OF ETHNICITY AND RACE

Ethnicity is based on the following categorization:

Hispanic or Latino: A person of Cuban, Mexican, Puerto Rican, South or Central American, or other Spanish culture or origin, regardless of race. The term *Spanish origin* can be used in addition to *Hispanic or Latino.*

Race is based on the following five categorizations:

American Indian or Alaska Native: A person having origins in any of the original peoples of North and South America (including Central America), and who maintains tribal affiliation or community attachment.

Asian: A person having origins in any of the original peoples of the Far East, Southeast Asia, or the Indian subcontinent, including, for example, Cambodia, China, India, Japan, Korea, Malaysia, Pakistan, the Philippine Islands, Thailand, and Vietnam.

Black or African American: A person having origins in any of the Black racial groups of Africa. Terms such as *Haitian* or *Negro* can be used in addition to *Black or African American.*

Native Hawaiian or Other Pacific Islander: A person having origins in any of the original peoples of Hawaii, Guam, Samoa, or other Pacific Islands.

White: A person having origins in any of the original peoples of Europe, the Middle East, or North Africa.

Note. Information from 2002 *Statistical Standards and Guidelines* (Chap. 1), by National Center of Education Statistics (NCES), 2002, Washington, DC: Author.

Guidepost

How do I develop lessons that celebrate students' diversity but inform them about U.S. culture?
Always keep in mind that minority students are proud of their culture. In this light, lessons should encompass the richness of other cultures while emphasizing their contributions to the American fabric of culture. Consult references that will instruct you on the different cultures represented in your classroom.

What teaching technique works best in a diverse classroom?
No single strategy is more or less effective when you are sensitive to your students' needs. However, allowing the class to work together to discover aspects of other cultures is one method of stimulating student interest and encouraging class members to become experts, sharing their knowledge with others.

are issuing strong warnings about the negative effects of sugar on the health of school-age children (Murray, Frankowski, & Taras, 2005).

The trend of obesity in 4- to 5-year-old children has increased to 10.1%, and another 10.7% are at high risk for obesity during their developing years (Pate, Pfeiffer, Trost, Ziegler, & Dowda, 2004). In addition, U.S. teenagers are more likely to be overweight than their counterparts in other nations. According to the National Institutes of Health (2004), 12.6% of 13-year-old boys and 10.8% of 13-year-old girls are considered obese. By age 15, these percentages increase to 13.9% and 15.1%, respectively. As a teacher, however, your main concern is the effect obesity has on your students' self-esteem, which consequently has an effect on their overall academic performance and classroom behavior.

STATING THE FACTS:

On Childhood Obesity: Children who are obese are more likely to have negative self-perceptions than are nonobese peers, and they misbehave more often (Strauss, 2000).

Not only has obesity among children become a national health issue, but, as just suggested, evidence indicates that it has a strong impact on self-esteem. As a result, low self-esteem can lead to behavioral problems in the school and in individual classrooms, and it can present special difficulties for student achievement. A longitudinal study conducted with students aged 9–14 years revealed significantly lower levels of self-esteem among Hispanic and White females who were obese (Strauss, 2000). A significant level of bias was also found against children who are obese by peers, teachers, and staff. Not surprisingly, adolescents who are obese are more likely to engage in at-risk behavior and have higher levels of depression.

In Real Time: **Role Model**

In the classroom, the teacher has a maturity and sensitivity to student differences that his or her students may not possess. Therefore, the teacher is both role model and monitor of appropriate behavior regarding children whose differences may incur derision through word or deed by other class members.

Body Modification A more recent occurrence of diversity is body modification and decoration. Teachers commonly see students with multiple piercings of their ears and other facial areas, as well as an increasing prevalence of tattoos, even in children as young as elementary school age. Although allowing a young child to have a tattoo may offend your personal sense of justice and decorum, not to mention your parenting style, the choice is personal, and in the case of schoolchildren, a choice condoned and approved by their parents. Once again, a teacher's personal opinion and views cannot be expressed in the context of the instructional program. Such views may be expressed in other venues, but the classroom is not one of them.

Sexual Orientation A child's sexual orientation—or that of his or her parents—is a form of diversity that has become part of the cultural fabric in the United States, and it is becoming decreasingly stigmatized. Research results reflect strong teacher support for children of gay and lesbian marriages, but male teachers have a significantly lower comfort level when interacting with gay and lesbian parents than do female teachers (Maney & Cain, 1997). The greatest threat, however, emanates from peers, who can be merciless to students who are gay or lesbians if they are identified as such. As a teacher, you *must* be sensitive to the child's needs, regardless of the child's parental configuration or the student's sexual orientation.

STATING THE FACTS:

On Parental Sexual Orientation:

- An estimated 2–8 million U.S. children have parents who are gay men or lesbians (National Gay and Lesbian Task Force, n.d.).
- At the end of September 2003, an estimated 523,085 children were in foster care, and 118,761 children were waiting to be adopted (U.S. Department of Health and Human Services, 2005).
- At least 1–9 million children have at least one parent who is a gay man or a lesbian (Perrin, 2002).

Religious Preferences In the public school environment, probably no issue is as sensitive as religion. Although the U.S. Supreme Court has consistently upheld individuals' rights to their religious preferences, it has also sent the clear message that separation between church and state is necessary. For classroom teachers, situations can arise that will challenge their social intelligence and their judgment. One such situation is the celebration of religious holidays like Easter, Hanukkah, Christmas, or Ramadan. As a teacher, be sensitive to a student's personal right to express his or her religious beliefs, ensuring that no other students are offended. Most important, respect the rituals, beliefs, and cultures of all religions.

VOICES IN THE CLASSROOM
Teacher Sensitivity

In seventh grade, I experienced prejudice so stark that I realized then how difficult it must be for Blacks to be considered different. At that time, my family had embraced the religion of Jehovah's Witness. As a result, we did not celebrate Christmas or birthdays and therefore didn't have trees or decorations at our house.

One day before Christmas vacation, my homeroom teacher asked the class what everyone was doing for Christmas. When she asked me and I told her that we did nothing, she said, "You're kidding. You don't celebrate Christmas?" Her tone was so sharply critical that some of the other students picked up on it and began harassing me about how dumb that practice was. The teacher intervened eventually, but not before most of the kids had made derogatory remarks about what a stupid religion Jehovah's Witness must be if its members didn't celebrate Christmas.

To make matters worse, after class the teacher then questioned me more deeply about my religion and why we didn't celebrate Christmas. Instead of telling me that she respected our views, she began to lecture me about how being a Christian meant celebrating the life of Christ. I went away confused and hurt, and I skipped school for the last 2 days before vacation rather than face her or the kids.

My parents' response to this situation was to send a member of our church to the teacher's house to try to convert her to our faith. Those years were tough for me.

—A former seventh grader

TEACHING THE MULTICULTURAL CLASS

For some minority groups, the struggle to assimilate is made more difficult by language barriers requiring greater effort from children already contending with cultural differences.

Researchers claim that the most important strategy for the teacher of a diverse class is to generate high expectations for every student (Catsambis, 1995). As a result of cultural and language barriers, children in minority populations require more time and patient instruction to become successful achievers.

Many teachers begin to "dumb down" the curriculum as they find these students lagging behind others who are not facing language or cultural barriers. Sometimes schools will track minority students into special classes for language instruction or into classes in which the material is presented more slowly (Catsambis, 1995).

Students Who Are English-Language Learners

Nearly every school in the United States has a number of students whose primary language is not English. Students who are English-language learners (ELLs) require additional services, not only from school personnel who specialize in language acquisition, but also from you, the classroom teacher.

The Needs of the Student Who Is an ELL The line between a child's being multicultural and his or her having special needs is often blurred because of his or her limited English proficiency (LEP), which can yield a false-positive result when the

Briefcase CD CH10-3—Checklist of Strategies for Teaching Students Who are English-Language Learners (ELLs)

student is tested for learning disabilities. Students who are ELLs are often classified as either having or not having a disability due to their language learner status (Baca & de Valenzuela, 1996). This classification creates an even more difficult situation for both the special education teacher and the classroom teacher as they struggle to craft lessons for students whose educational status thwarts their success with the curriculum.

You may be working with a student who is an ELL whose cognitive perceptions are high but whose language deficiency is preventing him or her from being successful. One solution to this problem is to challenge all your students to achieve at levels above their current proficiency. This strategy is supported by research that reveals that students who are tracked in classes for slow learners, where the expectation of achievement is reflected by overly simplistic instruction, conform to low proficiency levels (Oakes, 1985).

The primary strategy for instructing the multicultural class is to *teach to the student's strengths*. Rather than viewing the child's primary language as a cause for his or her lack of achievement, use the child's knowledge of two languages as a source of learning for all class members. Some tips follow:

- ☑ Encourage students who are ELLs to share their understanding of the material in their native language.
- ☑ Incorporate your students' cultural aspects into the instructional material.
- ☑ Ask students who are ELLs to share their perspective on historic events or to use examples from their home country to solve math problems or study science applications.
- ☑ Present difficult concepts with numerous graphics and illustrations that will help the student who is an ELL process the information. Have high expectations for all students.
- ☑ Challenge all students to achieve beyond what they might expect through independent study.
- ☑ Share with your students the differences in cultural and linguistic meanings.
- ☑ Encourage students who are ELLs to share their language with the class in a variety of ways:
    - To read newspapers from their native country
    - To share travelogues or brochures about their country
    - To help students who speak English learn words in another language
    - To have food fests in which everyone shares a favorite dish
- ☑ Allow your students to diverge on the topic being taught if they are integrating their personal experiences.
- ☑ Do *not* publicly correct oral English usage errors made by students who are ELLs.
- ☑ Use portfolio or authentic assessment in lieu of traditional testing methods.

Four Teaching Methods

In her book *Multicultural Education: A Caring-Centered, Reflective Approach,* Valerie Ooka Pang (2001) described four teaching styles related to the diverse classroom: the assimilationist teacher, the human relations teacher, the social action multiculturalist teacher, and the caring-centered multiculturalist teacher. She defined each as follows:

1. ***Assimilationist teacher:*** The assimilationist teacher teaches basic knowledge and skills that are time honored and Western in origin, using behaviorist techniques supporting the meritocratic system.
2. ***Human relations teacher:*** The human relations teacher teaches basic knowledge and skills as well as social harmony within the Western tradition, with value placed on diversity and tolerance.

3. ***Social action multiculturalist teacher:*** The social action multiculturalist teacher teaches social action skills, with emphasis on equality and questioning of the dominant culture; he or she focuses on life skills.
4. ***Caring-centered multiculturalist teacher:*** The caring-centered multiculturalist teacher teaches building a multicultural society, with an emphasis on ethics and justice and a strong focus on individual needs, democratic cooperation, and accommodation of all differences.

These four teaching styles are presented on a continuum that reflects traditional through student-centered teaching. The traditional teacher is defined as an instructor who disseminates information while the responsibility of learning is placed on the student, whereas the constructivist teacher encourages student engagement, personal interpretation, and development of the material presented. Pang followed the latter pattern, adding the multicultural factor and encouraging teachers to consider a more caring and sensitive mode of instruction.

Necessary Teacher Qualities

When assigned a diverse class, a teacher must be able to do the following:

- ***Be organized:*** Each class period must be extremely well structured to include ample explanation of the material being presented. The teacher must prepare abundant visual aids for the student who is an ELL.
- ***Have patience:*** Students who are ELLs process more slowly because they are unfamiliar with the jargon and idiom of the English language. The teacher must be aware of his or her instructional pace and be prepared to set aside extra time for such processing. A frenetic teaching style that relies on the speed of students' responses and the quickness of their grasp of the material will only confuse and frustrate the diverse learner.
- ***Teach relevant lessons:*** The teacher of the diverse class must have the ability to apply examples and problem solving that relate to real-life issues. Doing so helps the students more clearly understand the concepts being taught.

TEACHING CHILDREN WITH SPECIAL NEEDS

Briefcase CD CH10-4— Definitions of Learning Disabilities

The term *special education* is well known by both educators and the general public. Since **Public Law 94-142** was passed in 1975, special education has been an operational fixture in every public and private school system, involving practically every person in the building in one manner or another. Nationwide, between 4% and 6% of students are classified as having a learning disability as defined by federal statute, while approximately 12% of all students are classified with a disability. As a novice teacher whose certification is not in special education, you will undoubtedly work with teachers and support staff from the special education department.

Guidepost

What is the status of the special education teacher in my classroom?
The special education teacher is considered your coteacher and may become involved in the entire lesson presentation. Although his or her main concern is the students in the class who are classified as learning disabled, he or she may assist other students who are struggling.

Who is the person with whom I should confer when I have a question about accommodations for students in special education?
Always consult the special education teacher assigned to your class, but each district has a special education compliance officer whose responsibility is to guide the program for students who are disabled.

STUDENTS AGE 6–21 YEARS WITH DISABILITIES DEFINED BY THE INDIVIDUALS WITH DISABILITIES EDUCATION ACT (IDEA)

Disability	1990–1991	1999–2000
1. Specific learning disabilities	2,144,017	2,871,966
2. Speech or language impairments	987,778	1,089,964
3. Mental retardation	551,457	614,433
4. Emotional disturbance	390,764	470,111
5. Multiple disabilities	97,629	112,993
6. Hearing impairments	59,211	71,671
7. Orthopedic impairments	49,340	71,422
8. Other health impairments	56,349	254,110
9. Visual impairments	23,682	26,590
10. Autism	—	65,424
11. Deaf–blindness	1,524	1,845
12. Traumatic brain injury	—	13,874
13. Developmental delay	—	19,304
All disabilities	4,361,751	5,683,707

Note. From *Twenty-third Annual Report to Congress on the Implementation of the Individuals with Disabilities Education Act*, by U.S. Department of Education, 2001, Washington, DC: Author, p. II-23. http://www.ed.gov/about/reports/annual/osep/2001/section-ii.pdf

Under federal law, specifically the Individuals with Disabilities Education Act (IDEA), *specific learning disability* is 1 of 13 categories of disabilities described in the law [see the preceding table entitled "Students Age 6–21 Years with Disabilities Defined by the Individuals with Disabilities Education Act (IDEA)"]. In contrast, the term *learning disabilities* is an "umbrella" term describing a number of other, more specific learning disabilities, such as dyslexia and dysgraphia.

DEFINITIONS OF LEARNING DISABILITIES

Disability	Definition
Dyslexia	A language and reading disability
Dyscalculia	Problems with arithmetic and math concepts
Dysgraphia	A writing disorder resulting in illegibility
Dyspraxia (sensory integration disorder)	Problems with motor coordination
Central auditory processing disorder	Difficulty processing and remembering language-related tasks
Nonverbal learning disorders	Trouble with nonverbal cues (e.g., body language, poor coordination, clumsy)
Visual-perception and visual-motor deficits	Problems such as reversing letters; being unable to copy accurately; having itchy, hurting eyes; losing his or her place; struggling with cutting with scissors
Language disorders (aphasia and dysphasia)	Trouble understanding spoken language; poor reading comprehension

Note. Adapted from *Learning Disabilities: Signs, Symptoms and Strategies*, by Learning Disabilities Association of America, n.d., Pittsburgh, PA: Author. Retrieved February 28, 2006, from http://www.ldaamerica.us/aboutld/parents/ld_basics/ld.asp. Copyright by Learning Disabilities Association of America. Adapted with permission.

LEGAL SIDEBAR

Ruling on Tuition Reimbursement for Parents of Students in Special Education

The courts frequently hear cases on school district reimbursement of tuition paid by parents to send their children with special needs to private schools. In Oregon, a federal court ruled that parents who place their child in a private school without requesting services from or giving notice to the school district in their community are *not* entitled to reimbursement.

—*Forest Grove School District v. T.A.* (2005)

Although each state is complying with federal mandates, the level of inclusiveness and support varies depending on the will of, budget of, and parental advocacy in many districts. A private coalition of parents reached an agreement with the state of Pennsylvania after filing a federal lawsuit claiming the state's failure to provide mandated accommodations for students with special needs (Samuels, 2005). In 2002, the Department of Justice cited Wisconsin schools, specifically those in Milwaukee, for failing to provide mandated services to students with disabilities (Borsuk, 2004). These cases are just two of literally hundreds of lawsuits relating to special education that are reminders of the importance and presence of disabilities legislation and its impact on the daily operations of U.S. schools.

Briefcase CD CH10-5—Individualized Education Plan (IEP) Provisions

According to the federal mandates, the school district must have a **compliance officer,** who is responsible for the dissemination and supervision of special education services to students who are disabled. When possible, this person should be consulted when you are confused or troubled about delivering services or complying with testing and instructional modifications. However, any special education teacher in the building should be able to answer such questions and provide guidance.

Teacher Attitude

STATING THE FACTS:

On special education training: The results of a British study revealed that teachers who had special education training had lower stress levels when teaching students who were severely disabled, and more tolerance for the needs of students with learning disabilities (Avramidis et al., 2000).

A study of preservice teachers at Oklahoma State University revealed that those who were given training and exposure to students with special needs had a more positive attitude toward these students and were more comfortable relating to them in the classroom (Avramidis, Bayliss, & Burden, 2000). Other studies have revealed a significant discomfort level for both novice and experienced teachers with the presence of students who are severely disabled in their classrooms (Hammond & Ingalls, 2003). A number of studies indicated that beginning and experienced teachers alike

Guidepost

What instructional and testing modifications must I consider for students with special needs?
Each student in special education has a validated individualized education plan (IEP) that is on file with the special education office in your school and should have been given to you at the beginning of the year. This plan will provide specific instructions on the modifications necessary for the student. Among them may be a longer time to take quizzes and tests, assistance by a reader or writer for quizzes and tests, and advance notice with clear directions before quizzes and tests.

LEGAL SIDEBAR

Inclusion and Parents' Wishes

Parents of a son who was autistic did not want him mainstreamed in kindergarten. The Sixth District Court denied the parents' request, stating that the school district's action supported the intent of IDEA: to provide an opportunity for maximum learning potential.

—*Burilovich ex rel. Burilovich v. Board of Education of Lincoln Consolidated Schools* (2000)

report increased levels of stress in their attempts to design and deliver lessons that will reach students with disabilities (Cook, 2001).

Besides gaining training and exposure to students with special needs to lessen their stress over teaching these students and thus improve their attitudes, teachers need to understand the legalities of inclusion and mainstreaming. *Inclusion* is sometimes known as *mainstreaming,* although these two terms differ slightly. **Mainstreaming** is the practice of taking students who were in self-contained special education classrooms and placing them in "regular" classrooms. Often, such placement can mean that they are then separated into learning groups within the classroom. **Inclusion** means incorporating students with special needs into the classroom environment and structure with no separation within the room or the learning process.

Associated with the term *inclusion* is the famous reference in Public Law 94-142 to the **least restrictive environment (LRE).** Your district may deem the LRE for its students in special education to be a separate room with separate teachers. Some special education law is open to interpretation, but most of it is not. For example, Section 504 of the Rehabilitation Act of 1973 protects the rights of individuals with disabilities in programs and activities that receive federal funds; the language of that law is clear (U.S. Department of Education, 1999):

> No otherwise qualified individual with a disability in the United States . . . shall, solely by reason of her or his disability, be excluded from the participation in, be denied the benefits of, or be subjected to discrimination under any program or activity receiving Federal financial assistance. . . . .

Therefore, as a teacher, you are required to follow the letter of the law.

In Real Time: **Inclusion of Students Who Are ELLs**

Teaching students who are ELLs in the included classroom is not easy; however, excluding them from social interaction with their peers, where they can learn English naturally, is contrary to good teaching practice.

Briefcase CD CH10-6—Indicators of Sensitive Teaching

Sara Rimm-Kaufman has worked with preservice teachers and children who are disabled, especially in the area of sensibilities and attitude. She believes that a correlation exists between teacher sensitivity to children with special needs and these students' positive interaction with peers and achievement levels (Rimm-Kaufman, Voorhees, Snell, & La Paro, 2003). Body language and tone of voice are critical when you are teaching students with special needs and students who are multicultural. She developed an excellent array of techniques that, although geared for childhood educators, include strategies appropriate for middle and high school teachers as well.

INDICATORS OF SENSITIVE TEACHING

Behavioral category	Target global behavior	Specific indicator
Tone of voice	Uses warm, calm voice	Uses voice that is appropriately loud or soft Uses gentle, peaceful, mild voice when appropriate
	Conveys respect in voice	Uses a sincere, genuine voice that shows respectful interest Does not use a sarcastic or negative tone
	Shows no abruptness	Keeps moderate pace Does not "cut off" the student during conversation
Nonverbal communication	Conveys warmth and openness	Gets down to the children's level Touches children when appropriate Leans toward children
	Smiles and laughs with children	Smiles frequently Smiles naturally and warmly Laughs easily with children
	Maintains close physical proximity	Sits or stands near children Approaches or makes eye contact before talking to children
Listening, turn taking, and talking	Encourages children to talk	Uses gestures and verbal encouragers Pauses after asking questions Listens to children Comments on children's actions and words
	Gives directions sensitively	Does not repeat unnecessarily or "nag" Repeats or modifies as necessary
	Achieves balance between teacher and child talk	Does not talk so much that children cannot respond Joins activities when appropriate
Noticing	Notices the positive	Uses words and expressions to show approval Comments on something positive about children Directs attention to the positive Gives more attention to positive behaviors than to negative behaviors
	Scans broadly and often and adjusts behavior accordingly	Scans regularly Notices less effective activities and adjusts pace and provides encouragement Notices children's verbal and nonverbal cues
Responsiveness	Responds to children's cues	Acknowledges children's bids for attention Observes children's frustration or impatience and responds to it Reads children's gestures and facial expressions accurately
	Uses appropriate magnitude for type of response	Responds in ways that children can understand Responds with genuine expressions of concern and interest
	Responds evenly among children	Responds to children in ways that are commensurate with the action Responds evenly to girls and boys and children of all ethnicities Responds fairly evenly to both children who are "easy" and those who are demanding

Note. Adapted with permission from Rimm-Kaufman, S.E., Voorhees, M.D., Snell, M.E., & Paro, K.M. (2003). Improving the sensitivity and responsivity of preservice teachers toward young children with disabilities. *Topics in Early Childhood Special Education, 23,* 151–163.

Literacy Instruction

Literacy proficiency for the child with learning disabilities presents particular challenges to the elementary-level classroom teacher. Young children just learning to read who do not achieve success in the early stage are more likely to lag in reading development (Torgesen, 1998).

First graders can understand about 6,000 words but can read only 300–500 of them before entering second grade. Their comprehension increases as they progress through the grades, with word recognition always ahead of word comprehension until they become mature readers toward the eighth grade (Indrisano & Chall, 1995).

Many theorists attempt to explain how children learn to read. However, the theory of the four stages of reading development by Jeanne Chall (1996) is one of the most prominent and respected in the field.

For children with learning disabilities, reading instruction should engage strategies that stress active involvement and a great deal of structure that uses visual, kinesthetic, tactile, and auditory modalities. Known as the *multisensory method of literacy instruction,* this strategy aims to activate all "learning pathways in the brain (visual/auditory, kinesthetic-tactile) (VAKT)" (McIntyre & Pickering, 1995). Some programs that champion this method are Project READ, the Wilson Reading System, the Lexia Herman Method, and the Orton–Gillingham approach (Lerner, 2000).

Briefcase CD CH10-7—Chall's Stages of Reading Development

In addition, a strong correlation exists between vocabulary knowledge and reading proficiency (Walley, 1993). Having a large store of words provides the learner with a wider bank of references for trial-and-error analysis during the reading process. Increased vocabulary knowledge enhances the learner's experiential range, which thus has a strong K-W-L (*k*now, *w*ant to know, *l*earned) application when the student is engaged in academic work (Beals & Tabros, 1995). All students would benefit from vocabulary enrichment, but for students with special needs or those who are multicultural, this factor is vital to their success in the language-learning process.

A steady stream of research has been completed on reading development and deficiencies, stimulated by the language versus phonics war in the late 1980s and early 1990s. Although the war still wages in some sectors of the field, most practitioners and theorists believe that a balanced program of phonemic instruction and student-centered, interest-based reading establishes proficient reading levels. For children with special needs, instruction that incorporates an emphasis on phonemes and word constructions that relate to personal and cultural experiences is most successful. According to conventional wisdom, emphasizing decoding and phonemic awareness is essential for the early learner in reading; however, teaching these skills by using poorly related or unrelated word constructions, or from stories that are culturally biased, accomplishes little and may cause harm.

CHALL'S STAGES OF READING DEVELOPMENT

Stage no.	Stage name	Skill
0	Prereading	The learner can identify relationships between letters and sounds. *(Preschool–kindergarten)*
1	Initial decoding	The early learner separates the phonological aspects of words (phonics instruction). *(Early grades)*
2	Confirmation, or reading fluency	The learner acquires a rhythm of word recognition (accuracy of reading). *(Early grades)*

—Cont.

Stage no.	Stage name	Skill
3	Reading to learn—Meaning	The learner begins to understand individual words combined with others to form concepts. Prior knowledge is a key component at this stage, as the learner applies contextual inference to facilitate comprehension. *(Early and intermediate grades)*
4	Multiple viewpoints—Relationships	The learner uses metacognition, which leads to self-awareness of comprehension as well as evaluation of the text. *(High school)*
5	Construction—Synthesis	The learner takes the information gained from reading and formulates hypotheses. A great deal of base knowledge is required. *(College)*

Note. Information from *Stages of Reading Development* (2nd ed.), by J. S. Chall, 1996, Fort Worth, TX: Harcourt Brace College.

A CATALOG OF READING METHODS

Method	Web site and description
Project READ	www.projectread-redwoodcty.org This program was established in 1983. It provides free one-on-one tutoring through workshops and ongoing instruction, mostly for adult learners. However, it also works in local libraries and is available for use by high school learners.
Direct instruction	This approach is direct teaching with consistent reinforcement of key terms and concepts. The best known example of this method is *DISTAR*, a highly structured hierarchical system that builds on mastery at aggregate levels of achievement. Teacher instruction is scripted to stimulate the expected student response.
Lexia Herman Method	www.lexialearning.com Named after Renee Herman, this method links visual, auditory, kinesthetic, and tactile stimuli through encoding and decoding skills, sight word recognition, structural analysis, the use of contextual clues, dictionary access skills, and decoding of diacritical symbols.
Lindamood–Bell program	www.lblp.com This program is also known as the *auditory discrimination in depth (ADD) method*, which helps students become aware of their mouth actions while producing speech sounds. It is for students who need to self-correct in reading, spelling, and speech.
Orton–Gillingham approach	www.ortonacademy.org This structured, sequential multisensory method is for written language. It emphasizes how a letter or word looks, how it sounds, and how the speech organs or the hand in writing feels when the sound or word is produced. Common English language rules are stressed.
Slingerland Multisensory Structured Language Instructional Approach	www.slingerland.org This more in-depth multisensory program stresses the logic and structure of English by teaching the smallest unit of sight, sound, and feel of a letter. It includes all the language arts skills: oral expression, decoding, reading comprehension, spelling, handwriting, and written expression. Controlled guided practice is used prior to independent practice.

—*Cont.*

Method	Web site and description
Wilson Reading System	www.wilsonlanguage.com This 12-step remedial reading and writing program is multisensory and teaches strategies for decoding and spelling. It does not, however, provide the exaggerated emphasis on language usage and structure that other programs do.
Reading Recovery	www.readingrecovery.org Specifically designed for first graders, this program targets young low-level readers and provides one-on-one instruction for 30 minutes each day for 12–15 weeks. Heavy emphasis is placed on word identification through the use of simple books with predictable language-patterned structures.
Success for All	www.successforall.net This holistic program emphasizes prevention, early and intensive intervention, and tutoring for students with low reading levels. It integrates phonics, cooperative learning, storytelling, language development, and community involvement. It is known as a comprehensive method of improving literacy achievement.

Mathematics Comprehension Problems

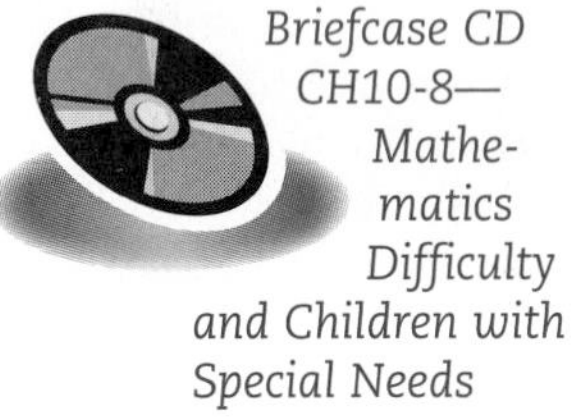

Briefcase CD CH10-8—Mathematics Difficulty and Children with Special Needs

Children with special needs, as well as many other learners, have difficulty comprehending the complexities of mathematics (Lerner, 2000). Some of the problems children have in this area are as follows:

- ☑ ***Spatial relationships:*** Some children are unable to manipulate objects in space, or to understand the concepts of *up and down, over and under,* and *front and back.*
- ☑ ***Visual-motor and visual-perception abilities:*** Children with the inability to differentiate objects in large or small groups must count items before they can visualize a total number. Another problem is the inability to recognize the difference between a hexagon and a rectangle.
- ☑ ***Time and direction:*** When a child has difficulty understanding the difference between time intervals, he or she may confuse morning with afternoon. The child may also be confused in terms of time allotted to reach a specific point and hence have problems with direction, which also affects time management.
- ☑ ***Memory deficiencies:*** Students with short-term-memory deficits have a great deal of difficulty computing math problems that require the ability to hold information in memory.
- ☑ ***Attention deficits:*** The inability to concentrate on specific procedures used to solve problems because of a short attention span is a major obstacle to learning mathematics.
- ☑ ***Cognitive processing:*** A student must be able to manipulate information cognitively as he or she solves math problems. A student's inability to process two or three details in a math problem leads to confusion, a sense of loss, and, finally, frustration.

Teaching that will accommodate these disabilities requires forethought and consideration of the overall lesson objectives. As you design your lesson procedures, incorporate practices that are mindful of the difficulties encountered not only by students with disabilities, but also by children who find mathematics beyond their understanding. The following practices have proved effective in working with students with special needs (Miller, Butler, & Lee, 1998):

- ☑ Provide numerous examples that explain all facets of the problem.
- ☑ Ensure that your instruction is specific regarding step-by-step procedure and that you repeat it at least twice during the lesson.

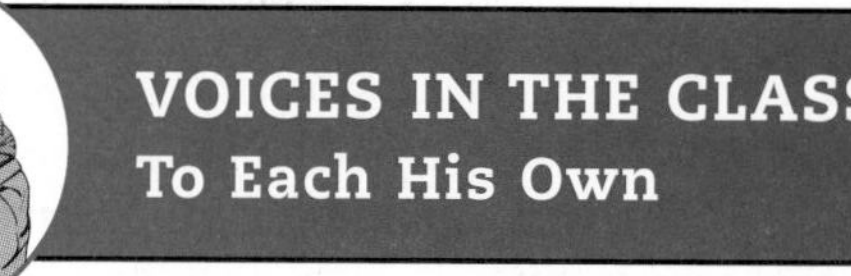

VOICES IN THE CLASSROOM
To Each His Own

My cousin Bob was not an exemplary student. He struggled through every grade and managed to get his high school diploma more with the political help of his parents than by his own achievements.

Bob had the misfortune of being the son of a driven man whose business life found primacy over his family. No matter how hard his father tried to shape him by teaching him the business, or putting a hammer in his hand to build a porch, or how to play a sharp game of pool, Bob's achievement was always mediocre.

However, in one aspect of his life he was exceptional: amateur radio. Through the encouragement of a few friends, he began his fascination with ham radio at an early age. He spent hours tuning his equipment and listening to faraway broadcasts through the dark tunnel of the 1950s. On Saturdays he was often "in the field" with an adult operator, erecting antennas or putting together radios. When Bob was a 16-year-old driver, his first modification to the old clunker his father gave him was to install a mobile radio, which made him among the first CB operators.

His achievements in this one area were exemplary, in fact exceptional. As an adult, he became a leader in the local amateur radio organization.

Not until years later, when Bob's son was diagnosed with a severe learning disability, did he realize that he, too, was learning disabled. He learned that all the terrible years in school were the result of his inability to process written language. Had Bob received the help now afforded children with learning disabilities, I cannot imagine where his genius might have taken him. He died suddenly of a heart attack at the age of 49.

—*The author*

Briefcase CD CH10-9—Checklist of Strategies for Teaching Mathematics to Children with Special Needs

- ☑ Identify the confusing elements of the lesson and explain them separately before applying them to the whole problem. Repeat the explanation while teaching the problem solution, and give many examples.
- ☑ Teach mathematics applications in a variety of settings (e.g., computing the number of pizza slices in a pizza or the number of stars in a quadrant of the autumn sky).
- ☑ Do not assume that students have a competent mathematics vocabulary. Work on increasing their word recognition of mathematical terms.
- ☑ Separate mathematics instruction by concept (e.g., ordering and relationships, numbering, patterns, categorizing).
- ☑ Incorporate stories into word problems.
- ☑ Combine visual and oral instructions with ongoing repetition of concepts.

Attention-Deficit/Hyperactivity Disorder

Although attention-deficit/hyperactivity disorder (ADHD) is not specifically listed as a separate category of disabilities in IDEA of 1997, it is considered an OHI, or other health-impaired, condition, which allows students classified with ADHD to receive special education services. Some facts about ADHD are as follows:

- ☑ An estimated 3% to 7% of all children aged 5–17 years have been diagnosed with ADHD. The highest incidence, 14%, is among White (non-Hispanic) children living in families with incomes below poverty level. It is 2 to 3 times more prevalent among boys than among girls (Pastor & Reuben, 2002).
- ☑ Thirty to 60% of children with ADHD have other learning disabilities, which complicates their adjustment in the classroom environment (Wood, n.d.). Although many students with ADHD are medicated, some are not and others avoid medication because of the side effects.

Briefcase CD CH10-10—Strategies and Suggestions for Teaching the Student with Attention-Deficit/Hyperactivity Disorder (ADHD)

No other learning disability is more misunderstood than ADHD is, probably because it is directly related to behavior. Too often, some teachers believe that what is being labeled as ADHD is actually an example of bad parenting. Nothing could be farther from the truth, as anyone who knows a parent with a child suffering from ADHD can attest. ADHD is a neurobehavioral disorder that impairs an individual's ability to focus and to manage social and emotional interactions (Lerner, 2000). As one veteran teacher who diagnosed himself with ADHD explained, "Imagine you had 15 people who all wanted to say something to you, as well as a song in your head. Now imagine that you cannot differentiate between whose voice is which; you cannot filter out thoughts; and you have just eaten a big bag of M&Ms" (A to Z Teacher Stuff, 2004). The strategies used for teaching a class in which one or more students is diagnosed with ADHD range from a combination of unusual tactics to a commonsense application of relating to people with different learning styles.

Briefcase CD CH10-11—Checklist of ADHD Characteristics

Characteristics of ADHD According to the American Psychiatric Association's (2000) *Diagnostic and Statistical Manual of Mental Disorders* (DSM-IV-TR), if a student exhibits six or more of the following symptoms of inattention for more than 6 months, he or she has ADHD:

- ☑ Is often easily distracted by extraneous stimuli
- ☑ Is often forgetful in daily activities
- ☑ Often fails to pay close attention to details or makes careless mistakes in schoolwork or other activities
- ☑ Often has difficulty sustaining attention in tasks or play activities
- ☑ Often does not seem to listen to what is being said to him or her
- ☑ Often does not follow through on instructions and fails to finish schoolwork or chores
- ☑ Often has difficulty organizing tasks and activities
- ☑ Often avoids or is reluctant to engage in tasks that require sustained mental effort
- ☑ Often loses items necessary for tasks or activities

STRATEGIES AND SUGGESTIONS FOR TEACHING THE STUDENT WITH ATTENTION-DEFICIT/HYPERACTIVITY DISORDER (ADHD)

Following are both suggestions and ideas from teachers who have worked with students with ADHD:

- ☑ "I designate a place in your room where the student can work quietly or noisily as the case may be."
- ☑ "I always provide extra time for completion of assignments."
- ☑ "I repeat directions a number of times in both an oral and [a] written manner."
- ☑ "I found that a bowl of fish placed close to where N _____ sat helped to keep him calm."
- ☑ "I bought one of those large rubber balls you sit on and bounce. Any student could use it instead of his or her seat, but N _____, my ADD student, was on it constantly. It was a great tool for keeping him with the class."
- ☑ "I placed a huge X with tape on the floor and told my ADHD student that that was his spot, and that no one could sit there but him. It really worked well."
- ☑ "Don't require the student to sit, if he or she prefers to stand while doing work."
- ☑ "Give him something to fidget with, or a piece of gum. I know this is unpopular, but by occupying himself physically, his brain is able to focus on the information you're delivering."
- ☑ "It helps for the student to have something in his or her hands to manipulate, such as Play-Doh, clay, or Silly Putty."

Note. From comments posted on a Teachers.Net forum found at http://www.teachers.net.

DOS AND DON'TS

Don't	Do
Classify your students by race or other diversities	Be conscious that all people are diverse in some way
Reference cultures, races, religions, or other diverse labels without knowledge of students' sensitivity	Be sensitive to the labels and preferences that some minority groups prefer
Ignore slights by other students toward those who are expressing their diversity	Establish an atmosphere of cooperation and tolerance for all diversities
Make baseless comments about religion	Use caution and restraint when referencing religious policies or beliefs
Allow students who are ELLs to remain outside the classroom environment of learning	Include students who are ELLs in every aspect of your instructional program and encourage their participation in their first language
Ignore the services, expertise, and professional assistance of the special education teacher	Work closely with the special education teacher and aides to provide the most effective instruction for students with special needs
Create tests or instructional work sheets that are not aligned with the IEPs of students who are classified	Work with the special education teacher to create tests and instructional work sheets that will align with classified students' IEPs
Categorize students by reading ability	Encourage group work and peer tutoring in your literacy program
Teach mathematics to the entire class at a pace that applies to all	Consider the probable difficulties that some students will encounter with abstract concepts related to math
Automatically associate bad classroom behavior with bad parenting	Consider that ADHD is a disorder that relates to behavior and requires a great deal of teacher patience with students who have it

WEB SITES OF INTEREST

http://coe.fgcu.edu/faculty/ray/red/vocabulary.htm
This excellent site provides numerous ideas for vocabulary lesson plans that may help with students who are ELLs.

http://www.colage.org
http://www.outproud.org.
Both these sites provide answers to sensitive questions about students who are gay or lesbian.

http://www.hispaniconline.com/hh/recipe.html
This excellent Web site describes Hispanic foods and their origin.

http://www.intime.uni.edu/multiculture/index.htm
This site provides an outstanding array of multicultural lessons, resources, and prompts.

http://www.washingtonpost.com/ac2/
wp-dyn?pagename=article&node=&contentId=A21167-2002Dec6¬Found=true
The article found on this site provides an interesting view on how all "races" are related.

http://www.cec.sped.org
This site is by the Council for Exceptional Children.

http://www.ldonline.org
This is a site on learning disabilities for parents, teachers, and other professionals.

http://www.nichcy.org
This site is by the National Dissemination Center for Children with Disabilities.

For Your Briefcase

To Do

- Review the appropriate way to address minority students in your classroom.
- Review your curriculum for sensitivity to student diversity.
- Prepare a strategy for teaching students who are ELLs.
- Confer with the special education teacher assigned to your classes.
- Identify the reading stages of your students who are ELLs.
- Familiarize yourself with ADHD indicators.
- Familiarize yourself with the eight basic learning disabilities defined in IDEA (see the table entitled "Definitions of Learning Disabilities").

Resources on Your Briefcase CD

Templates

- Checklist of Strategies for Teaching Students Who Are English-Language Learners (ELLs)
- Checklist of Strategies for Teaching Mathematics to Children with Special Needs
- Checklist of ADHD Characteristics

Tables

- Statistics on U.S. Minority Groups
- Proper Ways to Address Students of Different Ethnicities and Races
- Definitions of Learning Disabilities
- Individualized Education Plan (IEP) Provisions
- Indicators of Sensitive Teaching
- Chall's Stages of Reading Development
- Mathematics Difficulty and Children with Special Needs
- Strategies and Suggestions for Teaching the Student with Attention-Deficit/Hyperactivity Disorder (ADHD)

REFERENCES

A to Z Teacher Stuff. (2004). *Ideas to use with ADD/ADHD students.* Springfield, MO: Author. Retrieved September 21, 2004, from http://forums.atozteacherstuff.com

American Psychiatric Association. (2000). *Diagnostic and statistical manual of mental disorders* (4th ed., text revision). Washington, DC: Author.

Avramidis, E., Bayliss, P., & Burden, R. (2000). A survey into mainstream teachers' attitudes towards the inclusion of children with special educational needs in the ordinary school in one local education authority. *Educational Psychology, 20*(2), 191–211.

Baca, L., & de Valenzuela, J. S. (1996, July). *Practical and theoretical considerations for assessment of culturally and linguistically diverse students.* Washington, DC: U.S. Department of Education, Office of Special Education Programs. Retrieved February 23, 2006, from http://www.alliance2k.org/products/4005.pdf

Beals, D. E., & Tabors, P. O. (1995). Arboretum, bureaucratic, and carbohydrates: Preschoolers' exposure to rare vocabulary at home. *First Language, 15*(1), 57–76.

Borsuk, A. (2004, March 22). MPS faulted on special ed efforts. *Milwaukee Journal Sentinel,* p. A1.

Burilovich ex rel. Burilovich v. Board of Education of the Lincoln Consolidated Schools, 208 F.3d 560 (6th Cir. 2000).

Catsambis, S. (1995). Gender, race, ethnicity, and science education in the middle grades. *Journal of Research in Science Teaching, 32*(3), 243–258.

Chall, J. S. (1996). *Stages of reading development* (2nd ed.). Fort Worth, TX: Harcourt Brace College.

Cook, B. G. (2001, January). A comparison of teachers' attitudes toward their included students with mild and severe disabilities. *Journal of Special Education, 34*(4), 203–213.

Filipino. (n.d.). In *Wikipedia: The free encyclopedia.* Retrieved July 12, 2005, from http://en.wikipedia.org/wiki/Filipino

Forest Grove School District v. T.A., No. 04-331 (D. Ore. May 11, 2005).

Gratz v. Bollinger, 539 U.S. 244 (2003).

Grutter v. Bollinger, 539 U.S. 306 (2003).

Hammond, H., & Ingalls, L. (2003). Teachers' attitudes toward inclusion: Survey results from elementary school teachers in three Southwestern rural school districts. *Rural Special Education Quarterly, 22*(1), 24–31.

Indrisano, R., & Chall, J. S. (1995). Literacy development. *Journal of Education, 177*(1), 63–84.

King, M. L., Jr. (1963, August 28). *I have a dream.* Speech delivered at the March on Washington for Jobs and Freedom, Washington, DC.

Lerner, J. W. (2000). *Learning disabilities: Theories, diagnosis, and teaching strategies* (8th ed.). Boston: Houghton Mifflin.

Maney, D. W., & Cain, R. E. (1997, August). Preservice elementary teachers' attitudes toward gay and lesbian parenting. *Journal of School Health, 67*(6), 236–241.

McIntyre, C. W., & Pickering, J. S. (Eds.). (1995). *Clinical studies of multisensory structured language education for students with dyslexia and related disorders.* Salem, OR: International Multisensory Structured Language Education Council (IMSLEC). Retrieved August 12, 2004, from http://www.ldonline.org/ld_indepth/reading/mssl_methods.html

Mercurial [blog]. (2003, September 16). *Latino vs Hispanic.* Retrieved June 20, 2005, from http://www.confusedkid.com/primer/archives/2003/09/latino_vs_hispa_1.php

Miller, S. P., Butler, F. M., & Lee, K. (1998). Validated practices for teaching mathematics to students with learning disabilities: A review of literature. *Focus on Exceptional Children, 31*(1), 1–24.

Murray, R., Frankowski, B., & Taras, H. (2005). Are soft drinks a scapegoat for childhood obesity? *Journal of Pediatrics, 146*(5), 586–590.

NASW Press. (n.d.). Guidelines for writing about people. In *Writing for the NASW Press: Information for authors* (Chap. 8-3A). Washington, DC: Author. Retrieved March 9, 2006, from http://www.naswpress.org/resources/tools/01-write/guidelines_8.htm

National Center of Education Statistics (NCES). (2002). *2002 Statistical standards and guidelines* (Chap. 1). Washington, DC: Author. Retrieved February 26, 2006, from http://nces.ed.gov/statprog/2002/std1_5.asp

National Gay and Lesbian Task Force. (n.d.). *Parenting by LGBT people.* Washington, DC: Author. Retrieved March 9, 2006, from http://www.thetaskforce.org/theissues/issue.cfm?issueID=30#footnotes

National Institutes of Health. (2004, January 5). *U.S. teens more overweight than youth in 14 other countries* [press release]. Washington, DC: Author.

Oakes, J. (1985). *Keeping track: How schools structure inequality.* New Haven, CT: Yale University Press.

Olson, S. (2002, December 8). We are all related to Kevin Bacon. *The Washington Post,* p. B.02. Available from http://www.washingtonpost.com/ac2/wp-dyn?pagename=article&node=&contentId=A21167-2002Dec6¬Found=true

Pang, V. O. (2001). *Multicultural education: A caring-centered, reflective approach.* New York: McGraw-Hill.

Pastor, P. N., & Reuben, C. A. (2002, May). *Attention deficit disorder and learning disability: United States, 1997–98* [Vital and Health Statistics, Series 10, No. 206; DHHS Pub. No. (PHS) 2002-1534]. Hyattsville, MD: National Center for Health Statistics, Centers for Disease Control and Prevention, Department of Health and Human Services. Retrieved August 12, 2004, from http://www.cdc.gov/nchs/data/series/sr_10/sr10_206.pdf

Pate, R. R., Pfeiffer, K. A., Trost, S. G., Ziegler, P., & Dowda, M. (2004, November). Physical activity among children attending preschools. *Pediatrics, 114*(5), 1258–1263.

Perrin, E. C. (2002). Technical report: Co-parent or second-parent adoption by same-sex parents. *Pediatrics, 109*(2), 341–344.

Pipher, M. (2002). *The middle of everywhere: The world's refugees come to our town.* New York: Harcourt.

Rimm-Kaufman, S. E., Voorhees, M. D., Snell, M. E., & La Paro, K. M. (2003, September 1). Improving the sensitivity and responsivity of preservice teachers toward young children with disabilities. *Topics in Early Childhood Special Education, 23*(3), 151–163.

Rogers, F. (1994). *You are special: Words of wisdom for all ages from a beloved neighbor.* New York: Penguin Books, p. 14.

Samuels, C. (2005, January 5). Settlement reached in Pennsylvania special education suit. *Education Week, 24*(16), 23.

Snyder, T. D., & Hoffman, C. M. (2003, June). *Digest of education statistics, 2002* (NCES No. 2003-060). Washington, DC: National Center for Education Statistics, U.S. Department of Education.

Spring, J. H. (2001). *Deculturalization and the struggle for equality: A brief history of the education of dominated cultures in the United States* (3rd ed.). New York: McGraw-Hill.

Strauss, R. S. (2000). Childhood obesity and self-esteem. *Pediatrics, 105*(1), e15.

Torgesen, J. (1998). Catch them before they fall. *American Educator, 22*(1), 32–39.

Trimble, J. E., & Dickson, R. (2005). Ethnic gloss. In C. B. Fisher & R. M. Lerner (Eds.), *Encyclopedia of applied developmental science* (Vol. I, pp. 412–415). Thousand Oaks, CA: Sage.

United Nations Educational, Scientific and Cultural Organization (UNESCO). (1978, November 27). *Declaration on race and racial prejudice.* Geneva, Switzerland: Author. Retrieved February 23, 2006, from http://www.unhchr.ch/html/menu3/b/d_prejud.htm

University of Maryland. (n.d.). The University of Maryland definition of *diversity.* In *Diversity at UMCP: Moving Toward Community Plan 1995.* College Park: Author. Retrieved September 24, 2004, from http://www.inform.umd.edu/EdRes/Topic/Diversity/Reference/diversity.html

U.S. Department of Education. (2001). *Twenty-third Annual Report to Congress on the Implementation of the Individuals with Disabilities Education Act.* Washington, DC: Author, p. II-23. Retrieved March 9, 2006, from http://www.ed.gov/about/reports/annual/osep/2001/section-ii.pdf

U.S. Department of Education, Office for Civil Rights. (1999, July). *Free appropriate public education for students with disabilities: Requirements under section 504 of the Rehabilitation Act of 1973.* Retrieved September 24, 2004, from http://www.ed.gov/about/offices/list/ocr/docs/edlite-FAPE504.html#_edn1

U.S. Department of Health and Human Services, Administration for Children. (2005, April). *The AFCARS Report: Preliminary FY 2003 estimates as of April 2005 (10).* Washington, DC: Author. Retrieved March 9, 2006, from http://www.acf.hhs.gov/programs/cb/stats_research/afcars/tar/report10.htm

Walley, A. C. (1993). The role of vocabulary development in children's spoken word recognition and segmentation ability. *Developmental Review, 13*(3), 286–350.

Wood, D. (n.d.). *What is attention deficit hyperactivity disorder (ADHD)?* Kenmore, WA: Get Mental Help, Inc. Retrieved August 28, 2004, from http://www.mental-health-matters.com/articles/article.php?artID=49

Chapter 11

Involving Family and Community

I have frequently gained my first real insight into the character of parents by studying their children.
—*Sir Arthur Conan Doyle* (1892)

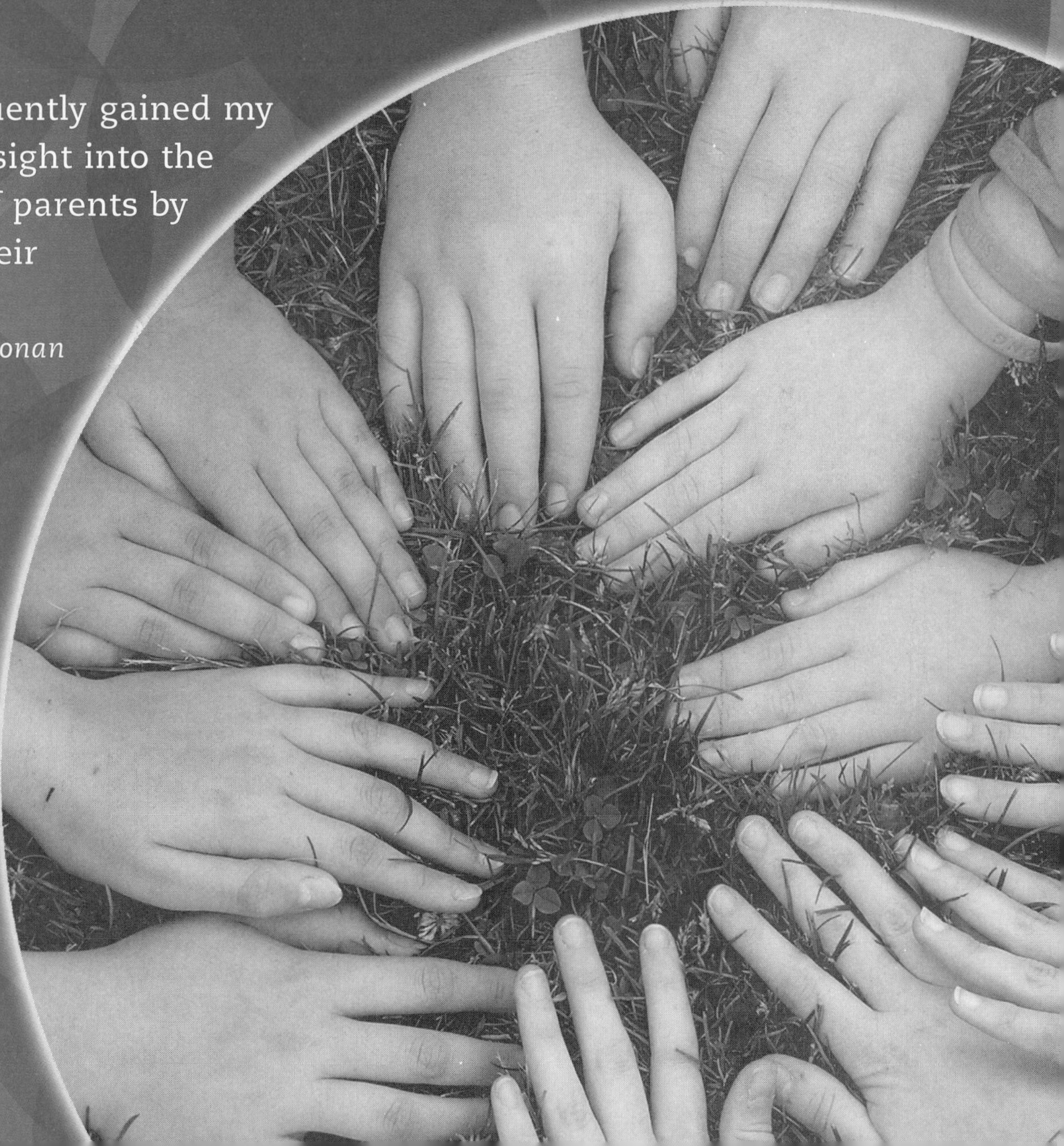

PARENTAL INVOLVEMENT

A great deal has been written, researched, and studied about the issue of parental involvement. Strong research results support the conclusion that parental involvement will improve student achievement and, some researchers believe, student behavior, values, and character (McNeal, 1999). In short, the importance of parents in the education formula cannot be overemphasized (Dwyer & Hecht, 1992).

Guidepost

To what extent are parents responsible for poor student achievement and behavior?
Your students are greatly influenced by parenting style and the economic structure of their homes. However, how you, the teacher, react to your students makes the difference in the classroom.

Should not parents be held responsible for their children's behavior and performance in school?
Parental responsibility is not something that can be legislated beyond protecting children from abuse. As a teacher, you must respect all parenting styles and work to provide an open line of communication with parents that will most benefit your students.

How do I maintain this open line of communication?
The best method of communication with parents is direct conversation, either in person or on the telephone. However, the time and place may not always permit such contact. Instead, using mail, handouts, weekly newsletters, and e-mail will require only a moderate level of your time and effort.

The Changing Pattern of Parental Involvement

The U.S. family has become diverse (Figure 11-1), and the nature and depth of parental involvement in the education of children has been transformed from the 1950s image of PTO membership and bake sales to the millennial reality of formalized parent conferences, community outreach, and amplified parental input. School districts are eager for parents to

***In Real Time:* Perspectives**

You will confront a wide spectrum of family configurations that rarely resemble popular images. Consequently, you must keep an open, nonjudgmental mind when encountering a student's behavior, demeanor, or performance that is in opposition to what is known as traditional.

SCENARIOS REFLECTING DIVERSE FAMILY STRUCTURES

- A third grader in your class is the daughter of a same-sex couple. She is puzzled when she continually hears the phrase "mom and dad."
- An eighth grader comes to school each day with a strong smell of wood smoke on her clothes. Some of the other students snicker at her. The student lives in a cabin heated by a woodstove.
- A fifth grader bows her head, joins her hands, and prays silently before eating anything; she does this during in-class birthday parties.
- Three of your students have not seen or do not regularly see either their father or their mother and are being raised by their grandparents.

LEGAL SIDEBAR

Protection of Children from Abuse

The Child Abuse Prevention and Treatment Act is based on the principle that if a child's parents fail to provide him or her with safe and appropriate care, the federal government may intervene. This act includes legislation to coordinate public and private services to assist the family and protect the child from abuse and neglect.

—*Child Abuse Prevention and Treatment Act (2003)*

STATING THE FACTS:

On Families:

- Current research shows that parental involvement positively influences a student's school readiness and performance and leads to higher academic achievement (McNeal, 1999).
- In March 2003, 68% of all households were families (children with two parents); this figure was down from 81% in 1970. Children living with relatives other than a mother and a father increased to 16% in the same period (Fields, 2003).

sit on committees, participate in program initiatives, and share in the governing process. Parent–teacher groups reflect more of a partnership than a support system. Often, principals seek parental opinions through surveys, telephone interviews, and large-scale meetings before implementing a new school rule or even adopting a new textbook. Parents are welcomed into the school not only to visit and observe, but also to participate in class and school activities. Although parents are still called when their children are having behavioral or academic difficulties, parent conferences are now formally scheduled on select days so that each parent receives at least a 20-minute overview of the student's work and progress.

The family and community are now seen as players in the entire school experience. The old paradigm of viewing families with low income as detrimental to student achievement has been transformed into recognition of cultural differences and identification of the strengths a family can bring to each student's success level (Davies, 1991).

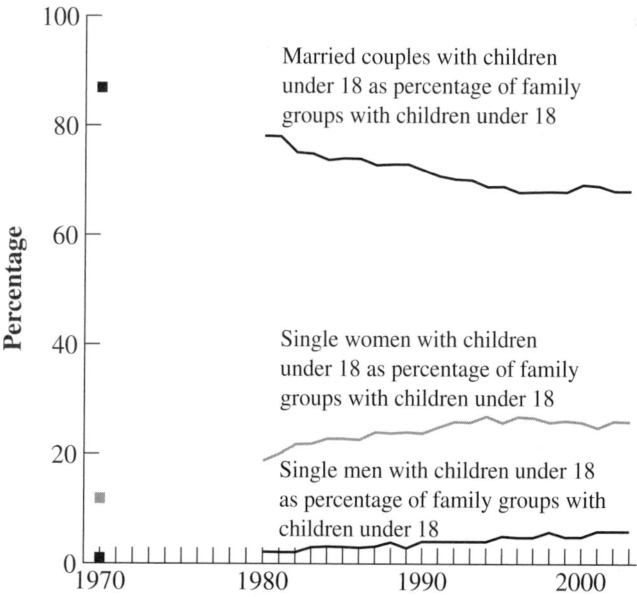

Figure 11-1. *Family groups with children, by type*
Data from U.S. Census Bureau, Current Population Survey, 1970 to March 2003 Annual Social and Economic Supplements.

Effective delivery of educational services is made possible through a collaborative communication among family, community, and school.

Community Outreach

The teacher's role in developing an environment of open communication and capitalizing on the physical and organizational resources of the school is an essential part of being an education professional. More than just involving parents, inviting the community to participate in school functions strengthens the pluralistic and democratic ideals that have been a part of the mission of education since the early days of our nation.

One working example is the National Network of Partnership Schools, sponsored by Johns Hopkins University, a program committed to establishing school–family–community relationships. Based on Dr. Joyce L. Epstein's model for parental involvement, the program consists of six types of involvement: parenting, communicating, volunteering, learning at home, decision making, and collaborating with the community (Epstein, Sanders, Simon, Salinas, Jansorn, & Van Voorhis, 2002).

Stating the Facts:

On parents who read to their children: The results of an early childhood longitudinal study in fall 1998 revealed the following percentages of parents who read to their kindergartners every day (Coley, 2002):

- All parents: 46%
- Parents with a high socioeconomic status: 62%
- Parents with a low socioeconomic status: 36%

EPSTEIN'S MODEL FOR PARENTAL INVOLVEMENT

- ***Parenting:*** Assist parents to understand the developmental stages of their children; help parents with child-rearing skills; work with school officials who work with families to strengthen parents' confidence in guiding children through the grades.
- ***Communicating:*** Increase two-way communications between school and home about school programs and children's progress.
- ***Volunteering:*** Recruit and train members of the family to volunteer in the school, within school programs, and in off-school locations.
- ***Learning at home:*** Provide information for families and develop activities for students to work with family members on homework assignments and projects.
- ***Decision making:*** Involve parents and other family members on school committees relating to governance, program initiatives, policies, and programs of partnership.
- ***Collaborating with the community:*** Link with community businesses and agencies to enrich students' experience, strengthen families, and support school goals.

Note. From *School, Family, and Community Partnerships: Your Handbook for Action* (2nd ed., p. 165), by J. L. Epstein, M. G. Sanders, B. S. Simon, K. C. Salinas, N. R. Jansorn, and F. L. Van Voorhis, 2002, Thousand Oaks, CA: Corwin Press.

Caution: Readblocks to Overcome in Involving Parents

- Parents are sometimes intimidated by school professionals and avoid contact unless summoned about their children's misbehavior. Having activities that are welcoming and asking parents to help design and conduct programs goes a long way toward ameliorating such intimidation.
- Many parents are unavailable to come to the school either during the day or in the evening because they are working or are caring for other children. Providing help for the care of younger children so that parents can participate is an essential role for the school truly interested in involving parents.
- Some parents simply do not want to become involved because they have their own lives and activities with their children. Respect parents' views without judgment. Keeping such parents informed of school activities, the school mission, and the willingness of the school to help may be sufficient.

Proactive Initiatives

Following are some of the initiatives that are examples of effective school–parent partnerships enhancing and supporting instruction and learning:

- ***Math Night:*** An idea sparked at a National Council of Teachers of Mathematics (NCTM) conference, Math Night is being used by teachers across the United States to engage their students after school and in the evenings. Teachers have students dress in theme costumes as they solve math problems. Some ideas are The Mathematical Wizard of Oz, Peter Pan in Mathland, and Alice in Math Wonderland. Parents are the key to the success of this initiative (Bafile, 2004).
- ***Family Reading Night:*** Children, parents, and teachers come together for pizza or other snacks on Family Reading Night and highlight specific themes such as Native American stories or tales of the sea.
- ***Parental Involvement Pledge:*** Originating with Project Appleseed, the Parental Involvement Pledge initiative has become popular in many schools across the United States because it directly involves parents as stakeholders in their children's education (www.projectappleseed.org/pledge.html). Many teachers use this pledge (fee required) or create their own to send home to parents.
- ***Parent-sponsored fun events:*** Parent-sponsored fun events are activities that generate from PTOs in which parents take the initiative to involve teachers, other parents, and students in events that nurture a sense of community. One example is Rosemont Middle School in West Linn, OR, where the PTO sponsored a Wet 'n Messy Barbecue as a September kickoff event.

PARENTAL COMMUNICATION

Even more so than schoolwide outreach programs, direct teacher–parent communication is essential. Each teacher can succeed in establishing meaningful and positive lines of communication through proactive efforts that seek to keep parents informed of their child's daily and overall progress (Epstein & Dauber, 1991).

In Real Time: **Parental Communication**

One truism of teaching is that you will hear more frequently from parents whose children are doing well in their studies and causing few to no behavioral problems than you will from parents whose children are achieving poorly or causing disciplinary problems.

Briefcase CD CH11-1—Parental Communication Initiatives

Best Ways to Communicate with Parents

Communicating with parents requires a conscious effort that takes time, thought, and preparation, as well as a great deal of extra work. However, the benefits for children can be enormous, even for peer-conscious adolescents, who, by virtue of their pubertal development, shun parental involvement in school affairs (Eccles & Harold, 1993).

PARENTAL COMMUNICATION INITIATIVES

Initiative	Description
Weekly progress reports (Grades K–3)	During the day, jot down brief notes on each child's accomplishments. At week's end, send home a report on the child's accomplishments, encouraging comments from parents and providing tips for parental assistance at home.
Daily reports (Grades 4–5)	Create a format that provides an overview of what was accomplished in class that day and a reflection piece written by each student. Have the students take it home to their parents each night and encourage parents to respond to it. Doing so has the double effect of providing a routine writing exercise while giving the students a chance to reflect on their daily activities.
Weekly or biweekly newsletters (all grades)	Using a desktop publishing program, create a newsletter that highlights the accomplishments of the class for that week (or two), noting individual efforts. Include samples of student work, advice to parents for helping the child at home, and general information on child development or educational initiatives.
Good news communication (all grades)	Proven to be a great student self-esteem builder, calling students' homes to report academic excellence to parents, or sending notices of outstanding achievement, is another option. Be sure to report improvement in areas previously defined as lacking.
Classroom invitations	Have students create open invitations for parents to visit the classroom to view projects or work. Be mindful of the child whose parent may not come, and be sure to provide a wide time slot to accommodate work schedules.
Weekly lesson objectives (all grades)	On Friday or Monday, send home with each child your plan for the coming week, with suggestions for parental assistance. Doing so has enormous potential for including parents because they may capitalize on your topic areas with family-related events or history.
Dining in (all grades)	Many teachers use food as a communal bridge. Invite parents for an in-class or in-cafeteria dinner in which parents contribute a dish or students do some of the cooking. Highlight student work at the gathering.
Reading salons (all grades)	Encourage parents to join a reading circle in which you suggest a book for them to read and a discussion session ensues. The books may be related to parenting or education themes, those that the children are reading, or even adult literature.
Community outreach (all grades)	Organize a gathering at a local community center such as a church, the YMCA, or even a home. Choose a topic common to child rearing or another educational issue. Invite speakers from other professions to provide an integrated link.
Parental participation (Grades K–5)	When feasible, invite parents to assist in a particular lesson, either in the classroom or as homework. Encourage parents to participate by giving them a specific assignment that involves working with their child. Seek out parents who have a particular interest or hobby that may apply to topics being taught in the class, and have them share with your students.
Parental participation (Grades 6–12)	Invite parents to present or speak about their jobs or hobbies that relate to topics you are covering in class.
Class Web site	Creating a class Web site is an effective means of communication that can easily be updated, is easily accessible, and is a powerful base of information. However, always remember that not all parents have computers or access to the Internet.

Briefcase CD CH11-2—Sample Letter of Praise and Accomplishment—Elementary School

Briefcase CD CH11-3—Sample Letter of Praise and Accomplishment—Middle School

Briefcase CD CH11-4—Sample Letter of Praise and Accomplishment—High School

Briefcase CD CH11-5—Template for Letter of Praise and Accomplishment

Briefcase CD CH11-6—Sample Letter Concerning Inappropriate Behavior

Following are some tips on communicating with parents of children at different levels in the school system:

- ☑ ***Kindergarten and elementary school:*** Daily progress reports for students in kindergarten through third grade can be a tremendous drain on a teacher's time; therefore, a specific period should be allotted each week to complete these reports. In Grades 4–6, having students write personal reflections on their progress is more time efficient and complementary to the learning process. Therefore, at the elementary level, communication with parents involves both your written reports and those of your students. The important point is that the parent is being informed of progress and is, by association, related to the learning process.
- ☑ ***Middle school:*** In middle school, parental communication shifts to a different mode. In view of the teaming strategy central to the middle school concept, parents are provided a wide perspective of their child's progress because parent conferences involve teachers from all or most of the student's subjects. This setup provides an opportunity for teachers to work closely on strategies to help students improve both their performance and their behavior. At the middle school level, communicating with parents is essential because young adolescents often have more issues requiring intervention and guidance.
- ☑ ***High school:*** Parental communication in high school is different from that in the previous grade levels. Older adolescents are more capable and are eager to assume responsibility for their behavior and performance, and they often resent parental intrusion. Another factor at the high school level is the structure of education (i.e., a student has five to seven teachers who do not meet as a team). Therefore, the parent communicates with different teachers for different subject areas.

  In addition, not all adolescents have a fully developed sense of responsibility, which makes parental intervention necessary. The primary mode of communication with the parent at this level is the report card, whose posting may trigger a parental inquiry. The guidance counselor is often involved in this communication and can be of enormous help as an intermediary between the student's many classroom teachers and the parents.

As a busy elementary teacher, do I have enough time to communicate with parents on their children's progress?
Parental communication is time consuming, especially for the teacher with upward of 25 students in class. However, the benefits are so strong that the teacher must find time to perform this important task. Try setting aside a specific time period each week solely for communicating with parents on their children's progress.

What particular issues affect young adolescents requiring more intervention?
The middle school student is on the crest of a physical and biological growth spurt that can generate emotional upheaval. Children at this stage are dealing with issues of identity, self-esteem, and social pressures that often overwhelm them to the point of dissension.

Is the high school teacher's role regarding parental communication different from that for other grade levels?
At the high school level, performance issues take on a strong meaning because students may be preparing for college entrance and are therefore grade conscious. Because communication with home is often more about performance than behavior, offering parents strategies to help improve achievement is a good policy at this level.

TELEPHONE CONFERENCE CHECKLIST

- ☑ Always remain calm and professional.
- ☑ Listen to the entire presentation by the parent.
- ☑ Ask questions that will provide more information: "What is your understanding of the assignment?" "What has [student's first name] told you about the assignment (or incident)?" "When did he (or she) say this?"
- ☑ Restate the overall assignment requirements or details of the incident to which the parent is referring. If the conversation is about an incident, always relate the complete truth.
- ☑ If the parent still does not understand the assignment requirement, ask him or her to meet with you in school. In reference to an incident or a disciplinary measure, if the parent is not satisfied, ask him or her to get in contact with the principal or the guidance counselor for further assistance.
- ☑ In the case of an incident or a disciplinary measure, never implicate another student by name or indicate to the parent that you are in agreement with the other student's misbehavior.
- ☑ Always assure the parent that your main concerns are class harmony, equity, and quality instruction.

***In Real Time:* Intensity of Parental Involvement**

Parents become less involved with school programs as their children grow older. Most parental interaction at the middle and high school levels is associated with sports. This phenomenon is evidenced by fewer organized parent–teacher groups at the secondary level than at the elementary level, and dramatically fewer classroom visits (Eccles & Harold, 1993). The main reason for such decreased involvement is that the adolescent, who is seeking autonomy and increasing peer collaboration, is less enthusiastic about a parental presence (Bafile, 2004).

Briefcase CD CH11-7—Template for Letter Concerning Inappropriate Behavior

Briefcase CD CH11-8—Telephone Conference Checklist

Telephone Conferences

Parents should be encouraged to get in contact with you about their child's performance or behavior. Most telephone calls from parents are attempts to clarify information their children bring home, such as homework assignments or field-trip particulars. Occasionally, you will receive a call about a problem with another child or a disciplinary matter. You must remember that children will relate their perspective of an incident, which may not include all the details that resulted in the disciplinary action.

Should you give out your private telephone number? No one can answer this question except you. Some veteran teachers will tell you to *never* reveal your telephone number or where you live. Others believe that if parents have the number, they may be more willing to talk to you about their children's progress or lack thereof away from the venue of school authority. This decision is a personal preference.

PARENTAL OBJECTIONS TO TEACHING MATERIALS

An increasing phenomenon is parental objections to the material being used for instruction. In one reported case, a parent refused to allow her daughter to read *The Hobbit* in her eighth-grade English class on the grounds that it was irreligious and taught fantasy. In a

RESPONDING TO PARENTAL OBJECTIONS TO TEACHING MATERIALS

- Meet with or call the parent to discuss the material content and your mode of instruction.
- Assure the parent that you are focusing on the literary or academic aspect of the material.
- Offer an alternative assignment if the parent insists that the material is too objectionable.
- Notify the principal of the protest in all circumstances.

related and more timely incident, a fourth-grade teacher was instructed by her principal not to use references to the popular Harry Potter books because their witchcraft themes are too controversial. In fact, the Harry Potter series ranks seventh on the 100 Most Frequently Challenged Books list compiled by the American Library Association (n.d.).

Other objections may arise from specific assignments that call on children to read or work on material that is contrary to the parents' beliefs. The most controversial topic is evolution. This issue is so sensitive and broad in scope that the beginning teacher should consult the principal, veteran teachers, and other professionals. Overall, parental objections to teaching materials should never be a matter managed by the teacher alone. Most helpful on these issues is the library–media specialist, who will know the exact procedures and legal guidelines to be followed in the event of parental objections.

THE PARENT CONFERENCE

Briefcase CD CH11-9— Parent Conference Checklist

Each teacher will eventually meet with almost every parent through the parent conference. In the elementary grades, a common practice is for parents to meet with the teacher individually in the classroom to review the child's work for a marking period. At this time, explain your assessment policy in detail and inform the parent about how effectively his or her child is meeting the class standard.

Veteran teachers follow some basic guidelines either when meeting with parents in a scheduled structure or when compelled to do so by the child's behavior or low academic achievement. Parent conferences should never be held in public. If you are confronted by a parent in a store or on the street, discourage the discussion on the grounds that without your student records you cannot be accurate about the child's performance.

The parent conference is an essential communication link in which a student's unsuccessful efforts in school can be reversed.

PARENT CONFERENCE CHECKLIST

- ☑ ***Before the parent conference,*** prepare a folder that reflects the child's academic and behavioral profile. It should include the child's attendance record; class-rule infractions; test, quiz, and homework scores; samples of class work; and an overall summary of the child's success in the class.
- ☑ ***Meet the parent in the classroom environment*** (if possible), either before or after school, but never when class is in session.
- ☑ ***Designate a time slot*** solely for dialogue between parent and teacher, even if the child is present during the conference.
- ☑ ***Always be truthful,*** but refrain from making derogatory remarks about the child's performance or behavior. Instead, construct your criticisms with regard to the child's appropriate developmental level and his or her achievement (academic or behavioral) with respect to these levels.
- ☑ ***If a parent becomes belligerent or disagreeable,*** remain calm and courteous and suggest that the principal or guidance counselor be called to provide more insight into the problem.
- ☑ ***Include the child's guidance counselor*** whenever you can to provide background information and direction.
- ☑ ***Include some positive information*** about the student's performance or behavior.

VOICES IN THE CLASSROOM
Two Diverse Parenting Styles

It was the usual type of parent conference—Mom, Dad, and Jimmy (not his real name). The complaints were the usual ones—his grades were down, he was kicking up in class, and he never did homework. The counselor was giving his usual routine, asking the parents about his home life and suggesting strategies to get him to attend to his work. Suddenly, the father yelled at Jimmy, "Sit up straight and listen when adults are talking." Jimmy kept his head down but slowly moved his body to a straighter position.

"Is it true, wise guy? Is it true that you lied to us about the homework?"

Jimmy mumbled something. Then the father gave him a blow to the back of the head with the flat of his hand, pushing Jimmy's face onto the table. The mother put her head down. I looked at the counselor and he at me—both of us frozen in disbelief. As we attempted to compose ourselves, the father was haranguing the kid, calling him a liar and a lazy good-for-nothing. Somewhere during that tirade, I got up, excused myself, and escaped.

From that day on, I never marked Jimmy's papers with slashing red marks. I gave him a baseline grade of 85 and accepted whatever he gave me. I never again chided him for his behavior. But I didn't need to, because after that he seemed to me to be a little less lively, a little less interested in where he was. Five years later, he committed suicide.

—An English teacher

Mrs. Hauk was an unusual person and therefore an unusual parent. I did not come into contact with her until the day the class was having a food festival celebrating the end of an extensive unit on Colonial America. Each student brought in a prepared dish reflecting colonial cuisine, along with his or her project. The class period was only 10 minutes old when the door burst open and in walked Mrs. Hauk dressed in complete colonial garb from shoes to bonnet. She was pulling behind her a little tyke of about 3 years old, who was similarly dressed as though they had just come in from Williamsburg. She brought pastry puffs and candies for all the students and came prepared to tell us a story of an Indian girl and a settler.

I was so overwhelmed with this woman's exuberance and vitality that I had forgotten about her son, whom I feared would be mortified in front of his friends to have his mother behaving so peculiarly. But my fears were groundless because it was evident that he was proud of his mother's behavior and joined in the merriment with the others.

Mrs. Hauk became a frequent visitor to our class, always bringing along some artifact or story to help in our lessons. She was a wealth of information and ever ready to assist either in or out of class. Although a working mom, she found time to be a part of her son's education and managed this in such a way as to make him feel that she was an integral part of his learning. What I found most telling was how her son saw his mother's participation as a natural part of his life. It never occurred to him that this was not the norm.

—A sixth-grade teacher

Guidepost

What strategies should I use in my class for students whose parents have a different behavioral philosophy from my own?
Your system of behavior management will likely run contrary to that of some parents. Some parents are indulgent of their children and do not support a strong teacher style of punishments and rewards. Other parents are authoritative and believe in a strict system of punishments and rewards. To maintain a balanced level of communication with parents, teachers need to be aware of these differences. Therefore, do the following:

- Provide all parents with a copy of your behavioral policy.
- Keep parents updated weekly on your lessons and the students' overall progress.
- Seek out parents' ideas on future projects through your weekly newsletter or flyers sent home with the students.
- Send home copies of newsworthy articles on child development or the latest research on learning.
- Remind parents of your policies on issues such as chewing gum, candy, appropriate attire for the weather, and classroom responsibilities.

DOS AND DON'TS

Don't	Do
Use school-level newsletters and flyers as the only avenue of communication between you and your students' parents	Initiate communication through personal letters, e-mail, or weekly updates directly from your hand and with information relative to each parent's child
Allow months to pass without notifying a parent that his or her child is having serious academic problems	Send frequent updates of all academic achievement to parents through a variety of information modalities—telephone, mail, e-mail, newsletter, flyers, group meetings
Automatically blame the parents for a child's misbehavior in your classroom	Consider the many factors that cause disruptive behavior, including your management of the class, the curriculum in general, or a specific lesson plan
Underestimate the power of the parent to influence his or her child to achieve	Be realistic about the extent of parental help and consider that parents have their own jobs and home problems to manage
Speak with parents on the telephone in your classroom during class time, or in the teachers' lounge or any public place	Return all calls to parents on the day they are received
Lecture a parent on the curriculum requirements if he or she objects to his or her child's reading a particular book or story	Encourage the parent to understand why the book or story is required and the importance for his or her child to engage the text
Lecture students in class about their particular beliefs on what is being taught (e.g., not believing in evolution)	Explain the facts surrounding the topic, making sure you have allowed for differences in opinion due to religious, cultural, or ethnic beliefs
Go to a parent conference without a folder containing information on the child's progress to that date	Thoroughly prepare yourself for the parent conference with data and background information on the child's achievement in other classes
Ignore any community-based programs or initiatives at which you might connect with parents on a personal level	Seek out community-based programs or initiatives, and when possible, design one of your own in an effort to reach out to marginalized parents

WEB SITES OF INTEREST

http://www.wlma.org/Professional/policystatements.htm#aasl
Maintained by the American Association of School Librarians, this site is a reference on the policy on challenged materials.

http://www.ncpie.org
This site, by the National Coalition for Parent Involvement in Education, is for individuals seeking to establish resources for individual schools or school districts.

http://www.pta.org/parentinvolvement/index.asp
This National Parent Teacher Association site has a great deal to offer both teachers and parents as they seek to improve communication and help for students.

http://www.nea.org/parents/index.html
This National Education Association site offers tips and resources for improving parent–school communication.

http://www.education-world.com/a_special/parent_involvement.shtml
Education World's site for parents provides a number of good ideas for fund-raising and other community–school-oriented projects.

http://www.projectappleseed.org
Disseminated by Project Appleseed, a national campaign for public school improvement, this site provides a checklist for effective parent–school partnerships.

http://www.ed.gov/pubs/FamInvolve/index.html
This site offers detailed information on family involvement in children's education by highlighting successful local approaches.

http://www.publicagenda.org/specials/parent/parent.htm
This site offers some interesting insights into the entire paradigm of parental involvement, supported by extensive public opinion polls.

http://www.ld.org/advocacy/parent_involve.cfm
This excellent site is for all teachers and parents of children with learning disabilities. It provides a compendium of information on how such parents can work with the school to assist their children.

http://www.gse.harvard.edu/hfrp/projects/fine/resources/research/homework.html
This article on parental involvement in homework provides some insight into why you should encourage parents to become involved with their child's homework.

http://www.csos.jhu.edu/p2000/default.htm
Teachers can obtain assistance in developing goal-oriented programs of family and community involvement from this site, by the National Network Partnership of Schools at Johns Hopkins University.

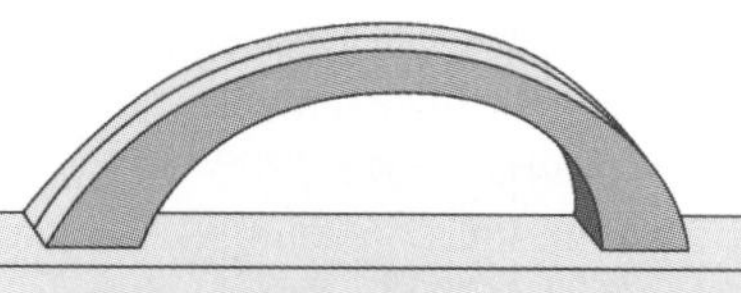

For Your Briefcase

To Do

- Familiarize yourself with your students' culture.
- Identify avenues through which you may encourage parental participation.
- Write up proactive initiatives to involve parents.
- Establish guidelines for parental communication.
- Consult with the library–media specialist about procedures on parental objections to the literature being read in class.

Resources on Your Briefcase CD

Samples

- Sample Letter of Praise and Accomplishment—Elementary School
- Sample Letter of Praise and Accomplishment—Middle School
- Sample Letter of Praise and Accomplishment—High School
- Sample Letter Concerning Inappropriate Behavior

Templates

- Template for Letter of Praise and Accomplishment
- Template for Letter Concerning Inappropriate Behavior
- Telephone Conference Checklist
- Parent Conference Checklist

Tables

- Parental Communication Initiatives

REFERENCES

American Library Association. (n.d.). *The 100 most frequently challenged books of 1990–2000.* Chicago: Author. Retrieved June 16, 2004, from http://www.ala.org/ala/oif/bannedbooksweek/bbwlinks/100mostfrequently.htm

Bafile, C. (2004). Math Night by the numbers. *Education World.* Retrieved July 8, 2005, from http://www.education-world.com/a_admin/admn/admin339.shtml

Child Abuse Prevention and Treatment Act, 42 U.S.C. § 5101 *et seq.*; 42 U.S.C. § 5116 *et seq.* (2003). Retrieved March 3, 2006, from http://www.acf.hhs.gov/programs/cb/laws_policies/cblaws/capta/index.htm

Coley, R. J. (2002, March). *An uneven start: Indicators of inequality in school readiness.* Princeton, NJ: Educational Testing Service.

Davies, D. (1991, January). Schools reaching out: Family, school and community partnerships for student success. *Phi Delta Kappan, 72*(5), 376–382.

Doyle, A. C. (1892, June). The adventure of the copper beeches. *The Strand Magazine, 3,* 613–628. Retrieved March 10, 2006, from http://eastoftheweb.com/short-stories/UBooks/AdveCopp.shtml

Dwyer, D. J., & Hecht, J. B. (1992). Minimal parental involvement. *School Community Journal, 2*(2), 53–66.

Eccles, J. S., & Harold, R. D. (1993). Parent–school involvement during the early adolescent years. *Teachers College Record, 94,* 568–587.

Epstein, J. L., & Dauber, S. L. (1991, January). School programs and teacher practices of parent involvement in inner-city elementary and middle schools. *Elementary School Journal, 91*(3), 289–305.

Epstein, J. L., Sanders, M. G., Simon, B. S., Salinas, K. C., Jansorn, N. R., & Van Voorhis, F. L. (2002). *School, family, and community partnerships: Your handbook for action* (2nd ed.). Thousand Oaks, CA: Corwin Press.

Fields, J. (2003). *America's families and living arrangements: 2003* (Current Population Rep. P20-553). Washington, DC: U.S. Census Bureau. Retrieved March 3, 2006, from http://www.census.gov/prod/2004pubs/p20-553.pdf

McNeal, R. B., Jr. (1999). Parental involvement as social capital: Differential effectiveness on science achievement, truancy, and dropping out. *Social Forces, 78*(1), 117–144.

Working with Your Colleagues and Support Staff

What advice would you offer new teachers? If I were to tell new teachers anything, it would be to function on the basis of hope rather than on optimism. Optimism is a conviction that things will work out for the best. Hope is a deep faith that the struggle for things to work out well might eventually succeed. Optimism will almost certainly fail, but hope never dies.

—Herbert Kohl (in Gomez, 2001, NEA Today.)

COLLEGIALITY

Teaching is unlike most other professions in that your colleagues can affect your daily life in a variety of ways while remaining so unobtrusive that you may not see some of them for days or weeks. Even in a small elementary school, a teacher can become so busy with his or her students and their activities that contact with colleagues is measured in moments at the photocopy machine or in hurried lunchroom dialogues punctuated with interruptions and telephone messages.

Environmental Impact on Collegiality

Where you teach influences collegial relationships. Teachers interact differently depending on their students' age and grade level and the buildings in which they teach. Teachers' views on their students will also vary depending on the age of the students they are teaching. Middle school teachers are apt to be more concerned with behavioral issues than are primary or high school teachers.

Elementary-Level Teachers Elementary teachers are generally isolated in their rooms most of the day, except for lunch and when their classes are either in recess or receiving instruction in art, music, or physical education. Accordingly, little time is available for collegial interaction beyond a few moments in the faculty lounge or at faculty meetings.

Middle School Teachers Middle school teachers see few members of the wider faculty on a daily basis beyond the members of their team. However, they work closely with their team members and often form strong collegial bonds.

VOICES IN THE CLASSROOM
You're on Your Own, Kid

It was 1970 and I was one of 19 new teachers hired at the junior high school, which in my youth was viewed like a local prison, complete with gangsters, mobsters, and criminals. We were gathered in the auditorium for the first faculty meeting of the year on the day before the urchins were to arrive. You could tell the rookies from the vets just by checking the fashion statements being made—formal to laid-back.

I sat next to another suited rookie seeking comfort from the gassing, sassing, T-shirted veterans who seemed to be downright cantankerous about starting the new year. Chief on their minds was, of all things, gum chewing. They were demanding to know if the principal was going to enforce the gum-chewing rule. Long minutes of heated discussion left the question in the air. This was followed by a spirited discourse on which of the faculty would get to park in the "varsity" lot—the one closest to the school. Also not resolved.

By this time, my seatmate and I were questioning our choice of professions. That year was big for the insurance business, and selling new cars was fast becoming a respected career. Fortunately, we avoided public humiliation by not asking the question that was foremost on our minds: When do we get our teacher's manual?

Later, we decided to put the question to our principal.

"Your what?" he said.

"You know, the book that tells you what to do," we inquired, both as deadpanned and serious as if we were choosing a coffin. At first he thought we were joking, then he said what became both his mantra and a prophecy: "Go check your room for leaks."

In those first days, we learned that there was no manual, that you should never ask the principal for something he doesn't want to give you, and that *faculty* is a euphemism for "the other people in the building."

—*A former teacher*

How can I get to know my colleagues? How do I break the ice?
Entering a social situation in which you are a stranger is always awkward. However, a school is a community of like-minded people.

- Begin by introducing yourself to the colleagues with whom you will be working most closely (i.e., those in your grade level or subject area).
- Join schoolwide committees or clubs in which you will work with other teachers or staff members.
- Volunteer for activities such as fund-raisers, sports events, or other programs in which teachers work with students.
- If you are assigned a mentor, spend some time talking with him or her about the school and the staff and how to function effectively as a colleague.

What questions should I ask my mentor, or any veteran teacher, during the first days and weeks of school?

- How do I get material photocopied?
- Where do I get needed classroom supplies? What is the limit?
- Who is the person who will help me when I have difficulty with a child who is misbehaving in my class?
- What are my responsibilities regarding the maintenance of my room (e.g., cleaning, fixing small items)?
- What are the specific procedures regarding grade keeping and report cards?
- How should I organize my parent conferences?

High School Teachers By virtue of their schedules, high school teachers will encounter more members of their faculty through period-long visits in central lounges as often as three times daily. As a result of having more time for collegial interaction with faculty from across four grade levels, high school teachers have an opportunity for a greater social and political bond.

Politics

High school and middle school teachers are generally more vocal on the issues that affect the workplace, which has varying results in terms of collegiality (Murphy, 1990). In one sense, the political environment found in middle schools and high schools can solidify a faculty as a group with common purpose, but in another sense it can also become divisive. The elementary school, by its nature, is less political because the duties and daily activities of its teachers lend themselves to a cohesiveness brought about by the intense demand of the young and developing student body. Elementary school–aged children require constant supervision and care, whereas older children are increasingly more independent, requiring less supervisory oversight.

INFLUENCES ON COLLEGIALITY

Getting to know your colleagues depends on a variety of factors:

- ☑ The leadership style of the principal of the building
- ☑ The level of cooperation between teachers and support staff
- ☑ The level of support from the parental community
- ☑ The level of perceived equity in teaching assignments
- ☑ The superintendent's leadership style, and support from the school board
- ☑ The school level: elementary, where teachers are somewhat isolated by grade structure; middle school, where teachers work closely in teams; high school, where teachers are isolated by subject area
- ☑ The size and demographics of the school building

INSTRUCTIONAL AND SUPPORT FACULTY

The Classroom Teacher

The *classroom teacher* is the professional who works with children in large or small numbers, teaching many subjects or a single subject, on a daily basis within the framework of an agreed-upon curriculum. This person is at the heart of any educational system and bears the characteristics of tradition that date from the ages of Socrates, Aristotle, and Confucius to those of Emma Willard, Annie Sullivan, and Christa McAuliffe.

In the modern classroom, you will likely have at least one other adult in the room while you teach, or you may be a teacher whose duties include coteaching. Coteaching was once an instructional strategy but is rapidly becoming a standard as a result of mainstreaming (inclusion) policies that call for special education teachers to work inside the classroom within the instructional program rather than as a pullout resource.

The Special Education Department

Almost 6%, or 2.8 million, of all school-age children receive services for a learning disability, while another 6% exhibit some form of learning disability but fail to meet the criteria for services (Gruber, Wiley, Broughman, Strizek, & Burian-Fitzgerald, 2002). Accordingly, the most visible professionals in the school building besides the classroom teachers are the special education teachers. Since the 1980s, the role of these teachers has expanded into a critical presence in all schools, public and private, but not without struggle and controversy.

Before the 1975 landmark legislation Public Law 94-142, students with disabilities ranging from physical to neurological were closeted in a classroom with one teacher and generally prevented from interacting with the student body. Prior to the 1975 legislation, each state formulated its own policy on the education of children with disabilities; however, in many states, these children were banned from attending public schools (Gaddy, McNulty, & Waters, 2002).

In Real Time: Special Education Teachers

Too often, classroom teachers think of special education teachers as professionals outside the educational program. Rather, they are real *teachers trained in all areas of the curriculum as well as extensive psychological testing procedures. Although they may be assigned only 12 students, they provide support for the entire academic program of these students.*

The phrase most quoted from the original Elementary and Secondary Education Act (now entitled *Individuals with Disabilities Education Act*) legislation is "least restrictive environment." This term means that every effort must be made to include a child classified with a disability in the main student body, within the entire spectrum of educational services.

Classifying children with learning disabilities is often a long, bureaucratic process involving a series of prescribed steps that include the classroom teacher, the parent, the school administrator, and the special education representative. For the novice teacher, the special education department may appear to be an enormous agency whose activities are visible throughout the school's entire educational program.

Role of the Special Education Teacher Since the 1990s, school districts have slowly been inching toward full inclusion of all students receiving special education. Prior to inclusion but following Public Law 94-142 in 1975, students with learning disabilities were taught separately but with some mainstreaming. In this capacity, the special education teacher acted as a resource professional who spent the day tutoring his or her assigned students in the major subjects, working with classroom teachers on time management and study skills, and administering the many required tests to the students who were classified.

DUTIES OF THE SPECIAL EDUCATION TEACHER

- Assisting students with learning disabilities with work from each subject area
- Acting as a liaison between the school and parents when reporting behavioral and academic progress
- Acting as a liaison between the student and the subject teacher
- Maintaining and upgrading the individualized education plan (IEP) of each student with a learning disability
- Testing and retesting students for learning disabilities

Special education teachers are unique in that their professional preparation has included a great deal of psychology and instructional technique surpassing that of classroom teachers. When working with their assigned students, these teachers must be conversant and relatively skilled in all five subject areas—math, science, English, foreign language, and social studies or history. They must also be skilled in literacy and compositional skills and understand the disabilities that block students from being successful in these areas.

One essential task special education teachers perform is the administration of various tests that are used to attempt to identify and gauge learning disabilities. This process is involved and includes observing and studying a student's current academic achievements and classroom behavior and administering a battery of tests of phonological-processing problems, of academic-skills discrepancies, and of cognitive achievement related to reading, writing, and computational skills. A few of the typical tests used are the Woodcock–Johnson Psychoeducational Battery, the Vineland Adaptive Behavior Scales, the Goodenough–Harris Drawing Test, and the McCarthy Scales of Children's Abilities. All these tests are geared to identify disabilities and plot educational programs that address the disabilities. This goal is accomplished through the IEP, or individualized education plan, which must be written for each student receiving special education services. The IEP is important for both the special education teacher and the classroom teacher because it describes in detail exactly what is necessary to accommodate the child's disability and helps blueprint a path to success. Most important, the IEP is a mandate for the classroom teacher to provide the services and accommodations as they are written by the special education teacher and supported by federal law.

Special Education Teachers as Coteachers As inclusion continues to become the rule, as well as the law, special education teachers are increasingly being embedded in the classroom in the role of coteacher. This arrangement goes beyond just having a couple of teachers in a room with 24–30 children. The term *coteach* implies cooperation, planning, and strategy; all three are necessary if teacher effectiveness and a harmonious learning environment are to occur. For the novice teacher, this experience will be unique because teacher preparation programs generally focus on helping the preservice teacher construct lessons and deliver instruction. When you are assigned to and responsible for a classroom of children, you will be the sole person in the room responsible not only for ensuring the safety of the children, but also for directing their learning. In the coteaching situation, these duties are divided in ways that must be optimal for the student and the instructional program.

As a novice, you may expect your classroom or area to include just you and the students. However, this scenario rarely occurs. Most likely, the special education teacher and possibly one or two teacher's aides will be in the room with you during the entire day. If you are assigned children who are severely hearing or visually impaired, or who have multiple disabilities, you may also have an additional person in the room with the child. Thus, you may have to rethink your idea of the teaching–learning scenario, and you will certainly need to write lesson plans and a classroom management plan that serves the needs of all your students.

In Real Time: **Coteachers**

The tradition of teaching in a room alone with 24–30 children is obsolete. Today's teacher can expect to have at least one or more other adults in the room on any given day. If you have students with learning disabilities on your roster, you may have both the special education teacher and an aide working with students during the lesson. You must design lesson plans that include these professionals as facilitators of your lesson.

The additional professionals in your room may work chiefly with students with learning disabilities, but they will also interact with the entire class, especially in cooperative learning groups. You must include these teachers in your lesson planning and work cooperatively with them to chart a course of instruction that is designed to meet the needs of all students. For example, a well-known study strategy for students who have difficulty processing many facts at once is to reduce the information into small paragraphs or outline form. This strategy is effective for everyone, not just students who process slowly; accordingly, your planning and preparation of material should include this technique. Be sure to consult the special education teacher for more techniques on material preparation and delivery.

Working harmoniously with others in close quarters for long periods is not always possible. Secondary teachers have the advantage of preparation periods or time between classes. Physical education, art, music, and careers or technology teachers often have flexible or staggered schedules to accommodate irregular numbers of students. However, the elementary teacher is physically with his or her children most of the day, along with one or two other adults in the room. Therefore, you must prepare yourself mentally to work with these adults as your instructional program unfolds. Mental preparation includes putting your students' needs before yours, thinking in terms of program efficiency rather than expediency, and establishing a cooperative classroom management style.

Teachers and Isolationism

The classroom teacher, including the teacher who "floats," does not teach in isolation. Every school has a culture of collegiality, albeit in varying degrees of intensity. A negative school culture has been traced as a cause of low student achievement, high student discomfort levels, and high dropout rates (Gruber et al., 2002). Your colleagues can be a great source of help during times of frustration and turmoil, or they can be the cause of your frustration and turmoil. The constant variables in the formula of collegiality are as follows:

- ☑ Your self-awareness
- ☑ Your confidence in your ability to be an effective teacher
- ☑ Your being true to the underlying purpose of the profession—helping children to learn

New teachers should observe veteran teachers and learn from them; however, implementing suggested strategies and tactics from the experienced teacher should be tempered with critical thinking and judiciously applied according to your values and personal philosophy. Former teacher Carolyn Bunting (1999) provided a good perspective on collegiality:

> Frequent communication with other teachers promotes self-confidence and self-reliance. Informal but regular teacher talk sessions inform and encourage teachers to become reflective about their practice.

PROFESSIONAL SUPPORT STAFF

Other Professionals

STATING THE FACTS:

On library–media specialists: Although 62,364 library–media specialists are in U.S. public schools, and 3,909 are in private schools, nearly 25% of public schools and 80% of private schools have none (Gruber et al., 2002).

Educating a child does take a village, and in a school, it takes more than just the classroom teacher. Most current public schools and some private schools are teeming with professionals not directly involved in classroom instruction; however, each professional plays an important role in the overall daily instructional program. The relationship between these professionals and the classroom teacher can have an enormous impact on whether a learning program is applied equally to all students.

PROFESSIONALS WHO SUPPORT STUDENTS AND CLASSROOM TEACHERS	
Description	**Duties and Support**
Library–media specialist: A professional who maintains and organizes the library system, information technology, and multimedia resources	• Conducts literacy sessions with young readers • Provides instruction on reference source material and citations • Provides guidance on new computer software programs • Is an instant resource on the latest print and electronic media material • Is the first source for professional development material
School nurse: A licensed or registered nurse who maintains a health facility in the school and is responsible for the immediate and preventive health care of students assigned to a school building	• Provides first-aid to injured children • Provides health policy information for students and teachers • Is the on-site official for reporting child abuse • Provides health care information on personal hygiene and nutrition • Maintains and administers prescription and nonprescription drugs for students • Maintains health records for all students assigned to a school building • Is the official source for information on individuals with disabilities regulations and procedures
School psychologist: A licensed psychologist who conducts psychological and remedial testing of children and provides a counseling service for all students deemed in need	• Tests students for disabilities or those who have been identified as needing remediation • Conducts counseling sessions with students classified under the Americans with Disabilities Act or as requested by parents and school officials • Provides a source of support for students needing immediate attention as a result of behavior breakdowns • Is a liaison among teachers, school officials, and parents
Social intervention specialist: A professional who is trained in the social support network	• Works with school officials and local social agencies to assist students from needy or dysfunctional homes • Is a source of information and procedures regarding home and family problems • Counsels students demonstrating stress from problems related to the home environment
Physical therapist: A licensed therapist who works specifically with children who have motor, neurological, or sensory difficulties	• Provides physical therapy for students with physical disabilities • Provides once- or twice-a-week physical exercise sessions for all students
Instructional support teacher: A fully licensed teacher who develops curriculum and coordinates instructional programs	• Provides information and resource material for instruction • Introduces new instructional programs through workshops, seminars, and in-class demonstrations

Briefcase CD CH12-1—Checklist for Professional Support

When to Call for Help

A prudent teacher knows that some situations or lessons require help from other people, especially from individuals trained in specific areas. Following are typical situations that generally require outside help:

CHECKLIST FOR PROFESSIONAL SUPPORT

Situation	Professional support staff
• You need assistance explaining to your students the difference between *primary* and *secondary* source material. • Your students are doing a major project requiring various multimedia sources. • You need electronic graphics on a particular topic. • You need a reference to support a paper you are writing for a course. • You want your students to get first-hand knowledge of how to use the library. • You need a selection of books to recommend to your students for outside reading. • You want to take professional development courses and do not know which to take to continue your certification. • You need grant money and want to know how to apply for and obtain it. • You need your students to understand how to research topics and write a critique.	☑ Library–media specialist
• A student injures him- or herself in such a way that the skin is broken, a fracture is likely, obvious pain is involved, or an adhesive bandage is needed.	☑ School nurse and principal
• A student has a headache and requests aspirin.	☑ School nurse
• You suspect physical or sexual abuse.	☑ School nurse and school psychologist
• A student is displaying behavior characteristic of deep depression or a lack of energy.	☑ School nurse, school psychologist, and social intervention specialist
• You plan to teach a lesson involving health issues and need an expert speaker.	☑ School nurse
• You have a student with a personal hygiene problem.	☑ School nurse and school psychologist
• A student in your class (or wherever you are in the building) suddenly goes out of control and is in danger of injuring him- or herself or others.	☑ School psychologist, school nurse, and principal
• A student is chronically misbehaving despite your best efforts.	☑ Vice-principal and school psychologist
• You suspect a student of behavior that may harm him- or herself or others.	☑ School psychologist, school nurse, and principal
• You suspect a student has attention-deficit/hyperactivity disorder.	☑ School nurse, school psychologist, and special education teacher
• You cannot interpret the test scores of a student with special needs.	☑ School psychologist, special education teacher, and guidance counselor
• You suspect that a student is undernourished.	☑ School nurse and social intervention specialist
• A student wants to speak with you about a home environment issue such as divorce, sibling abuse, or problems relating to care and nourishment.	☑ Social intervention specialist

—*Cont.*

Situation	Professional support staff
• You are implementing a physical exercise program in your class.	☑ Physical therapist
• A student who is physically disabled cannot function well in your classroom.	☑ Physical therapist
• You want to initiate a new curriculum requiring many resources.	☑ Instructional support teacher
• You need help coordinating instruction with testing requirements or state standards.	☑ Instructional support teacher
• You need help designing lesson plans for a particular class that may not be responding to instruction.	☑ Instructional support teacher

NONINSTRUCTIONAL SUPPORT STAFF

Secretaries and Clerks

Briefcase CD CH12-2—Checklist for Noninstructional Support

The secretaries in all school offices are extremely important to the efficient functioning of the education program. They are the first line of communication among all staff and communicate the implementation of the daily schedule. The secretary is the person who first receives telephone messages from parents, other professionals from around the district, salespeople, maintenance staff, and teachers.

Office clerks do the odd jobs around a school that help keep the organization moving. These people include the copy-machine person, the attendance clerk, the detention clerk, the library assistant, and the media transport person.

Have consideration for the copy-machine clerk. Do not dump a huge copying job on him or her 15 minutes before you need it. Plan ahead.

How They Help You For the novice teacher, the secretary can be your sole connection to procedure and resources. His or her knowledge of the system will help you navigate the often-hectic first days and will keep you on track regarding administrative requirements. For you, the teacher, the copy-machine clerk is also enormously important to implementation of your daily lessons.

The office secretary is a key person in the operation of the daily school program.

Go to The secretary for the following:

- Forms and information on employment records, such as W-4s, health insurance forms, and payroll dates
- Information on and procedures for taking attendance
- Scheduling an appointment with the principal
- Procedure on obtaining common classroom supplies (e.g., staplers, tape, scissors, and major purchases such as textbooks, DVDs, or videotapes)
- Schedules for reserving the auditorium or other facilities
- Information on parking and passes

The Custodian

Veteran teachers can attest to the value of knowing the custodian well. The custodial staff of a school contributes a great deal to the efficiency of the educational program and the safety of the entire school community, yet it is generally unseen during the school day. The custodian's job description extends across a wide spectrum within the system that ranges from dealing with unpleasant cleanups to performing major maintenance and repair jobs.

How He or She Helps You The custodian cleans your room every day after school. He or she also performs minor repairs, in and out of the classroom, on a range of mechanics such as pencil sharpeners and locker doors. The custodian also hauls your textbooks from the delivery room to your room. Therefore, the effective teacher takes time to establish a rapport with this vital person.

Go to The custodian in the following instances:

- When windows stick, drapes fall down, or desks break
- When you need a map hung in your room
- To fix a piece of furniture that may injure a student
- To fix unworkable light fixtures, light sockets, or other electrical items
- When a nearby lavatory toilet is overflowing or poses hazards to students
- When a child vomits in or near your classroom

The custodian is an active and essential member of the school community.

Teacher's Aide and Monitor

The teacher's aide is now more frequently referred to as a *paraprofessional*. Thirty-four states have some type of regulation or certification requirement for paraprofessionals, who number approximately 900,000 in the nation; also, the No Child Left Behind (NCLB) legislation has outlined a higher standard for certification to be imposed by 2006 (U.S. Department of Education, 2004). However, many school districts have their own requirements that may range from an associate's degree to a high school diploma or less. In some schools, parents are enlisted as aides, especially at the primary level, and they may or may not undergo an indoctrination program.

Monitors are being used more frequently in schools to assume what are known as *nonprofessional* duties. However, they are also enlisted to assist teachers by working with individual students and performing clerical duties. Most monitors still perform traditional duties such as bus, hall, and cafeteria supervision.

How They Help You A teacher's aide can be an enormous help to you in the classroom. Besides functioning as a tutor for your students, an aide is another adult in the room to help with classroom control.

Go to The teacher's aide in these instances:

- To work with individual students on their dependent-practice part of the lesson
- To sit by and assist a student who is disruptive because he or she does not understand the material
- To help in daily planning (especially for brainstorming ideas on instruction)
- To conduct minilessons on a part of the lesson for students who may be struggling with the material
- To work in the library with a group of students on projects or individual assignments

Go to The monitor in these instances:

- To accompany an unruly child to the main office
- For photocopying or retrieving files
- To work with a student who is struggling with a part of the lesson
- To accompany a group of students to the library or computer center

School Resource Officer

A recent addition to the school staff is the school resource officer, who is usually a uniformed police officer assigned, as part of his or her duties, to spend part or all of the school day in the building. The officer's presence is meant to generate a positive image of law enforcement officials as well as to protect students through prevention education.

The presence of a school resource officer sends a positive message to students about law enforcement as part of the support team.

How He or She Helps You The resource officer will most likely not have an impact on your daily classroom lessons but will provide assemblies related to drug and alcohol abuse and present positive ways to spend leisure time. The officer will also provide in-class presentations on issues that may relate to your lesson. His or her presence within the building will generate a sense of security for both students and staff.

Food Service Personnel

Often overlooked as partners in education, the food service personnel begin their day early to prepare for the morning breakfast program and then lunch. Their job is essential to providing students with the nourishment necessary for them to be alert and prepared for the rigors of the day.

How They Help You Food service personnel may make your day when you desperately need a bagel, coffee, and a friendly smile. Never forget to thank them.

THE UNION

Whether to Join the Union

Briefcase CD CH12-3— Unions: An Overview of the Debate

If you begin work in a school district that has a union, making the decision to join can be a cause for angst. For the novice teacher, the issue can be confusing because of the nature and relationship of the union as a bargaining agent and the administration as the employer. Some districts have a *closed shop* agreement, which means you have no choice but to join; however, most have what is known as *agency fee payers,* which means you can refuse to join the union but must pay a fee to the union as your bargaining agent. Often, this fee is equal to union membership dues.

Positive and Negative Views on Unions Joining the union is often a personal decision because many people believe strongly in a worker's right to unionize, whereas others believe as strongly that unions have no place in the public school system.

Opinions on teacher unionism range wide on both sides of the spectrum. New teachers should examine their views and feelings on this issue. The presence of unionism in public schools is a simple sociological fact; groups seek both security and autonomy when operating in a closed system governed by an agency of considerable power (Lieberman, 1997). Despite strong rhetoric by national union officials that their high priority is quality education and reform, a labor union's first allegiance, in fact its duty as a collective

UNIONS: AN OVERVIEW OF THE DEBATE

Pro	Con
Unions are bargaining agents for increased pay and benefits.	Collective bargaining often results in greater gains for veteran teachers.
Contracts provide guidelines to prevent teacher–administration disputes.	Rigid contract language often blocks individual teacher initiatives.
Political activism ensures that the legislature focuses on educational issues and financing.	The National Education Association and the American Federation of Teachers contribute more to Democratic candidates, which alienates Republican and Independent voting members.
Unanimity allows for more effective reform initiatives.	A union's stance on issues such as vouchers, charter schools, and religion in schools is contrary to many members' views.
Without a union, school district administrators would govern through dictums and mandates, without teacher input.	Administrative officials value teacher input and would violate the spirit of professionalism by ignoring it.
Organized educators stimulate research and studies of educational issues.	National union advocates focus on issues that result in more teachers and less student contact time.
Unions work to improve teachers' pay and benefits, which in turn attracts more highly skilled and qualified teachers.	Most gains unions negotiate benefit the long-term veteran; negotiated salary packages are often skewed to the top levels of seniority.
Unions offer lower car and life insurance rates, lower loan rates, and discounts on luxury items and services.	Union membership offers members opportunities for savings, but many of these opportunities are also available from companies and programs open to the public.

QUOTATIONS ON TEACHERS' UNIONS

If we could get rid of the union, we'd be able to get these programs to work.
—Middle school principal discussing new program initiatives

I've been teaching for 35 years and make $62,000. Do you think they'd think twice about replacing me with a young teacher who'd make $32,000 a year?
—Veteran teacher on why unions are necessary

Teachers should get respect and good pay, but I don't believe they should be allowed to strike like a factory worker.
—Financial adviser

Teacher unions must take responsibility for the quality of teachers and for the learning environment in schools.
—Bob Chase, former National Education Association president (in Peterson, 1997)

Lest anyone misunderstand, there is a huge difference between teachers and teachers' unions. . . . A union . . . is not a teacher but a service business. Its goal is its own success, accomplished by providing something of value to their [*sic*] consumer, the teacher.
—Brent Morrison, journalist and critic (in Morrison, 2000)

bargaining agent, is to protect its members' job security and enhance their overall working conditions. In the process of attaining this goal, a union also generates benefits for the students and the educational system as well.

How the Union Helps You

Unions arose because of a need for services and benefits that teachers were not getting by simply asking for them. Overall, the union provides protection and ensures fair and reasonable practices between employer and employee. Teachers' unions do the following:

☑ Negotiate with the local school board on these issues:
- Wage and benefits parity
- Reduced class sizes
- Fair remuneration for extracurricular activities
- Fair scheduling of the school day
- Safety of the school environment
- Academic freedom
- Fair hiring and firing practices
- Reasonable provisions for sick or personal leave
- A fair grievance process to settle disagreements arising within the instructional and noninstructional environment

☑ Provide legal counsel in any disciplinary action against a teacher

☑ Provide a host of discounts and special offers from a variety of agencies and companies selling services and merchandise

☑ Provide in-service courses, seminars, and workshops on instruction and other education-related topics

As you can see, reducing class size is clearly a beneficial goal for teachers' unions because it increases the teacher force and subsequent union membership. However, having smaller classes also benefits the student. A wealth of research supports higher student achievement in classes with fewer than 20 students (Mosteller, 1995). This example

VOICES IN THE CLASSROOM
Making Personal Decisions

It was my first year of teaching—in fact my eighth day. I didn't even have all of my textbooks yet, and there I was on the pavement—striking. It went against everything I ever believed in for a teacher. This is what autoworkers did, not teachers. There was something terribly wrong.

It was Friday, September 17, 1971, and 95% of our 550 teachers were on the picket line throughout the entire district. This was the culmination of months of failed collective bargaining and strident language between the administration and the teachers' union. Our mailboxes were flooded with flyers from the union, complete with caricatures of board members made to look silly as they unilaterally ruled our lives. The union message was simple but insistent. We were getting a salary less than that of most factory workers; our medical insurance was filled with loopholes; sabbaticals were given at the whim of the administration; sick days were limited to two without a doctor's note; and bus duty, cafeteria duty, and hall duty were mandatory and beneath the dignity of college-educated professionals.

The district settled the contract on Sunday afternoon—the 1-day strike had secured all but a few minor points of our demands. We had won.

But I was depressed. I had betrayed my beliefs of what a teacher is supposed to be. I had taken a cut in pay working in industry to become a teacher because I wanted to work with kids. I had argued against the strike with my colleagues, but in the end they made me an offer I couldn't refuse—you're either with us or against us. Unfortunately, "against us" meant a concrete wall of silence and collective derision. For those who did not strike, their lives were never the same. A few quit, many became physically ill, and some, even 10 years later, were being shunned and detracted as "scabs."

—*A former teacher*

demonstrates how the interests of the union can parallel the interests of the teacher; however, in some instances, the interests are contradictory.

The Union and You

When a teachers' union strikes against a district, the big losers are the students. Substitute teachers, administrators, and even hall monitors try to hold together a schedule of instruction that is often nothing more than maintaining order. Even when the union implements a modified job action such as work-to-rule, when members perform their duties to the letter, often shutting down extracurricular activities, the students are the losers. Ultimately, such actions hurt you as a teacher because they put a strain on your relationship with your students. Going out on strike certainly flies in the face of the definition of a teacher.

The union's purpose and role can often step between you and the ideals to which you may subscribe as a teacher. Following are three examples:

1. Contract language may forbid you to establish a club or an activity because you would not be remunerated. Doing the activity or club for free weakens the union's position on demanding money for other clubs and activities.
2. Accepting more students in your class than the contract allows (usually 30) undermines the union's negotiating strategy. You will likely not be allowed to accept one or two extra students even if they need your class to graduate.
3. Performing services for the district such as helping out in the cafeteria or monitoring halls violates the contract. This prohibition prevents you from contributing your energy and ideas to the solutions of problems you believe are part of your personal ideals.

These examples are just several situations that can cause you personal angst as a result of unionism. However, depending on the contract language and the strength of the union's grievance team, you may have fewer or more situations that will put you at odds with the union.

In Real Time: **Novice Teachers and the Union**

A novice teacher is wise to remain vigilant but aloof from the politics that stir between the union and the administration. The first 3 years of a teacher's career should be focused on becoming an effective teacher within the guidelines provided by the administration and the teachers' contract.

Briefcase CD CH12-4—Background Information on the Two National Teachers' Unions

The Union Representative (The Rep)

In school districts in which a union is the bargaining agent, you will be approached early in the year by a representative of the local, who will provide you with a packet of information about becoming a member. Many locals have informational sessions embedded into the orientation given by the district, or they host an evening event to introduce you to union officials. Each school has a union representative (rep) who is the in-house liaison between the local and the district. The rep does the following:

- ☑ Represents the union and its members on issues that may arise requiring an interpretation of contract language
- ☑ Is a resource person for questions concerning the duties and responsibilities of teachers and administrators relative to the contract
- ☑ Accompanies teachers to meetings with school officials when disciplinary action may be the result

When You Should Consult the Union Rep New teachers are often unaware of procedures and expectations within the district and the building. You should see your rep for information and guidance regarding the following:

- ☑ Your responsibilities related to a duty or an activity
- ☑ A reprimand from a supervisor or the principal
- ☑ An incident with a student in which you are unsure of your rights and responsibilities
- ☑ Questions about dues payment, deductions, or other union benefits
- ☑ Information related to the union's contract, the union's constitution, and your rights and responsibilities

BACKGROUND INFORMATION ON THE TWO NATIONAL TEACHERS' UNIONS

National Education Association (NEA)	American Federation of Teachers (AFT)
Founded in 1857, the NEA began as a professional organization for all educators, including administrators, with few ties to labor activities.	Founded in 1916 by rank-and-file teachers, the AFT has a history of being closely associated with labor, especially the AFL–CIO (American Federation of Labor–Congress of Industrial Organizations).
The NEA is open to all education-related organizations, including higher education, and has 2.7 million members nationwide.	The AFT has more than 1.3 million members, including health care professionals, paraprofessionals, and higher education faculty.
The NEA is organized around a representative assembly of 9,000 delegates from locals in all 50 states.	The AFT is organized around a representative assembly of approximately 3,000 delegates from locals in 43 states.

Note. Union locals are affiliated with either the NEA or the AFT. Such affiliations may vary within states as well as between states. Data from www.aft.org/about and www.nea.org/aboutnea/index.html.

DOS AND DON'TS

Don't	Do
Spend entire preparation periods visiting in the teachers' lounge, listening to or participating in grousing sessions	Ask veteran teachers questions on any area in which you are confused or having problems
Choose as a role model the teacher who is vocally antiadministration, is critical of students, or has an overall negative demeanor	Seek out veteran teachers who are working to solve problems, enjoy being with students, and are still learning from their mistakes
Send students to the school nurse without judging the need for his or her help	Consult the school nurse when you are in doubt about whether a child needs professional help in school or at home
Exclude the special education teacher in your room from your curriculum plan, policies, and strategies	Include the special education teacher and allow him or her to perform his or her duties as a professional
Refuse any student who is designated as learning disabled his or her testing modifications	Provide the special education teacher or his or her aide with the necessary directions and guidelines for all your quizzes, project work, and tests
Join the union without first talking with peers, administrators, the union rep, and your family	Carefully consider the pros and cons of joining the union before signing up for dues deduction
Make a decision about joining the union on purely emotional or ideological grounds	Consult peers, veteran teachers, and supervisors before joining the union
Take part in any union job action until you are given clear assurances that your job is not in jeopardy	Support your colleagues, after careful examination of the issue, if you deem their struggle is just and honorable for both teachers and students
Treat custodial staff as servants or low-level workers	Establish a working relationship with all custodial staff and treat them with respect for the job they do
Allow the teacher's aide in your room to set disciplinary policy	Allow the teacher's aide to participate in the policymaking process and help him or her to enforce it
Allow the students in your class to "play off" you and your aide on disciplinary matters	Inform students about the authority status of the classroom and let them know that you and your aide speak in one voice on disciplinary issues

WEB SITES OF INTEREST

http://www.aare.edu.au/01pap/jar01124.htm
On this site, you will find an article relating to teacher collegiality and the link between teacher collaboration and student learning outcomes.

http://specialed.about.com
This site provides information on a wide range of special education topics. The information is practical, and the site is user friendly.

http://www.nea.org/esphome/index.html
This site, sponsored by the National Education Association, provides support and information relating to all noninstructional staff personnel.

http://brookings.nap.edu/books/0815753039/html
At this site, you will find the complete text of Tom Loveless's book *Conflicting Missions? Teachers Unions and Educational Reform.* It provides balanced information about teachers' unions in general.

http://www.nea.org/index.html
This site is the official National Education Association (NEA) Web site.

http://www.aft.org
This site is the official American Federation of Teachers (AFT) Web site.

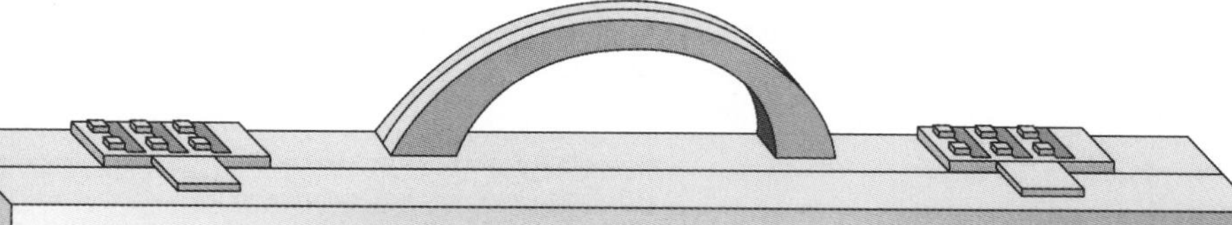

For Your Briefcase

To Do

- At first, introduce yourself to the colleagues with whom you will be working most closely.
- Initiate a meeting with your mentor.
- Meet with your coteacher (special education).
- Introduce yourself to the professional and noninstructional support staff.
- Speak with your union representative for more information about the union.

Resources on Your Briefcase CD

Templates

- Checklist for Professional Support
- Checklist for Noninstructional Support

Tables

- Unions: An Overview of the Debate
- Background Information on the Two National Teachers' Unions

REFERENCES

Bunting, C. (1999, August). Teacher, Improve thyself. *Classroom Leadership, 2*(9). Retrieved March 9, 2006, from http://www.ascd.org/portal/site/ascd/menuitem.2a4fb56d79bd30a98d7ea23161a001ca

Gaddy, B., McNulty, B., & Waters, T. (2002, April). *The reauthorization of the Individuals with Disabilities Education Act: Moving toward a more unified system* [Policy brief]. Aurora, CO: Mid-continent Research for Education and Learning (McREL). Retrieved April 7, 2006, from http://www.mcrel.org/PDF/PolicyBriefs/5022PI_PBReauthorizationIDEA.pdf

Gomez, D. S. (2001, March). New teachers and social justice [Interview]. *NEA Today.* Retrieved April 7, 2006, from http://www.nea.org/neatoday/0103/intervw.html

Gruber, K. J., Wiley, S. D., Broughman, S. P., Strizek, G. A., & Burian-Fitzgerald, M. (2002, May). *Schools and Staffing Survey, 1999–2000: Overview of the data for public, private, public charter, and Bureau of Indian Affairs elementary and secondary schools* (Rep. No. NCES 2002-313). Washington, DC: U.S. Department of Education, National Center for Education Statistics. Retrieved March 9, 2006, from http://nces.ed.gov/pubsearch/pubsinfo.asp?pubid=2002313

Lieberman, M. (1997). *The teacher unions.* New York: Free Press.

Morrison, B. (2000, July). *Teacher unions vs. teachers.* Retrieved March 15, 2006, from http://www.brentmorrison.com/0007Teacher_Unions.htm

Mosteller, F. (1995). The Tennessee study of class size in early school grades. *Future of Children, 5*(2), 15.

Murphy, M. (1990). *Blackboard unions: The AFT and the NEA, 1900–1980.* Ithaca, NY: Cornell University Press.

Peterson, B. (1997, Summer). We need a new vision of teacher unionism. *Rethinking Schools Online, 11*(4). Retrieved March 15, 2006, from http://rethinkingschools.org/archive/11_04/union.shtml

U.S. Department of Education, Office of the Secretary, Office of Public Affairs. (2004, October). *A guide to education and* No Child Left Behind. Washington, DC: Author. Retrieved March 6, 2006, from http://www.ed.gov/nclb/overview/intro/guide/index.html

Chapter 13

Growing Professionally and Personally

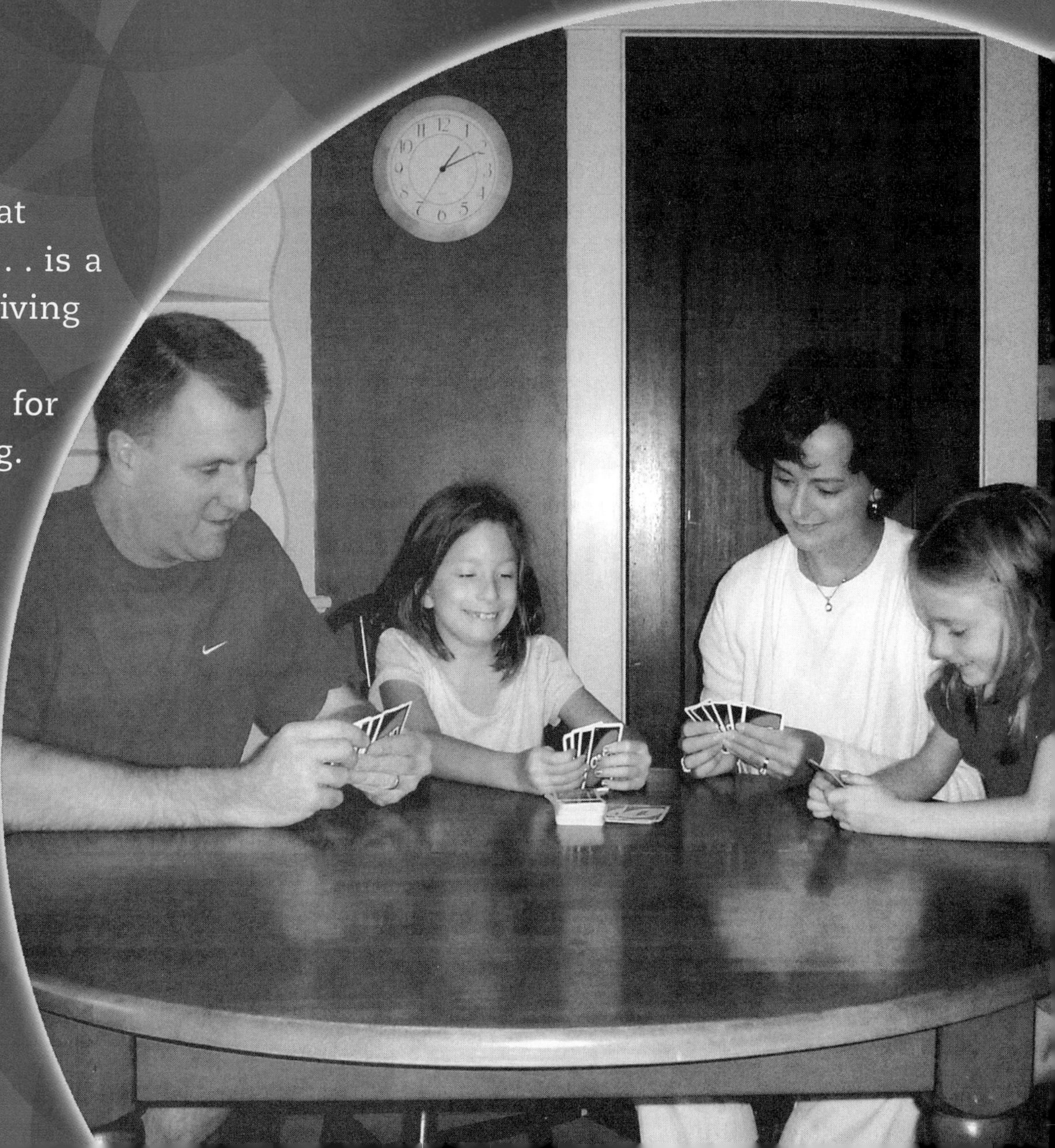

I believe that education . . . is a process of living and not a preparation for future living.
—*John Dewey* (1897)

PROFESSIONAL DEVELOPMENT

Teachers' job is to educate, to train, to enjoin, and to prepare. Yet, to accomplish these tasks, teachers must be educated, and although they are given a certificate validating that they have some expertise with which to teach students, the nature of becoming educated reveals another reality: "Education is a progressive discovery of our own ignorance." This statement—attributed to the philosopher William James ("Will") Durant—implies that education is never complete, is never finished, is really an ongoing opening of doors that reveals ever new and interesting facets of life. Consequently, the wise teacher knows that students teach as well as learn.

Throughout your professional career, you will be engaged in the ongoing learning process. Some of this learning will come from your students; some may be presented at workshops, at seminars, and in committee work; and some will come from your personal initiative and discovery.

STATING THE FACTS:

On teacher qualification: Under the No Child Left Behind Act (2002), schools that are eligible for Title I aid must employ "highly qualified teachers" by 2004, and all public schools must do so by 2005–06.

Obtaining the *continuing education unit*—or what is known as the *CEU* in many other professions—is a requirement designed to upgrade practitioners' knowledge and skills. In education, fulfilling this requirement is referred to as *professional,* or *staff, development,* and across the United States, it is growing rapidly amid No Child Left Behind (NCLB) mandates. Most states—except Oregon, North Dakota, New Hampshire, and Arizona—and the District of Columbia mandate some degree of professional development (Quality Counts, 2003). The NCLB stipulation that all school districts upgrade the quality of their teaching staff has resulted in a flourish of after-school and summer programs to improve teaching skills in general areas of instruction and standards alignment. In 2000, 80% of all public school teachers participated in some form of professional development activities focused on state or district curriculum and performance standards (Parsad, Lewis, & Farris, 2001). Other professional development courses were given in the areas of technology integration, teaching methods, discipline, and strategies for teaching students with learning disabilities.

In Real Time: Staff Development Mandates

Most new teachers are mandated to attend staff development workshops to indoctrinate themselves in programs adopted by the district. Often, new teachers are joined by veteran teachers who were given new assignments in which these programs are in effect. Veteran teachers sometimes resist and resent both the reassignment and the forced workshop and present a negative attitude toward staff development that may not be totally justified.

The stated purpose of professional development is to provide upgraded content information, to review and integrate new instructional skills, and to establish environments in which teachers and staff work together as part of the learning community. However, teacher quality is at the core of the objective. A great deal of evidence indicates that districts do not always hire qualified teachers, especially in specific subject areas. The results of a highly respected survey known as the *SASS* (*Schools and Staffing Survey*) revealed that "22 percent of secondary school students nationwide take at least one class with a teacher who did not even minor in the subject taught" (Quality Counts, 2003, p. 7). Reports such as this have energized criticism of teacher qualifications and raised doubts about the quality of education that U.S. children are receiving. Congress took these criticisms seriously when it mandated districts to hire and train qualified teachers.

Often, school counselors can assist staff with professional development choices.

Yet, the National Center for Education Statistics (NCES) found that "teachers typically reported that they had spent 1 to 8 hours or the equivalent of 1 day or less on the [development] activity" (Parsad et al. p. iv). As you would expect, teachers who spend more time on professional development activities are more likely to use the newly learned strategies in class. Although the wisdom of providing increased hours of professional development is obvious, the expense is prohibitive. Besides footing the costs of materials and consultants, most districts pay step-in-salary increases for *X* number of hours accumulated in professional development. For most teachers, this system of step increases built on hours acquired is the only path to augmenting salaries other than negotiating pay raises when contracts expire. Accordingly, professional development is a necessary but expensive proposition.

Reinvention of the Wheel

Workshops, seminars, in-service days, retreats, and after-school training sessions form the structure of professional development. As a novice teacher, you can expect to begin these sessions almost immediately, if not before the school year begins. Many districts provide a new-teacher induction program that includes workshops on specific instructional techniques that correlate with their own or state standards. Thus, much of what you learned in your junior- and senior-year methods classes will be repeated in some form or another. As frustrating as this repetition may be for you, keep in mind the necessity of having all teachers working together toward the same goals and objectives.

Despite this noble purpose, however, teachers—novice and veteran alike—often find some of the workshops or seminars lacking in original construction or, as so many teachers like to say, "Why are we reinventing the wheel?" A workshop can be instructive, informative, and genuinely helpful in some or many ways. However, if a teacher has a system of instruction that works for him or her and is organized and considered proficient, he or she may take umbrage at having to attend a seminar on brain-based learning calling for rethinking his or her methods. The simple answer to the question about reinventing the wheel is that the goal of most workshops or training sessions is *not* to try to change a teacher's mind or teaching style, but to help him or her find better ways to motivate students or improve an already-excellent style. This is the point: Unless teachers are exposed to the developing research on instruction and learning and have a chance to get together to discuss the issues that affect their daily work, even the most effective teacher will become staid and stale because students do not live in a vacuum. The teacher who does not think he or she needs to change or adopt new techniques, or to read about what is happening in the field of education, is only creating a vacuum in which the student may be more informed than the "sage on the stage."

At the heart of every professional development program is a concept or an idea. It may be behavior management, or assessment, or student health and safety, but it will always be about how to improve, reform, or repair the system. Professional development has been compared metaphorically to *building the plane while flying it*. Although this analogy is clearly an exaggeration, districts often do introduce new techniques, textbooks, and curricula that require a great deal of training and commitment. For some teachers, taking a radical turn in methodology is cause for stress and anxiety as they attempt to engage in a system or strategy that may reflect badly on their skills. For this reason, a teacher should keep him- or herself informed of district policy and program objectives and be open minded about new techniques, but also be critical of any aspects that appear to work against an effective learning experience for his or her students.

Improvement of Skills

The teaching profession is often associated with the word *traditional.* Some time-honored beliefs about school seem to survive the tides of change. An example is the use of technology in the classroom. Despite the widespread availability of computers and Internet access, only 39% of U.S. teachers use it for classroom instruction in some way, and only 11% of teachers with 20 years or more experience report using computers or the Internet (Rowand, 2000).

In 56% of all U.S. schools, 50% of the teaching staff is proficient in technology at the intermediate level. However, all these figures improve substantially when teachers are given training and instruction in the use of computers and software programming (Rowand, 2000).

For many teachers, resistance to using technology is rooted in their teaching preferences and unwillingness to integrate techniques that seemingly provide no benefit beyond an attraction to students. However, given that student interest is piqued through technology, the modern teacher must at least accept training that will provide a modicum of technological expertise for use in the instructional program.

Just as doctors must review the latest pharmacological products and inform themselves of the most recent procedures in healing, so must teachers stay informed of the research and findings that affect a child's learning. Unlike physicians, however, teachers do not face liability if they do not stay informed. Therefore, keeping up to date becomes a voluntary act somewhat stimulated by district offerings on professional development. Herein lies the spirit of the word *professional.* Teachers often lament over the public's lack of recognition of them as professional; yet, one of the criteria necessary for them to be viewed in that light is to possess and sharpen their skills in the field.

Teachers who do not meet regularly to discuss problems with the program or with individual students, and who do not seek updates on research findings that affect student learning, will follow their own paths. Ultimately, teachers who follow their own paths will develop separate and isolated modes of instruction that never reap the fruits of collegiality.

In Real Time: **Working Together**

When teachers work together on a common goal that ultimately improves the education system, everyone benefits—principals, teachers, parents, and especially the students.

WAYS TO IMPROVE: PROFESSIONAL DEVELOPMENT

- Serve on district committees for curriculum or other programs.
- Attend conferences, seminars, and workshops on topics related to your field.
- Volunteer to be on in-school committees with your colleagues.
- Find ways to involve students in educational projects outside the classroom that help promote the mission of the school.

Avenues for Development

Various avenues are available for teachers to improve their skills and expand their overall knowledge base on educational and developmental subjects. Most districts have an in-house department or director of curriculum and staff development. This person's job is to promulgate material to all teachers and staff regarding new programs and techniques that become available. In some states, county and state governments promote programming and informational sessions to upgrade their teachers' skills. More personally, teachers can discover a great deal about the latest instructional techniques from the Internet, the local library, or a nearby college or university library.

VOICES IN THE CLASSROOM
Working Together

I do not like what our district calls "staff development workshops." I think they're a waste of time and just give kids yet another vacation from school—sort of ironic, don't cha' think? But, last year, the union and the administration came up with an idea that finally made sense. Our annual teacher conference day was organized jointly with principals and district staff and geared to promote practical applications of instruction and classroom management. The day was planned out many months in advance, and the cost of speakers and consultants was borne by both the union and the administration.

On the day of the conference, a continental breakfast was served at a downtown banquet hall and was followed by opening remarks from a state assemblyman who has been a friend of education. We then went to the local middle school, where a wide variety of seminars and lectures were available on the topics of improving classroom instruction and promoting effective classroom management. Three of the sessions were hands on; the others a combination of lecture and discussion. However, the presenters were all asked to keep speeches and sermons at a minimum and to evoke audience participation.

The result was an astounding success as proved by the high grades given at the survey at day's end. Many of the discussions that had originated at the conference were continued through hour-long staff development sessions after school in the months that followed. Teachers were asked to comment on what they had learned and how improvements could be made. In the spring, an ad hoc committee followed through with a report on suggested changes and increased resources. No mandates were made, but the lines of communication were opened and a new channel of support was established as a result. I can honestly say that something positive came from spending that one day out of school and in staff development.

—A veteran teacher

The two national teacher organizations—the National Education Association (NEA) and the American Federation of Teachers (AFT)—also provide sources of information and research through their professional journals, seminars, workshops, and course offerings. Teachers should belong to at least one national professional organization that relates specifically to the age group of children whom they are teaching. The following organizations are generally considered the best that support education:

- Phi Delta Kappan International (PDK): www.pdkintl.org
- Education Week: www.edweek.org
- Association for Supervision and Curriculum Development (ASCD): www.ascd.org
- National Association for the Education of Young Children (NAEYC): www.naeyc.org
- National Middle School Association (NMSA): www.nmsa.org
- National Association for Sport and Physical Education (NASPE): www.aahperd.org/naspe
- National Council of Teachers of English (NCTE): www.ncte.org
- National Council of Teachers of Mathematics (NCTM): www.nctm.org
- National Science Teachers Association (NSTA): www.nsta.org
- National Council for the Social Studies (NCSS): www.ncss.org
- Music Teachers National Association (MTNA): www.mtna.org
- American Council on the Teaching of Foreign Languages (ACTFL): www.actfl.org
- Learning Disabilities Online: www.ldonline.org
- American Library Association (ALA): www.ala.org
- National Art Education Association (NAEA): www.naea-reston.org

Another way to improve your skills is to serve on district committees that are involved in program initiatives. Not only will doing so give you the opportunity to explore an issue in depth, but it will also involve you in the process of instruction through planning and design. Service on these committees often requires attendance at regional and national conferences, where you will meet and collaborate with teachers from various districts who may be engaged in extremely successful instructional and management initiatives. Conferences are a rich source of information and enable you to make contacts in your field that can help you find new ways to engage your students and enrich your teaching strategy.

Working outside the classroom, or even the school, with students is another excellent avenue for professional development. As you work with students on a community project, you are serving as a role model for them and are contributing to your knowledge about students. Seeing them in an environment outside school is seeing them in ways often hidden in the classroom.

Your Portfolio

Briefcase CD CH13-1—Teacher Portfolio Contents Checklist

A concept for teacher assessment that is becoming increasingly common is the **teacher portfolio.** The emphasis on teacher effectiveness has been highlighted by such organizations as the Interstate New Teacher Assessment and Support Consortium (INTASC) and the National Board for Professional Teaching Standards (NBPTS), both of which structure evaluation around performance standards. The traditional assessment of teacher competence through three or four classroom observations is giving way to a broader evaluation of performance by examining all aspects of teaching duties. Teacher assessment based on multiple-choice questions on state tests is now only one part of a more holistic evaluation of teacher work. This type of evaluation necessitates a teacher portfolio of performance.

The workshops and seminars you attend, the committees on which you serve, and the courses of higher education that you complete are all signs of your self-improvement as a teacher. Collecting this information in a professional portfolio and keeping it up to date provides both you and your employer with a journal of your personal and professional development.

Principals using the portfolio to assess your performance rely on a set of standards structured around the INTASC standards (Council of Chief State School Officers, 1992). When compiling your portfolio, prepare documents that reflect your integration of these standards.

Your portfolio is a history of your teaching career. During a single academic year, you will achieve a great deal professionally that is just part of your daily regimen. For example, working with students during study hall time or lunch or preparation periods on projects, homework, or other class work is consistent with INTASC Standard 3, understanding how students differ in their approaches to learning; Standard 4, understanding and using a

TEACHER PORTFOLIO CONTENTS CHECKLIST

- ☑ Current résumé
- ☑ List of graduate courses completed, with brief descriptions
- ☑ List of workshops and seminars attended, with brief descriptions
- ☑ Samples of student work from lessons considered successful
- ☑ Teacher work sample
- ☑ A list, with descriptions, of work done or currently being done with students in extracurricular activities
- ☑ Identification of INTASC (Interstate New Teacher Assessment and Support Consortium) standards or state standards as they apply to course work, workshops, and seminars you completed or attended
- ☑ Past observations and evaluations, including those completed during student teaching
- ☑ In an appendix, copies of licenses, certificates, and honors and awards received resulting from and since earning your undergraduate degree

SAMPLE STANDARDS FOR LICENSING

Wisconsin Standards for Teacher Development and Licensure

1. Teachers know the subjects they are teaching.
2. Teachers know how children grow.
3. Teachers understand that children learn differently.
4. Teachers know how to teach.
5. Teachers know how to manage a classroom.
6. Teachers communicate well.
7. Teachers are able to plan different kinds of lessons.
8. Teachers know how to test for student progress.
9. Teachers are able to evaluate themselves.
10. Teachers are connected with other teachers and the community.

Note. Reprinted from *Wisconsin's Standards for Teacher Development and Licensure* with permission from the Wisconsin Department of Public Instruction, 125 S. Webster Street, Madison, WI 53702; 800-266-1027; http://dpi.wi.gov.

INTASC STANDARDS

1. **Content pedagogy:** The teacher understands the central concepts, tools of inquiry, and structures of the discipline(s) he or she teaches and can create learning experiences that make these aspects of subject matter meaningful for students.
2. **Student development:** The teacher understands how children learn and develop, and can provide learning opportunities that support their intellectual, social, and personal development.
3. **Diverse learners:** The teacher understands how students differ in their approaches to learning and creates instructional opportunities that are adapted to diverse learners.
4. **Multiple instructional strategies:** The teacher understands and uses a variety of instructional strategies to encourage students' development of critical-thinking, problem-solving, and performance skills.
5. **Motivation and management:** The teacher uses an understanding of individual and group motivation and behavior to create a learning environment that encourages positive social interaction, active engagement in learning, and self-motivation.
6. **Communication and technology:** The teacher uses knowledge of effective verbal, nonverbal, and media communication techniques to foster active inquiry, collaboration, and supportive interaction in the classroom.
7. **Planning:** The teacher plans instruction based upon knowledge of subject matter, students, the community, and curriculum goals.
8. **Assessment:** The teacher understands and uses formal and informal assessment strategies to evaluate and ensure the continuous intellectual, social, and physical development of the learner.
9. **Reflective practice—Professional growth:** The teacher is a reflective practitioner who continually evaluates the effects of his or her choices and actions on others (students, parents, and other professionals in the learning community) and who actively seeks out opportunities to grow professionally.
10. **School and community involvement:** The teacher fosters relationships with school colleagues, parents, and agencies in the larger community to support students' learning and well-being.

Note. The Interstate New Teacher Assessment and Support Consortium (INTASC) standards were developed by the Council of Chief State School Officers and member states. Copies may be downloaded from the Council's Web site at http://www.ccsso.org.

Council of Chief State School Officers. (1992). *Model standards for beginning teacher licensing, assessment, and development: A resource for state dialogue.* Washington, DC: Author. http://www.ccsso.org/content/pdfs/coretrd.pdf. Reprinted with permission.

variety of instructional strategies to encourage student development; and Standard 5, creating a learning environment that encourages active engagement in learning.

Volunteering for school theatrical productions, music programs, academic assemblies, or presentations is also a contribution to your professional growth. In addition, your work to promote any activity or program that helps develop the social, emotional, and cognitive growth of children is part of your professional development. Included in such development is your work with colleagues and community leaders to promote activities and programs that benefit both the school and the local community.

A final note to beginning teachers: Faithfully keep a written or an electronic journal of your daily activities, thoughts, ideas, jottings, and achievements from the first day of your teaching career forward. A number of electronic journal software programs can help you keep a daily diary. Microsoft Office has an integrated journal that can be synthesized with your Web and office e-mail accounts, as well as your address book and task list.

Master's Degree Versus Job

One crucial question in the minds of many teacher preparation graduates is whether to continue on to acquire a master's degree or to try to secure employment immediately. The foremost consideration will be whether your state requires a master's degree. If so, your options are more limited, especially if you have a time requirement. If your state does not mandate securing a graduate degree, but doing so is your personal goal, you have the leisure of working on it during a longer period. Following is a simple *if . . . then* formula that might help you think through the decision:

- ☑ ***If you plan on getting married or have recently been married,*** then securing employment immediately will mean that you will be working full time while taking evening courses toward your master's degree. Any veteran teacher will tell you that first-year teaching is tough enough without the added pressure of doing graduate course work. If you have the option, delay the graduate work for at least a year. Being married can also mean parenthood, so having children, teaching in your first year, and doing graduate work is a nearly impossible task.
- ☑ ***If you have heavy undergraduate loans to pay,*** then finding employment immediately is probably an urgency for you. Federal loans come due 6 months following graduation unless you are enrolled in a graduate program. In addition, graduate programs are generally expensive, even for state institutions. However, you may be able to acquire assistantships or work study contracts that will reduce your tuition.
- ☑ ***If you do not have loans and your finances are stable,*** then continuing on and completing your graduate work makes sense. Delaying means that life will catch up with you. The longer you are away from the rigors and routine of study and research, the more engrossed you will become in the other activities of life, and the more difficult returning to the academic regimen will become.
- ☑ ***If your employer offers financial assistance,*** then consider going on to graduate work. Many districts offer incentive programs for acquiring a master's degree. They may offer to pay for the course entirely or partially, or they may offer salary increases for credits accrued. However, take courses sparingly—one per semester during your first years of teaching.

You may need to take other considerations into account when deciding whether to pursue graduate work or get a job. In November 2004, President George W. Bush signed into law the Taxpayer–Teacher Protection Act, which boosts the limit on loan forgiveness to $17,500 for high school math and science teachers and for elementary and high school special education teachers *who work in high-poverty schools*. To qualify, a teacher must be "highly qualified" under the No Child Left Behind Act (2002) and must have taken out his or her loans prior to October 1, 2005. NCLB loan forgiveness is an excellent incentive to go directly to work, but you must be prepared for rigorous teaching conditions.

PERSONAL ISSUES

The Job, You, and the Family

Teachers are generally family-oriented people. They may be raising a family, may intend to raise a family, or are supportive of the concept of family and community. This characteristic of teachers, though not universal, no doubt arises from their personal desire to work and promote the development of children. Therefore, a teacher naturally values and cherishes his or her own family and wants to nourish its development. Often, the job of teaching can interfere with such nourishment if it takes you away from your spouse and children and creates a problem of priorities.

Teaching: The Take-It-Along-Home Job

Teaching is a take-it-along-home job. Teachers do not leave their jobs in the classroom when they go home. They must work outside the classroom to prepare the lessons for the next day and review and evaluate the students' submitted work. Teaching is about people, and sometimes people have problems that accompany them to school. A child in your class who is obviously hungry or constantly falling asleep cannot escape your notice. Children often hurt one another emotionally through name-calling and physical assaults that sometimes can be unusually cruel. Depending on your sensibilities, these daily traumas may have a greater or lesser effect on your emotional state. Ultimately, these emotions get dragged into your home and may have an impact on your family.

VOICES IN THE CLASSROOM
A Personal Crisis

My first year of teaching was one I will never forget, because it brought me to the brink of divorce. My husband worked as a sales agent for an insurance company and, luckily for me, was home every day at 5 p.m. When I got hired as a seventh-grade English teacher, we had two boys at home, aged 5½ and 3. The youngest was in nursery school and the oldest was beginning kindergarten. I threw myself into the job, spending the last 2 weeks in August busily preparing my classroom. When school began, I found a good babysitter and didn't come home until 4 or 5 o'clock each day. And when I was home, I was correcting compositions and preparing lessons for the next day. This was in 1970, when the wife was still expected to put supper on the table and keep the house clean. Needless to say, those duties began to fall by the wayside of my trek to become the best teacher in the world.

What added to the stress of the situation was the fact that the faculty at my school happened to be party happy; so, every Friday I gleefully went to the local "teacher" bar to share the week's classroom stories over a gin and tonic. Of course, I also volunteered to work on the school play and be the adviser for the literary club. This pulled me away from home at least two nights a week and then on Saturdays for car washes and can drives.

At the Christmas party, my husband pulled me aside and told me that he was seriously considering leaving me. I remember just looking at him as though he were some kind of stranger. He then cataloged what I had been doing for the past 5 months and how the children no longer saw their mother and he was technically without a wife. It was a sobering moment, and during the Christmas break I took a long, hard look at what I was doing.

In January, I made some changes and began spending less time on schoolwork and more time concentrating on my family. I learned how to get more work done in school and took less home with me. I also learned how to say "no" when the crowd was heading for happy hour. It helped, but it was still a struggle. We continued to have marital problems throughout my first years of teaching, and it wasn't really until my third year that I had a routine down that accommodated both family and profession. For sure, though, it's a ton harder for the woman than the guy.

—A veteran English teacher

In Real Time: Career Stress

Teaching is the kind of job that follows you home. Not only must teachers prepare for the next day's classes, but often students who have social, emotional, or learning difficulties generate an emotional strain that can be extremely stressful.

The Helpfulness of a Mentor

Every teacher must remember that he or she cannot save all the children. Teachers cannot extract the children living in disheveled, chaotic homes and adopt them. Instead, teachers can only do their jobs well enough so that such students get 7 hours of caring, professional help that may make a difference and offset some of the dysfunction in their lives. Often, a teacher's caring and intervention has made the difference, has helped a child find a better living situation and brought him or her to higher levels of comfort and success. Hundreds of case histories tell of teachers making such a difference. A good example is Annie Sullivan's triumph with Helen Keller. Sometimes, a teacher is the difference between success and failure for the rest of a child's life.

Nevertheless, these children's problems should not become *your family's* burden or concern. In fact, a teacher should not discuss a child's personal problems with family members or discuss any aspect of a student's life in public.

Yet, discussing the plight of these children with someone is often helpful. In most buildings, at least one person is a good listener, a person who sometimes offers excellent advice. This person may be the school nurse, or the librarian, or another teacher or administrator, but he or she can help teachers balance their feelings of helplessness and frustration that so often flow from dealing with children at risk. You should routinely seek out this mentor, and if you encounter an especially gruesome situation, possibly even seek professional help.

A Focus on the Family

A principal once observed that often the man or woman who is not married or in a relationship spends more time working at the school after hours and on weekends. A family requires time and effort, and most husbands and wives have rich lives outside their jobs. For the teacher, this fact is not only true, but also essential. Having the support of a family will help you balance the rigors and stress of the day. A focus on family is an important part of your health and will ultimately have an effect on your professional life. Therefore, be sure to do the following:

- ☑ Set aside time for you and your family to participate in activities that have nothing to do with school.
- ☑ Have your family members join you in extracurricular activities in which the community is welcome (e.g., fund-raisers such as car washes, fun runs, walk-a-thons).
- ☑ Allow your children to help you with posters and bulletin board design.

Reflection on Year 1

Briefcase CD CH13-2—Year-End Reflection Checklist

When the first year draws to a close, you will likely have doubts, have a little regret, and do a good deal of second-guessing. If you look back on the year and see no mishaps, have no regrets for decisions you have made, and are convinced that you did an outstanding job, you may be thinking you are now a veteran. However, the truth is that even 20-year veterans have regrets, mishaps, and remorse over a bad decision or two. Being critical of your performance is part of the self-reflection process that helps build effective teaching.

YEAR-END REFLECTION CHECKLIST

- ☑ How would I rate my overall performance (on a scale from 1 to 10) during the past year?
- ☑ Do I know the names of every teacher, staff member, and administrator in the building?
- ☑ When contemplating my conversations with parents, what regrets do I have?
- ☑ Can I think of one or more times when I treated any student with disrespect?
- ☑ Which of my single lessons was a total bomb?
- ☑ Which of my single lessons was a roaring success?
- ☑ Did I give a test that was completely ineffective?
- ☑ What was the best test I gave?
- ☑ Did my students' overall content understanding improve?
- ☑ Did my students have observable learning moments? How many?
- ☑ What is my single main regret?
- ☑ What will be at the top of my list to change for next year? Why?
- ☑ Which of my colleagues did I admire the most? Why?

This reflection must include more than a review of your students' scores on final exams, reading and mathematics tests, or standardized tests. Other criteria affect your evaluation. Among these are student comfort level with your teaching style, parental communication (frequency and outcome), collegial interactions, your contribution to extracurricular activities, the outcome of an exciting lesson that engaged your entire class, and your personal life.

DOS AND DON'TS

Don't	Do
Believe that your education finished with your master's degree	Continue to take courses and workshops and attend seminars
Take courses or workshops that do not pertain to some facet of your field or some aspect that will enhance your overall effectiveness as a teacher	Take courses and workshops that support your field and will enhance your skills
Become the cynic who decries district initiatives to provide staff development	Find areas in which you can participate actively in a workshop or seminar and, when possible, provide your expertise
Overload yourself with course work and schoolwork	Balance your time so that you can do both effectively
Isolate yourself in your own corner of the school	Seek out your colleagues and engage in dialogue with them both professionally and personally
Forget your family and other interests	Work on managing quality hours with your family outside the school environment
Forget that teachers are not one-dimensional beings	Seek out multiple avenues of developing your areas of expertise (e.g., volunteer to work with students outside the classroom)
Forget that you are a teacher with responsibilities	Remember that all teachers have responsibilities other than teaching

WEB SITES OF INTEREST

http://www.ed.gov/nclb/methods/teachers/teachers-faq.html

This site is good for reviewing what the U.S. Department of Education views as quality teachers.

http://www.eduscapes.com/tap

This site is a rich resource of information on professional development.

http://www.eduscapes.com/tap/#1

This site shows you how technology can help you with your electronic portfolio.

http://www.eduscapes.com/tap/#2

This Web page has a potpourri of Internet addresses within and related to the teaching profession.

http://www.alleducationschools.com/featured/masters-education.php?src=goo_ma_ed20

This site provides a comprehensive list of master's in education programs.

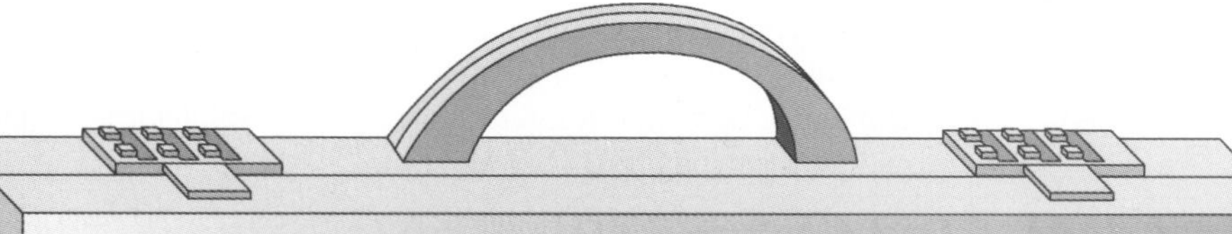

For Your Briefcase

To Do

- Ask your principal or personnel in the district office about professional development requirements.
- Check with office personnel or the union rep on how acquisition of credit hours affects salary scales.
- Join at least one professional association.
- Begin to maintain your teaching portfolio.
- Investigate district policy on remuneration for the master's degree.
- At year end, evaluate your successes and failures.

Resources on Your Briefcase CD

Templates

- Teacher Portfolio Contents Checklist
- Year-End Reflection Checklist

REFERENCES

Council of Chief State School Officers. (1992). *Model standards for beginning teacher licensing, assessment, and development: A resource for state dialogue.* Washington, DC: Author. Retrieved April 7, 2006, from http://www.ccsso.org/content/pdfs/corestrd.pdf

Dewey, J. (1897, January 16). My pedagogic creed. *The School Journal, 54*(3), 77–80.

No Child Left Behind Act of 2001, Pub. L. No. 107-110, § 2361, 115 Stat. 1425 (2002).

Parsad, B., Lewis, L., & Farris, E. (2001, June). *Teacher preparation and professional development: 2000* (Rep. No. NCES 2001-088). Washington, DC: U.S. Department of Education, National Center for Education Statistics. Retrieved March 9, 2006, from http://nces.ed.gov/pubsearch/pubsinfo.asp?pubid=2001088

Quality counts 2003: To close the gap, quality counts. (2003, January 9). *Education Week, 22*(17), 7. Retrieved March 9, 2006, from http://teachermagazine.com/sreports/qc03/templates/article.cfm?slug=17exec.h22

Rowand, C. (2000, April). *Teacher use of computers and the Internet in public schools* (Rep. No. NCES 2000-090). Washington, DC: U.S. Department of Education, National Center for Education Statistics. Retrieved March 9, 2006, from http://nces.ed.gov/pubsearch/pubsinfo.asp?pubid=2000090

Wisconsin Department of Public Instruction. (n.d.). *Wisconsin's standards for teacher development and licensure.* Madison, WI: Author. Retrieved March 9, 2006, from http://dpi.wi.gov

Glossary

Abstraction A cognitive technique closely associated with indirect instruction in which the student makes assertions about a concept or topic that are applicable to other topics or completely different from the context being presented.

Assertive discipline A method of classroom management that relies on the behaviorist conception of human behavior. Designed by Lee Canter, it is based on a belief that students must be made aware of their responsibilities regarding their behavior and that the teacher must recognize the differences and patterns particular to each student. Implementation includes heavy use of extrinsic motivators.

Assessment A means of obtaining data as feedback to help shape decisions about student progress. Assessment is an indicator of learning that guides teacher planning and instruction.

Authentic assessment A form of assessment that asks students to respond to information based on real-life or authentic experiences or situations. In this assessment technique, students are asked to *show* what they learned. It presents them with tasks that mirror the priorities and challenges found in the best instructional activities and makes every attempt to relate them to real-life situations and problems. Strategies include researching, writing, analyzing, collaborating, and presenting.

Big Question An instructional schema in which a probing or an expanding question is asked as a means of immersing students in a topic.

Brain-based learning A method of learning that emphasizes factors of brain development. Instruction based on brain development focuses on the external factors that affect the learning process as it relates to the capacity of the brain to process information.

Career placement office An office on most college campuses offering a service to graduates that includes maintaining a portfolio of the graduate's transcripts, résumé, recommendations, and other data relative to his or her achievements as a student.

Choice theory Theory by William Glasser based on a humanistic approach to classroom management and built on the recognition of four basic needs: survival, love and belonging, power, and freedom and fun. By understanding that each child has these needs, the teacher then builds a behavior management system that helps students to *act* on good behavior, to verbalize their *feelings* and *thinking* about that behavior, and to consider their *physical body reactions* to said behavior.

Cloze A technique, used in the indirect instruction model, in which students are given a paragraph or more of information with missing words that are completed through either dependent or independent work.

Compare–compare grid A chart that compares the characteristics of two subjects.

Compliance officer A school official responsible for overseeing the district special education program to ensure that procedures related to special education students are being administered according to state and federal laws.

Concept mapping A technique mostly associated with indirect instruction in which the student brainstorms the many topics related to a specific concept.

Concept teaching An instructional technique calling for the categorization of concepts in an effort to bring the student to an understanding through relationships. It inspires students to seek relational ideas and formulate new ones as a result of their brainstorming efforts.

Congruent communication An idea popularized by Haim Ginott. The essence of his plan is that children deserve sane messages from adults related to behavior expectations. His belief is that the teacher is a model of behavior and that verbal communication plays an important role in establishing appropriate behavior.

Cooperative learning A type of learning in which students are placed in various-sized groups and given a task related to meaning or specific problems, or to the analysis and refinement of concepts. Characteristic of this method of learning is the group dynamic, in which students have an impact on one another's efforts as they work through the assignment.

Direct instruction A model of instruction with these basic elements: presentation of material, explanation, and reinforcement.

Discovery and inquiry-based learning A type of learning in which the essential aspect is that the student performs an active search of information and then draws conclusions and inferences from what was discovered.

Discrepant facts The use of unusual or extraordinary facts, which tends to stimulate curiosity.

Discrimination A cognitive technique closely associated with indirect instruction in which the student parses the differences between what may be applicable to a concept or event relating to the material being taught.

Discussion A strategy used in both direct and indirect instruction in which the student is encouraged to speak on the material being presented.

Diverse instruction The use of a variety of teaching modes such as lecture, cooperative learning, discussion, and demonstration.

Diversity A modern concept that now includes gender, disabilities, personal preferences, body differences, religion, politics, and sexual preference.

Document-based question (DBQ) strategy A technique in which the class answers a question by researching primary source materials. The students' findings are then reported through presentations, newsletters, posters, dioramas, skits, short stories, or combinations thereof.

Electronic portfolio A portfolio similar to the portfolio binder but rendered electronically. The compilation is presented in a variety of formats and stored on hard disks or a CD-ROM.

Essay test A mode of testing whereby the student must respond in writing to a prompt. This form of testing has a wide spectrum of application and can target both general and specific areas of the material that was taught. Essays can be designed for short or lengthy responses. They also measure skill areas such as writing and organizational abilities.

Estimation A cognitive technique, closely associated with indirect instruction, in which the student is asked to make estimations or predictions about ideas related to the material being taught.

Exit slips A teaching strategy that provides students with a reflective summary of what was learned during the lesson. At the end of the subject period, each student writes one or more points that he or she learned during the lesson that day.

Formative assessment The ongoing or immediate judging a teacher performs during the instructional process. Although it could be in the form of quizzes and tests, it is often observational as teachers gauge how well students are responding to the instruction.

Generalizing A cognitive technique, closely associated with indirect instruction, in which the student constructs general statements relating to the material being taught.

Graphic organizers Graphics that highlight concepts, ideas, names, facts, dates, and pertinent information, usually in the form of shapes and diagrams.

Gregoric's cognition model A model of learning through which cognition is believed to be channeled through four basic modes: concrete, sequential, abstract, and random. These modes interplay and generate specific behaviors related to their definitions.

Inclusion A technique calling for support services such as assistance and tutoring from special education teachers and aides to be brought directly to the student in the classroom.

Indirect instruction Any form of instruction in which the student is an *active* rather than a *passive* learner. Central to indirect instruction is student involvement through either discovery or problem solving. It is often facilitated through cooperative learning.

Individualized education program (IEP) A plan specific to each student in special education that outlines the types of services and modifications he or she will receive as a result of his or her disability.

Induction programs The term currently being used to refer to teacher mentoring. The major difference is that many school districts are instituting comprehensive mentoring programs that use a holistic approach to orienting the new teacher.

Inquiry An indirect instruction technique in which the class is presented with a problem that stimulates inquiry into the topic.

K-W-L An anagram meaning "What do I already *know* about the topic? What do I *want* to learn about the topic? What have I *learned* from studying this topic?"

Learning modalities The various categories of how people learn (e.g., multiple intelligences, brain-based strategies, audio stimuli, and visual stimuli).

Learning standards A core curriculum generally designed around content and skills. What makes learning standards different from the prior scope-and-sequence method is that they are written to reflect outcomes and are more specific to grade, subject, and skill level.

Learning styles The manner in which a child learns. The three main styles are auditory, visual, and kinesthetic.

Least restrictive environment (LRE) A term referring to the mandate that originated with Public Law 94-142 requiring all students to be taught in an environment that achieves as much parity as possible. In effect, this law was passed to eliminate the practice of teaching children with disabilities in rooms separate from that of the mainstream student body.

Literature circles A teaching strategy in which students share their reading in small groups. It is student directed, and the structure and tempo are set by the members of the circle. The format is open ended. Students design and share their questions and comments with students in other circles. Sometimes, students create posters, book covers, or other materials to use to present their book to other members of the circle.

Mainstreaming A technique by which a child with disabilities is brought into the regular education classroom without any particular assistance or support. It has given way to the method of inclusion, which calls for integrated support for the mainstreamed child.

Matching test A type of test in which students are given a set of terms that are matched, to some level of accuracy, with another set of terms. Some of the types of matching tests most frequently used are word searches, crossword puzzles, location maps, and straight matching columns.

Millennial Generation A label believed to be coined by William Strauss and Neil Howe that refers to people born after 1979 and who seem to possess certain common characteristics.

Multicultural A term that refers to a variety of cultures and languages. It has given way to the more comprehensive term *diversity*.

Multiple-choice test A testing mode whereby students are given choices when they are responding to a prompt. These choices can be constructed in various ways so as to include or exclude information relating to the topic, which thus gives the tester the ability to target specific areas and levels of cognition taught during the lesson.

Multiple intelligences A theory promoted by psychologist Howard Gardner, founded on the notion that all people possess more than one intelligence. Gardner believes that each person has varying degrees of proficiency in one or more of the following intelligences: linguistic, logical-mathematical, kinesthetic, spatial, musical, interpersonal, intrapersonal, and naturistic.

No Child Left Behind (NCLB) Federal legislation that reauthorized the Elementary and Secondary Education Act of 1965. The main points of this act are increased accountability for all states and the District of Columbia through greater testing of their students; a choice for parents to move their children from low-achieving schools; and a more rigorous emphasis on literacy.

Pacing Teaching in a measured and balanced manner that takes into consideration the child's developmental and interest levels.

Performance assessment A type of assessment closely associated with authentic assessment but also used in traditional formats. The student must demonstrate some level of proficiency with the material taught. Such performance can take the form of PowerPoint or poster presentations, demonstrations, or experiments.

Portfolio assessment A mode of authentic assessment whereby the student places work in a portfolio for a period to demonstrate a spectrum of improvement. Also included are teacher comments, peer evaluations, and other items that demonstrate the student's growth.

Portfolio binder A compilation of your qualifications as a teacher. It may contain your résumé, education philosophy, teaching-style beliefs, classroom management plan, sample student work, a sample lesson plan, and a sample thematic or unit plan.

Portfolios A form of assessment that logs student work through a progression of assignments. It is geared to help the student chart progress and note development of his or her skills.

Positive discipline A discipline method built on the behaviorist concept of human behavior. Fred Jones originated this method, which requires teachers to record student actions to establish a baseline. From there, the use of extensive rewards for proper behavior is necessary for the success of this program. Also emphasized is the use of a teacher's body language to curtail inappropriate behavior.

Preinstructional techniques Exercises used to determine student knowledge or perception of the material to be taught. These techniques also help engage the student immediately.

Project-based learning and problem-based learning (PBL) A form of instruction centered around real-world situations. It asks students to solve a problem by using observational and critical-thinking skills. Its basis is John Dewey's experiential learning model.

Public Law 94-142 A federal bill passed in 1975 that is considered the landmark turning point for children with disabilities. Its statutes require all children classified with disabilities to be given a free, appropriate education (FAPE). This law more clearly defined the term *disabilities* and the role of special education in the education system.

Readers' theater A teaching strategy whereby literature is presented through drama. The drama is usually simply staged, with children reading their parts in minimally developed roles. However, depending on the book chosen, the teacher may expand on the theater concept.

Reliable test A test that can be replicated with the same students or other students who are taught the same material. A reliable test can produce the same or similar results.

Rubrics Standards or baselines of criteria provided to the student as a guide. Rubrics can be constructed as grade specific, content specific, or skill specific. Rubrics are also used in both traditional and nontraditional assessment. They are structures of objectives presented for competence levels and frame the specifics of achievement within a skill level.

Socratic method An ancient technique of instruction whereby the teacher asks a series of questions relating to a topic to elicit student participation and understanding. The best way to understand how this method works is to read the account between Socrates and Meno in Plato's dialogue *Meno*.

Sponge activity An introductory or concluding activity that either transitions students into the class as soon as they arrive or has them on task when the bell rings at the end of the day. It also is an instrument that engages students in independent work related to the lesson that day.

Storyboard A graphic used to analyze a work of fiction or nonfiction in which the work is depicted in chronological and characteristic order.

Summative assessment The instrument used to determine, as best as possible, student comprehension of the material taught. Summative assessments usually take the form of unit tests, final essays, or standardized tests. They may also be performance specific.

Teacher portfolio A personal account of your work preparing to become a teacher, your student-teaching experiences, and a record of your achievements as a teacher. It should include your résumé, sample lesson plans, certificates acquired in your field, workshops and seminars in which you participated, awards given for your work with children, and program initiatives with which you have been involved.

Teacher recruitment incentives Incentives offered by individual districts, the state, and the federal government to recruit teachers for low-income schools.

Traditional assessment The term used to define assessments that are most commonly used by schools and industry. They include multiple-choice, matching, and true–false tests, and the short answer essay. Although their main purpose is to assess factual- or literal-level knowledge, the skilled test maker can design effective traditional assessments that measure high-order thinking skills.

True–false test A mode of testing whereby students are given a 50% chance to answer correctly. This type of test allows the tester to focus on specific details of a lesson.

Valid test An effective assessment of the material that was taught. A valid test measures student achievement related to the content and processes that were presented during the lesson. Also, the test should conform to or align with state or district learning standards.

Venn diagram A graphic organizer that usually consists of circles intertwining to reveal commonalities among concepts.

Webbing The use of a graphic with shapes to brainstorm a specific concept or topic.

WebQuest An instructional technique that requires students to use the Internet and its many search engines to formulate a map of information relating to a topic. The topic is usually presented through a series of questions that lead the student to discover a wide spectrum of information related to the topic.

Teaching Resource A

SAMPLE DAILY LESSON PLAN

Lesson Topic: Comparing the original text of *Romeo and Juliet* with an artistic (cinematic) representation and gaining insight into the creative process

Goals: To promote student awareness of artistic tone and design through an application of critical analysis and evaluation; to generate recognition of the social, historical, and cultural features of the text

(New York State Language Art Standard 2.1 and 3.1—Intermediate)

Main Objective of Instruction: To demonstrate the constancy of artistic design across social, cultural, and historical contexts and how each context depends on the human drives of survival, community, and love

Objectives:

- Students will be able to write a critical review of the 1996 movie *Romeo and Juliet,* using the original text as a frame of reference.
- Students will formulate a comparison framework, identifying the dramatic points presented by the original text and the attempted effect of the film.
- Students will orally discuss and provide conclusions on the characterizations of the original text and those of the film.
- Students will articulate the cultural aspects of the Elizabethan Age as expressed in the play and the cultural aspects of the modern age as expressed in the film.
- Students will articulate, through written response, the social factors affecting the theme of the play and the film.

Materials:

Films: *Romeo and Juliet* (1996); *Romeo and Juliet* (1969) (Zeffirelli)
Text: Folger Shakespeare Library's *Romeo and Juliet*
Overhead projector
Markers and paper for group presentations

Procedure: *NOTE: This lesson follows the completed reading of the entire play.*

Focusing Activity: Students will view the opening scene of the 1969 film version of *Romeo and Juliet,* then view the opening scene of the 1996 version.

1. The viewings will be followed by open discussion on points of similarities and dissimilarities:
   - What did you find most different between the two movies?
   - What was the effect of using guns as opposed to swords?
   - Why was that effect used?

- What did you notice about the character of Tybalt in the modern film?
- How does his character as a Hispanic man play to diversity?
- How did the director of the modern film attempt to sustain Shakespeare's original tone?
- How can we describe tone when speaking of films?
- Which film had the greater dramatic effect?

During the discussion, students' comments and critical points will be placed on an overhead for them to copy to their notes.

2. The opening scene will be read aloud, with students participating as characters. The same questions will be asked relative to the original text and the two films.
3. Students view the remainder of the 1996 film.
4. Students view portions of the Zeffirelli film.
5. *Dependent practice:*
   a. Students write the opening paragraph of a film critic's review of the 1996 version of the film and share it with the class.
   b. Students work in cooperative groups to formulate criticism of the play and the film and prepare comparison charts.
6. *Independent practice:*
   a. Students complete the review of the film.
   b. Students complete handouts on Shakespearean theater.
   c. Students complete handouts on the textual differences between modern and Shakespearean language.
   d. Students write an editorial on teenage suicide.

Assessment:

1. Students write a comparative essay, choosing a single character from the play, and demonstrate the characterizations in the film and in the original play.
2. Students complete short essay answers on the application of terms such as *tone, mood,* and *dramatic irony* as they are used in both the film and the original play.
3. Students present oral arguments as to whether or not the film captured the essence of Shakespeare's intent and purpose. This exercise is accomplished in teams of three.
4. Students present their research on the Elizabethan Age through a written analysis of how aspects of that age are woven into the context of the play.
5. Students present a critical analysis, in written form, on the social and cultural aspects of the film and what impact they had on the artistic expression of the play as intended by Shakespeare.
6. Students present oral arguments as to the mores and values present during the Elizabethan Age and the modern age and how they were depicted in both the play and the film.
7. Students create a speculative work (newspaper, magazine, play, radio play, television show, videotape) that demonstrates a single theme or plot out of context (e.g., Shakespeare doing a television sitcom; Mark Twain conducting a talk show; Longfellow writing a poem about a space shuttle mission, etc.).
8. *Culminating activity!* Students submit their final analysis as to the motives of the characters in the play and analyze the relative impact of context and sociocultural influence on these motives.

Teaching Resource B

SAMPLE UNIT PLAN

(Following are segments of a full interdisciplinary unit on the study of basic geometry, developed by Erin Buel of Elmira College, Elmira, NY. They are reprinted with her permission.)

Topic: Study of Basic Geometry

State Standards:

- #3—Students will understand mathematics and become confident in communicating and reasoning mathematically, by applying real-world settings, and by solving problems through the integrated study of number systems, geometry, algebra, data analysis, probability, and trigonometry.
- #6—*Interconnectedness: Common Themes*—Students will understand the relationships and common themes that connect mathematics, science, and technology and apply the themes to these other areas of learning.
- #7—*Interdisciplinary Problem Solving*—Students will apply the knowledge and thinking skills of mathematics, science, and technology to address real-life problems and make informed decisions.

Main Overarching Goal and Essential Question:

- The goal of this unit is for students to become familiar with and confident in their mathematical ability in the area of geometry.
- The essential question students will be able to answer after completing this unit is: *What aspects of geometry do I see and use in my everyday life?*

Unit Objectives:

- Students will define the names of various geometric terms both orally and in written form.
- Students will classify figures into their respective categories, using visual charts.
- Students will analyze a work of art and recognize the various geometric aspects used in the piece.
- Students will apply their knowledge of geometry to their everyday lives by writing a journal entry outlining their use of geometry throughout their day.
- Students will follow rules and procedures for constructing geometric figures by hand.
- Students will verify given formulas by making models of geometric figures.
- Students will assist one another through group work and discussion during class and small-group activities.
- Students will physically construct geometric figures, using paper and folding techniques.
- Students will construct a miniature-golf hole using geometric formulas and design.

Interdisciplinary Applications:

- *Art:*
  - Students will research examples of mathematics in art.
  - Students will construct different logos and designs, using a compass and a straightedge.
- *Social Studies:*
- Geography—Students will find the diameter across the world to certain countries.
  - Students will discuss latitude and longitude lines: parallel and perpendicular.
  - Students will read about Native American geometry using circles.
- *Science:*
  - Students will determine the distance to the core of the earth.
  - Students will understand the importance of perpendicular lines in a construction and its ability to withstand much pressure and force.
- *English:*
  - Students will write a paragraph explaining the labels *units, units squared,* and *units cubed.*
  - Students will write a short paper on their favorite work of art that displays geometric aspects and describe which aspects are used.
  - Students will complete a journal entry in which they outline their use of geometry throughout their day.
- *Technology:*
  - Students will use the digital camera to take pictures during the Launch Activity.
  - Computers, the Internet, and a projector will be used throughout the unit for visual demonstrations.
  - Students will use the Internet for information and examples of geometry in art.
  - Students will use a compass, a protractor, and a straightedge for constructions and measuring.

Questions to Be Answered:

- Where do I see geometry in my everyday life?
- How do I construct figures such as circles, polygons, and polyhedrons?
- How do I classify these figures?
- What are *congruence* and *similarity?*
- From where are the area and volume formulas derived?
- Why is knowledge of geometry important in the world?

Content to Be Covered:

I. Basic Geometric Ideas
   - A. Line Segments
   - B. Parallel and Perpendicular Lines
   - C. Congruency

II. Angles
   - A. Measurement
   - B. Construction
   - C. Classification
   - D. Angle Bisectors

III. Polygons
   - A. Perimeter
   - B. Area

C. Classification
D. Similarity
E. Construction of Triangles
IV. Circles
A. Area
B. Circumference
V. Three-Dimensional Figures
A. Surface Area of Polyhedron and Cylinder
B. Volume of Prism and Cylinder

Launch Activity: An activity to lead students to become more observant of geometry in their environment.

Students and teacher take a walk around their school and surrounding community, observing geometric shapes in everyday objects. Some examples will be

- Windows, which include shapes (squares, rectangles, parallelograms, semicircles, hexagons), also angles, symmetry, congruence
- Brick structures (e.g., patios and walls)
- Roofs
- Fountains

This activity was inspired in part by information provided at the following Web site: (www.pbs.org/teachersource/mathline/concepts/architecture/activity2.shtm)

Instructional Activities:

- *Measuring and Classifying Angles:*
  - Students will use protractors to measure angles.
  - Students will choose three objects and draw the approximate angle of each object on their papers.
  - Students will measure the angles of their drawings.
  - Students will take turns presenting one of their angles to the class by drawing their angles on the board and classifying them into the Acute/Right/Obtuse chart.
- *Parallel and Perpendicular Lines:*
  - Students will discuss the latitude and longitude lines of the earth, using a globe.
  - Students will explore the use of Euclidean geometry relative to latitude and longitude.
  - Students will compare table and desk designs to determine the relationship of perpendicular lines.
- *Congruence:*
  - Students will test congruency, using measurements (angle and length) and tracing.
  - Students will complete the optical illusion handout, for which they will need to use their rulers to test congruency.
  - Students will make tangram pieces and will construct figures congruent with those proposed by the teacher.
- *Geometry-in-Art Lab:*
  - In the computer lab, students will examine various aspects used in art, such as angles, similarity, two-dimensional and three-dimensional figures, parallel lines, etc.
  - Students will visit the following Web sites to choose a piece of artwork for which they will write a description of the geometric patterns found in it:
    - www.mathacademy.com/pr/minitext/escher/
    - www.math.nus.edu.sg/aslaksen/gem-projects/maa/0203-2-03-Escher/main.html

- http://en.wikipedia.org/wiki/Image:Melancholia_I.png
- www.mcescher.com

- *Constructing Segment and Angle Bisectors:*
  - Students will make constructions of angle bisectors, using the tracing-paper method in which paper is folded so sides align, which creates a bisector, and the compass method.
  - Students will make constructions of segment bisectors, using the tracing-paper method and the compass method.
- *Constructing Triangles:*
  - Students will construct triangles, using the compass method and the ruler-and-pencil method.
  - In groups of four or five, students will construct 20 equilateral triangles, using the compass method, and derive a pattern to connect triangles to form a regular icosahedron.
  - Students will use construction paper to cut and fold their own icosahedron.
- *Classifying Triangles:*
  - Students will draw a number of triangles and measure the sum of the inside angles.
  - Students will recognize that (in a Euclidean plane), the sum of the measured angles equals 180°.
  - Individually, students will complete a triangle chart, giving examples of different triangles and their classification. The chart will be 3×3, with acute, right, and obtuse at the top, and scalene, isosceles, and equilateral along the side.
- *Classifying Polygons:*
  - Students will separate polygons into triangles by drawing diagonals from the vertices. This exercise will be followed by a discussion on the number of degrees in each polygon.
  - Students will discuss which polygons they see and use in their daily lives.
- *Similar Polygons:*
  - Students will determine the congruency of given polygons and fill in the missing angles and side lengths of similar polygons.
  - Students will complete a Similar Triangle chart, which includes the triangle name and spaces to complete, using shortest, middle, and longest sides.
- *Circles:*
  - Students will practice drawing circles of different radii, using a compass.
  - Students will draw the "CBS" eye logo and the yin–yang symbol.
  - Students will discuss and practice ways in which people drew circles in the past, without compasses.
- *Three-Dimensional Figures:*
  - Students will discuss polyhedrons used in real life (basketball, videotape, etc.).
  - Students will construct a cube and a dodecahedron, using patterns.
  - Students will complete a chart that includes the following information: polyhedron, no. faces, no. vertices, no. edges, shape of base or bases, shape of other faces.
- *Geometry-in-Art Presentations:*
  - Students will present their art piece from their research in the computer lab and share with the class the aspects of geometry included in the work.
- *Perimeter of a Polygon:*
  - Students will measure the perimeter of various objects around the room and those brought to class that are common to everyday life.
  - Students will begin their "Everyday Geometry Journal," in which they will write entries listing all the geometric objects they have viewed during a typical day. There should be a minimum of 25 objects.

- *Circumference and Area of a Circle:*
  - Students will measure the circumference and diameter of a number of different-sized circles, using a ruler and string. Measurements will be entered into a chart and students will visualize pi as approximately equal to 3.14159.
  - Students will then configure the distance to the center of the earth (radius) and the distance between various countries of the world.
- *Area of a Rectangle:*
  - Students will design a floor plan of the classroom, including all rectangular and circular objects as seen from above. They will then calculate open space in the classroom.
  - Students will draw a floor plan of their house, using knowledge of circles and rectangles.
- *Area of a Parallelogram and of a Triangle:*
  - Students will draw as many figures as they can on graph paper, using a perimeter of 16 units. They will then discuss which figure shapes have the largest area.
  - Students will draw a parallelogram, using graph paper, and find the area.
- *Area of an Irregular Figure:*
  - Students will practice finding areas of shaded regions on a handout.
  - Students will make their own shapes by cutting out graph paper or configuring through drawings to make their figure fit the given dimensions.
- *Surface Area of a Polyhedron:*
  - Students will be asked how much wrapping paper is needed to cover a shoebox.
  - Students will calculate the areas of polyhedron patterns on paper, cut them out, and then fold them into a three-dimensional polyhedron shape.

Handouts: *Optical Illusion Handout*—This handout is used to illustrate the concept of congruency.

Native American Geometry Designs—This handout contains samples of designs from which the students will replicate their shapes and identify the variety of mathematical variations.

Assessment: This is an authentic assessment.

Students construct a miniature golf course hole in the classroom, using pieces of wood and duct tape.

- *Step 1:* Students draw designs of a golf course on graph paper, working in groups of four. *Requirements:* Perimeter must be at least 20 and no more than 30 feet. You must use polygon shapes and no circles.
- Students must submit their design.
- *Step 2:* The group must calculate the area of all pieces of the course, then find the perimeter of the outside figure.
- *Step 3:* Students begin construction of the miniature golf course. They play the course and consider angles, obstacles, and sidewalls.
- *Step 4:* Reflecting on the design. Students report on their work by describing the process and noting the obstacles and problems they had to overcome to achieve their goal. Students indicate how geometry played a role in the project.

RUBRIC OR MINIATURE GOLF COURSE ASSESSMENT

Design	1	2	3	4
Area computations	Student does not attempt to complete the problem	Incorrect formula or answer given, with no work shown	Student answers are correct, but no work is shown or small errors in computation were made	Student answer is correct, with all work shown
Perimeter computation	Student does not attempt to complete the problem	Incorrect formula or answer given, with no work shown	Student answers are correct, but no work is shown or small errors in computation were made	Student answer is correct, with all work shown
Scale	No scale given	Design not drawn to scale; units not labeled	Design drawn to scale with small errors; units labeled	Design drawn to scale with correct units labeled
Neat, complete	Incomplete drawing, disorganized, shows little effort	Slight effort shown; stray marks covering paper; straightedge not used	A few stray marks; a few lines not drawn; straightedge used; effort shown	Design neat, complete; straightedge used; pleasing to the eye
Construction				
Course is neatly constructed	No effort shown	Slight effort made; pieces unattached to floor	A few loose pieces; course still usable	Pieces secured to floor; solid angles made; sturdy construction
Course follows design	No effort shown	Construction simply thrown together without design	Follows design with slight errors	Follows design and neatly changes drawing when needed
Group Activity				
Collaboration of designs	Refuses to work with group members	Works with group members with arguments over design characteristics	Works with group members but follows own plans without compromise	Works well with all group members; open to all ideas shared
Construction of course	Refuses to work with group members	Works with group members with arguments over construction	Works with group members but follows own plans without compromise	Works well with all group members; open to all ideas shared

Teaching Resource C

SAMPLE LETTERS TO PARENTS

Sample Letter of Praise and Accomplishment—Elementary School

Date:

Ms. Harriet Stohl
Glimmering Glass Elementary
104 North First Street
Middletown, U.S.A.
555-555-5555

Dear Mr. and Mrs., Ms. ___________________

It is my great pleasure to inform you that Jackie has had an extremely successful week in our fourth-grade class. In math, she completed all her assignments on time and achieved a high score on the weekly quiz. In social studies, Jackie's presentation on Hiawatha was exciting and informative.

Overall, Jackie has been participating actively in class and has helped many other students finish their tasks.

I hope you join me in giving Jackie an enthusiastic round of applause for her accomplishments.

Sincerely,

Harriet Stohl

Sample Letter of Praise and Accomplishment—Middle School

Date:

Ms. Bert Rustle
Gladdings Middle School
111 West Street
Middletown, U.S.A.
555-555-5555

Dear Mr. and Mrs., Ms. ________________

I am happy to report that Stanley did a remarkable job in math throughout the unit on measurement that we just completed. Not only did he demonstrate an understanding of the material, but he completed every homework assignment and major project related to the unit.

I consider Stanley a positive role model in my seventh-grade class and am certain that he will be successful throughout the remainder of the year.

I congratulate him on his accomplishment, and I applaud your support and concern.

Thank you.

Sincerely,

Bert Rustle

Sample Letter of Praise and Accomplishment—High School

Date:

Ms. Ginny Wolfe
Orland High School
53 East Avenue
Middletown, U.S.A.
555-555-5554

Dear Mr. and Mrs., Ms. ________________

Our 10th-grade English class just concluded a unit on the theme of human conflict in literature. Your daughter, Gertrude, demonstrated an exemplary understanding of the works we read, and she wrote some outstanding papers reflecting her thoughts. Her work has been a model for others in the class and certainly indicates her hard effort and her focus on her studies.

Although I am sure Gertrude will receive many honors in her future academic career, I believe recognizing her individual efforts is important at this time.

I congratulate her on this accomplishment and applaud your support and concern.

Thank you.

Sincerely,

Ginny Wolfe

Sample Letter Concerning Inappropriate Behavior

Date:

Ms. Jean Autry
Canyon Elementary School
1435 Canyon Road
Out West, U.S.A.
555-555-5555

Dear Mr. and Mrs., Ms. ________________

I am writing to you concerning Ginger's behavior in my seventh-period science class. I regret having to do so, but during the past few weeks, she has been increasingly disruptive to the point of interfering with both my teaching and other students' learning. She has repeatedly ignored my requests to cooperate and apply herself to the work.

Specifically, in the past week I spoke to her about throwing paper in class, loudly disrupting the class during a test, consistently coming into the classroom late, and frequently instigating other students to misbehave.

The school's discipline policy calls for all students to cooperate and respect one another's right to learn. I have asked Ginger to review the code, which can be found on the back pages of her plan book.

I am hoping that you might speak with her about this behavior and encourage her to apply herself to the tasks assigned. You may want to review the discipline code with her and suggest some areas in which she might improve. Ginger's success in this class depends on her completing her work and focusing on the material being presented.

I am willing to discuss this situation with you further by telephone or in a conference. My telephone number here at school is 555-555-5555. To set up a conference, please call Ms. Tangible, our Guidance Office secretary, at 555-555-5544.

Thank you for your help in this matter. I assure you that my chief concern is Ginger's success this year.

Sincerely,

Jean Autry

Teaching Resource D

END-OF-YEAR CHECKLIST

- ☑ Did my strategic teaching plan align with state and district standards?
- ☑ Was my class behavior plan effective?
  - ☑ What about it needs to be changed?
  - ☑ To whom may I speak about making improvements?
- ☑ Was my room arrangement serviceable during the entire year?
  - ☑ Should I look for a different furniture style?
  - ☑ Should I change the physical layout of the room with additional or less furniture?
- ☑ What materials did I lack that would have helped me have a more successful teaching year overall?
  - ☑ Do I need more audiovisual materials?
  - ☑ Are workbooks available that would support my program?
  - ☑ Do I need more art and craft materials?
- ☑ How can I better communicate with my students' parents? (See Parental Communication table in Chapter 11.)
- ☑ Which staff members can I consider true sources of help and support?
- ☑ Which staff members should I engage for more support?
- ☑ How can I improve student participation in the learning process?
  - ☑ Should I change my teaching style?
  - ☑ Are my assessments effective?
  - ☑ Can I find a more engaging way to present the material?
  - ☑ What outside help can I get to improve my instruction?
  - ☑ What can I do this summer to prepare myself for next August–September?
- ☑ What books can I read this summer to help me improve professionally?

Teaching Resource E

SUPPLY OF AND DEMAND FOR TEACHERS

Region Codes: 1—Northwest; 2—West; 3—Rocky Mountains; 4—Great Plains/Midwest; 5—South Central; 6—Southeast; 7—Great Lakes; 8—Middle Atlantic; 9—Northeast; 10—Alaska; 11—Hawaii
Demand Codes: 5.00–4.21 = Considerable Shortage; 4.20–3.41 = Some Shortage; 3.40–2.61 = Balanced; 2.60–1.81 = Some Surplus; 1.80–1.00 = Considerable Surplus

SUPPLY OF AND DEMAND FOR TEACHERS

Field	Region											
	1	2	3	4	5	6	7	8	9	10	11	U.S.
Art/visual ed.	2.29	2.18	2.67	2.88	2.79	2.75	2.61	2.53	2.91			2.68
Bilingual ed.	4.17	3.93	4.67	4	4.38	4.2	3.88	4	4.67			4.12
Business ed.	2.5	2.63	2.8	3.11	2.86	3	2.56	2.88	3		3	2.87
Pre-K	2.17	2.89	3.2	2.3	3.26	2.93	2.14	2.39	2.82		4	2.57
Kindergarten	2.11	2.65	3	2.29	3.27	3	2.13	2.34	2.6		4	2.51
Primary (1–3)	2.2	2.65	3.38	2.19	3	2.95	1.97	2.36	2.29		4	2.43
Intermed. (4–5)	2.33	2.63	3.67	2.35	3.14	3.1	2.32	2.58	2.54		4	2.63
Middle	2.38	2.82	4.2	2.88	3.48	3.47	2.74	3.03	2.58		4	3
Eng. sec. lang.	4	3.55	4.5	4	3.94	3.79	3.29	4.15	3.6			3.8
Health ed.	2.29	2.5	3.5	2.63	2.69	2.5	2.27	2.11	3			2.51
Home ec.	3	2.67	4	3.67	3.2	3	3	4	2			3.17
Class. lang.	3	3	3	3.4	2.67	3	2.83	3.6	3			3.11
French	2.71	2.8	3.67	3.28	3.2	3.46	3.12	3	2.75	3		3.14
German	2.57	2.88	2.33	3.12	3	3.57	3.1	3.24	2.33	3		3.11
Japanese	2.25	3	3	3	3.33	3.8	3.5	4	2	3		3.23
Spanish	3.38	3.33	4.5	3.85	4.22	4.09	3.77	3.94	3.56	3		3.86
Mathematics	3.78	4	4.43	3.98	4.28	4.3	4.15	4.26	4.71	5	5	4.19
Music instru.	3	3.1	3.67	3.63	3.04	2.9	3.04	2.93	2.83			3.15
Music gen.	2.71	2.83	4	3.46	2.76	2.86	2.96	2.78	2.86	3		3
Phys. ed.	2.43	2.15	2	2.37	2.52	2.33	2.17	2.1	2.71		3	2.32
Literacy	3	3.08	3	3.32	3.26	3.27	3	3.26	3.1	3	4	3.18
Biology	3	4.22	3.2	3.6	3.86	4	3.66	3.77	4.06		4.5	3.78

—*Cont.*

Field	Region											
	1	2	3	4	5	6	7	8	9	10	11	U.S.
Chemistry	4	4.31	3.2	3.94	4.16	4.16	4.04	4.07	4.4		5	4.7
Earth/physical	3.5	3.79	3.4	3.62	3.74	3.84	3.71	3.78	4.29			3.73
Physics	4	4.24	3.2	4.18	4.29	4.27	4.23	4.27	4.57			4.22
General sci.	3.38	4.08	3.88	3.49	3.73	3.96	3.6	3.55	4	5	4	3.69
Social studies	2	2.18	2.83	2.54	2.53	2.66	2.15	2.09	2.77	3	3	2.37
Special ed.	4.17	4.83	5	3.96	3.9	4.53	4.08	4.42	4.88			4.3
Speech ed.	2.67	3.8	3	3.11	3.5	3.45	2.8	3.13				3.2

Note. From 2004 *Job Search Handbook for Educators* (p. 8), by the American Association for Employment in Education, 2003, Columbus, OH: Author. Copyright 2003 by the American Association for Employment in Education. Reprinted with permission.

Teaching Resource F

STATE-BY-STATE TEACHER CERTIFICATION REQUIREMENTS CONTACT INFORMATION	
State	**Contact information**
Alabama	Alabama Department of Education, Teacher Education and Certification Office 5201 Gordon Persons Building, PO Box 302101, Montgomery, AL 36130-2101 Phone: (334) 242-9977 E-mail: teached@alsde.edu Web site: www.alsde.edu/html/home.asp
Alaska	State of Alaska, Department of Education & Early Development, Teacher Certification 801 West 10th Street, Suite 200, Juneau, AK 99811-0500 Phone: (907) 465-2831 E-mail: tcwebmail@eed.state.ak.us Web site: www.educ.state.ak.us/TeacherCertification/home.html
Arizona	State of Arizona Teacher Certification 1535 Jefferson Street, PO Box 6490, Phoenix, AZ 85007 Phone: (602) 542-4367 Web site: www.ade.az.gov/certification
Arkansas	Arkansas Department of Education Rooms 106B & 107B, Arch Ford Education Building, 4 Capitol Mall, Little Rock, AK 72201 Phone: (501) 682-4342 Web site: http://arkedu.state.ar.us/teachers/teachers_licensure.html
California	Commission on Teacher Credentialing, California Department of Education 1430 N Street, Sacramento, CA 95814 Phone: (916) 445-7254 Web site: www.ctc.ca.gov/default.html
Colorado	Educator Licensing 201 East Colfax Avenue, Room 105, Denver, CO 80203 Phone: (303) 866-6628 Web site: www.cde.state.co.us/index_license.htm
Connecticut	Bureau of Educator Preparation, Certification, Support & Assessment PO Box 150471, Room 243, Hartford, CT 06115-0471 Phone: (860) 713-6969 E-mail: teacher.cert@po.state.ct.us Web site: www.state.ct.us/sde/dtl/cert/index.htm
Delaware	Delaware Department of Education 401 Federal Street, Suite #2, Dover, DE 19901 Web site: http://deeds.doe.k12.de.us/certificate/deeds_er_instruct.aspx

—Cont.

State	Contact information
District of Columbia	Office of Workforce & Professional Development 215 G Street, NE, Washington, DC 20002 Phone: (202) 698-3995 Web site: www.k12.dc.us/dcps/logan/dcpswpdhome.html
Florida	Bureau of Educator Certification Suite 201, Turlington Building, 325 West Gaines Street, Tallahassee, FL 32399-0400 Phone: (800) 445-5739 Web site: www.fldoe.org/edcert
Georgia	Georgia Professional Standards Commission Two Peachtree Street, Suite 6000, Atlanta, GA 30303 Phone: (404) 232-2500 Web site: www.gapsc.com/home.asp
Hawaii	Hawaii Teacher Standards Board 650 Iwilei Road #201, Honolulu, HI 96871 Phone: (800) 468-4644 Web site: www.htsb.org
Idaho	Teacher Certification, Idaho Department of Education 650 West State Street, PO Box 83720, Boise, ID 83720-0027 Phone: (208) 332-6880 Web site: www.riverdeep.net/educators/certification/cert_id.jhtml
Illinois	Illinois State Board of Education 100 North 1st Street, Springfield, IL 62777 Phone: (866) 262-6663 Web site: www.isbe.net/certification
Indiana	Indiana Department of Education, Division of Professional Standards Room 229, State House, Indianapolis, IA 46204-2798 Phone: (317) 232-6610 Web site: www.doe.state.in.us/dps
Iowa	Department of Education Grimes State Office Building, Des Moines, IA 50319-0146 Phone: (515) 281-5294 Web site: www.state.ia.us/educate/directory.html
Kansas	Teacher Education & Licensure Team 120 SE 10th Avenue, Topeka, KS 66612-1182 Phone: (785) 296-2288 Web site: www.ksde.org/cert/cert_members.html
Kentucky	Education Professional Standards Board 100 Airport Road, 3rd Floor, Frankfort, KY 40601 Phone: (502) 564-4606 Web site: www.kyepsb.net/certification/index.asp
Louisiana	Division of Teacher Standards, Assessment and Certification, Department of Education PO Box 94064, Baton Rouge, LA 70804-9064 Phone: (225) 342-3490 Web site: www.doe.state.la.us/lde/offices/rsc.html
Maine	Maine Department of Education, Certification Office 23 State House Station, Augusta, ME 04333-0023 Phone: (207) 287-5944 Web site: www.riverdeep.net/educators/certification/cert_me.jhtml

—*Cont.*

State	Contact information
Maryland	Division of Certification & Accreditation, Maryland State Department of Education 200 West Baltimore Street, Baltimore, MD 21201 Phone: (888) 246-0016 Web site: www.marylandpublicschools.org/MSDE/divisions/certification/
Massachusetts	Department of Education 350 Main Street, Malden, MA 02148-5023 Phone: (781) 338-3000 Web site: www.doe.mass.edu/Educators/e_license.html?section=k12
Michigan	Michigan Department of Education 608 West Allegan Street, PO Box 30008, Lansing, MI 48909 Web site: www.michigan.gov/mde/0,1607,7-140-5234_5683_14795-22288-,00.html
Minnesota	Minnesota Department of Children, Families, and Learning 1500 Highway 36 West, Roseville, MN 55113-4266 Phone: (651) 582-8200 Web site: www.riverdeep.net/educators/certification/cert_mn.jhtml
Mississippi	Teacher Licensure 359 North West Street, PO Box 771, Jackson, MS 39205-0771 Phone: (601) 359-3483 Web site: www.mde.k12.ms.us/ed_licensure/licensure_guidelines.htm
Missouri	Missouri Department of Elementary & Secondary Education PO Box 480, Jefferson City, MO 65102 Phone: (573) 751-4212 Web site: www.dese.state.mo.us/divteachqual/teachcert
Montana	The Montana Office of Public Instruction PO Box 202501, Helena, MT 59620-2501 Phone: (888) 231-9393 Web site: www.opi.state.mt.us/cert/index.html
Nebraska	Teacher Certification 301 Centennial Mass South, PO Box 94987, Lincoln, NE 68509 Phone: (401) 471-0739 Web site: www.nde.state.ne.us/TCERT/index.html
Nevada	Department of Education, Teacher Licensing Office 1820 Sahara Avenue, Suite 205, Las Vegas, NV 89104 Phone: (702) 486-6458 Web site: www.doe.nv.gov/licensing.html
New Hampshire	New Hampshire Department of Education 101 Pleasant Street, Concord, NH 03301 Phone: (603) 271-3494 Web site: www.ed.state.nh.us/education/beEd.htm
New Jersey	New Jersey Department of Education PO Box 500, Trenton, NJ 08650 Phone: (609) 292-2070 Web site: www.state.nj.us/njded/educators/credentials.htm
New Mexico	Secretary of Education, Public Education Department 300 Don Gaspar, Sante Fe, NM 87501-2786 Phone: (505) 827-5800 Web site: www.sde.state.nm.us/div/ais/lic/index.html

—*Cont.*

State	Contact information
New York	New York State Department of Education 5N Education Building, Albany, NY 12234 Phone: (518) 474-3901 Web site: http://ohe33.nysed.gov/tcert/certificate/index.html
North Carolina	North Carolina Department of Public Instruction 301 North Wilmington Street, Raleigh, NC 27601 Phone: (919) 807-3300 Web site: www.dpi.state.nc.us/licensure/lifaq.htm
North Dakota	North Dakota Education Standards and Practices Board 2718 Gateway Avenue, Suite 303, Bismarck, ND 58503-0585 Phone: (701) 328-2264 Web site: www.nd.gov/espb/licensure
Ohio	Office of Certification/Licensure 25 South Front Street, Mail Stop 105, Columbus, OH 43215-4183 Phone: (614) 466-3593 Web site: www.ode.state.oh.us/teaching-profession/teacher/certification_licensure
Oklahoma	Oklahoma Commission for Teacher Preparation 4545 North Lincoln Boulevard, Suite 275, Oklahoma City, OK 73105-3418 Phone: (405) 525-2612 Web site: http://sde.state.ok.us/pro/tcert/profstd.html
Oregon	Academic Affairs PO Box 3175, 1431 Johnson Avenue, University of Oregon Campus, Eugene, OR 97403-0175 Phone: (541) 346-5700 Web site: www.ous.edu/acadaf_TeachEd.htm
Pennsylvania	Bureau of Teacher Certification & Preparation, Division of Candidate Evaluation Services 333 Market Street, Harrisburg, PA 17126-0333 Phone: (717) 787-3356 Web site: www.teaching.state.pa.us/teaching/site/default.asp
Rhode Island	Office of Teacher Preparation, Certification & Professional Development 255 Westminster Street, Providence, RI 02903-3400 Phone: (401) 222-4600 Web site: www.riverdeep.net/educators/certification/cert_ri.jhtml
South Carolina	South Carolina Department of Education, Division of Teacher Quality Landmark II Office Building, 3700 Forest Drive, Suite 500, Columbia, SC 29204 Phone: (803) 734-1418 Web site: www.scteachers.org/global/Contact.cfm
South Dakota	South Dakota Department of Education 700 Governors Drive, Pierre, SD 57501 Phone: (605) 773-3134 Web site: http://doe.sd.gov/oatq/teachercert/index.asp
Tennessee	Office of Teacher Licensing, Tennessee Department of Education 4th Floor, Andrew Johnson Tower, 710 James Robertson Parkway, Nashville, TN 37243-0377 Phone: (615) 532-4885 Web site: www.state.tn.us/education/lic/index.php

—*Cont.*

State	Contact information
Texas	State Board for Educator Certification 1701 North Congress Avenue, 5th Floor, Austin, TX 78701-1494 Phone: (512) 936-8400 Web site: www.sbec.state.tx.us/SBECOnline/default.asp?width=1024&height=768
Utah	Utah State Office of Education 250 East 500 South, PO Box 144200, Salt Lake City, UT 84114-4200 Phone: (801) 538-7753 Web site: www.usoe.k12.ut.us/cert/default.htm
Vermont	Vermont Department of Education 120 State Street, Montpelier, VT 05620-2501 Phone: (802) 828-2445 Web site: www.state.vt.us/educ/new/html/maincert.html
Virginia	Virginia Department of Education, Division of Teacher Education & Licensure PO Box 2120, Richmond, VA 23218-2120 Phone: (800) 292-3820 Web site: www.pen.k12.va.us/VDOE/newvdoe/teached.html
Washington	The Professional Certification Office Old Capitol Building, PO Box 47200, Olympia, WA 98504-7200 Phone: (360) 725-6000 Web site: www.k12.wa.us/certification
West Virginia	West Virginia Department of Education 1900 Kanawha Boulevard East, Building 6, Room 252, Charleston, WV 25305 Phone: (800) 982-2378 Web site: http://wvde.state.wv.us/certification
Wisconsin	State Superintendent of Public Instruction, Department of Public Instruction 125 South Webster Street, PO Box 7841, Madison, WI 53707-7841 Phone: (800) 441-4563 Web site: http://dpi.wi.gov/tepdl/licguide.html
Wyoming	Professional Teaching Standards Board Suite 400, 1920 Thomes Avenue, Cheyenne, WY 82002 Phone: (800) 675-6893 Web site: www.k12.wy.us/ptsb/certification.htm

Teaching Resource G

BOOKS AND JOURNAL ARTICLES FOR EDUCATORS

Following is a short list of books and journal articles from the many that have been published about the education system. These resources can be considered a beginning for individuals wanting to become informed about the state of modern-day schools and the children whom teachers serve.

Books

Roland Barth

Barth, R. (1991). *Improving schools from within: Teachers, parents, and principals can make the difference.* San Francisco: Jossey-Bass.

Linda Darling-Hammond

Darling-Hammond, L. (1997). *The right to learn: A blueprint for creating schools that work* (2nd ed.). San Francisco: Jossey-Bass.

Darling-Hammond, L., & Bransford, J. (Eds.). (2005). *Preparing teachers for a changing world: What teachers should learn and be able to do.* San Francisco: Jossey-Bass.

Howard Gardner

Gardner, H. (1983). *Frames of mind: The theory of multiple intelligences.* New York: Basic Books.

William Glasser

Glasser, W. (1993). *The quality school: Managing students without coercion* (2nd, exp. ed.). New York: Harper Perennial.

John I. Goodlad

Goodlad, J. I. (1984). *A place called school: Prospects for the future.* New York: McGraw-Hill.

E. D. Hirsch, Jr.

Hirsch, E. D., Jr. (1988). *Cultural literacy: What every American needs to know.* New York: Vintage Books.

Alfie Kohn

Kohn, A. (1999). *Punished by rewards: The trouble with gold stars, incentive plans, A's, praise, and other bribes.* Boston: Mariner Books.

Jonathan Kozol

Kozol, J. (1992). *Savage inequalities: Children in America's schools.* New York: Harper Perennial.

Kozol, J. (1996). *Amazing grace: Lives of children and the conscience of a nation.* New York: Harper Perennial.

Deborah Meier

Meier, D. (2000). *Central Park East and its graduates: Learning by heart (School Reform, 29).* New York: Teachers College Press.

Meier, D. (2002). *In schools we trust: Creating communities of learning in an era of testing and standardization.* Boston: Beacon Press.

Marjorie Murphy

Murphy, M. (1991). *Blackboard unions: The AFT and the NEA, 1900–1980.* Ithaca, NY: Cornell University Press.

Gunnar Myrdal

Myrdal, G. (1996). *An American dilemma: The Negro problem and modern democracy.* New Brunswick, NJ: Transaction. (Originally published in 1944)

Diane Ravitch

Ravitch, D. (2003). *The language police: How pressure groups restrict what students learn.* New York: Knopf.

Seymour B. Sarason

Sarason, S. B. (2004). *And what do you mean by learning?* Portsmouth, NH: Heinemann.

Theodore Sizer

Sizer, T. (1997). *Horace's school: Redesigning the American high school.* Boston: Mariner Books.

Theodore Sizer & Nancy Faust Sizer

Sizer, T., & Sizer, N. F. (1999). *The students are watching: Schools and the moral contract.* Boston: Beacon Press.

Grant Wiggins & Jay McTighe

Wiggins, G., & McTighe, J. (2001). *Understanding by design.* Upper Saddle River, NJ: Prentice Hall.

Journal Articles

Educational Leadership

Hoerr, T. R. (2005, May). Meeting new teachers' personal needs. *Educational Leadership, 62*(8), 82–84.

Price, L. F. (2005, April). The biology of risk taking. *Educational Leadership, 62*(7), 22–26.

Rooney, J. (2005, April). No failure to communicate. *Educational Leadership, 62*(7), 90.

Salvo, J. C., Kibble, L., Furay, M. A., & Sierra, E. A. (2005, May). Surviving day one . . . and beyond. *Educational Leadership, 62*(8), 24–28.

Scherer, M. (2005, May). The right new teachers. *Educational Leadership, 62*(8), 7.

Vaughan, A. L. (2005, April). The self-paced student. *Educational Leadership, 62*(7), 69–73.

Educational Review

Belfield, C. (2005, May). The teacher labour market in the US: Challenges and reforms. *Educational Review, 57*(2), 175–191.

Pediatrics

Barlow, S. E., & Dietz, W. H. (1998, September 1). Obesity evaluation and treatment: Expert committee recommendations. *Pediatrics, 102,* 29–39.

Brown, R. T., Amler, R. W., et al. (2005, June 1). Treatment of attention-deficit/hyperactivity disorder: Overview of the evidence. *Pediatrics, 115,* 749–757.

Collins, R. L., Elliott, M. N., Berry, S., et al. (2004, September 1). Watching sex on television predicts adolescent initiation of sexual behavior. *Pediatrics, 114,* 280–289.

Millman, R. P. (2005, June 1). Excessive sleepiness in adolescents and young adults: Causes, consequences, and treatment strategies. *Pediatrics, 115,* 1774–1786.

Phi Delta Kappan

Braun, N., & Roth, M. (2005, June). Top Web sites for elementary school teachers. *Phi Delta Kappan, 86*(10), 801.

Burris, C. C., & Welner, K. G. (2005, April). Closing the achievement gap by detracking. *Phi Delta Kappan, 86*(8), 594–598.

Christie, K. (2005, June). Chasing the bullies away. *Phi Delta Kappan, 86*(10), 725–726.

Comer, J. P. (2005, June). Child and adolescent development: The critical missing focus in school reform. *Phi Delta Kappan, 86*(10), 757–763.

Marshall, K. (2005, June). It's time to rethink teacher supervision and evaluation. *Phi Delta Kappan, 86*(10), 727–735.

Supovitz, J. A., & Christman, J. B. (2005, May). Small learning communities that actually learn: Lessons for school leaders. *Phi Delta Kappan, 86*(9), 649–651.

Teaching Resource H

EDUCATION FAST FACTS	
Public school districts	14,315
Elementary schools	95,201
Secondary schools	38,161
Total public schools (including academies)	94,112
Charter schools (number fluctuates)	3,000
Private schools	27,223
Catholic schools	8,102
Enrollment—All schools	51,610,631
Elementary	36,168,631
Secondary	13,989,239
Academies	1,452,937
Public school enrollment	47,917,774
Charter school enrollment	750,000 to 825,000
Private school enrollment	5,262,849
Home school enrollment	1.1 to 3.0 million
Public school teachers	2,997,748
Elementary teachers	1,686,336
Secondary	1,078,501
Others	232,911
Private school teachers	395,317
Catholic school teachers	149,600
Student–teacher ratio, public schools	16.3 : 1
Private school ratio (Catholic as well)	16.8 : 1
Total public school expenditures (including federal, state, and local)	$411.5 billion
Federal funding for public schools	$ 29.1 billion
State funding for public schools	$199.1 billion
Local funding for public schools	$172.7 billion
Per-pupil expenditure (public school)	$8,922
Private school tuition, average	$4,639
Catholic school tuition, Average	$3,236

—*Cont.*

Average salaries	
Superintendent, public school	$126,268
High school principal	$86,452
Middle school principal	$80,708
School counselor (licensed)	$100,052
School nurse	$60,000
Public school teacher	$39,857
Private school teacher	$27,210
Catholic school teacher	$36,630

Note. Data from *The Condition of Education 2003* (Pub. No. NCES 2003-067), by J. Wirt, S. Choy, S. Provasnik, P. Rooney, A. Sen, and R. Tobin, June 2003, Washington, DC: National Center for Education Statistics; *Schools and Staffing Survey (SASS): 2003–2004* (Pub. No. NCES 2003-409), by B. Holton, September 2003, Washington, DC: National Center for Education Statistics; *Schools and Staffing Survey (SASS): 1999–2000* (Pub. No. NCES 1999-349), by K. A. Reynolds and J. Thompson, August 1999, Washington, DC: National Center for Education Statistics; and "Table B-1. Employees on Nonfarm Payrolls by Industry Sector and Selected Industry Detail," in *Employment, Hours, and Earnings from the Current Employment Statistics Survey (National)*, by U.S. Department of Labor, Bureau of Labor Statistics, 1999, Washington, DC: Author, http://www.bls.gov/webapps/legacy/cesbtab1.htm.

Index

Note: Locators in italics indicate figures.